# Hari Om Tat Sat

## The Divine Sound: That Is the Truth

Extemporaneous talks given by Osho at OSHO International Meditation Resort, Pune, India

# OSHO

# Hari Om Tat Sat

## The Divine Sound: That Is the Truth

MACMILLAN

First published in the Indian subcontinent 2016 by Macmillan
This updated edition published 2024 by Macmillan
an imprint of Pan Macmillan Publishing India Private Limited
707 Kailash Building
26 K. G. Marg, New Delhi 110001
www.panmacmillan.co.in

Pan Macmillan, The Smithson, 6 Briset Street, Farringdon, London EC1M 5NR
Associated companies throughout the world
www.panmacmillan.com

ISBN 978-93-82616-62-7



The material in this book is a transcript of a series of original OSHO Talks, *Hari Om Tat Sat – The Divine Sound: That Is the Truth*, given to a live audience. All of Osho's talks have been published in full as books, and are also available as original audio recordings. Audio recordings and the complete text archive can be found at www.osho.com

1 3 5 7 9 8 6 4 2



Typeset in Adobe Garamond Pro by R. Ajith Kumar, New Delhi
Printed and bound in India by Gopsons Papers Pvt. Ltd., Noida

# Contents

# Preface

Nothing can be added to truth. Truth is always pure, nude, alone. And there is great beauty, because truth is the very essence of life, existence, nature. Except for man, nobody lies. A rosebush cannot lie. It has to produce roses; it cannot produce marigolds – it cannot deceive. It is not possible for it to be other than it is. Except for man, the whole existence lives in truth. Truth is the religion of the whole of existence – except man. The moment a man also decides to become part of existence, truth becomes his religion. It is the greatest revolution that is possible to happen to anyone. It is the glorious moment.

When I say that except for man everything is living truth – the ocean, the clouds, the stars, the stones, the flowers; everything is nothing but truthfulness, nothing but just itself with no mask, and only man is capable of deceiving others, of deceiving himself – it has to be remembered that this is a great opportunity. It has not to be condemned, it has to be praised because even if a rosebush or a lotus wants to lie, it cannot. Its truth is not freedom; its truth is bondage. It cannot go beyond the boundaries. Man has the prerogative, the privilege of being untrue. That means man has the freedom to choose. If he chooses to be truthful, he is not choosing bondage, he is choosing truth and freedom. Freedom is his privilege.

In the whole of existence, nobody else has freedom. But there are dangers when you have opportunities. When you have freedom, you can go wrong. No rose can go wrong, no rock can go wrong. You can go wrong; hence a deep awareness of each act, of each thought, of each feeling, has to penetrate you. To me that is the meaning of "a seeker of truth." Only man needs to seek it; everybody has already got it, but the glory of freedom is not there. You have to seek it, and find it. In that very seeking and finding you are glorious, you are the very crown of existence.

*Beyond Psychology*
Osho

# A Note about Language

**Spoken Words:** Osho's books are not "written" but rather are transcribed from recordings of his talks. These talks are extemporaneous, without reference to notes other than copies of questions, stories or scriptures he has been asked to comment upon, or jokes he might use to drive home a particular point. He has asked his editors to preserve that quality of the spoken word in his printed books.

**Pronouns:** When hearing him speak, it is quite clear to the listener that generally when Osho talks about "man" he is referring to "human beings." His use of "he" as a default pronoun simply serves an ease and flow of speaking – in no way does it imply that "she" (or "they") is being dismissed or disregarded.

Osho's unique vantage point is good to keep in mind:

*A meditator is neither a man nor a woman,*
*because meditation has nothing to do with your body;*
*neither does it have anything to do with your mind.*
*In meditation you are simply and purely consciousness.*
*And consciousness is neither male nor female.*

– Osho

# 1

# The Sound of Truth

Osho,
I have heard you say, *hari om tat sat* – the divine sound: that is the truth. When you speak, I hear the sound of truth resonating in me, yet I am not enlightened. How is it that I can recognize that which I haven't realized?

*Hari om tat sat* – the divine sound: that is the truth. It is one of the *mahavakyas*, the great sayings which have been embedded in the hearts of the mystics since eternity. It is not something theoretical, not something philosophical, it is something existential.

Those who have gone within themselves have always heard a strange sound, which can only be called the sound of existence itself. It is difficult to reduce that sound into language. Hence for centuries, as far back as we can go, om, the sound, has been represented not by any alphabetical word but by a symbol.

That symbol is beyond any alphabet. It does not belong to any language. Hence the Tibetans can use it, the people who are writing in Sanskrit can use it; Mahavira, who was using a language called Prakrit can use it; Gautam Buddha, who was speaking in a language called Pali can use it. There is no other symbol in the whole world which does not belong to any particular language, but is simply symbolic of a certain experience that can happen to anyone. And why have they not reduced it to some linguistic form? It is not without reason.

The sound of om is heard only when your mind is completely silent, when you have gone beyond all language, all thinking, and when there is pure silence, not even a ripple. Suddenly you hear music. There is no instrument playing it; it seems it is simply the very heartbeat of existence. That's why it doesn't matter whether someone is a Buddhist, a Hindu, a Jaina. It does not depend on your philosophy, on your religion. It depends on the depth of your reach toward your very inner center. There, suddenly, you are overwhelmed.

It is not exactly om, but om comes the closest to expressing the sound. And the sound has been called the divine sound because it is not man-made. It is eternally herenow. Whoever wants to enter the stream of eternal existence is bound to hear it. It says nothing, but it vibrates your being to such joy, to such celebration, to such a dance that you have never dreamed of before.

The word *hari* is used as one of the names of God. I don't want to bring God in; I want to avoid God completely because it brings all kinds of lies behind it. No one has ever experienced any God. There is no evidence, no proof, no argument to support it. It is an absolutely useless hypothesis – not only useless, but immensely harmful because so much bloodshed has happened because of the name *God*. It is time that we forget the word and start using something else fresh.

The word *hari* in itself has another meaning which is far more beautiful than the word *God*. *Hari* in Sanskrit means the thief. And the sound of om, once you come close to it, certainly proves the master thief because it simply steals your very heart forever. Then you are part of existence and you are no longer a separate personality. You are not. Existence is.

Certainly this can be done only by a master thief: you are completely stolen, absorbed, not even a mark is left behind. Those who have used the words *hari om* would rather say that it is the divine sound. My own preference is to say that it is the master thief sound, which has stolen millions of hearts. But whatever you say, one thing is certain: *tat sat – tat* means that, and *sat* means truth.

This sound of om is our very truth, is our very being. We are made of it. The whole existence vibrates, and through different vibrations of the same sound there are different things, but they are simply different vibrations. A certain vibration creates a tree, another vibration creates a bird, another vibration creates a man, but the whole existence, according to the mystics, is made of sound. This sound is certainly the most sacred, the most divine, because there is nothing more beautiful, nothing more ecstatic. Once you have heard it, even from far away... Just a glimpse and you will never be the same person again.

All that we are searching for in meditations is nothing but this master thief. We are searching in our being: What kind of dance, what kind of music goes on there in the living center of your life? Strangely enough all those who have entered inward have found the same answer, without exception – *hari om tat sat.*

You are asking, "When you speak, I hear the sound of truth resonating in me, yet I am not enlightened. How is it that I can recognize that which I have not realized?" There are many things in this small portion of your question. When you hear me you are hearing existence itself, just the way you hear the wind passing through the pine trees or you hear the sound of running water. I have nothing to say to you, that's why for years I go on speaking continually. If I had something to say, I would have said it. And because I don't have anything to say, I can continue for eternity.

When you hear my sound and truth starts resonating in you, it is simply the bridging between the master and the disciple. If what is coming from me originated in existence itself and you are in love, in trust, feeling one with me, you will start resonating with the same truth that is making me a vehicle. It does not need you to be anyone special. It just needs a loving heart, a trusting heart with open doors so the breeze that is coming is not obstructed, and the fragrance that is flowing can overwhelm you, can surround you, can open your heart like a rose opening its petals.

But your problem is: "How is it possible because I am not yet enlightened?" Who said that to you? I am saying every day you *are* enlightened, and you are so stubborn that sometimes I also start feeling it would be better I join you and become unenlightened. Why keep this separation? Either you become enlightened or I am going to become unenlightened. There is a limit to everything!

I don't know who the person is who goes on spreading these rumors that you are not enlightened. What is the source of this knowledge? I know this source – because for thousands of years you have been told you are not enlightened. The people who were telling you that you are not enlightened were on an ego trip – they were enlightened, you were not enlightened; they had arrived, your journey is going to be very long, perhaps many, many lives.

Their whole effort was to create a great distance between you and themselves so they could be superior to you. They are divine, they are God's incarnation, they are enlightened; they are messengers, they are messiahs, and you… You are just an ignorant person moving from one life to another, carrying the same load of ignorance that goes on increasing with every life. These people have insulted the whole humanity.

As far as I am concerned, I want to say that not only are you enlightened, the trees, the rivers, the mountains, the stars are all enlightened. Otherwise is not possible. I want it absolutely clear to you, that to be alive is to be enlightened. Wherever there is life, wherever there is love, enlightenment is just hidden underneath. You may not recognize it. The whole effort is to help you to recognize it.

All the meditations are nothing but an effort to feel your enlightenment – which is already the case; whether you feel it or not it does not matter. If you feel it, you will rejoice and your life will become a dance, moment to moment, of tremendous glory and majesty, of grace and gratitude. If you don't recognize it, you will remain miserable, asking all kinds of idiots, frauds, "How can I become enlightened?"

There have been masters like Bodhidharma. You ask him how to become enlightened, and you will get such a good slap on your face that you will wake up immediately, saying, "I am sorry, I had just fallen asleep. I *am* enlightened." Those days were beautiful, when it was perfectly accepted that a master can slap the disciple. Now people have completely forgotten those beautiful moments and those beautiful days and those beautiful people.

It is said about Chuang Tzu…

When for the first time he entered the hut where Lao Tzu, his would-be master was living, Lao Tzu looked at Chuang Tzu and said, "Remember one thing: never ask me how to become enlightened." The poor fellow had come for that very purpose. But Lao Tzu made it clear, "I will accept you as my disciple only on this condition."

There was a moment of silence. Chuang Tzu thought, "It is strange. I have come to become enlightened. That is the very purpose of becoming a disciple. And this old fellow, so beautiful and so graceful, is asking such an absurd thing: 'If you want to be my disciple, promise me that you will never ask about how to become enlightened.'"

But it was already too late. He had fallen in love with the old man. He touched his feet and said, "I promise I will never ask how to become enlightened, but accept me as your disciple."

Immediately came a hard slap, "You idiot! If you are not going to become enlightened, then for what purpose are you becoming a disciple? I was asking this promise because I could see in you such beautiful intelligence that you might have immediately realized the point of my asking. You are enlightened; there is no way to *become* enlightened. There is no need. In fact, even if you want to become unenlightened, there is no way."

Then why has this whole humanity become unenlightened? How have they managed it? – just by forgetting, just by being too involved in other things. The world is vast, and the mind goes on taking you into new desires, longings, achievements, greed. Slowly, slowly a curtain falls between you and your mind, and the mind completely forgets your being. It forgets completely that there is an inner world also, not only an outer existence.

The outer is very poor in comparison to the inner. But once you get involved with the outer, it is so vast that there is a possibility you may wander around in the universe for millions of lives. And you may not realize that you are wasting your time, and that it is time to look in.

Promise me to never ask again: "I am not enlightened, how to become enlightened?" I have my own ways of slapping, far more sophisticated. I don't use my hand because I am a lazy man; moreover I don't want to hurt my hand. But I have my own ways, and I go on slapping people – and you know it well!

And the last part of your question is, "How is it that I can recognize that which I have not realized?" – you can recognize it; that is an absolute guarantee that you must have realized it in some unconscious way. Perhaps you have forgotten your realization. Each child is born with the realization.

I have condemned Gautam Buddha's story many times, but this time I am going to appreciate it, just to put things in balance. The story is: Gautam Buddha is born while his mother is standing under a saal tree, and he is born standing. And the first thing he does is to take seven steps in front of his mother and declare to the universe, "I am the most enlightened person ever." I have condemned it for different reasons; now I want to appreciate it for different reasons.

In fact, if he could, every newborn child would say the same thing: "I am enlightened." If every newborn child could walk, he would take seven steps and declare to the whole world: "I am the most enlightened person, unique." Perhaps the story is simply a symbolic way of recognizing each child's innocence as his enlightenment, as his ultimate experience. But he will be lost in the world. Perhaps once in a while someone comes back to his childhood again. My effort is to bring you back to your innocent childhood again. What you have not done in your first birth you can do in your second.

After I have gone from here tonight, everyone has to take seven steps and declare to the whole world, "I am the most enlightened person!" Try it, and you will really rejoice. And never fall back again into the old ignorance and start looking for how to become enlightened. Finish it tonight!

You are asking, "How one can recognize if one has not realized?" It is a question like if you are given a rotten egg in a restaurant and you say, "This is rotten." And the manager comes and says, "Are you a hen? Have you ever produced an egg? If you have never produced an egg, on what authority are you saying that this is rotten?"

There is no need. You can recognize things which you may not have consciously realized but which must be an undercurrent of realization within you. Except that, there is no other way. How do you realize when you fall in love that it is love? Certainly somewhere deep inside you there must be a hidden corner that already knows what love is. How do you recognize when you see a roseflower and say it is beautiful? Have you ever seen beauty? Have you ever realized what beauty is? But certainly you realize that the rose is beautiful. I am simply saying that there must be a certain realization in your being about beauty, about truth, about the ultimate sound of existence. That's what makes you recognize. You are much more than you think you are.

You are not what all the religions have made you – sinners, condemned, just sitting in the waiting room for the train to take you to hell. And the waiting room itself is giving you enough experience of hell!

The word *sin* is used by all the religions without paying attention to the root meaning of the word. The root meaning of the word is to forget. It has nothing to do with morality, it has nothing to do with your good actions or bad actions; it has something to do with forgetting who you are. And if you have forgotten, you can remember.

Gautam Buddha continually says to his disciples, "It is not a question of realization, it is only a question of remembering. What you have forgotten you have with you." Just a little search in all your pockets – also in the pockets which you are keeping secret even to yourself.

I have told you the story of Mulla Nasruddin…

Mulla is traveling in a train and a ticket checker comes, and Mulla looks into everything for his ticket. He opens all his suitcases and bags. And creates so much fuss that almost half of the passengers have to move to make space for all his things that he is taking out to look for the ticket.

Tired, the ticket checker says, "Forget all about it, just answer me one question and I will be satisfied. You have been looking in everything, in places where the ticket cannot be lost – you have even looked in your shoes. Why should the ticket be lost in your shoes? But you have not looked in the right pocket of your coat."

Mulla replied, "Don't mention that. I am not going to look in that pocket. That is my only hope, that perhaps the ticket is there. I can look everywhere in the world, but not in my right pocket."

Everyone in the compartment said, "This is strange, the fellow thinks that perhaps… If you think that perhaps the ticket may be there, then that is the first place to look. But no, there are different kinds of logic and different kinds of arithmetic. The man also has a point. He says, 'That is my only hope, don't destroy it. Let me look in the whole world first. That is the last resort.'"

Tired of his search, the ticket checker says, "Simply be quiet and collect your things, because you are disturbing all the passengers, and I will not ask anything about your right pocket."

Mulla said, "That's right. No one should ever make any indication toward my right pocket because I am not going to look there."

Most of us are searching for things exactly where we know they are not. Now, people are searching for God in churches, in temples, in stone statues, and no one ever thinks, "Is God going to be met there?" The statues are man-made, the temples are man-made and no one is looking inside himself, which is the only space not manufactured by man, the only place where perhaps the ticket is. It is simply a question of remembering. But you, whether you remember or not, are by nature part of the whole.

The experience that "I am part of the whole" is enlightenment. If you recognize it, you start dancing. If you don't recognize it, you go on crying unnecessarily. Things which are very simple have been made unnecessarily complicated, just to cheat you, exploit you. Religion has functioned in the world as the greatest business; the greatest in two senses: it accumulates more money than any other business and it goes on selling things which are invisible.

Now, selling things which are invisible is a great business. You purchase something invisible, you keep it carefully in your suitcase, afraid that it may get lost; then to find it will be very difficult. So keep the suitcase locked, never open it, because who knows? – the invisible thing may have wings, may fly out.

The most intelligent people in the world are also purchasing God – who is absolutely invisible – and purchasing tickets for heaven, depositing bank balances in paradise. And everything they give, they see with their own eyes going into the pockets of the priests. But perhaps from those pockets there are invisible ways. The money that they are giving to the pope will reach. In the Vatican the pope has a bank. It is really a branch of the original bank; you deposit in the branch and it will reach the original bank. You need not be worried about it.

And this pope goes on wasting your money in unnecessarily traveling here and there. He came to India, and wherever he goes the first thing he does is to kiss the earth. He could have done it in the Vatican. There was no need, the earth is the same everywhere, but certainly the tastes are different... When he touched down at

New Delhi airport, I was in Nepal and I said to my people, "This is his first taste of Hinduism." Because you cannot taste earth in India unless you taste cow dung, and that is the only essential Hinduism.

And he wastes your money, which you think is going to be deposited in paradise. On a single trip to Australia he wasted six million dollars – twice the visit of Elizabeth, the Queen of England. He has been around the world three times, wasting six million, eight million dollars on each trip. This is your money.

Once Bernard Shaw was asked, "Do you think a man can live joyfully just keeping his hands in his pockets and doing nothing?"

Bernard Shaw said, "Yes, it is possible. Just one thing has to be remembered: the hands must be yours, and the pockets must not be yours. Just keep your hand in someone else's pocket."

That has been the whole of religion. And they are giving you things which even an idiot can understand…

The Italian consul from Kolkata was here. Before he came here to be slapped by me he had gone to Satya Sai Baba. He seems to think himself a seeker of truth. And what happened in Satya Sai Baba's place? There they have an arrangement that you fill in a form with your name, your country, your job in the office, and what your essential question is, what you have come to ask. The Italian consul was taken in.

Many other people were sitting waiting for Satya Sai Baba. He was given a special place. Satya Sai Baba came in and directly pointed to him, saying, "You live in Kolkata. You are Italian. You work in the consulate." A great miracle! And he had filled in all the information.

These idiots like Satya Sai Baba are surrounded by other idiots not only of this country, they come from far away in search of truth. And he was immensely impressed: "This is your question. You want to know this, this is your inquiry. You are a great seeker of truth."

Now, naturally he is going to write a book. I will wait for his book. Here he also got special treatment, but I don't think he will have the guts to even refer to it. He was so afraid; he had an appointment to go to dinner with one of our sannyasins, Azima, but he simply escaped. He never reached the hotel where Azima was waiting for him for dinner; afraid that Azima was bound to ask, "What do you think about Osho?"

And it is not that he will not think about me. He will think about me day in and day out! He will see me in his dreams because he avoided seeing me here. When I pointed at him, he was holding his hand over his face. I could not believe that such cowards... When I was looking from the window of my car, I passed by his side; he had changed the position of his hand. Now he was keeping his hand over the side of his face. These are the people who are your diplomats, your politicians, your priests.

If religiousness means anything, it means fearlessness. It means taking a risk, putting at stake all that you have, all that is familiar, for the unknown; leaving the known and moving into the unknown. That simple step makes you religious. No other discipline is needed.

I have continually to postpone those funny and strange questions... Their time never comes. One is so great that I think tomorrow morning I will begin with it.

Now a few things to contemplate seriously...

Gorbachev, Margaret Thatcher, and Ronald Reagan are the guests of the king of Saudi Arabia, who has a magic swimming pool. The magic is that if you name a liquid while jumping into the empty pool, it will immediately be filled with that liquid.

Gorbachev goes first, and ripping off his clothes, he shouts, "Vodka!" and leaps into the pool, which is miraculously full of the finest Russian vodka.

Thatcher goes next, and bouncing along in her bra and panties, she yells, "Whiskey!" She lands with a splash in a pool filled with the finest, twelve-year-old scotch.

Not to be outdone, Reagan races toward the pool in his jockey shorts, stubs his toes on the edge of the pool and falling headlong, he screams, "Oh, shit!"

# 2

# Lovemaking Should Be a Meditative Process

Osho,
My girlfriend told me that I am a little boring, not very juicy, very dependent and a victim. Then I felt very guilty and depressed and utterly unworthy. I began to feel inside me a big "No" toward existence, life, love, you. Meanwhile, I observed in me this destructive energy and I felt that I somehow enjoyed it! Is it possible to use this energy in some creative way?

Your question is an example of the stupid conclusions that the mind comes to. Perhaps you may not have looked into it and its contradictions. I would like to go into the very psychology of such questions. They are not only within you, they are within many. You are courageous to expose yourself.

The exposure begins: "My girlfriend told me I am a little boring…" Your girlfriend is very compassionate because each man finally becomes *very* boring, not a little boring. Do you realize the fact that what you call love is a repetition, the same stupid gymnastics again and again? And in this whole stupid game the man is the loser. He is dissipating his energy, perspiring, huffing, puffing, and the girl keeps her eyes closed, thinking, "It is only a question of two or three minutes and this nightmare will be finished."

People are so uninventive that they take it for granted that going through the same actions is making them more interesting. That's why I say your girlfriend is very compassionate – she only told you that you are a little boring. I say to you, that you are utterly boring. When the Christian missionaries came to this country, people discovered that they knew only one posture of making love: the woman underneath and those ugly beasts on top of the delicate woman. In India that posture is called the missionary posture.

India is an ancient land and the birthplace of many sciences, particularly sexology. A book of tremendous importance, by Vatsyayana, has been in existence for five thousand years. The name of the book is *Kamasutra*, hints for making love. And it comes from a man of deep meditation; he has created eighty-four postures for lovemaking. Naturally the love posture should change, otherwise you are bound to be boring.

Vatsyayana recognizes the fact that the same love posture creates boredom, a feeling of utter stupidity, because you are always doing the same thing. He invented eighty-four postures to make the love life of couples a little interesting. No one in the whole world has written a book of the caliber of *Kamasutra*. But it could only have come from a man of immense clarity, of deep meditativeness.

What is your lovemaking? If you look at your lovemaking, you yourself will feel that it is all boring. And particularly for the woman it is more boring because the man is finished in two or three minutes and the woman has not even started. All around the world, cultures have enforced in the minds of women that they are not supposed even to enjoy or move or be playful. That is called "dirty"; prostitutes do it, not ladies. Ladies have to lie down almost dead and let that old guy do whatever he wants to do; it is nothing new, there is nothing new even to see.

You should not take it as a personal disrespect. Your girlfriend is telling you something really sincere and honest. Have you given her orgasmic joy? Or have you only used her to throw out your sexual energy? Have you reduced her to a commodity? She has been conditioned to accept it, but even this accepting cannot be joyful.

You make love on the same bed where you fight every day. In fact fighting is the preface: throwing pillows, shouting at each other, arguing about everything and then, tired, some negotiation is needed. Your love is only a negotiation. If you are a man of aesthetic sensibility, your love chamber should be a sacred place because it is in that love chamber that life is born. It should have beautiful flowers, incense, fragrance; you should enter it with deep respect.

And love should not be just an abrupt thing – just grabbing the woman. This hit-and-run affair is not love. Love should have a preface of beautiful music, of dancing together, of meditating together. Love should not be a mind thing, where you are continuously thinking of how to make love and then go to sleep. Love should be a deeper involvement of your whole being, and it should not be projected by the mind but should come out spontaneously – beautiful music, fragrance, you are dancing hand in hand, you have again become small children playing with flowers... If love happens spontaneously in this sacred atmosphere, it will have a different quality.

You should understand that the woman is capable of multiple orgasms because she does not lose any energy. Man is capable of only one orgasm and he loses energy, looks depressed. Even the next morning you can see his hangover, and as he goes on growing older it becomes more and more difficult.

This difference has to be understood. The woman is on the receptive end; she has to be, because she has to become a mother, she needs more energy. But her orgasm has a totally different way of happening. Man's sexuality is local, like local anesthesia. A woman's body is sexual all over. And unless her whole body starts trembling with joy, with each cell of her body becoming involved, she cannot have an orgasmic explosion.

So it is not only in your case, it is the case for almost ninety-nine percent of women around the world. The whole situation has to be changed. The woman should not be under the man. In the first place it is ugly; the man has a stronger body, the woman is more fragile. She should be on top of the man, not the man on top of the woman.

Secondly, man should remain silent, inactive, so that his orgasm is not finished within two minutes. If you are silent and let the woman go crazy on top of your chest it will give her good exercise and it will bring her to an explosion of orgasmic energy. It takes time for her whole body to warm up, and if you are not inactive there is no time. So you meet, but the meeting is not of beauty, of love, but just utilitarian.

Try what I am saying with your girlfriend. You be the inactive partner and let her be the active partner. Allow her to be uninhibited. She has not to behave like a lady, she has to behave like an authentic woman. The lady is just created by man; woman is created by existence. You have to fill the gap between your orgasms. The gap can be filled in only one way: you remain very inactive, silent, and enjoy her going crazy. And she will have multiple orgasms. You should end the game by your orgasm, but you should not begin with it.

Then your woman will not call you a little boring. You will be a really interesting, real wonderful guy who is behaving like a lady! Keep your eyes closed so that she is not inhibited by your eyes. So she can do anything – movement of the hands, movement of the body, moaning, groaning, shouting... Unless she says, "*Hari om tat sat*!" you are not allowed to be alive, you simply remain silent. This should be the indication. *Hari om tat sat* simply shows: this orgasmic explosion, this is the truth. Then she will be going mad after you. Right now you must be behaving stupidly, as most of the men in the world do.

The second thing you say: "My girlfriend is saying that I am not very juicy..." So become a little more juicy! To become juicy is not very difficult. The juice of all kinds of fruits is available everywhere. Drink more juice, less solid food. She is giving you good advice and you in your stupidity are thinking that she is condemning you. When she says, "...you are very dependent and a victim,"

I can see even through your question that she is right. You are a victim, just as every human being is a victim – a victim of stupid ideologies, which have created strange guilt feelings and do not allow you to be playful. Although you may be making love, you know you are committing a sin and that hell is not far off.

Becky Goldberg was telling Goldberg, "You are a great lover."

Goldberg said, "But you never told me this before. I was waiting for someone to say that I am a great lover, but I dropped the idea because it seems I am not."

Becky Goldberg said to him, "No, you are a great lover, and I wanted to say it to you many times, but you were not there!"

...making love to Becky, and Goldberg is not there. He is counting his money, doing his accounts, and his mind is doing thousands of things. In every bed where there are two lovers there are at least – I mean minimum – four people. There are more inventive people; they may have a whole crowd in the bed. The woman is making love to Goldberg and thinking of Muhammad Ali. Goldberg is making love as a duty and is thinking of so many beautiful actresses. But his mind is not there, and neither is his wife's mind there. Their minds are in their dreams.

A man told his friend, "Last night I had a tremendous dream. I have to tell you. I have been waiting for the morning to tell you the dream."

The man said, "What kind of dream?"

He said, "I went fishing in my dream and I caught such big fish that even to draw in one big fish was a strenuous job for me, and I caught so many fish. I don't know where these fish disappear to in the day."

The other man said, "Stop all this nonsense, you don't know what I have dreamed. In my dream I found, on one side of me, Sophia Loren, absolutely nude. And I said, 'My God, have I reached heaven?' On the other side was another beautiful woman. It was impossible to judge who was more beautiful."

The other friend became very angry and said, "You idiot! You pretend to be my best friend. Why didn't you call me?"

He said, "I did call, but your wife said you had gone fishing."

No one is where you think he is. No one is at home. While making love make it a meditative process. Your whole presence has to be there, showering on the woman you love. The woman has to be there, showering all her beauty and grace on her lover. Then you will not be a victim, otherwise you are a victim.

Love is not accepted by your so-called, utterly idiotic religions to be a natural and playful experience. They condemn it. They have made it a condition: unless you leave your woman, you will never attain truth. And the conditioning has been going on for so long that it has almost become a truth, although it is an absolute lie.

You are a victim of traditions and you are certainly dependent. When I read on with your question, you will see how you are dependent – dependent on a girlfriend who tells you that you are boring, not very juicy and a victim.

Your dependence shows further: "Then I felt very guilty and depressed and utterly unworthy." If your girlfriend, by saying such simple truths, can make you very guilty and depressed and utterly unworthy, she certainly seems to be your master. "I began to feel inside me a big 'No'…" And this is where your girlfriend has been kind, not to say to you, "You are a little bit of an idiot too."

You are saying, "I began to feel inside me a big 'No' toward existence…" Now, what has existence done? Do you think your girlfriend is existence? "…toward life." Do you think your girlfriend is life? "…toward love." And finally, "…toward you." Why involve me? I have not been giving all these ideas to your girlfriend; I don't know her. She is not getting these lessons from me about what to tell you.

This shows your utter idiocy. Are you here for me or for your girlfriend? I go on saying things every day and nothing changes in you. Your girlfriend just said that you are a little boring and you don't doubt her. Perhaps you have come here following your girlfriend. And in what way can you say no to existence, to life, to love and to me? That really is hilarious. I had not said anything and you have included me – on what grounds?

Rather than listening to your girlfriend who was saying sincerely that you are just a little boring, you should have asked her, "In what way can I become a little more interesting? Do you have any suggestions? If I am not juicy then tell me how I can become juicy." That would have been an intelligent step. But instead of asking the girl you started having "...a big 'No' toward existence, life, love, you." Sometimes I think that... I don't even know you personally, nor your girlfriend. In what way am I involved in it?

But I can understand the reason. Perhaps you may not be able to explain it, but I can see the underlying reason for your "big No." You believe in your girlfriend too much; naturally you could not ask her. That shows your dependence. You must be afraid to make much fuss about these things with the girl, because girlfriends are not your permanent wives, no law prevents them from moving with someone who is more juicy. And in the beginning everyone is juicy, but just a few days together and the whole juice dries up. You start looking around for some other girl, from some other man, because they are all looking juicy.

You will repeat the same thing life after life; you have done it already, without understanding the foundation. Living with one man more than a week, then the problem arises of how to get rid of him. He is also thinking about how to get rid of you. But it does not look right to say so to each other, so you start creating trouble; that somehow some other idiot may become interested in your girlfriend because you both go on seeing that other girls are more juicy, other men are more juicy. It is an old story that the grass on the other side of the fence of your bungalow looks greener than your own grass. Distance creates that phenomenon.

Any woman may look juicier to you than your wife – she is just a pain in the neck. But what you don't know is that all these women are following the same philosophy. For one or two days they are so groovy, and once they have caught hold of you the real story starts – they start becoming a pain in the neck. And the same is true about men. Meeting a girl on the sea beach, in the garden, by the side of a river, he pretends to be Alexander the Great; he walks like a lion, and within two days the same fellow is reduced to a rat.

No one talks about the reality of why this is happening, why so many people are unnecessarily made miserable. This society will never be happy if we don't allow people to move and not get stuck in marriages, not get stuck in their own promises. Meet with each other out of freedom, and the moment you feel that you have explored the whole topography of the woman and the woman knows that she has experienced whatever is possible to experience in the man, then it is time to say good-bye to each other in deep friendliness. There is no need to hang around each other's neck.

A world completely free from any contracts between man and woman will be immensely lovely, beautiful, unboring, interesting. But we have created institutions, and to live in an institution is not a very great experience. Your marriage is an institution – although the newer generation is moving a little more freely, before settling after the age of thirty. I have been looking around the world to find a hippie who is at least of the age thirty-five. I have not found any. Nearabout thirty all hippies disappear, they become just square people whom they were fighting against before.

Seeing the situation, that living in institutions – of marriage, community, society, the Lions Club, the Rotary Club – you cannot live joyously, you have experimented. This is the first time in history that we have a younger generation. I don't mean that in the past there were not young people, but there was no "younger generation." A small child, seven years old, would start following the father's business, would start going to the fields, would start taking care of the cows; or if the father was a carpenter, would start helping him. At the age of seven he had already joined the society.

For the first time in history there is a generation which can be authentically called younger and which has created a generation gap. Schools, colleges, universities are there and it takes twenty-five years, twenty-six years to come out of the university with a postgraduate degree or with a doctorate. But by that time you are no longer young. By that time you start having responsibilities: professorial, professional, family, marriage.

But between the time that you spend in the hostels and in the universities, before entering life, there is a long gap in which you are not engaged in any utilitarian, purposive activity. That has created the generation gap. Men and women become sexually mature – women at the age of thirteen, men at the age of fourteen – and they will be married perhaps ten years afterward or twelve years afterward. These twelve years have created girlfriends and boyfriends.

It is a great opportunity for the future to understand the whole phenomenon and its psychology. You have the choice to change the old habits, to create trouble but drop old habits. Every man needs to be aware of many women. Every woman needs the experience of many other men before deciding to marry. Their experience will help them to find the right person with whom they can melt and merge without any difficulty.

You are saying, "Meanwhile, I observed in me this destructive energy and I felt that I somehow enjoyed it!" Everyone has destructive energy because energy, if left to itself, is bound to be destructive – unless it is used with awareness and becomes creative.

But the most important thing that you are saying is that, "... somehow I enjoyed it!" Then how are you going to change it? With anything that you enjoy you are bound to remain on the same level; you cannot change it because you may not enjoy the change. And all this has come to your mind only because your girlfriend told you that you are "...a little boring, not very juicy, very dependent and a victim."

You have energy. To enjoy destructive energy is suicidal, to enjoy destructive energy as destructive is in the service of death. If you are aware of it, you have to go through a transformation.

Use your energy creatively, perhaps that will make you less boring, more juicy, less dependent, less of a victim. And the most important part will be that you will not feel guilty and depressed. No creative person feels depressed and guilty. His participation with the universe by his creative actions makes him tremendously fulfilled and gives him dignity. That is the very birthright of every man, but very few people claim it.

Moreover, this big no will become a big yes if the energy moves into creative dimensions. And there is no difficulty, it is so easy to use energy in creative fields. Paint, garden, grow flowers, write poetry, learn music, dance. Learn anything that changes your destructive energy into creative energy, and immediately the big no will become even a bigger yes. Then you will not be angry at existence, you will be grateful. You will not be against life. How can a creative person be against life, love? It is impossible, it has never happened. It is only the uncreative people who are against everything. If you can be creative, life-affirmative, you cannot be against me, because I am giving you the directions for becoming an authentic, sincere, celebrating individual.

Your girl has raised very important questions for your life. The easiest way would be to change the girlfriend, but I suggest that your girlfriend is certainly a friend to you and that whatever she has said is absolutely sincere, authentic. Be grateful to her and start changing things. The day your girlfriend accepts you as juicy, as interesting, will be a great day in your life. So don't be a coward and change girlfriends because "This girlfriend creates trouble in the mind, find some other girlfriend."

You must know of my disciples here. You are fortunate to find a very compassionate girl. Your next choice will be very difficult; she will make you feel absolutely guilty and unworthy. Because what have you done to be worthy? What have you done not to be boring? What have you done to declare your independence? What have you done not to be a victim? It is time you should do it. You will remain always grateful to your girlfriend.

I would like to tell your girlfriend, "Go on hitting this fellow until you are satisfied that he is not boring, but full of juice, utterly interesting, playful, celebrating. You may lose him somewhere on the path of life, but you will have prepared him for some other woman; otherwise the way he is now he is going to torture many women and torture himself."

He is even planning to torture me! I am absolutely out of the game, I am not a partner in your relationship. In what way have you managed to think that a no arises against me? I understand why it arises. It arises because I respect women in every dimension as being equally capable as men. They have been beaten down the ages; they have never been able to say a single thing about their husbands.

Just three days ago it has been reported that even in America husbands are beating their wives. But the wives have been hiding the fact up to now because it does not look as if you have been beaten and you cannot do anything, nor does it look good to defame the husband. It does not look good to the children, if they come to know. I used to think that wives are only beaten in India.

One of the great Hindu saints, Tulsidas, who is worshipped and read all over India by every Hindu, has a strange statement: "*Dhol ganwar pashu aur nari. Ye sab taran ke adhikari.*" He is categorizing women with drums – *dhol* means drum, *ganwar* means idiots, *pashu* means animals, and *nari* means woman. All these four are constantly to be beaten. The *dhol*, the drum, will not work if you don't beat it. So for thousands of years Indian women have been beaten. It has been taken for granted, there is no question.

I have come across situations where a husband was beating his wife and I could not tolerate it. I entered their house, and I was amazed that more than the husband, the wife was against me, saying, "He is my husband, you cannot interfere in our affairs. If he is beating me, it is perfectly okay."

The conditioning has gone so deep. Here, I am taking out all your conditionings; I am preparing the future man who will respect the woman as equal to himself, who will give opportunity for her growth as he takes opportunity for his own growth. And there will not be any kind of bondage. If two people can live in love their whole life, no one is going to disturb them. There is no need of any marriage and there is no need of any divorce. Love should be an absolute act of freedom. But you have been told for thousands of years, "If you really love, then your love has to be permanent." I don't see that anything in life has the quality of being permanent. Love cannot be an exception.

So don't expect that love has to be permanent. It will make your love life more beautiful because you know today you are together, tomorrow perhaps you will have to part. Love comes like a fresh, fragrant breeze into your home, fills it with freshness and fragrance, remains as long as existence allows it and then moves out. You should not try to close all your doors or the same fresh breeze will become absolutely stale.

That's what people's lives have become: stale, ugly. And the reason lies in their idea of permanent love. In life everything is changing. Change is beautiful; it gives you more and more experience, more and more awareness, more and more maturity.

Just to change the subject…

The male dinosaur has been going out with the female dinosaur for two thousand years and finally he asks her for a kiss. She agrees.

Four thousand years later he asks if they might hug a little, and she agrees.

Three thousand years later he says, "Look, honey, we have been seeing each other for about nine thousand years. Don't you think it is about time we…er…you know, get it on?"

She looks at him shyly, and says, "Oh, darling I would love to, but I'm having my decade."

A little Jew is wandering through the Sahara Desert carrying a watermelon under his arm. He stares into the distance where he thinks he is seeing a mirage. But no, it turns out to be Pope the Polack walking toward him, carrying a car door.

They greet each other and the pope asks the Jew why he is carrying the watermelon.

"Every time I get thirsty I eat a slice," explains the Jew. "And what are you doing with that car door?"

"Well," says Pope the Polack, "every time I get too hot I just roll down the window."

# 3

# Enlightenment Is Your Very Being

Osho,
When you said last night that I am enlightened, it really freaked me out. It looks like I'm much more at ease with being unenlightened and searching for it, rather than just being enlightened. I don't know what the question is, but I feel I need a slap to wake me up!

The question you have asked must be reflecting the question of many people. It is significant in the sense that being enlightened brings a full stop to your desires, longings, searchings. All that you have done down the ages is only desiring, seeking, dreaming, hoping. And one is afraid to come to a point where suddenly you find there is no way to go, nowhere to go: you have arrived.

You are saying, "When you said last night that everyone is enlightened it really freaked me out." It freaked many out, it freaked many *in*, but it certainly freaked. And it brought to the surface something that you must have been carrying within your unconscious. Without this freaking out it may not have come to the surface.

You are saying, "It looks like I'm much more at ease with being unenlightened and searching for it, rather than just being enlightened." You are saying something immensely significant, not only about you, but about the human mind as such. It is at ease in hoping, it is at ease if there is a tomorrow. The goal may be far away, but if the goal is there it is at ease. It does not want to come to a standstill – that feels very uneasy because we have become accustomed to dreaming, running after goals, never arriving but always trying to arrive. The goal seems to be just close by, but the distance between you and the goal remains the same whatever you do. It is almost like the horizon. You go toward it; it goes on receding back in the same proportion. This has been the training of our minds, this is what we are; hence although you are just a beggar dreaming about kingdoms, you are at ease.

It happens in many ways. You will not find poor people thinking about the meaning of life, you will not find poor people even bothering whether there is something like enlightenment or not. Only when a civilization becomes richer – people become educated, their bodily needs are fulfilled – do they suddenly start thinking about faraway goals. Then they start searching in many dimensions. They are searching, but deep down they don't want to arrive at the conclusion. This is a strange dilemma, but if you understand rightly, you can see the point. The point is that the mind can live only in movement. When there is no movement time stops, the mind stops, and only you are.

It was not you who freaked out, it was your mind, with which you are absolutely identified. Unless you create a distance between the mind and you – you the witness – then you will remain searching. Money, power, prestige, God, paradise, enlightenment; anything will do, just it should keep you going onward. Any direction is okay; just stopping is dangerous because the moment you stop, the mind dies. The moment you stop your personality dies. The moment you stop you disappear into the oceanic existence; hence the fear.

I have told you a beautiful story about Rabindranath…

In one of his poems he has the same glimpse that is expressed in your question. In the poem he says, "I have been searching for God for many, many lives. Sometimes I saw him near a faraway star, and I was immensely happy that although the star was far away, it was not impossible to reach. And I started moving there, but by the time I reached the star God had moved to some other place. But he was visible – although so far away, but inviting, creating hope. I went on running around the universe for many, many lives.

"One day it happened that I came to the house of God. I could not believe that I had arrived. It was such a shock, but still I stepped toward the door. As I was going to knock on the door my hand suddenly froze. A thought arose in me: just wait a minute and think it over. It is written outside the door, 'This is the house of God.' If by chance, it turns out to be *really* the house of God then you are finished. What are you going to do then?

"For millions of years your training has been only for searching. You are perfectly disciplined as a seeker, but finding? That is absolutely new; you are not acquainted with it. And moreover, finding the ultimate, the absolute God, beyond which there is nothing to search… What will you do then? What will you be? And it is going to be forever – an eternal situation of a full stop."

He took his shoes in his hands. He was afraid that as he was going back down the steps, if God heard some noise outside and opened the door… And then he ran away, not looking back.

The poem is beautiful because it says, "I am again searching for him. I know him, his house; I go on avoiding it. I go in every direction, but I keep myself far away from the house where he is because I know that meeting him is going to be my disappearance."

Enlightenment is nothing but your disappearance. It is nothing but a pure silence. Naturally one feels afraid and one starts thinking, "It is better to remain unenlightened and searching for it." The story that I told you from Rabindranath's poem is your story. It is everyone's story. That's why I say that you *are* enlightened, but you don't want to recognize it. You want to find some way so that you can start searching for enlightenment again.

In the search is the mind, the ego, the personality; in the search are all the saints, the sages, the prophets, the incarnations of God. The moment you arrive, you are just a pure silence, a nothingness – alive, abundantly alive, overflowingly alive, full of fragrance, but now there is no movement. You will remain in this silence for eternity. I think every one of you has returned from the house; knows the way, knows the house and is still searching and seeking and asking, "Where is the house of God? Where can I find him?"

The moment you understand that the reason for your search is not that you are not enlightened, the reason for your search is that the mind wants to go on living, and it can live only in your unenlightenment... You have to choose. You can choose the mind and go on seeking for eternity that which is available right now, this very moment. Or you can choose the state of no-mind, no-movement and disappear in the cosmos, in the eternal peace, in the splendor of the universe. But it all depends on you; it is your freedom.

The biblical story that God drove Adam and Eve out from paradise is certainly wrong. It is Adam and Eve who escaped because in the garden of paradise there was no possibility of being a prophet, no possibility of being someone special, no possibility of any ego arising. In the garden of paradise, you, the trees, the animals are all equal. Seeing this situation, my own understanding is that Adam and Eve escaped, they were not driven out. It was a revolt against a state where everything was available and there was no way to find anything new. Escaping from that kingdom, man started searching.

I have reasons to say that: in India the twenty-four tirthankaras of the Jainas are all kings who renounced their kingdoms. Gautam Buddha was going to be a king, the only son of his old father. He escaped before he was crowned as the king. The ceremonies were ready because the old man wanted Gautam Buddha to be crowned before him; he wanted to see his son on the throne. Seeing the situation, Gautam Buddha escaped. He had seen everything, he had all that was possible for anyone to have in his possession in those days.

The most beautiful women of the kingdom were collected just for his pleasure. His father had made three different palaces in different places, for different seasons.

In India, just in my childhood, the seasons were absolutely certain. They became disturbed only after the Second World War; otherwise, each season was four months long. And it was absolutely determined: the winter comes exactly on one date, the winter goes exactly on one date.

The old king had made three beautiful palaces in his kingdom, so when it was summer Gautam Buddha could move to a hill station; when it was winter, too cold, he could come to the plains, near a beautiful river; when it was too rainy, he had found a place for him where it was a pleasure, not in any way a trouble.

There is a place just nearby where Gautam Buddha was born. Perhaps in the whole world that is the place where it rains the most – five hundred inches per year! In Pune it rains only seventy inches per year. Even to live in a nearby place, Khandala, is very difficult; it rains two hundred inches per year. That means for days it goes on raining, you cannot come out; for days there is no sun, for days it is just rain and rain. Just conceive, five hundred inches… For four months continually there will perhaps not be a single day when it is not raining, and great floods. Gautam Buddha's father had found a faraway place where the rainfall was nearabout forty or fifty inches per year; just a pleasure. Gautam Buddha became tired, bored because everything that he needed was handed over to him, even without his asking.

It is a strange situation. When you are poor you want to be rich, and when you are rich suddenly you feel that you have gained everything, but you have lost hope. Now there is nowhere to go; you have come to the last rung of the ladder. Sitting there on the last rung of the ladder you look simply foolish and nothing else.

This accounts for the differences in the religions which were born in India and the religions which were born outside India. It needs a tremendous psychological insight. Jesus was a poor man. Moses was also not a rich man; he could have been a rich man, but he discovered that he was a Jew and he wanted to be with his own race. He renounced all his powers and went into a great revolt against the Egyptian kings. Mohammed was also a poor man. These three poor men created three religions outside India. The three religions created in India were all created by kings. Rama and Krishna are kings; Mahavira and Adinatha are kings; Gautam Buddha is a king. And you can see the difference between the religions because of these people's situations.

Gautam Buddha does not promise you any paradise where beautiful women will be available to you, where rivers of wine will be flowing – strange, but not inexplicable. He is fed up with women, he is fed up with wine, he is fed up with everything that money can purchase. All that he can promise his disciples is a pure silence.

But Mohammed cannot do that, Jesus cannot do that. Jesus has to provide in his paradise all those beautiful things which poor people are missing on the earth. Mohammed provides rivers of wine, beautiful women. And you will be shocked to know, because homosexuality was very much prevalent in Saudi Arabia, that in paradise beautiful boys are also provided for the sages.

Jesus provides everything that a poor man can dream of and can hope for. Mahavira provides only absolute aloneness. This will not appeal to a poor man. He is already very lonely, and you have come… And to attain that aloneness he has to go through all these disciplines. Are you mad? He wants things: he wants beautiful women, he wants beautiful men, he wants beautiful houses. You have come here saying, "You have to fast, you have to train yourself in Yoga, you have to meditate. Then finally you will get pure nothingness."

This can appeal only to the very rich. They are tired of things, they want just silence; they are tired of people, they want pure aloneness. The poor man is not tired; he has not even had the chance to be tired of money. He is hoping that someday he will have money, have a beautiful house.

One day I was going to the university and I was stopped on the road by a beautiful woman who gave me a pamphlet. "What is it?" I asked,

She said, "Everything is explained in it, and if you are interested the phone number is given."

Driving to the university, I looked at the pamphlet; it showed a beautiful house by the side of a mountain river, great tall trees, and a question: "Do you want this house?"

I thought, "In this city, at least, there is no such house; perhaps I don't know it? If it is available, it is worth looking at the details."

I turned the page and inside the details were given: "If you become a follower of Jesus Christ, in the kingdom of God you will have even better houses than the one you have just seen on the other side of the page."

When a poor man creates a religion it is bound to be full of your desires, greed, lust, and a promise that everything will be fulfilled. When a rich man creates a religion his religion is going to be purity, silence, a beautiful space. But you are one with that beautiful space, not separate. Looking at the religions, their holy books, you can decide whether those holy books came from poor people or from people who have known riches. And remember one thing, the poor man's paradise is just a projection. That's why all the religions that have been created outside India – just by coincidence – don't have the quality, the superiority, the grandeur that Indian religions have.

But India is no longer rich. Those religions were created some seven thousand years ago, some five thousand years ago, some twenty-five centuries ago. Today even the Indian masses have turned to Christianity. Christianity is now the third greatest religion in India. They have turned to Mohammedanism, which is now the second greatest religion in India. Hinduism goes on shrinking, and more and more people go on turning toward Christianity, Mohammedanism, because more and more people are poor. Hinduism has nothing to offer the poor people. They are not interested in nirvana, they are not interested in meditation, they are not interested in their inner being. You can see it here. If anyone descends from Mars and looks at this commune, he would not think that this commune exists in India. How many Indians are here?

The religion that I am providing for you is the highest possible. It is not for those who are seeking employment, not for those who are hungry, starving. It needs intelligence to understand me. It needs a kind of frustration with the world: the kind of experience that all this world provides is meaningless, that it leads nowhere, that it is a sheer wastage of life. Something more is needed – something that money cannot purchase, something that science cannot produce, something that is not available in the market, something that you have to find within yourself.

Why are people not interested in themselves? Perhaps at some moment in their past lives they had reached the house of God, and ever since they have been running away from it. Although they give good names for their running: they are running in search of God, they are running in search of self-realization, they are running for enlightenment. In fact they are running away from exactly these things, as far away as possible.

But you cannot run because your enlightenment is your very being, whether you like it or not. Existence has not asked you whether you want to be born or not; neither has existence asked you whether you want enlightenment in your innermost core or not. Existence does not treat you as separate; hence there is no question of asking you. You are part and parcel of this beautiful universe. And this universe goes on moving into different forms, but the innermost core remains the same: the same light, the same joy, the same celebration.

It is frightening to you because then there will be no movement. But I have been in this full stop for thirty-five years and not for a single moment have I felt that I am in a wrong situation.

People ask me, "You don't move your legs for two hours..." I have also thought, "Why don't I move my legs?" Then finally I discovered that there is no need. I am not walking, why should I move them? It is not only here that I am sitting like that, the whole day I am sitting in my chair just like that. You must be puzzled about what I am doing in my room – just sitting. And there is not even grass growing!

Nothing is happening and I am perfectly happy; even for a single moment there is not a desire – even to go into the ashram and see what kind of stupid things are happening. Just last night when you all had become enlightened... Nirvano told me, "You should have been there."

I heard the noise. I said, "This is enough for me: that my people have become enlightened, I'm just worried what will happen to their enlightenment in the morning." And I can see that you shouted unnecessarily; not even a single one has become enlightened! You can try it today again because this is the place where you *have* to become enlightened. Just watch Sardar Gurudayal Singh. Most probably he will become enlightened before anyone else. He shouts better, he laughs better, what more is needed?

Pope the Polack and a nun, riding a very fresh and alive looking camel, arrive in a small town in the middle of the Sahara Desert. The pope is completely exhausted and decides to have a few days' vacation. He checks into a caravanserai for the night and the next morning comes out of the tent wearing his underpants and carrying a towel across his shoulder.

"Excuse me," he asks one of the Bedouins, "but can you tell me how far it is to the water?"

"Oh," the Arab replies, "a few hundred miles."

"Shit," says Pope the Polack, "I guess I will have to stay on the beach today."

...hundreds of miles away, then it is better to stay at the beach.

Amos Saperstein dies suddenly with an enormous erection. The undertaker, Moishe Finkelstein, tries everything to make it shrink.

He puts cold water on it, then packs it in ice cubes, but nothing works. Finally they decide that they have only one option: they cut a hole in the lid of the coffin and cover it with a sheet.

On the way to the cemetery the coffin is carried past two little old ladies sitting on a bench. "Well, there goes old Amos," says grandma Kravitz. "I hope his family gave him a proper send-off."

Just then a gust of wind blows the sheet off the top of the coffin.

"The tight-fisted bastards," says grandma. "Look at that! Only one lousy flower."

And the last, before you start becoming enlightened again…

A priest with a huge prick has terrible trouble getting any woman to sleep with him. At the local whorehouse it is always the same answer, "Sorry father, I wish I could, but that monster is much too big for me."

In desperation, the priest thinks up a cunning scheme. He visits a whorehouse on the other side of the town where no one knows him, picks out a girl and takes her to the bedroom.

Once they are inside the priest tells the girl he is very shy and then says, "Do you mind if I undress with the lights out?"

She agrees. Then as he climbs on top of her she says, "Do you know, father, I am really glad this is what you came here for. When you first walked through the door I was sure you were just going to talk to me about… Jesus Christ!"

# 4

# Fear Is a Byproduct of Your Unconsciousness

Osho,

I always thought that one had to conquer fear, and then death would not be scary anymore. The other day I was sitting in a place in the hills where people were killed and I saw that death is sweet. Now I think it must be more like this: that death helps one to understand fear; that first you experience death and she helps you see what fear is all about. Is it like this? Can you talk about it please?

Your question is based on complete misunderstanding, confusion. First, you will have to understand where your confusion is. You say, "I always thought that one had to conquer fear…" This is the first point of misunderstanding. You cannot conquer fear. Fear has to be understood. The moment you start thinking of conquering it, you have already accepted its existence, its power over you. And fear is just like a shadow: you can fight with it, but you cannot win. On the path, one has to be very aware whether one is fighting with something that does not exist but is only your own projection; otherwise the journey goes on becoming longer and longer.

Secondly, the language of conquering is not the language of a meditator, it is the language of a soldier. We have nothing to conquer. We have to certainly understand everything concerning ourselves, our mind, its workings. For example, fear has never existed. That does not mean that people have not been afraid. That is a totally different thing. People have been afraid because they don't understand many things, and fear arises out of their ignorance.

You have seen death – you think so. Death can be seen only in deep meditation, where it withers away like darkness withering away when the light is brought in. But everyone thinks he has seen death because he has seen someone dying.

To see someone dying is not to see death, because what is happening inside the person is invisible to you. He is only changing house; he is moving from this body to another body. But once the consciousness that is his life moves out of the body, the body is dead. The body has always been made of dead, material things. It is the consciousness within which radiates through all that the body is constituted of, and makes it look alive.

And you know perfectly well, when you are depressed, sad, you look less alive. When you are joyous, blissful, laughing, you look more alive. Life comes from the inner sources of your being and life is eternal; hence, death cannot exist. Death is only a change which you cannot see with your eyes.

There have been experiments done. If there is something like consciousness or soul in man… They have weighed a dying person. Certainly if something leaves him he will lose weight – it does not happen. And because he does not lose weight, the people who have been experimenting with such stupid things have concluded that there is no consciousness. Consciousness has no weight.

So first you have to understand that fear has not to be conquered; otherwise you will remain always afraid of the conquered fear, because the conquered fear is there. You may be on top of it, but things change. You may, in a certain weak moment, be defeated by the nonexistent fear again and it will be on top of you. You do not always have the same vitality, the same aliveness; there are ups and downs. In every state when you are not feeling a well-being, fear will come back. And the miraculous thing is that fear has no existence except in your imagination.

You have not seen death. To see death there is one possibility, and that is deep meditation; the other possibility is to die. But the other possibility is not certain because death is such a great surgical phenomenon – the whole consciousness has to leave the body – and nature has made an arrangement that before people die they become unconscious.

Medical science learned very late that when you operate, first make the man unconscious. Either local or general, but some anesthesia, some unconsciousness has to be there. He will not be able to bear the pain. And this is about small surgery. Death is the greatest surgery. Your whole consciousness is taken out of your body. Naturally you become unconscious before it happens. So even if you die – and you have died many times – you don't remember. How can you remember? You were unconscious, and your memory has not made any record of it.

So the only certain way – a hundred percent proof – is meditation. Meditation creates the situation in which you know that you and your body are absolutely separate. They are working together in deep harmony, in great synchronicity, but they are not one. Once you understand that they are not one, you know your consciousness is your life. And the moment life leaves the body, people think the body is dead.

It is always someone else who dies. Have you observed it? You never die. One feels really great that someone else has died and you have been alive for eighty years and still death has not come. In fact, the longer you live, the less is the possibility of your dying.

The data is that most people die nearabout seventy-five. Then the ratio of death starts falling. Nearabout the age of eighty, less people die. Nearabout the age of ninety, even less people die. Nearabout the age of one hundred, very few people die. Nearabout the age of one hundred and fifty, it is very rare to find someone dying. And nearabout the age of two hundred, there is no precedent. So if you can go on pulling yourself up to two hundred, you will not die. You will see everyone else dying and you will enjoy!

But seeing someone else dying is not an experience of death. You have to go so deep inward that you are only pure consciousness. The body is surrounding you, but it is not inseparable from you. You can see the gap. That very moment you have seen that death is a fiction – the greatest fiction. But it goes on haunting people because no one meditates, and when they die, the fear of death makes them so unconscious that it becomes impossible for them to experience what is happening.

You cannot experience from the outside; you can experience only with awareness from the inside. But that kind of awareness is very rare. Those who have managed to create, through meditation, that crystallization of awareness are agreed on the point: that death does not exist. There is no question of fear.

You go on saying that if you conquer the fear, then death will not be scary anymore. No one knows anyone in the whole of history who has conquered fear. Even your greatest warriors are trembling inside. And you are making it completely upside down. First you will conquer fear... That is a Don Quixote experiment. How are you going to conquer fear? – aikido, jujitsu, archery? Even nuclear weapons in your hand will not allow you to conquer fear.

Fear is a by-product of your unconsciousness, so the only way to get rid of it, to know its bogus reality, is to become conscious. It is not a question of conquering; fear has nothing to do with it. Once you know what death is, fear disappears.

You are saying, "The other day I was sitting in a place in the hills where people were killed, and I saw that death is sweet." Great! Other people are killed and you feel that the death is sweet. If it is so sweet, why are you living? Join those dead people in the hills, get killed. And in India there are such simple ways of getting killed; just on the MG Road, the traffic will kill you, you don't have to manage... Strange laws exist in the world. If you are caught committing suicide, the punishment is to send you to the gallows. A strange society we have created. The poor fellow was himself doing the same thing – that was a crime. And now the punishment is the same crime. Now it is being done by the government, by the justice department. He himself may have failed, but now there is no possibility of any failure.

Death can be sweet if you move from one body, one existence, one form, with pure awareness into another and higher. Then it is sweet, really sweet. But not for others, only for you. And you go on intellectually creating the whole question, based on absolute fallacies. You say, "Now I think…" Remember, thinking does not make any sense here. Here you have to know, not to think; here you have to experience, not to think.

Thinking is a poor substitute for experience; a dangerous substitute because it will prevent you from experiencing. Do you say to your girlfriend, "I think I love you"? Either you love or you don't, but from where does this "I think" come? And if the girl belongs to my commune, she is going to give you a good slap to wake you up from your thinking. Love is not a thinking.

But you say, "…I think it must be more like this…" Just imagination, guesswork, that death helps one understand fear. Death makes one understand fear, but it is not the death of someone else; it is your own death, and that too with the condition that you are conscious. "…that first you experience death and she helps you see what fear is all about." Seeing the death of other people should create a sadness in you, not sweetness. And it is not going to help you to understand what fear is all about. Only your death… That too with an absolute condition. Moving out of the body with full awareness will not only allow you to understand fear, it will allow you to forget all about fear. It does not exist.

But people go on thinking about things which can only be experienced. It is one of the greatest problems, that thinking gives you substitutes. And if you become satisfied with those substitutes, guesswork, then you will never encounter the real. It is because of this that I emphasize: first get rid of all your thinking. Be in a silent clarity, a transparency, so that you can see things as they are – not that you think about them or guess about them.

Then not only fear, many other things will disappear and many new things will appear in your experience. The same energy that was involved in fear, when released, may blossom into flowers of love in your being. The same energy involved in anger may become a fragrance of tremendous joy in the silences of your heart.

You don't have many energies, you have only one energy. But that energy is invested in fear, anger, greed, jealousy. This same energy, once you are alert, centered in yourself, turns into blissfulness, ecstasy, gratitude, love. And a strange thing which no religion has ever talked about: every fiber of your being becomes prayerful, wordless, not addressed to any phony god. All gods are phony. Simply out of gratitude arises prayer toward this beautiful existence. Except for this existence, you don't have any sacred place. This is the only holy, sacred temple. There is no other temple. All other temples are false substitutes to deceive and cheat you.

So get out of your misunderstanding and guesswork. Reality cannot be discovered by thinking and guesswork. You will come to stupid conclusions. And the difficulty is that you may cling to them.

Edna and Zabriski have a lovely Polish wedding in Chicago.

"Let us be good Americans," says Zabriski, "and have a black baby."

"Okay," says the young bride.

Nine months later Edna gives birth to a beautiful white baby. Next year their second baby is white, and a year later she gives birth to another white baby.

"We must be doing something wrong," says Zabriski. "I will ask my friend at work."

So Zabriski meets his friend, Dougie, the huge black foreman, and asks him why they could not have a black baby.

"Hey, man," says Dougie. "Have you got a prick that is fifteen inches long?"

"No." answers Zabriski.

"Is your prick five inches wide?" asks Dougie.

"No." replies Zabriski.

"Well, that's your answer then," says Dougie. "You are letting in too much light."

Osho,

Could you please say something about curiosity? I often have experienced it as something which makes me feel alive and excited. But when I tried to meditate, it turned out to be a disturbance. And now, when I sit in your presence, getting more and more silent, I don't want to know anything anymore.

Curiosity is childish. It certainly keeps you excited, but it has never made anyone wise, in tune with himself and the universe. Curiosity is a kind of itching in the head. You scratch, it feels good, but don't scratch too much; scratch in different places. But itching is not going to make your intelligence purer, clearer, more far-reaching. That's why in meditation it becomes a disturbance. It is your old habit, so you go on being curious about everything: What is it?

But in meditation you have to remain centered within yourself: no curiosity, no thinking, no questioning. I am happy that you managed and that you can say, "And now, when I sit in your presence, getting more and more silent, I don't want to know anything anymore." To not want to know anything anymore is to be at the stage of a sage. He knows nothing, he becomes again a child; he becomes immensely silent, no thought arises. He enjoys existence for the first time because that old disturbance of knowing is no longer there.

There used to be a very knowledgeable man, Mahatma Bhagwandin. I came in contact with him when I was very young and he was very old. We used to go for walks in the forest and he knew about everything. He knew the names, Latin names, of all the trees, the flowers and their uses, medicinal uses; what miracles can be done with the roots, the trees, flowers, leaves. The first day we were in the forest, I heard him speaking continually for three hours.

The second day I said to him, "You know so much, I don't think you are going to die."

He said, "What gave you this idea?"

I said, "Your great knowledge will certainly help you. I don't know anything, but I enjoy the trees. I don't know the names. And I don't see the point that the name is needed to enjoy the tree, to enjoy the flower, or to know its medicinal qualities."

He was a very intellectual man, but when I said this to him as we walked, there was silence for a few moments. And then he said, "Perhaps you are right. In fact I have never enjoyed anything, everything has been a problem: what are its qualities, what are its medicinal properties, how can it be used, in what quantities... You are perhaps right, that I have missed enjoying existence. I always look, curious for more knowledge."

Just by accident, the day he died, I happened to be in the same city. I was passing by and someone informed me that Bhagwandin was on his deathbed. He was nearabout eighty years old. I rushed; I had not seen him for five years. He had almost become a skeleton. His last words to me were, "You were right. I wasted my life in unnecessary curiosity, I burned myself with knowledge. Innocence is the way to enjoy."

It is perfectly good that now you are not interested in knowing anything anymore. Keep alert about it. The mind is cunning, it comes from the back door. It will try a few times at least, but remain alert. Knowledge is of no use. When knowledge is not there, wisdom blossoms.

Meditation is only a technique to throw out all knowledge and make you capable of seeing with innocent eyes. Then everything – the sounds of the birds, this immense silence, the sun passing through the bamboos – becomes such a joy that one wants to sing, one wants to play a guitar, one wants to dance, or one wants simply to sit silently and enjoy the tremendous miracle of this existence.

You are moving in the right direction. Keep on moving. Never forget for a single moment that the mind will try… It is old, long, long cultivated by you. It takes a little time for it to understand that it is no longer welcome. Up to that moment one has to be very alert.

A Viking longship comes to the shore and out jumps a large, hairy Viking in full battle dress. He strides across the beach, climbs the cliffs, and trots into the nearest village. Finding no one around, he hammers on the door of one of the huts and a pretty girl opens it.

The big Viking grabs her by the arm and snarls, "Have you been raped lately?"

"No!" shrieks the terrified girl.

"Okay," says the Viking, "has your village been pillaged or burned down recently?"

The girl shakes her head. The Viking releases her and runs as fast as he can back to his ship. The ship sails further up the coast to another deserted cove. Exactly the same things happen.

The Viking arrives in another village and grabs the first girl he finds. "Have you been raped lately?" he asks. "And has your village been burned to the ground in the last three weeks?"

The terrified girl says no to both questions and runs away.

The Viking takes off his helmet and scratches his head. "Well," he mutters to himself, "I wonder where the boys have got to?"

Osho,
Why do I have so much difficulty when I have to decide something. For instance, whether I should go or stay here longer? I do not seem to be able to solve such problems.

You are asking the question to a wrong person because I don't have any experience of that type. Either I do it or I don't do it, but I am never wavering. This is the wavering mind: to be or not to be. But that is the nature of the mind. It cannot decide anything, it goes on and on… But have you noticed one thing? Whether you decide or not, something happens. Either you go or you remain. So why waste time? Just look directly into the situation, balance the alternatives. This is the only possibility right now for you.

If you have succeeded in being in deep meditation, there is no need. Meditation has a clarity – unwavering, unhesitating. It knows no alternatives, it simply goes on doing what the whole being says to do; it is undivided. But the mind is split.

Now you are saying, "Why do I have so much difficulty when I have to decide something. For instance, whether I should go or stay here longer? I do not seem to be able to solve such problems." These are not problems. They indicate your divided mind, the split mind, and the trouble with the split mind is that whatever you do, you will repent. If you stay here you will continually think, "It would have been better to have gone." If you go away, you will look back and you will think, "What kind of stupidity have I done? I should have stayed."

When you ask such questions to me, you put me in great trouble. I cannot decide whether you should go or you should stay. On the level of the split mind just weigh it up – what are the cons and what are the pros? Why do you want to go? What is there that is pulling you? And why do you want to stay here? What is there that is stopping you from going?

Watch very impartially, as if it is not your problem but someone else's problem. You have to work it out, and whichever side seems to be the weightier, do it. It will not be a hundred percent total, but at least you can attain seventy-five percent. If you want a hundred percent totality then this question, or any other question, is not the issue.

Meditate, so that the split mind disappears. Then the meditator simply goes, does things. He has no regret, no repentance; he never thinks for a single moment that he should have done something else which would have been better. He has put his whole totality in – nothing could be better than that.

When you put your whole totality there, that experience becomes one of tremendous transformation. If you can be totally here, be here, then forget about going anywhere else. If you want to go, then go totally, and forget about me and this place. But do things with a totality of being; otherwise you will be always feeling guilty that you have not done the right thing, that you have missed the train unnecessarily. I have never worked that way.

I was teaching in the university. And without taking any leave from the university I was traveling all over the country, because leave was only twenty days per year and I was traveling twenty days per month. The vice-chancellor called me and said, "I don't want to lose you. You are part of our beautiful university; without you… No one is going to replace you. But just take a little care; everyone thinks you are here, and in the newspapers we hear that you have been lecturing in Chennai, Kolkata, Amritsar, Srinagar. It makes me embarrassed. People bring those news cuttings to me, saying, 'Look, he is in Srinagar.'"

I immediately wrote my resignation and gave it to him. He said, "What are you doing? I am not asking for your resignation."

I said, "You are not asking, but this is what I am doing with totality."

He said, "I was always afraid… That's why I was not mentioning it to you. Please take it back."

I said, "Now that is impossible, you will have to accept it. As far as my work in this university is concerned, I have completed it. You cannot call a single student who can complain against me. What people do in thirty days, I can do in one week, so the work has not suffered. What concern is it for you, where I am?"

He said, "It is not my concern. Just take your resignation back; otherwise the whole university, particularly the students, will kill me!"

I said, "There is no harm in it. You need to be killed, it is time. You are seventy-five."

He said, "You are a strange fellow."

I said, "I have been nine years in this university. Have you only come to know *now* that I am a strange fellow?"

In the evening he came to my home and said, "Just take it back; I have not told anyone. This resignation will hurt me."

I said, "I don't want to hurt you. What you said was true. You cannot give me that much leave – it is almost the whole year I am wandering around the country. But you cannot tell me that I am not teaching. I am teaching your people and I am teaching all around the country. I am teaching twenty-four hours a day."

He said, "I understand. Take the resignation back."

I said, "That is impossible, I never take anything back. And I am not angry at you; in fact, I wanted to get rid of this teaching job. When I can teach fifty thousand people, why should I bother with twenty people? It is a sheer wastage. You have helped me, you should feel good about it. You should have done it before!"

When my father heard about it, he came from his village to the university city and said, "I know, with you nothing can be changed. I have not come to say to you to take your resignation back. Your vice-chancellor has written to me, saying, 'Come and try to convince him to take his resignation back,' but I know you more; he does not know you. So I cannot say anything about it. I have come only to say that if at any time you need money, I will always be available, as long as I am alive."

I said, "I will not need money. I have never contributed anything to the family except trouble. And you have enough financial problems."

He said, "If you have said you are not going to take any money, there is no point in arguing with you. I will do something on my own without asking you."

I said, "That is up to you."

What he did was to make a beautiful house with all the facilities that I would need; he put money in a bank account so that in case I wanted, I could come back. He created a beautiful garden around the house; he knew my likings. And I was not even aware of it. I became aware of it when he died. When he died, my brothers informed me, "This property is in your name and we all want to go to the ashram. So you have to sign a letter giving authority so that it can be sold and the bank account can be closed."

I said, "I don't possess anything and I have told my father not to do any such thing, but he never asked me." So I had my secretary give an affidavit on my account, saying that I don't write, don't sign anything, and she is allowed to do all kinds of transactions for me. The officials of that village knew me perfectly well, so they did not create any trouble. The house was sold, the account was closed.

If you have clarity, you simply follow your light that goes on leading you; you don't go astray here and there, you don't become accidental. What you are asking is to remain split, is to remain accidental. My suggestion is to meditate a little more so that this whole conflict disappears. Then whatever the result, whether you stay here or you go somewhere else, you have my blessings. It does not matter. What matters is your clarity and a decision, a conclusion out of that clarity.

Today let me leave you in silence. Be utterly quiet, as if there is no one here.

# 5

# One World Government Is Needed

Osho,

At various times I have heard you describe your work as "an experiment to provoke God" and "a model city for the future." Then there was the world tour. In the present context of the accelerating global crisis, how would you describe your work now, and what is happening to those who have gathered around you here?

You have asked many things. The most fundamental thing is to remember that whatever is happening here is not work. To call it work implies tension, worry, and a fear of failure. It is not work, but a playful relationship with existence.

As far as the world of man is concerned, I don't think there is much chance of converting the masses against their own past. They are creations of the past, and their past will come to its crescendo in the coming crisis. The masses will be drowned in that crisis. I feel sad about it, but the truth has to be said.

Only a few people in the world will be able to survive after this global suicide, and those will be the people who are deeply rooted in consciousness: alert, aware, loving, and ready to disconnect themselves from the past completely and unconditionally. And be ready to begin the New Man and the new humanity with the freshness of a child. I have been enjoying the fact that there are many people in the world who are capable of going deep into themselves. Their only hope is a self-realized being.

It is too late to do anything to protect the immense destruction that is going to happen. If we can protect only a few genuine human beings, that will be enough, more than enough. The past of humanity has been absolutely accidental; they have been doing things without knowing their consequences. Now we are suffering the consequences and there is no way to change those consequences.

For example, the whole ecology around the earth has been destroyed. Life does not exist as separate islands; not a single man is an island. Everything is interwoven. You have heard these two words, *dependence* and *independence*. Both are unreal; the reality is interdependence. We are all so interdependent on each other – not only men on other men, not only nations on other nations, but trees and man, animals and trees, birds and the sun, the moon and the oceans... Everything is interwoven. The past humanity has never thought about it, that it is a cosmos. They went on thinking in terms of taking everything separately. It was impossible for people in the past to think that man and the trees are connected, that they are interdependent.

You cannot live without trees, and neither can trees live without you. But it is too late. Hundred-year-old, two-hundred-year-old, even four-thousand-year-old trees have been destroyed and cut to create more newsprint for all kinds of stupid newspapers, without ever giving any consideration to what you are doing. You will not be able to replace them.

Just in Nepal... Unfortunately it is the poorest country in the world. It has nothing except the eternal Himalayas and the deep forest, ancient and old. It has been selling its forest to different countries – that is the only commodity it can sell. In the last thirty years, half of the trees of Nepal have disappeared, and for the coming thirty years, Russia has purchased the rights to the remaining forest. And they are cutting trees not in the old way, with an ax, but by very modern techniques so that, in a day, thousands of trees simply disappear. Miles of land are becoming desert.

Those trees were preventing the rivers of the Himalayas from coming down with too much force, because the rivers had to pass all these trees and every tree was lessening the force, slowing down the flow of water. By the time they reached Bangladesh, where they meet with the ocean, the quantity of water coming was exactly as much as the ocean could absorb. But now those trees have disappeared.

Rivers are coming with such great force, and with such a quantity of water, that the ocean cannot absorb it so quickly. It returns it, and Bangladesh is suffering continually, every year, from great floods, strange floods – rivers flowing backward because the ocean will not accept the water. They destroy all the crops of Bangladesh. Bangladesh is poor and the floods are killing thousands of people, thousands of animals, destroying thousands of houses. And now Bangladesh cannot do anything. It is beyond its power to tell Nepal, "Please don't cut down the trees."

In the first place, even if Nepal stops cutting down the trees, the wrong has already been done. And in the second place, Nepal cannot stop cutting those trees; it has sold them even for the future thirty years. It has taken the money to survive.

A similar kind of situation exists in many areas of the world. There are many gases which are being produced by our factories which have made us aware of a strange phenomenon. Those gases move upward and make holes in a certain layer called the ozone layer: a variety of oxygen, which covers the earth twenty miles up, the whole area of air. Ozone is absolutely necessary for humanity, for animals, for trees because not all sun rays are life-giving. There are a few sun rays which are life-destructive. Ozone turns those life-destructive rays back and allows only life-affirmative rays. Now great holes have been created by the gases that our factories and industries create, and from those holes death rays from the sun are entering our atmosphere.

This earth has never been so sick; it has never been in such danger of new diseases. Now, the vested interests are not ready to listen, to stop these factories or find alternatives. And scientists are engaged only in creating more war material. No government is ready to give them support so they can create more ozone and fill up the gaps which, unconsciously, we ourselves have created.

My emphasis is that our problems are international but our solutions are national. No nation is able to solve them. I take it as a great challenge and as a great opportunity: nations should be collapsed into one world government. It was tried by the League of Nations before the Second World War, but it could not succeed. It simply remained a debating club. The Second World War destroyed the very credibility of the League of Nations. But the necessity was still there; therefore they had to create the United Nations organization, the UN. But the UN is as much a failure as the League of Nations was. Again, it is still a debating club because it has no power. It cannot implement anything, it is just a formal club.

I would like a world government. All nations should surrender their armies, their arms to the world government. Certainly if there is a world government, neither armies nor arms are needed. With whom are you going to have a war? To find the closest neighbor among the planets for some kind of war is almost impossible.

Nations have become out of date, but they go on existing. And they are the greatest problem. Looking at the world just like a bird looks, a strange feeling arises: we have everything, we just need one humanity.

India has so much coal – and coal is not created in a day; it takes millions of years for wood to become coal. Then after millions of years the same coal becomes diamonds. The elements that make up the coal and the diamond are the same. It is the coal under pressure for millions of years that creates the hardest thing in the world, the diamond.

India has so much coal; Russia has no coal at all, but they have an overproduction of wheat. Half the population of India goes on starving; it needs wheat, it certainly cannot eat coal. But in the Soviet Union in the time of Stalin they were burning wheat in their railway trains instead of coal. They don't have coal, but now they have a super-technological production of crops, fruits. It was easy for them to burn the wheat, but they didn't know that they were burning millions of people, who were dying because they didn't have anything to eat. The problems are worldwide. The solutions have also to be worldwide.

And my understanding is absolutely clear, that there are things… In one place they are not needed and somewhere else the very life depends on them. A world government means looking at the whole situation of this globe and shifting things where they are needed. It is one humanity.

In Ethiopia one thousand people per day were dying and in Europe they were drowning billions of dollars' worth of food in the ocean, because they have better technology for production. Anyone looking from the outside will think that humanity is insane. Thousands of people are dying and mountains of butter and other foodstuff is being drowned in the ocean. One recent year when America drowned its foodstuff, just the expense of drowning it was two billion dollars. It was not the cost of the product, it was just the cost of carrying it to the ocean and drowning it.

America itself has thirty million people who cannot afford enough food. It is not a question of giving to someone else, it is a question of giving to its own people. But the problem becomes complicated because if you start giving free food to thirty million people, then others will start asking, "Why should we pay for our food?" Then the prices of things will go down. With the prices going down, the farmers will not be interested in producing food anymore – what is the point? Afraid of disturbing the economy, they let thirty million people die on the streets and go on drowning the overproduction in the ocean.

Not only that, exactly thirty million people are dying in American hospitals, nursing homes, from diseases caused by overeating.

They cannot be allowed at home because at home it is very difficult to protect the fridge from those people! They are dying because they eat too much, and on the street there are people dying because they have nothing to eat. An exact number: thirty million dying of overeating, and thirty million dying with not enough food. Sixty million people can be immediately saved with a small understanding.

A bird's-eye view is needed to look at the world, all over, as one unit. Our problems have brought us to a situation where either we will have to commit suicide or we will have to transform man, his old traditions, his conditionings. Those conditionings and those educational systems, those religions that man has followed up to now, have contributed to this crisis. This global suicide is the ultimate outcome of all our cultures, all our philosophies, all our religions. They all have contributed to it. And in strange ways because no one ever thought of the whole; everyone was looking at a small piece, not bothering about the whole.

For example in India, Jainas only do business. They don't cultivate, but they need food. They can't cultivate because Mahavira, their teacher, has told them that if you cultivate you will have to cut plants and plants have life, and his teaching is nonviolence. So they cannot be warriors, they cannot be cultivators. And of course, no one wants to become a sweeper, to become a cleaner, because in India these people are condemned as almost inhuman.

So the only alternative left for Jainas was just to do business, sell things, accumulate money. All their violence became their greed. That is the reason why they are the only people in India who don't have beggars; they are the richest people in India. But this is a kind of sucking of the blood of the society. Everything else is being done by someone else, and the money somehow goes on moving into hands which don't do anything.

Mahavira simply thought about *his* philosophy, but he never thought that this philosophy could not become universal. And that which cannot become universal cannot be true. People will have to cultivate, and certainly plants will have to be cut, crops will have to be cut. This violence cannot be avoided just by not doing it yourself; someone else is doing it for you.

The situation is the same around the world. Everyone has taken a certain portion of life, ignoring the remaining parts which are essentially joined with it. There are people… For example, the man who created the Nobel Prize committee was the greatest arms producer in the First World War. He earned so much money out of the production of war materials that he created a Nobel Prize for peace.

There is so much money that every year dozens of Nobel Prizes are given. With each Nobel Prize two hundred and fifty thousand dollars are also given, and this all comes only from the interest on the money. The basic money remains in the banks of Switzerland. It will continue forever to give twelve Nobel Prizes per year for creating the arts, for creating peace, for creating great poetry, painting, science. And the man who created the money made it by producing war materials. The whole of the First World War was fought with his weapons; both sides were purchasing from him. He was the greatest arms producer. He was responsible for all the people that died in the First World War.

The same is happening today. No one is interested in the coming crisis, which is not far away. This century is going to end just in twelve years. Twelve years is not a long time; almost everyone present here will be able to see the end of this century. You will be fortunate if you don't see the very end of life on this earth. Preparations are on the way to destroy the whole earth. And the people who are doing it are doing it behind great names: nations, religions, political ideologies, communism.

It seems man exists for all these kinds of things – communism, democracy, socialism, fascism. The reality should be that everything should exist for man, and if it goes against man it should not exist at all. The whole past of humanity is full of stupid ideologies for which people have been crusading, killing, murdering, burning living people. We have to drop all this insanity.

If nations disappear, the second great disease is religions because they have been fighting, they have been killing. And for reasons in which no one is really interested. I have never come across a man who is really interested in God. If you give him five rupees in one hand and God in another, he will take the five rupees and he will say, "God is eternal, we will see later on. For the moment, five rupees will be helpful." Who is interested in God except the priests? Because that is their business, and they want their business to spread.

When I was being harassed in America, taken from one jail to another jail, my airplane passed over a beautiful city, Salt Lake City. It looked tremendously beautiful in the night, very planned. It is very intelligently managed by a certain Christian sect, the Mormons. Their leader was killed in America; shot dead because Mormons were teaching something against the old orthodox Christianity. They were saying that their president, their leader, had direct contact with God. That cannot be allowed. Only the pope has direct contact with God.

Now, all kinds of idiots become leaders, and because their leader was shot and killed – it always happens – the followers became very fanatical. They created this Salt Lake City. Ninety-eight percent of the people in Salt Lake City are Mormons and all around the world there are millions of other Mormons. It is the duty of every Mormon to send at least one dollar every day to Salt Lake City, which is the capital of their religion. One million dollars reach Salt Lake City every day.

What is being done with those one million dollars? The empire is spreading; Salt Lake City is becoming almost a big empire. The people who believe in it are so fanatical – are bound to be because their leader was saying the same stupid kind of thing as Jesus was saying. If Jesus could create such a vast Christianity... They choose their president. And every president, once he is chosen, has direct contact with God, and whatever he orders has to be followed.

I would not have come to know all this about the Mormons and their city, if not just by chance, where our commune was situated in Oregon, three magistrates had to decide whether to give it the status of a city or not. One of them was a Mormon, and he was the most influential of the three. One was against; the other was just wavering, but because of the Mormon he voted for the city.

The Mormon judge used to come to the commune, and he loved the place. He himself told my secretary, "You should be alert and aware because of what happened to our leader. We were not doing any harm to anyone, but our leader was shot. And the man you are following is saying such outrageous things that the danger is always there."

And what happened? – because of this Mormon judge, the city was recognized. For two years the city was on the map of America, in geography books. The federal government was giving money to it, as to any city; the state government was giving money to it. Then they managed a very tricky thing; they persuaded the president of the Mormons to send a message to the judge saying, "You have been chosen by God to go to Nigeria for missionary work."

I wrote a letter to him, saying, "It is very strange that in the whole world God has chosen you to go to Nigeria. I suspect there is politics behind it – Ronald Reagan wants you to be removed from the place. The only way to remove you is a direct order from God." And what I had visualized happened. The moment he was removed another person was appointed and the three judges decided that the city was no longer a city. That's what Ronald Reagan and his government wanted: first take away the recognition, then it is easy to destroy it. They destroyed it. I had sent a message to the magistrate, saying, "You will be responsible for the destruction. You don't understand that it is a political strategy."

When the Mormon magistrate came back after one year, he recognized that something strange had happened. The people who destroyed the commune were also angry with the magistrate who had recognized it. When he came back from Nigeria, they caught hold of him and there was a case against him, alleging that he had taken a bribe from us. And what was the bribe? He had fifty cows. When he was going to Nigeria, after the city was recognized, he wanted to put those fifty cows somewhere and we were purchasing cows, hens, all kinds of things for the commune. He was ready to sell them as cheap as possible; he was even ready to contribute them. Because we had purchased those fifty cows, he was dragged to court: "You recognized the city because those people purchased your cows." Those cows could have been sold anywhere.

Strangely enough, those cows were purchased after the city was recognized, months after. When he received a direct order from God, now what will he do with fifty cows, where will he take them? Where to find a purchaser so quickly? And because he was told, "Move to Nigeria immediately..." He thought that we were in need of them – and we were in need.

They took revenge on him. They removed him from his post; he lost his job and then he was condemned for taking a bribe. I came to know about the Mormons because of this judge, when I heard that God had sent him a direct message. But God is so crazy. He goes on sending different messages against Hindus, Mohammedans, Christians. Even different messages to different sects of Christians. Either there are many Gods or there are many pretenders.

And how do these people receive these messages? No one gives any evidence. They have been killing, butchering, doing all kinds of things which are inhuman. They have destroyed the one humanity, divided it into pieces. First, if the world is to survive, the nations should go; second, the religions should go. One humanity is enough; there is no need of India, England, Germany. One religiousness is enough: meditation, truth, love, authenticity, sincerity, which do not need any name – Hindu, Christian, Mohammedan... Just one religiousness, a quality, not something organized. The moment organization comes in there is going to be violence because there will be other organizations in conflict. We need a world of individuals without any organizations. Yes, people who have similar feelings, similar joys, rejoicings, can have gatherings. But there should not be any organizations, hierarchies, bureaucracies.

First nations, second religions, and third, a science completely devoted to a better life, to more life, to better intelligence, to more creativity; not to create more war, not to be destructive. If these three things are possible, the whole humanity can be saved from being destroyed by its own leaders: religious, political, social.

In a way, this crisis is good because it is going to force people to choose. Do you want to die or do you want to live a new life? Die to the past, drop all that has been given as heritage from the past and start fresh, as if you have descended on this earth for the first time. And then start working with nature not as an enemy but as a friend, and the ecology will soon be functioning again as an organic unity.

The damage can be removed; it is not difficult to make the earth greener. If many trees have been cut, many more trees can be planted. And with scientific help they can grow faster, they can have better foliage. Different kinds of barriers can be created in the rivers so that they don't flood poor countries like Bangladesh. The same water can create much more electricity and help thousands of villages to have light during the night, to have warmth in the cold winters.

It is a simple thing. All problems *are* simple, but the basic foundation is the trouble. Those three things will try in every way not to disappear, even at the cost of the whole world disappearing. They will be ready for this disappearance, but they will not be ready to declare, "We surrender all our arms, all our armies to a world organization."

The function of nations will remain only simple: railway lines, post offices, a small police force to take care of internal affairs. There is no need of armies. Millions of people are involved in armies, which are useless. They can be put to creative arts, to farming, to gardening. And they are trained people, they can do jobs which no other people can do. An army can make a bridge so quickly – that is its training; it can create more houses for people.

Science is capable now, if it is no longer engaged only in war and creating more war material, to create so much food that five times more people can live happily on this earth than exist today. Today there are only five billion people. Twenty-five billion people can live joyously without hunger, without suffering from diseases. But science should be released from the hands of nations, which are forcing their scientists to create more war material. Scientists are functioning almost like prisoners.

I want it to be known to the whole world that if you are not ready to be one, be ready to disappear from this planet. But I hope there are intelligent people who would like to survive, who would like this beautiful planet to grow more beautiful, this humanity to grow more intelligent. I am afraid perhaps the whole of humanity is not even aware of the danger that is coming closer every moment.

You are asking me, "At various times I have heard you describe your work as 'an experiment to provoke God...'" It is still the same. I am still trying to provoke the God within you, the divine within you. More consciousness, more light, more aliveness, more ecstasy.

Miserable people are dangerous, for the simple reason that they don't care whether the earth survives or not. They are so miserable that deep down they may feel that it is better if everything is finished. Who cares if you are living in misery? Only happy people, ecstatic people, dancing people would like this planet to survive forever. So my effort continues to be the same: an experiment to provoke God. "...and 'a model city for the future.' In the present context of accelerating global crisis, how would you describe your work now, and what is happening to those who have gathered around you here?" It is the same; nothing has changed because the world crisis has not changed.

The people who have gathered around me are learning how to be more happy, how to be more meditative, how to laugh more, live more, love more, and to spread love, laughter around the world. This is the only protection against nuclear weapons. If the whole globe can learn to love and laugh and enjoy and dance, then Ronald

Reagan and Gorbachev will look surprised: "What has happened? The whole world seems to have gone mad!"

People who are happy, contented, are not the people to be forced to kill other people who have not done any harm to them. It is not strange that all the armies, down the ages, have been kept sexually repressed. Because sexually repressed people are bound to be destructive. Their very repression forces them to destroy something.

Have you ever watched in your own being that when you are happy, joyful, you want to create something; when you are miserable, suffering, you want to destroy something. It is revenge. All armies are kept in repressed sexuality so the moment they get to kill that becomes their joy; at least their repressed energies are expressed. Of course in a very ugly way, inhuman way, but some expression is there.

Have you noticed that painters, poets, sculptors, dancers are never sexually repressed people? In fact, they are over-sexual. They love too much, they love too many people. Perhaps one person is not enough to exhaust their love. They have been condemned by the priests down the ages: these poets, painters, sculptors, musicians are not good people. And these are the only people who have made this humanity something beautiful, who have contributed some flowers of joy, some flowers of music, some beautiful dances to the world. What have the priests done to the world? – they have burned women, calling them witches; they have killed people who belong to other faiths. They have not been creative people. They have not enhanced the earth and they have not enhanced life.

We need, with these three fundamental changes, a great respect for creative people of any dimension. And we should learn how to transform our energies so that they are not repressed, so they are expressed in your love, in your laughter, in your joy. This earth is more than a paradise, you don't have to go anywhere. Paradise is not something that has to be achieved, it is something that has to be created. It depends on us. This crisis gives a chance for courageous people to disconnect themselves from the past and start living in a new way – not modified, not continuous with the past, not better than the past, but absolutely new.

Find ways to relate in a new way. Forget marriages, start thinking of how to inquire into life. Forget all your beliefs, start to meditate in search of finding exactly who you are, because by finding yourself you will have found the very essence of existence. It is immortal and eternal, and those who have found it, their bliss and their benediction is inexpressible. We need more happy people around the earth to prevent the third world war. You will be amazed, surprised by my answer. You may not be able to find immediately what connection there can be between nuclear weapons and people's laughter – there is. These nuclear weapons and these destructive war machines cannot work by themselves. They are being worked by human beings, behind them are human hands.

A hand that knows the beauty of a roseflower cannot drop a bomb on Hiroshima. A hand that knows the beauty of love is not the hand to keep a gun loaded with death. Just a little contemplation and you will understand what I am saying.

I am saying: spread laughter, spread love, spread life-affirmative values, grow more flowers around the earth. Everything that is beautiful, appreciate it, and everything that is inhuman, condemn it. Take this whole earth away from the hands of the politicians and the priests and you will have saved the world, and you will have changed the world into a totally new phenomenon, with a new human consciousness. And it has to be done now because the time is very short. By the end of the twentieth century, either we will enter the first century of a new history of man or there will be no one left alive, not even a single wildflower. Everything will be dead.

There are experiments going on in Russia, and perhaps in America too, with death rays. Rather than dropping a bomb, it is far easier to spread death rays, which simply kill the living people, animals, birds, trees. Only dead things – houses, temples, churches – will remain. It will be really a nightmare. And those death rays are not visible. We know that death rays exist; they are just trying to find out how to spread them, to reach a certain destination and destroy all living beings that come across them.

Man has to be freed from these monsters. Our work here is to teach people consciousness, more awareness, love, understanding, joy, and spread the dance and celebration around the earth. Reduced to a single statement, I can say: "If we can make humanity happier, there is not going to be any third world war."

Giovanni wants to have a ride on a bicycle so he decides to go and ask his friend Mario if he can borrow his. On the way he starts to think, "For sure, Mario will tell me to be careful with the bike, but I will tell him not to worry. Then he will tell me that his sister wants to use it, but I will tell him that I will be back in time; then I know Mario will get scared and tell me it is not the time of year for riding bikes…"

Meanwhile Giovanni arrives at Mario's house and he looks up to the window and shouts, "Hey, Mario! Go and fuck yourself, you and your bike!"

Hamish MacTavish has not seen his old friend, Gordon MacPherson for forty years. So when they bump into each other in the street one day, they rush to the nearest pub to celebrate.

"It will be wonderful to have a drink together after all these years," says Gordon.

"Aye, it will," says Hamish. "But don't forget, it is your round."

There is an accident on the construction site. Seamus runs over to where Paddy is lying in a heap of rubble.

"Are you dead, Paddy, after such a terrible fall?" asks Seamus.

"Yes, certainly I am," replies Paddy.

"Ah, bejabbers!" says Seamus, "you are such a terrible liar, I don't know whether to believe you or not."

"That proves I am dead, you idiot," says Paddy. "If I was alive, you would not be calling me a liar to my face."

The last…

Hamish MacTavish is careening down the road in his old Ford car when a policeman pulls him over.

"Excuse me, sir," says the cop. "Would you mind blowing into this bag?"

"By all means," says Hamish. "Would you like me to play a jig or a reel?"

"No, no," says the cop. "This bag tells you how much you have been drinking."

"Oh, there is no need for that," says Hamish. "I have got one of my own at home – I married her!"

No, you need one more…

Pope the Polack is very sick. Doctors come from all over the world to try and diagnose his illness, and finally a little Jewish psychiatrist from New York finds the cause of the problem.

He tells the pope, "Your holiness, because you have had nothing to do with women all your life, your hormones are unbalanced and there is only one possible cure. You must make love with a woman."

"No, no!" cries Pope the Polack, "I can't. All the vows I have taken… I just *can't*!"

"But, your holiness," replies the shrink, "you must or you will die, and this too is a mortal sin."

The pope retires for a few days to consider his fate, and then calls the psychiatrist again.

"Okay," says Pope the Polack, "I have reached my decision. I will do as you ask. But please, be sure that the girl has nice, big tits."

# 6

# Celibacy Is the Real Perversion

Osho,
Every time you call homosexuality a perversion, even though you do not condemn homosexuals, I feel hurt as I am a gay. I have tried to look, to watch, to meditate on it but still my feelings, my love go naturally toward men. Since being with a man I like and trust, I have felt silence and happiness. But it is difficult to accept myself totally, joyfully. How can I live these moments without feeling perverted? What is the difference between being totally accepted by you and not being condemned?

The question is immensely important because the whole future of humanity depends on a few factors. One is homosexuality. First, I would like to explain to you why I call it a perversion. And once you understand it, things will be simpler.

There is no biological program in you for homosexuality. The biological program in your sperm is heterosexual. I am simply stating a fact, that homosexuality has arisen under ugly pressures in the monasteries of all religions; where it is forced to happen in the name of the purity of celibacy. And also in the schools, colleges, and universities where boys and girls are kept separate; where teachers and professors function as gods so that no heterosexual relationship happens.

Men and women become sexually mature at the age of thirteen or fourteen. The natural thing would be to allow them the expression of their new area of exploration. Of course, all precautions can be taken so that small boys and girls don't get into any trouble – particularly the girls, that they should not become pregnant at such an early age.

In the past there was no way, but now we are in a better position. According to me, the pill is the greatest revolution that has happened in history. And now, even better pills are available. The first pill was not a hundred percent foolproof. You have to take it continuously and if you miss one day and by chance you meet your lover… The human tendency is to think that one does not get pregnant every time, "Why should it happen at this time? Take the chance." But if hundreds and thousands and millions of people are taking chances, then a few pregnancies are bound to happen.

The society managed to forcibly keep the two sexes apart. And I wondered myself, when I came to know that between the ages of sixteen and eighteen, as it happens, sexual energy is at its peak. It will never be the same power again.

When boys and girls return from the universities, aged twenty-four, twenty-five, twenty-six, we have arranged their marriages. Their peak point of energy has already passed six or eight years before. They are on the decline. Because of this decline… And I suspect that religions wanted this decline to happen because with this declining force you cannot have an orgasmic experience. An orgasmic experience is a flood. You are so flooded that you disappear. I respect the orgasmic experience because my understanding is that all meditations have arisen out of it. All spirituality has arisen out of it, because it has given a taste of the beyond.

First, by preventing young people from having a sexual experience until they are twenty-five or twenty-six, they will never experience orgasm. Second, they will never think that there is any possibility of a higher consciousness, of a more beautiful space within themselves; that they are not what they see in the mirror, that they are much more. In an orgasmic experience they become almost one with the whole. It is the first glimpse – a window opens and they start searching for ways to widen the window, to fly in this open sky.

No one has worked out how man found meditation, how he started thinking of a spiritual experience of ecstasy. To me, it is very simple. First, once the boys and girls have an orgasmic experience, they have already tasted the spiritual, the divine, the sacred. Now in their whole life nothing is going to be of that height.

Secondly, in an orgasmic experience one comes to know that thought stops, time stops. You come to a standstill – no movement. Those who were wise enough tried it in another way: How to get rid of thoughts, time and movement and become absolutely still? They were surprised that it works both ways; you attain the same orgasmic experience. But when the orgasmic experience is sexual you are dependent on the other person, and when the orgasmic experience comes out of meditation you attain a tremendous dignity as an individual: independence.

Religions did not want this orgasmic experience to happen to people. And to prevent it, they created the idea of celibacy. It is ugly and very cunning, but priests *are* cunning. Their whole concern was their own business. If people start experiencing the spiritual and the sacred individually, then the brahmin priest is no longer needed; neither is the rabbi or the catholic priest needed. They have come in direct contact with the universe in such an intimate way that there is no need for any mediator.

There were two ways to destroy this possibility. In the past, they used early marriage: seven years, eight years old. Now, a seven-year-old boy is not sexually mature, and neither is the girl. But because they are married, slowly, slowly they are being taught by their relatives and friends and they start playing. Sex becomes just a play to them, and at the most just a method to produce children. They don't have any time to experience what could have turned them in a spiritual direction. This has been followed for centuries. They are so burdened too early. And the birth of children does not depend on an orgasmic experience.

So sex has to be understood in two ways: on the one hand it reproduces the species, which is a biological phenomenon; on the other hand, it creates an energy experience which no religion, no politician would like people to have. Because that will create the greatest revolution in the world. People will have a direct contact with existence – no hell, no holy scripture, no priest, no mediators. And these are the people who have been the parasites of humanity. But the times changed, education came into the world; students had to leave their homes and live in hostels, boys with boys, girls with girls. That also contributed to the perversion.

I am not condemning it, I am simply telling you how it happened. And when I say perversion, I don't mean any condemnation. I simply mean going away from the natural course of things. If a boy from fourteen to twenty-five – that is a long period – becomes homosexual, then that becomes a deep-rooted habit in him, so even when he is married his interest is not in women. Religions don't want men to be interested in women, nor do they want women to be interested in men. Slowly, slowly they have made a very detailed strategy over thousands of years.

In the present, monasteries, universities, armies create homosexuals. Wherever one sex gathers, sooner or later they start finding ways to release each other's energies. So the first thing to remember is that I will continue to call it a perversion because it is a perversion. It is against nature. Nature never produces anything which is useless. Homosexuality is useless; it does not generate anything in you. Neither can it produce children, nor can it give you an orgasmic experience. Have you ever heard of homosexuals having an orgasmic experience? All they have is a sexual release. The energy accumulates and becomes a tension, and it needs some release.

Homosexuals know only ejaculation, they don't know what they are missing: the orgasm.

So sexual energy runs parallel in two ways. On the one hand it produces children, on the other hand it can produce a new being in you. Homosexuality destroys both. And do you want me to call it a natural thing? It is destructive, it is perversion. I can understand that it may be hurting you. But if you have cancer and the doctor says to you, "It is cancer," it hurts, but it has to be said; otherwise there is no way to operate on you, to remove the cancer. Homosexuality has become far more dangerous than cancer. No one was intentionally moving in that direction, but that's how things happen – in the unknown, in the darkness.

Homosexuals, because they were perverted, created the disease AIDS. Heterosexuality creates life; life for your children and a divine life for you. Homosexuality is absolutely barren; it does not create anything. Slowly, slowly as it spread... Perhaps it has been happening and we were not aware of it. The awareness came just within the last five years, when doctors found that homosexuals with AIDS lose their resistance against any infection, and their life span is not more than six months to two years.

I was the first in the whole world to make people aware of it. Governments were hiding it, doctors were not wanting to talk about it, scientists were not revealing it to the people. They had their reasons; it looks ugly if the nation has to declare that it has thousands of homosexuals. It is not a glory, it simply means that so many people have become perverted. And because of AIDS, the danger became more.

To accept that one million people are suffering from AIDS in one country... The problem is, what are the politicians going to do about it? Nothing can be done about it. According to the scientists, there is no possibility to cure it. It is just like death, a slow death. You cannot cure death, slow or fast. And it looks ugly for nations to recognize it. Many nations have not even bothered to have a census about how many people are homosexual because they are potential AIDS patients. Doctors are afraid to tell anyone they have AIDS because then they will have to be admitted to a hospital. The disease is such as man has never known. Anything infected coming out of the body… Even kissing, because a way for the virus to be passed on through saliva is from one mouth to another mouth.

It is very strange that only one primitive tribe of Eskimos have never kissed. When Christian missionaries first arrived to convert them to Christianity, the Eskimos could not contain themselves laughing when they saw them kissing each other. Such a dirty habit! Saliva carries all kinds of viruses, all kinds of diseases. Particularly kissing is nothing like the poets have been praising it to be. It is certainly a dirty habit.

Eskimos also express their love. But love should be expressed in a cleaner way: they rub their noses with each other. Noses are very clean, clean and cool – unless they are running. Those periods are avoided; Eskimos never kiss with their noses if their noses are running!

Sexual contact is bound to give AIDS to the partner who did not have it. A mother's milk can give AIDS to her children. You will be surprised to know that there are now children who were born with AIDS. Because the father must have been suffering from AIDS and the sperm carried the virus into the mother's womb – small children… When I condemned it in a world press conference, journalists laughed at me, politicians laughed at me. They said that I was unnecessarily making a small thing too big, because I said that two-thirds of humanity is going to die through AIDS. I proposed what precautions should be taken, and now many civilized countries have adopted the same procedures; without, of course, mentioning my name.

My name seems to be dynamite. Even my own people are afraid to utter it, what to say about others? Now the same journalists are reporting in great praise about their governments, that they are taking precautions. This could have been done three years ago and would have saved millions of people from catching the disease. Now, as far as I can see, it is uncontrollable.

Doctors don't want to admit it, so they simply give a certificate saying that the person does not have AIDS, because to admit an AIDS patient is dangerous: for the nurses, for the doctor. Coming in contact with such a man, the best way is simply to say, "We examined you and you are negative. You don't have AIDS. You don't need to worry." They have shifted their responsibility, but they have created a danger for the society. Now this man will move...

Here, there are a few sannyasins... Because I have made it an absolute rule that no AIDS-positive person should be allowed to enter the gate. If he wants to go anywhere, he should go to the Vatican. The Vatican is the most responsible for creating AIDS. And the pope's position has to be changed – not as a representative of God but as the superintendent of an AIDS hospital! All people suffering from AIDS should move toward the Vatican.

I have prohibited their entry. People have to bring a certificate saying that they are negative. But you will not believe how irresponsible man can be. There are many doctors who are selling negative certificates. You simply give some money: "There is no need to be worried, take the certificate." It seems we will have to make our own lab to test people before we allow them on the campus. Their certificates can be bogus. In Mumbai, you can just give a few rupees and you can get a certificate. And this is happening all around the world. But such irresponsibility has never been seen. They only think of themselves and the money that they are getting. They are not worried what harm this man can do to his friends, to his family, to his children, to his wife.

People are trying to get negative certificates because they don't want to be condemned by the society, and they don't want their wives, their children, their parents to feel embarrassed that they have got AIDS. Friends will no longer be friends. So to protect one's ego, people are trying to hide the fact. And because of the hiding of the fact, it is spreading like wildfire all over the world.

Do you want me to not call homosexuality a perversion because it hurts you? If it hurts you, I am not responsible for your hurt. Your priests who have been teaching celibacy are responsible. But strangely, governments are making laws against homosexuality, that it is now a crime. Anyone found to be homosexual can be sent to jail. But homosexuality is not the real root, the real root is the idea of celibacy.

Celibacy is the real perversion, but not a single man in the whole world has condemned celibacy because no one wants all the religions to be against him. But I am at ease because the whole world is already against me. What more can it do? I say it definitively: celibacy should be made one of the most heinous crimes. The religions which teach it should be banned. And all celibates in the monasteries, the monks of different religions, should be told, "Get married, or at least find a girlfriend. You have lived with boyfriends long enough." The people who have AIDS should be segregated. They should have their own small cities, where all are suffering from AIDS: the doctors, nurses, patients, scientists. Then there is no danger. You cannot have, like double pneumonia, double AIDS – single is enough!

If humanity functions sanely, then AIDS patients should be taken care of in remote places. They can work, they can earn, but their cities should be closed cities. They cannot move around in the world, spreading a fatal disease. It is out of compassion that I am saying this. If the people who are suffering from AIDS understand the meaning of compassion, and if they want to save humanity, they themselves should move out of the crowd, live with the same kind of people who are suffering; make small villages, islands. Otherwise, even without nuclear weapons humanity will be destroyed. And this destruction will be very ugly.

If you feel hurt, book a ticket to Rome. Hit the pope as hard as you can with: "You are not the representative of God, you are the representative of the homosexuals; particularly the people who have reached the point where homosexuality has created AIDS." The name of the Vatican should be changed to: "AIDS Camp" – seems to be perfectly good. And I don't want the pope to be demoted. He should remain the superintendent of the AIDS Camp.

But you cannot stop me just because you feel hurt. I am not only concerned with you, I am also concerned with the whole of humanity. To avoid hurting a single person and create a dangerous situation for many... I cannot do that.

You say, "I have tried to look, to watch, to meditate on it. But still my feelings, my love go naturally toward men." It is a very strange perversion. The natural attraction is always for the opposite polarity. Man and woman are opposite polarities, like negative and positive electricity. If you are only attracted toward men, something is wrong in you. You should go through some therapy groups, you should learn how to love a woman. In fact, it is so ugly even to think that a man is attracted toward a man and not toward a woman.

Women are doing the same because they want to be equal. The women involved in the liberation movement have become lesbians; their idea is to boycott men completely. Lesbianism is old, but not very widespread. There is a possibility that there may not be any harm in it, because two negatives cannot create anything – neither a child nor a painting. For creating anything two positives are needed. So perhaps lesbianism may not create a disease like AIDS, but one never knows. Up to now we were not aware that homosexuality was going to create AIDS. Perhaps it takes a certain time. And it will take a longer time for the negative. It is possible they may even create a far more dangerous disease.

But this is sheer insanity. The people who are homosexuals should move and create homosexual communes, the women who are lesbians should move and create lesbian communes. But leave the whole of humanity. Why torture them? Why destroy them? You don't have the right. You are completely free to do what you want to do, but don't interfere in any one's life. I have every condemnation when someone interferes in others' lives.

You are asking me, "Since being with a man I like and trust, I have felt silence and happiness." That's good – just go to a homosexual, gay commune, feel happy and feel silence. "But it is difficult to accept myself totally joyfully." Why shouldn't you accept? If you sow the seeds, you should accept the flowers too. If you accept homosexuality joyfully, and you feel happy with men and you trust men and like them, then there is no need to feel any guilt. You have chosen to die within two years. It is your choice. Make as much happiness as you can within these two years. But you are not feeling totally joyful – feel totally condemned. I am preaching totality; it does not matter *what* is total. Feel totally condemned, feel totally corrupted, feel totally perverted and rejoice with all the perverts.

You ask me, "How can I live these moments without feeling perverted?" There is no need. You *are* perverted. Why should you live these moments without feeling perverted? Live these moments knowing fully that you are perverted. Just as someone is a man, someone is a woman, someone is a bird, someone is a tree, you are a pervert.

You are asking, "What is the difference between being totally accepted by you and not being condemned?" I do everything totally. I accept you totally in your natural flowering, and I condemn you totally in your perversion. And for me there is no problem, I am always total. My yes is total, my no is total. But if you have chosen the no, then I will condemn you totally. You cannot question my totality.

But the simple thing is – and homosexuals around the world are not doing it… In Texas they created a law against homosexuality, that homosexuals can be jailed for years. One million homosexuals protested outside the parliament. I don't think that homosexuality should be punished by jail. Homosexuals should be given different localities. They can live in their own world, in their own way, and be happy, but they should not be allowed to move in the wider society, spreading all kinds of dangerous viruses.

But no one seems to do anything about it. There are deserts, there are uninhabited islands. Just give them to homosexuals. Divide the world into heterosexual and homosexual. And there should be no communication between them. Or change yourself. I know changing is difficult. Once you have become accustomed to a certain sexual behavior it becomes very difficult to change the behavior. Ten, twelve years are enough to make it your second nature; unless you are courageous enough, can discipline yourself, to drop that perversion and be natural. It is possible, but you will need guts for it.

I am not only answering you, I am answering all the homosexuals of the world. It is their duty to declare that they are homosexuals. It is their duty to say that they want their own communes. It is the duty of lesbian women to say that they want their own communes. And then it is perfectly okay; you leave the world at peace. Otherwise, my prediction that two-thirds of humanity will die from AIDS is coming closer.

In poor countries, we don't even have any idea how many people are homosexuals, how many people are suffering from AIDS. The government is not interested in your life. So almost all the poor countries have no data; only the very rich countries have now become aware of the fact. And they are collecting data but the data should be multiplied by at least five because it is very difficult to find someone who will say that they are gay.

Now the very word has become condemned and homosexuals are going underground. They had their restaurants, their clubs; they have changed their names. The whole process is going on. And most of the people who create the law are homosexuals. It is a very difficult situation. Teachers, professors, principals are mostly homosexual because they have access to beautiful boys. The people of power, whether they are priests or politicians, have power and they can manage very easily. But they don't know that they are risking the whole life of this planet.

If there is a choice to commit suicide, I would rather people are given poison than have an ugly disease like AIDS. If we decide to destroy the planet then destroy it. But destroy it as peacefully, as beautifully as possible, not with ugly diseases and everyone feeling guilty. And I know you are only a victim. You should not feel guilty, you should feel revengeful. Guilt is inverted revenge. Make it change into authentic revenge.

Who are the people who have created the situation? These people should be punished. If the government does not punish them, then make committees and punish them. If there are one million homosexuals just in a small state, Texas, how many millions of homosexuals are there around the world? These millions of people should make their own committees and punish the priests and the people who have been teaching celibacy. They have perverted you. You need not feel guilty, you need to feel totally revengeful because it is not only your question. The whole life on this planet is reaching an end from many directions.

We can prevent politicians from using nuclear weapons, but what to do with AIDS? And people, even though they are intelligent, behave very unintelligently. One of my sannyasins and therapists, Veeresh, allows people suffering from AIDS into his groups. Just now I have been told that he tells people, "Osho teaches compassion, so all of you be compassionate to this fellow. Hug him, kiss him, love him."

Now, this is a great interpretation of compassion! He should have told the man who is suffering from AIDS, "Osho teaches compassion. Now, it is your compassion not to touch people. Tell them that you are suffering from AIDS and you don't want to spread it." Rather than telling him that, he is telling other group participants to hug him, and they are hugging him. That fellow may spread AIDS to the whole group. And because he is respected there, naturally he will feel very good.

Here, we will be creating an institute to check your AIDS report, whether it is authentic or not. I want my people to be saved not only from nuclear weapons, but also from inner causes that can destroy the whole humanity.

Hymie Goldberg is telling Moishe Finkelstein about the new town brothel.

"It is fantastic," says Hymie. "You can screw all night, and when you leave they give you breakfast and twenty dollars."

"Have you actually tried it?" asks Moishe.

"No," admits Hymie, "but Becky has."

A lawyer has been trying for months to get Mendel Kravitz to pay a bill, but all his letters and telegrams are disregarded. Finally, in desperation he sends Mendel a tear-jerking letter, with a photograph of his little daughter. The lawyer writes under the photo: "Here is the reason I must have the money you owe me."

Mendel replies by sending a photograph of a beautiful redhead in a bathing suit. The caption on this picture says: "Here is the reason I can't pay."

Mendel Kravitz is trying to make out with his secretary. He wines her and dines her and when he gets her back to his apartment, he whispers sweet promises in her ear.

"If we get it together," murmurs Mendel, "a fur coat or perhaps a trip to Europe."

The secretary takes him by the hand into the bedroom and they are soon in bed together. Later, while dressing, she asks him when she will get the fur coat he promised.

"What fur coat?" asks Mendel.

"You promised me a fur coat," insists the girl.

"When I am horny, I will promise anything," says Mendel. And putting one hand over his heart and the other over his prick, he says, "When he is soft, he is hard. When he is hard, he is soft."

# 7

# The Difference between a Master and a Teacher

Osho,
I was with a very strict enlightened teacher, Lee Lozowick, in America for six years. While in Boulder, Colorado, I fell in love with your sannyasins, and then you. Now, after one week in Pune, a nagging feeling has arisen in me: Have I truly taken sannyas, and are you truly my master?

The question asked by you... You will have to be prepared for a shock. I am going to analyze it point by point. You say, "I was with a very strict enlightened teacher, Lee Lozowick..." I know Lee Lozowick very well. Neither is he strict nor enlightened. And you remained with him in America for six years. That shows that you are not even intelligent either. If you were really with a master, there was no need to come here. Your innermost being would have been fulfilled, contented, blessed. If you could fall in love with my sannyasins in Boulder, Colorado, Lee Lozowick is not even worthy enough to be compared with my people there.

If you have looked into your question deeply, unprejudicially, silently, then my answer will be very clear to you. In the first place, a teacher is never enlightened. A teacher has teachings; he has a whole system of beliefs. A master is not a teacher. A master is a fire you have to go through so that all that is not gold in you is burned, and only the pure gold comes out. To be with a master is not an easy job. It is the most difficult journey one can go on.

You wasted your six years. Lee Lozowick himself was with Da Free John. He is not only a fraud, he also betrayed his own teacher. Da Free John is also not a master, but at least he is a teacher of a far higher quality than Lee Lozowick. It happens all the time. People see that so many people are attracted toward certain doctrines, certain personality characters, and they feel they can also manage – if not so many people, then a few at least. Lee Lozowick betrayed Da Free John because he does not even mention his name or that he has been a disciple himself. And how did he become a master? His own teacher has not recognized his enlightenment.

But in America everything is possible. I have heard a wise man saying, "A fraud is someone who can tell you to go to hell so tactfully that you start packing for the trip." That's what Da Free John and his disciple Lee Lozowick are. And when I am saying these things, remember, I have no personal antagonism toward anyone. But I have simply to say the truth to you, even if it goes against all manners, etiquette, culture. I am not here to teach you manners, I have to hit directly into your heart with the truth, however much it hurts.

These people have sprung up all over the world. India has suffered from these people for many centuries, but this century is seeing a new phenomenon. The Indian frauds have created similar kinds of people all over the world – pretenders, who know nothing except some strategy that influences people to believe in them. And particularly at this time, when everyone is going down into a deep psychological crisis. Everything seems to be silent on the surface. You may not even be thinking about the third world war, the ecological crisis; you may not be thinking about AIDS. At least consciously you may not be concerned at all what is going to happen to humanity tomorrow, but deep down you cannot avoid it.

Your consciousness is a separate personality, but your unconscious, as you go deeper, becomes more and more part of the whole ocean. So whatever is happening in the soul of the cosmos has ripples in everyone's unconscious. If you can read your own unconscious, you can read the whole future that is going to happen. But you may know or you may not know about your unconscious situation.

These frauds – the Indians and their by-products, mostly American – are doing a good business. It is said that psychologists build castles in the air, psychoanalysts live in them, and psychiatrists collect the rent. But I wonder who pays the rent? – you! I say again, you! You pay the rent, and there are many others who are paying the rent. Those castles do not exist, no one lives in those castles.

But in a psychological crisis of this intensity – in which we are – everyone is shattered inside, is somehow holding himself together, and anyone who pretends to teach you the way toward the beyond immediately attracts you. You don't have any way, any criterion, any measurement to figure out whether the man is true or not, whether the man is authentic or not. In the East, because the tradition is more than ten thousand years old, slowly, slowly we have figured out a few indications of an enlightened master. Those indications may be helpful to you.

The authentic master is not at all interested in disciples, in the crowd, in the numbers around him. He does not brag about it. He attracts only the very intelligent because what he teaches and whatever he is, is understandable only by very highly intelligent people. Have you ever checked what intelligence quotient you have? Before figuring out whether a master is true or not, you should have a psychological test to find out what your mental age is.

The average mental age of humanity is fourteen years. Now, people with a mental age of fourteen years are not the people to understand something of the transcendental, the spiritual, the inner. It is time for them to play football, watch boxing matches, sit before their TV, glued to it for seven and a half hours every day. I have always wondered that no one ever thinks about how much intelligence they have. Is it enough to be a disciple? Is it enough to be accepted by a master?

A master is not in any way interested in converting you to a certain system of beliefs. If any master is doing that, he is only a teacher. And a teacher carries only borrowed knowledge. He can say beautiful things, but they are all parrotlike. Sometimes he can talk even better than the masters because masters are spontaneous and the teacher has gone through much rehearsal. He is well prepared, he has done his homework, and he goes on teaching the same thing again and again to different people.

A teacher remains continuously consistent with a certain current of ideology. The master is basically contradictory, inconsistent. He has to be because what he is saying is not within his hands. It is in the hands of the universe itself, he is only a vehicle. Whatever kind of song existence brings to his lips, he cannot edit anything out of it or make any additions, improvements. A master is very raw in the sense that he brings whatever comes from existence exactly as it is. He is never a polished man.

The master does not in any way humiliate you by making you disciples. By accepting you as disciples, he gives you dignity and individuality. He asks nothing from you and he goes on giving you things which have no price but are immensely valuable. The effort of a master is to become a certain milieu, a certain presence so that he need not even say anything to you. Just sitting by his side, your heart slowly, slowly starts falling in tune with the master. And the master's heart is in tune with the heart of the universe. Being in tune with the master, you are also in tune with the universe. It is not knowledgeability that makes a master, it is innocence.

And I know absolutely, with certainty, that this fellow, Lee Lozowick, is not an innocent man. He has betrayed his teacher – and you are doing the same here. You have betrayed him. But one cannot blame him because when he went to Da Free John he must have thought of him as a master and slowly, slowly discovered that he is only a teacher. But if a teacher can attract so many disciples, what is the point of remaining with him? He started collecting his own disciples.

If you have been with a master, it is almost impossible to desert him. Your love will prevent you from doing that. Your trust will become a Himalaya between you and the whole world. Your master is your whole universe. And it is strange that you are asking, "Now, after one week in Pune, a nagging feeling has arisen in me: Have I truly taken sannyas, and are you truly my master?" What happened to Lee Lozowick? It took you six years and still you want to go back to him. The reason is clear: it is not that you have found a master in him, you have found in him a recognition for your ego.

Here, your ego is going to be destroyed every day. Unless you disappear completely, leaving only your essential being, you are not a sannyasin. What happens when a person like you, after six or seven days, takes sannyas? What is going on in his mind? – he is thinking that by taking sannyas some miracle is going to happen to him. You are absolutely wrong. This sannyas that you take is not going to bring any miracle, it is simply entering a commune of seekers, making yourself available, becoming an insider and not just a spectator. Then step by step learn the ways of love, the ways of trust; then step by step learn how to enter your own being. The day you enter your own center will be the true sannyas. This is only a formality.

With a true sannyasin, an authentic being who has come to his own, the question will not arise, "...and are you truly my master?" There is only one way to find out whether someone is truly your master. If in his presence, if in his universe of seekers, if in his caravan of searchers, you suddenly stumble upon yourself, and you find the ecstasy that you have never experienced, and the blessing that has not been even in your dreams. And after this experience no question arises in you... That is the very definitive thing, that no question arises in you. All questions have simply fallen, as leaves fall in the fall time from the trees. Only in that experience of the disappearance of questions, and with them thoughts and the mind, will you have the answer: that you have found the true master. You cannot decide beforehand because it is not a market; it is not that someone has written on his door, "I am the true master."

You will have to learn patience and waiting. One never knows, it can happen today, it may take years; it all depends on you. The master simply creates a certain subtle atmosphere. That atmosphere is here. If you can get in tune with it, you are a sannyasin. And if you become slowly, slowly dissolved and become part of the dance and the celebration that is going on here, of the meditation and the ecstasy, suddenly you will realize you have come close to an authentic master.

If it does not happen, there can be two reasons: either the master is not authentic or your disciplehood is not authentic. Rather than jumping to the idea that the master is not authentic, it is better first to look at your disciplehood. What have you done by becoming a sannyasin? What changes have happened to you? In what ways have you become more involved in the movement; in what way have you entered yourself, in what way has your lifestyle changed?

Everything depends on you. Giving you sannyas simply means that we accept you, our doors are open to you, not more than that. Now, what is happening inside the temple will depend on you: your intelligence, integrity, sincerity, your authentic search for truth. And I cannot think that in six days you have found that meditation leads nowhere, that you have touched the presence of my being. But I will suggest to you that perhaps you should go back to Lee Lozowick. Because I am not interested at all in gathering a crowd of unintelligent, impatient people, in a hurry.

You will come back – about that I am certain. But this time go back first, and be finished with Lee Lozowick. That is what is nagging you. You are thinking that perhaps you have left your right master and here you have come into a strange world: "Why not go back home?" I never want anyone to be here half-heartedly. Either you are here or you are not here; there is no other choice. So you can think it over.

Either say good-bye to your so-called teacher, strict teacher; strictly enlightened. That I have heard for the first time. There have been enlightened people, but *strictly* enlightened! So it seems a few are lousy. Gautam Buddha is not a strictly enlightened person – a lousy person in comparison to Lee Lozowick. Just go back to him because that is the only way to be finished with him.

Now that you know me and you know my people, and you know the space that is being created here, when you go back to Lee Lozowick, you will have something to compare him with. If you feel to come back, then come with totality. Your totality will be respected and loved. And only your totality can make you discover the master that is here.

I am not a teacher, not at all. I have no teaching. I have simply a presence that I want to share with you – in my words, in my silences, in my presence, in my absence. I want you to feel that this small place is not part of the neurotic world outside the gate; that a different kind of consciousness is growing here. It is a nursery. But perhaps... It happens to many people that when they come the second time, then they recognize.

It is just like a joke. There are very few people who understand a joke when they hear it for the first time. Most of the women, particularly, who get it the first time... It simply means that they have good teeth; it does not mean that they have understood the joke. The Englishman never understands when he hears a joke for the first time. He wonders what it is. He gets it in the middle of the night. Thinking about it this way and that way, figuring it out, suddenly he catches the glimpse. He says, "My God!" And then he laughs in his bedroom silently so that no one can hear.

The German never gets it. He laughs because everyone else is laughing, and if you don't laugh they will think you are German. The Indian never gets it either. But he does not laugh like the German, just to give company to other people who are laughing. It seems to the Indian that he is too serious a person, far above, spiritual, how can he laugh? It is not that he is spiritual or far above, the real fact is that he does not understand the joke.

I have been searching for a purely Indian joke. I have gone through almost thousands of books in search of a purely Indian joke. I have to confess that there exists no such thing. All jokes that are available in Indian literature are imported. Only the Jew understands it. But he understands it before you have even finished it. And to tell a joke to a Jew is a very embarrassing experience because in the middle of the joke he will say, "Shut up! It is an old joke, and moreover you are telling it all wrong."

I have been watching. Many people have come here for the first time, and only the very intelligent have remained – and remained silently, without ever thinking that any other world exists except this commune.

A few remained here just to learn enough so they could go back and become great masters in their own right. They are not interested in truth, they are interested in their own egos. And now there are a few people around the world – they will not mention my name and they have lived with me for ten years. They are afraid that someone may recognize: "You have been Osho's disciple." They want to erase that part of their life completely so that they can say they are a master, unique; that they have discovered the truth themselves and they are not repeating it.

I go on receiving their pamphlets and their leaflets and I wonder: these people are either blind or utterly unconscious. They are quoting me, in their name, and they are sending those pamphlets to the sannyasins. And the sannyasins send them to me, saying, "Look what your people are doing." They have never been my people. They were here just to learn some strategy so that they could be masters.

The third type is more sincere. They come and they don't feel at ease. It is natural. When you change from one commune to another commune, it is changing from one river to another river. The taste of the water changes, the flow of the river changes. The climate changes, the trees on the banks are different, a different fragrance… Everything changes. Naturally one feels to be back in the old, which you have become accustomed to.

I want you to go back because that will reveal to you that your six years have been a wastage, and your six days here have given you a greater insight. And when you come again, you will come clean – clean of your past hanging on you. This will bring you a certain maturity that you need.

Little Ernie and little Elmer are outside the whorehouse, and after seeing the comings and goings their curiosity is aroused. So they knock on the door and ask the madam if they can come in and find out what it is all about, but she tells them the price is ten dollars.

After saving their pocket money for weeks they amass the sum of seventy-nine cents and approach the madam again. Being a businesswoman and sensing the possibility of future clients, she takes their seventy-nine cents and tells one of the girls to give them a quick flash of her pussy for their money.

Two minutes later they are leaving the place when Ernie turns to Elmer and says, "I didn't like the look of that, did you?"

"No," replies Elmer, "I'm glad we didn't have ten bucks' worth."

Osho,
Why are you against marriage? Women have been, certainly, the cause of their husband's enlightenment.

It is certainly true that without women no man would have ever been enlightened. They create such hell that there is no way out except to become enlightened. This also explains why very few women have ever become enlightened – and not very strictly enlightened, just so-so. The reason is that husbands are not capable of creating that great a hell. Who is going to help women to become enlightened?

I am certainly against marriage. My being against marriage has many reasons. One of them is that if there is no marriage, man and woman will be moving freely with each other. And soon you will see there are an equal number of women enlightened as men; this disparity will disappear. There have been thousands of enlightened men and perhaps five enlightened women; you can count them on five fingers. Still, their enlightenment is lukewarm. Once you have released the man and the woman from this bondage, you will be creating a situation in which no one nags you into enlightenment.

Enlightenment that has come out of nagging is not much of an enlightenment; it is simply escape. I want authentic enlightenment, and that needs absolute freedom from nagging. No one is nagging you, no one is telling you to become enlightened; everyone is accepting you as you are, enlightened or unenlightened. Out of this freedom will come more authentic men and authentic women becoming enlightened. But this will be out of freedom, not out of bondage. Not out of misery, despair, agony, but out of joy, love, orgasmic experiences.

You can see that the quality of enlightenment will be totally different. The first kind of enlightenment is bound to be dry, juiceless – he will be unable to laugh because he is completely afraid, continually defending his achievement because anyone can pull him back into the world.

Gautam Buddha says to his disciples, "Never look more than four feet ahead while you are walking, so that you will never see any woman's face." What kind of fear...? And these people are going to become enlightened.

A disciple is going on a journey and Buddha says to him, "Remember never to look at a woman."

The man seems to be a stubborn type. He says, "But there may be an accidental situation when, not knowing, I may have looked at a woman. Then what am I supposed to do?" He is right, because going into the world, there is every possibility of seeing a woman. You can close your eyes then, but you have seen her.

Buddha says "Okay, you can look, but never touch."

But the man is not in any way of a lesser quality than Gautam Buddha. He says, "There is a possibility that one may have to touch a woman. For example, what if a woman falls into a ditch and I am alone on the road, and unless I help her, she is going to die. Do you want me to let her die?"

Certainly Buddha cannot say that, so he says, "Okay," reluctantly. "You can touch in certain emergencies. Don't make it a common practice. But even if you touch, don't speak."

The man said, "This is putting me into a difficult situation. If the woman says something, do you want me not to answer? If a woman asks me where this road goes, should I remain silent, knowing perfectly well where this road goes, that she is going on the wrong road and may suffer for miles and miles and will never reach?"

Just desperate with this man, Buddha says, "Do whatever you want to do!"

But putting people under such conditions to make them enlightened is not my way, and I don't think it is the right way either. Any kind of experience that may happen in this way cannot be joyous; it cannot blossom into flowers, it cannot release fragrance. It will be dry, dirty, escapist, fearful, always on guard. No, I don't support any such enlightenment.

I want you to withdraw all miserable conditions from the world, and marriage is one of the most miserable conditions. Let love be freed from the chains of marriage. Allow humanity to love, to laugh, to enjoy, to celebrate life, to experience life to its very depth. And out of this intensive experiencing of life will arise a totally different kind of enlightenment, which will be able to dance, which will be able to sing, which will be able to laugh. It will have a beauty of its own, a glory, a splendor. I am introducing a totally new kind of enlightenment to the world. The old one, to me, looks rotten. That's why I am against marriage. It will go on creating the rotten enlightenment.

An optimist is a man who marries his secretary and thinks he will still be able to dictate to her.

If married life was supposed to be fun, it would not start in church.

Love is temporary insanity, curable by marriage.

Marriage is permanent insanity, curable only by enlightenment. But that enlightenment will come out of an insanity; its roots, its juices, all will be poisoned.

A single man is one who runs around and gets into all kinds of trouble. A married man does not have to run around. He is already in trouble. This trouble creates the possibility of thinking of a life beyond, because this life is finished. If there is not a life beyond, that would be a very terrible and shocking situation.

A wedding day is when rings are put on the finger of a woman and in the nose of a man.

Laugh and the world laughs with you. Weep and you sleep alone.

I am describing these different aspects of marriage…

Notice in a restaurant window: Don't stand outside and be miserable, come inside and be fed up!

Not to take women seriously is to ask for trouble. To take them seriously is to get it!

All marriages are happy, it's living together afterward that causes all the trouble.

He that will not reason is a bigot, he that cannot reason is an idiot, and he that dares not reason is a husband.

If you want to attain enlightenment, the best training up to now has been marriage. But that enlightenment will be as miserable as the sources from which it is coming. I want sages who can dance, sages so innocent that they can laugh, sages so innocent that they can enjoy small things of life with such joy; sages who can live on this earth as if it is paradise, not asking for any paradise beyond. But up to now our sages have all been psychologically sick.

A little time for enjoying enlightenment… If you cannot enjoy it forever, there is no harm in enjoying it temporarily, even for a few moments. When you laugh you all look almost like Gautam Buddhas. When you sit silently, you look like a congregation in a church!

Mendel Kravitz arrives at a cabaret club and asks the doorman who he should see to get a booking for his singing act.

"You should see the concert secretary," says the doorman. "By the way, you're not a hypnotist, are you?" Mendel assures him that he is not, and goes in.

The concert secretary looks up suspiciously and says, "I hope you are not going to tell me you're a hypnotist, are you?"

Mendel assures him he is only a singer, and is sent to find the organist for a tryout. The organist likes the songs but looks uneasily at Mendel. "You don't do any side acts by chance, do you?" he asks. "No hypnotism for instance?"

Mendel is tired of the question and demands an explanation.

"Well," says the organist, "last week we had a hypnotist here. He was so good that he had at least two hundred of the audience in a trance."

"What's wrong with that?" asks Mendel.

"Nothing," continues the organist, "but halfway through his act, he fell over the microphone, hurt his foot, and yelled out, 'Shit!' The cleaners have only just cleaned the hall."

Kowalski and his wife are celebrating their thirty-first wedding anniversary. As a surprise he comes home with a little monkey.

"What's that?" asks his wife.

"It's a monkey," replies Kowalski. "What did you think it was? This is my anniversary present to you."

"You are crazy!" she cries. "What are we gonna do with a monkey?"

"Well," says Kowalski, "he's gonna eat with us, he's gonna sleep with us..."

"Sleep with us?" shouts Mrs. Kowalski. "What about the smell?"

"Listen," says Kowalski, "after twenty-five years, if I could get used to it, so will the monkey."

# 8

# Love and Meditation Is Going to Save the World.

Osho,
The other morning, the discourse left me feeling terrified and desperate: desperate to save this incredible, beautiful planet, and terrified because the odds against us seem so high. I feel so insignificant, and helpless to do anything. The only thing I can see to do is to be here with you as much as possible, nourishing my consciousness and supporting your vision. Is there any more that can be done?

I can understand your desperation, your helplessness. This is perhaps how every human being who is aware of the crisis feels. But you are not aware of a greater power: destruction is a low category power, creation is a high category power. Destruction is out of hate, creation is out of love.

You have seen where hate can lead humanity – to its ultimate suicide. But you have not seen the possibility of love growing to its height; it may simply prevent this crisis from happening. No one is insignificant because everyone has a heart and everyone has love, sensitivity, consciousness. And he can reach the very ultimate peak of existence. A single individual can prevent this great crisis, what to say of millions of people full of love and joy and silence?

I am reminded of an Old Testament story about two cities, Sodom and Gomorrah…

The people in both cities became absolutely sexually perverted; all kinds of perversions prevailed. The story is very beautiful; it will give you courage, it will take away your desperation. It will make you stand up as an individual, representing life and love which cannot be destroyed by any nuclear weapons, by any politicians. Even God could not destroy Sodom and Gomorrah.

I have to remind you at this point that in the Old Testament version he destroyed the cities. It was impossible to change those people; they had become so accustomed to perverted ways. You may not know that the word *sodom* means making love to animals. That's why the whole city was called Sodom. And even today making love to animals is called sodomy. Just the vibration of the word *gomorrah* is enough to give you the sense of what it means: gonorrhea.

But the story takes a very special turn, and that's my point to emphasize. In the Judaic religion there is a small stream of revolts by rebels, revolutionaries. They are called Hasids. They are not accepted by the orthodoxy as authentic because they go against anything in orthodoxy, anything in a tradition which does not appeal to the human heart, to reason, to sensitivity, to consciousness. They have written their own story.

Their story is that there lived a man – a Hasid – who used to live six months in Gomorrah and six months in Sodom. He approached God and said to him, "Have you taken into account the possibility that there may be one hundred absolutely natural, wise people in these two vast cities? Are you going to destroy them also because others are perverted? Then it will be a great injustice, a pure injustice and it will be a condemnation on you. So reconsider!" God had not thought of the possibility. Certainly in those two big cities, almost like Hiroshima and Nagasaki, there must be one hundred intelligent, natural, alert people. They will also be destroyed, and this will not be in tune with God's divineness, it will be simply ugly.

So God said, "If you can prove that there are a hundred such people, I will not destroy those two cities."

The Hassid said, "And if there are only fifty, are you going to destroy?"

God was caught by the mystic Hasid. He said, "Even if you can prove fifty…"

The mystic said, "If there are only twenty-five? What does it matter? Does the number matter to you or the quality? – quantity or quality?"

God said, "Certainly the quality."

And the Hasid said, "If it is the quality then to tell you the truth, I am the only man who is not perverted, who is living a natural, blissful life. But I live six months in Gomorrah and six months in Sodom. Are you going to destroy those cities?"

God had never come across such a clever person. From a hundred he had brought him down to one. Only a Jew can do that! They know how to bargain – and he bargained. In the Jewish version of the story God destroyed those cities, but not in the Hasidic version. The cities were saved because God could not destroy even a single person of quality, a single person of wisdom, just because the whole city had become perverted.

I am telling you this so that you need not be terrified. You have to be only alert. I will read your question: "The other morning, the discourse left me feeling terrified and desperate…" There is no need to feel desperate and there is no need to feel terrified. If one Hasid can persuade existence to protect two cities, we have thousands of Hasids with us. Every sannyasin is a Hasid. Existence cannot allow a few idiots like Ronald Reagan to destroy this world.

But that does not mean that you have to remain just silent. You have to create a great atmosphere of love around yourself which will be the protection; you have to learn to dance and to sing. Let these politicians know that this earth is still full of beautiful people – so many songs, so much music, so much creativity, so many people meditating. They are bound to have a second thought.

On our part, we don't need bigger nuclear weapons to stop the war; that's the problem. We need something totally different. Love will provide the energy, meditation will provide you with tremendous strength. You will not feel so insignificant, you will feel dignified and significant, because your love, your meditation, your blissfulness is going to save the world.

And don't be worried that you are helpless to do anything. The idea of helplessness has arisen because you have never been told what your resources are. You have never looked into your resources: your love, silence, peace, compassion, joy. You have never looked into all this inexhaustible potentiality of your being. If thousands of people blossom in love, music, dance and the whole earth becomes a celebration, then any Ronald Reagan is not going to destroy this world. He will feel helpless; he will feel guilty to destroy such beautiful people and such a beautiful planet.

You ask me, "The only thing I can see to do is to be here with you as much as possible, nourishing my consciousness and supporting your vision. Is there anything more that can be done?" – it is enough. More is not needed; more will keep you unnecessarily worried. And worry is like a rocking chair: it keeps you going but gets you nowhere! There is no need to worry and there is no need to feel desperate, helpless. A few idiots have prepared death for the planet; there are millions of intelligent people who can prevent it just by their love, joy, beauty, ecstasy. These are far more powerful experiences, because atomic energy, or nuclear energy, is part of the material world. It is the explosion of the atom, the lowest, smallest particle of matter.

We have not yet understood that nature has an absolute balance. If a small atom exploding can destroy… Have you ever thought about a living atom of your being and its explosion? In other words, we have been calling it enlightenment. It is nothing but an explosion of your being into light. And then suddenly you have a far higher and superior power. It need not fight with the lower, its very presence will make the lower impotent.

It has not been tried on a vast scale, only once in a while. But those rare instances are certainly a proof that if tried, every human being can become an explosion of consciousness – which is a far superior energy – and make all these nuclear weapons and the people who hold them utterly impotent and guilty.

A few instances will help you. They look nonfactual because they are rare, and because not many people have tried them.

A follower of Gautam Buddha, Devadatta – his own cousin-brother – was naturally jealous of the immense glory, impressiveness and the impact of Gautam Buddha on people. Whoever came to Buddha never returned the same. Something changed in his very being. Buddha had sown a seed; the man would return at the right time, when the first clouds started raining.

But this was invisible to the blind Devadatta; not physically blind, but spiritually blind. He could not understand what the matter was. He was as beautiful as Gautam Buddha – his cousin-brother – as educated, as cultured in the arts of those days. There was no question that Gautam Buddha was superior and he was not; he could not see the superior aroma that surrounded Gautam Buddha.

Finally he asked him, "I would like to be declared your successor."

Buddha said, "Whoever is capable of succeeding me will succeed me, I am not going to declare him. Anyway I am still alive, just in middle of my life. And this is not my way to choose! Who am I to choose a successor? Existence itself will choose."

Devadatta became so hurt that he left the commune and made many attempts on the life of Gautam Buddha. Those attempts look fictional because we don't know the power of love and we don't know the power of awareness; we don't know the beauty of ecstasy and its tremendous power of protection.

Buddha used to meditate on a small rock at the bottom of a vast mountain. Devadatta tried to roll a big rock down from the mountain in the direction of Gautam Buddha, so that that rock would kill him completely and no one would be blamed; no one would even think that someone had killed him. The rock came rushing down the mountain and everyone who was present was surprised, could not believe that it could happen: the rock stopped just two feet away from Buddha, changed its route and moved away from him. Then it went on falling. This behavior of the rock was very strange; one would never think that a rock would do that. Even Devadatta was puzzled.

Devadatta himself was the king of a small kingdom, and he had a mad elephant. The mad elephant was always kept in chains in the prison because he used to kill people. Devadatta saw another opportunity. The elephant was brought near Gautam Buddha and released. He rushed toward Gautam Buddha, the way he would have rushed toward anyone else. But as he reached near him, he suddenly stopped, and with tears in his eyes he bowed down to Gautam Buddha and touched his feet with his head. No one could believe that an insane elephant… How is he making a distinction? But blind people are blind people! Devadatta could not see what the rock could see, what the mad elephant could see – a subtle, invisible aura of love.

A few years ago when a man threw a knife at me in the morning meeting… And it seems it was an absolute conspiracy because just before the meeting, fifteen minutes before, the police informed the office, "Today there is a danger; a man is going to throw a knife at Osho. So twenty police officers should be allowed in."

Now, this is stupid. If they knew that a certain man was going to commit a crime, they should have arrested him. Rather than that, they informed the office. As the story went on it became clear that it was absolutely a conspiracy. Those twenty police officers with loaded guns surrounded that man. The sannyasins thought that perhaps they were for our protection – that was wrong. They were for the protection of the man who was going to throw the knife. They were afraid that ten thousand sannyasins would kill that man if anything happened.

That man shouted – which is on record – "Osho, you are against Hinduism and we cannot tolerate your existence anymore." Then he threw the knife at me. And because he was shouting, I stopped and listened to him, what he was saying. It is on tape. He threw the knife from just fifteen feet away and it was strange, the knife fell eight feet away from me. Not only did it not touch me, it did not even touch anyone in the crowded Buddha Hall; the knife touched no one.

The police said, "It is a police case. We will arrest this man and bring him to the court."

This was all strategy. You can see how politicians work – cunningly, inhumanely. They prevented us from putting a case against the man. They said, "There is no need. Ten thousand witnesses, his words are recorded, even the sound of the falling knife is recorded, and twenty police officers of high rank are witnesses. You need not be worried; it is going to be a police case. We will take him and bring him to court."

They took him away, presented him before the court, and the court released him, saying, "Such a thing has not happened at all." And because we had not put any case against him, then it was too late. The police managed it in such a way that they did not insist that the case happened.

But I have been thinking about it: in such a crowded place, even if a blind man throws a knife it is going to hit someone. The knife behaved exactly like the rock and the elephant. It was a police conspiracy and you can see the justice. When twenty police officers are present, when ten thousand people are ready to be witnesses; the knife is there, his shout is recorded, the sound of the knife falling on the floor is recorded...

And what was the judge's reason to reject the case? The reason was, "If it was an attempt on Osho's life, then why have they not brought the case? Why have they not reported the case to the police? Secondly, if a man was trying to murder Osho, those ten thousand sannyasins would not have let him go so easily." We had not done anything because the police had prevented us, saying, "There is no need."

Still, one of the most important criminal advocates of the supreme court of India, Ram Jethmalani was there. We had asked him to be present. He wanted to say something. The judge said, "You cannot speak, it is not your case." And certainly it was not our case. But I have seen things which make me certain that what appears to be a miracle is not a miracle.

I am absolutely certain that I was poisoned in Oklahoma with a certain metallic poison, thallium, but it has not been able to kill me.

They put a bomb under my chair in the jail in Portland while I was at the court; they were expecting me to come any moment. I came, and the man there indicated to me to sit on a particular chair. That was also strange because there were many chairs, I could have sat on any chair. He immediately locked the door from the outside and said, "I will be coming back within fifteen minutes." I had no idea that I was sitting on a bomb! But something went wrong; the bomb did not explode.

If millions of people are full of love and meditation, there is no need to feel desperate or helpless. You are given tremendous power by nature which can nullify any nuclear weapons. And that's what I'm trying to do: to prepare you to love, unconditionally, to prepare you for friendliness even with strangers; to prepare you to drop your organized religions because they create conflict, to drop even the belonging to your nations. Formally you will have to carry their passport, but this is just a formality. Deep in your being you should not be a Hindu, an Indian, a German, a Christian.

If this wave spreads – and I have every hope that it is going to spread – then you can forget all about the third world war; the second was the last. The third is possible only if there is not enough love and meditative energy to prevent it.

Osho,
Alone, insecure, scared, I can see a door – to God's house or death or insanity, I don't know which. Sitting with you, intoxicated by

your freedom, though my mind is like a cattle train, my heart knows no question. Can the curtain rise and the world stop amid such beauty?

If your mind is silent, if you are feeling in deep synchronicity with existence and with a great love for the beauty of this planet, then the door you are standing before is neither of death nor of insanity nor of God. Because God died long ago. It is the door of your own inner being, of your own inner consciousness. Don't stand before the door, enter and you will find yourself. There is no greater joy in the world than to find yourself. It brings such a serenity, such a settlement with everything. It simply puts you in harmony with nature, with existence, and life becomes a moment-to-moment ecstasy.

You need not feel alone, insecure, scared. It is natural to feel that way because you are standing before the door and you don't know who is inside – God, death or insanity. I say to you on my authority that there is no God, no death, no insanity, but an eternal rejoicing of life, love, celebration. Just enter through the door.

Don't go on standing there because the fear is that feeling alone, insecure and scared you can escape from the door. And then it may take lives for you to find it again – and with the same problem. Be courageous and enter through the door, and you have entered the most sacred place, the most sacred temple that exists.

Osho,
Your gestures move me more deeply than your discourses. Your grace and beauty touch me even more than your silence. Osho, wiggle a toe or give us a wink.

My God! You are asking very difficult things of me. I don't know how to give a wink; I have never given a wink to anyone. And to do it for the first time will be very difficult. I know how to use both eyes together, but a wink means one eye has to remain open.

Once in a while if I have mistakenly put some shampoo or some soap in my eyes and made them red, Nirvano puts some drops in them. You can see, today this eye is a little red. She puts in the drops, but her problem is that either I can open both eyes or I can keep both eyes closed. So she keeps one eye closed with one hand, and opens the other eye forcibly – just inexperience.

I cannot hope to succeed and give you a wink; I never do anything in which there is a little suspicion of failure. I will start trying alone in my room. When I am an expert I will give you a wink. As far as the toe is concerned, it is so lazy that even if I want to move it, it will not move. But I will make every effort to satisfy you. But you seem to be a strange person, to ask me for such gestures. Do you want me to look funny? I can do that because I'm not concerned at all with the world, what they think. You will just have to give me a little time to practice.

I have never moved my toe. It simply remains always enlightened, unmoving! Now to persuade it to come down from enlightenment is going to be very difficult, but I will make every effort to persuade it: "Just once in a while taking a holiday from enlightenment is not a sin! And you are not committing any sin, just moving…" Of course the problem with the wink is more difficult: Who to give it to? Because anyone who gets it will become enlightened. And with all you people, I love you so much that I cannot choose someone to give the wink to. So I will have to figure it out. It is a very difficult job.

Everyone knows how to wink because they have been doing it all the time; it is a language. The toe is more spiritual than the eye, because I don't think anyone takes any offense if you move your toe. But if you wink, particularly at a woman – and here homosexuals are not respected… So I will have to find a woman who does not get disturbed by the wink. It is a very complicated question.

Sign on a bookstore: Going out of business – words failed us!

That is the beauty of the gesture, it never fails. Although no one teaches it, it simply is understood naturally.

A statement of Picasso: "The world today does not make sense, so why should I paint pictures that do?"

Now, these are absurd gestures: winking an eye, whistling at a woman. And the toe is absolutely your own invention. I have never heard that to attract a woman you have to move your toe. Perhaps it is to distract her – seeing that the man is mad... Instead of winking his eye he is moving his toe!

I am very inexperienced in such great affairs. But I promise you, I will try with the trees, I will try with the rocks because they will not feel offended. And they will not fall in love with me either. Once I am satisfied, then I will give you a wink – not to anyone in particular. That is my way.

Nirvano was asking me, "Do you see people?" Even when I am looking at you, I am not seeing you. It is so tiring a job. You cannot expect such a thing of me! I love you, but I don't know you. I know only very few people who came in the very beginning and stayed with me for all these fifteen years. But others, who have come afterward, have the same share of love.

But when I am speaking, I am just speaking to the walls. I love Bodhidharma for that particular gesture: he was sitting facing the wall for nine years. His audience was sitting behind him and he would speak to the wall. Emperor Wu asked him, "What strange kind of thing is happening here? I have never seen a speaker talking to the wall and the audience sitting behind listening to it."

Bodhidharma's answer was, "It doesn't matter. Even if I face them, I am facing a wall. But that wall is a little disturbing – someone moves, someone changes his posture. That distracts me. So I decided on a new method: I speak to the wall. They can go on changing their postures, coming and going, whatever they want to do. Whether they are listening or not, I am not concerned. And it is strange that since I have started speaking to the wall, there is utter silence behind me because everyone wants to get what I am saying. No one is moving."

So I will have to find a way how to wink. Perhaps I can wink at the wall. The toe is more difficult because it is absolutely new. In the whole history of man, no one has moved his toe as a gesture – gesture for what?

There is an incident in Gautam Buddha's life…

A great king, Prasenjita, had come to listen to him. Of course, being a great king, he was sitting in the front. Buddha suddenly stopped in the middle of a sentence and said to Prasenjita, "Why are you moving your toe?"

When he asked this, the movement stopped and Prasenjita said, "I don't know, it just happened."

Buddha said, "Your whole life is just like that. It is just happening, accidentally. You are not conscious."

But except for that incident, I have never come across any incident where the toe is even mentioned. But for your satisfaction I will practice. By the way, are you a student of psychology? Because only psychologists ask absurd questions.

In America in the 1970's, each year twice as many psychiatrists committed suicide compared to mental hospital patients. The number has grown since the '70's – it is now '88 – now four times as many psychiatrists are committing suicide as people from any other profession. Naturally, if you are concerned with absurd things… The eyes are not meant to wink, and the toes are not meant to be moved. When you do such things you disturb the inner ecology of your body.

But once in a lifetime it won't hurt me. Just how long it will take for me to practice, that I cannot say. You will have to learn patience. And if in your patience some understanding arises and you withdraw your question, I will be immensely happy. That patience, absolute patience, may turn out to be a new birth for you. You may be reborn.

There is only one problem with going through a second childhood: this time you can't blame your parents.

Just two jokes, not related to your question, but certainly related to you…

Paddy lurches out of the pub and bumps straight into Father Murphy, the village priest.

"Patrick," says the priest, "I am so sorry to see you come out of such a place as that!"

"Well, then," says Paddy, turning around, "I will go right back."

Uncle Albert is staying for the weekend, and little Ernie is asking him all sorts of questions.

"Uncle Albert," he asks, "why are some men bald on the front of their head?"

"Well," replies Uncle Albert, "these men are the great thinkers."

"And what about the men that are bald on the back of their head?" asks little Ernie.

"These men," explains Uncle Albert, "are the great fuckers."

"So what does it mean," continues little Ernie, "when they are bald all over?"

"That's obvious," replies Uncle Albert, "these men think they are great fuckers."

# 9

# Existence Is Reality, God Is Simply Fiction

Osho,

What is existence? Is it something like what people call God?

Existence is that which is, and God is that which is not. Existence is a reality, God is a fiction. Existence is available only to meditators, people of silence; God is a consolation for the sick minds, sick psychologies. Existence is not your production – God is. That's why there is only one existence, but thousands of gods. Each according to his needs, his suffering, his expectations, creates a god or accepts an old belief about God.

God is a great consolation, but it is not a cure. Existence is not a consolation. To be in tune with it is to be healthy and whole. All the religions of the world have been teaching God; I teach you existence. I teach you to be in tune with that which surrounds you, which is within you and without you. Once you are in tune with it, there is no death for you, no misery, no tension, no worry, but a tremendous peace surrounds you, a contentment which you have never even dreamed of.

God is for those who cannot grow in consciousness, who are retarded as far as consciousness is concerned. It is a kind of toy;

retarded people need it. And the moment I say it is a toy, then it is up to you how you want to make it – to look like a monkey or to look like an elephant. It is just up to you whether to give him four hands or one thousand hands. It is your creation. Strangely enough, man believes God created everything. The truth is that God himself is a creation of man's imagination.

God is the greatest lie you can ever find because on that lie thousands of other lies depend. Churches, religious organizations go on multiplying lies upon lies, just to protect one lie. You have to understand the psychology of lying. The first thing about lying is that you need a good memory because you have to remember. You lie to someone about something, to someone else about something else; you have to remember what you have said to one and what you have said to the other.

Truth needs no remembrance. Truth is always there, just the same. You don't have to cram it in your memory. Memory gives you a bondage, a prison; it clings around you, covers you so much that slowly, slowly you disappear completely. Truth is uncovering yourself from all lies. And there is a sudden revelation that you are part of the immense truth I am calling existence.

You don't need any churches, temples, mosques; you need only a prayerful heart, a loving heart, a grateful heart. That is your real temple. That will transform your whole life. That will help you to discover not only yourself, but the very depths of this immense existence.

We are almost like the waves of the ocean; just on the surface, and the ocean may be miles deep. The Pacific Ocean is five miles deep. But a small wave on the top will never know the depth – her *own* depth because she is not separate from the ocean. She will cling to her small entity: be afraid about death, be afraid of losing herself in the vastness, the oceanic infinity. But the truth is that the death of the wave is not a death but the beginning of an eternal life.

God has been invented. It was people's need; people needed a protector. In the immensity of the universe, a man feels so alone, so small. The vastness creates trembling in him. What is your existence?

I am reminded of a story by Bertrand Russell...

The archbishop of England sees in a dream that he has reached the pearly gates of paradise. On the one hand he is immensely pleased, and on the other hand he is very troubled because the pearly gates are so vast, in all directions, that he cannot see the whole gate. It is so high that it is beyond the capacity of his eyes to see. And he himself seems to be just like a small ant, compared to this great gate. He is a little bit afraid. He is no ordinary man, he is the archbishop of England. He feels humiliated just by the gate, and the fear arises, "If this is the situation at the gate, what is the situation going to be inside?"

With fearful hands he knocks on the door, but in the immensity of that space only he can hear his knock. It takes days for him, but he goes on knocking harder and harder. Finally a small window opens in the gate and Saint Peter looks out with one thousand eyes, trying to figure out who has been making a noise. Those one thousand eyes are so shiny, like stars, that the archbishop feels even more reduced – almost to a nonentity.

Saint Peter asks, "Please, whoever you are, wherever you are, come in front of me."

The archbishop declares himself. He says to Saint Peter, "Perhaps you don't know me. You can check with Jesus Christ, I am the archbishop of England."

Saint Peter says, "Never heard of any such thing as England."

The archbishop says, "Perhaps you may not have heard about England, but you must have heard about our beautiful planet, Earth."

Saint Peter says, "I don't want to hurt your feelings, but unless you give me the index number of your Earth, I cannot figure out what you are talking about. I will have to go to the library and look – if you give me the index number – to which solar system you belong. Because there are millions of solar systems and each solar system has many planets."

But the archbishop had never thought that the earth had any index number. He says, "I don't know any index number, but I am the archbishop. Just go and tell Jesus Christ."

Saint Peter says, "You are giving me puzzle after puzzle. Who is this fellow Jesus Christ?"

The archbishop is very shocked. He says, "You don't know Jesus Christ, the only begotten son of God?"

Saint Peter says, "As far as I am concerned, I have never seen God; I don't know whether he exists or not. I am just a doorkeeper. Perhaps somewhere in the most interior parts of paradise someone exists who thinks that he is God, but I have never come across…"

It is such a shock that the archbishop wakes up perspiring.

The story is significant because it shows how small we are and how big the universe is. Naturally, primitive man was not able to adjust himself to this vastness of the universe without giving it some personality, and without making himself in some way related to that personality.

God is an effort of the primitive mind of man to give existence a personality. Then he becomes God the father, and you can make some relationship with him. You may even be against him, but at least there is someone you can be for, you can be against; there is someone who is greater than you, who is going to protect you, who is your guarantee. God is simply the poverty of human consciousness.

The people who attained their inner consciousness and its highest peak, like Gautam Buddha, denied the existence of God. Anyone who has ever become inwardly healthy, gone beyond the mind which is basically sick, has denied God. God as a fiction is good for kindergarten school children. They need it – parables, fables, stories. But very few human beings have gone beyond the kindergarten school.

God exists because you are not aware of yourself. God exists because you have not made any contact with your own center. The moment you know yourself, there is no God and there is no need of any God. On the contrary, I am in absolute support of Friedrich Nietzsche: "God is dead."

The second part of his sentence is even more significant, "God is dead and man is now free." That second part has not received much attention from the philosophers, the mystics, the psychologists, but the second part is the most important; the first part is not much. In fact, the first part is basically wrong. God cannot die; fictions never die. The moment you know they are fictions there is no question of their death. They are neither born nor do they die. God was never born in the first place. How can he die? Death is the other extreme of birth.

So the first part is not very important, but that has been given much importance by theologians because they became afraid: "This is sacrilegious, to tell people that God is dead. That means that now no religion is needed." They became afraid for their own business. But they forgot the second part which is more important. It has tremendously significant implications. It means that God was a bondage, God was a retardedness, God was out of fear. God was not a treasure but a heavy, mountainous weight on your heart and on your growth.

Once God is removed, man's possibility to grow and blossom is absolutely free. A God is a despot, a fascist. Without God, the world becomes freedom. Existence becomes a tremendous dignity to every individual. From the smallest blade of grass up to the greatest star in the universe, it gives immense significance and love. It makes no difference; there is equality and equal opportunity. And there is no need unnecessarily to pray and waste your time, to read the holy scriptures, which are the most unholy books in the world. There is no need to be exploited by the priests. You are certainly and suddenly free from all these chains. Now you can be yourself.

With God in existence you can never be yourself. You are just a puppet, your strings are in the hands of God. The ancient saying in India is that not even a small leaf of a tree moves unless God's order is received for it to move. Whatever you are, according to religions you are made out of mud. The word *human* comes from *humus*, which means mud. And the word in Hebrew, Arabic, Urdu, Hindi, is *admi*; it is used as the name of the first man, Adam. *Adam* means the earth. God made man out of the earth and then breathed life into the puppet.

Now, what kind of freedom do you have? Someone has breathed life into you, and it is in his hands at any moment to stop breathing life into you. Whatever you are doing, the religions believe it is your fate; it is written on your forehead. And there have been many con men who have even been trying to read what is written on your forehead. Astrologers, palmists, all kinds of cunning people have been exploiting the simplicity and innocence of humanity. There are people who are reading your hand, looking at the lines, telling you what those lines mean. The whole emphasis is that you are not living a life of your own; you are just a part in a drama, and the part that you are playing has been decided beforehand.

That was the argument that Krishna, the Indian god's incarnation, gave to his disciple Arjuna in the great Indian war, Mahabharata. Seeing the immense massacre that was going to happen, Arjuna simply lost his nerve. He was a man of immense courage and great intelligence.

He said, "I don't see any point in this war. Even if I win… And I am certain I am going to win." There was no other warrior of his quality. "But sitting on the golden throne of victory surrounded by the corpses of all my friends and all my enemies, all the beautiful people, does not appeal to me at all. The scene makes me feel insane. Rather than fighting, I will leave it to the other party – who is no one, another cousin-brother. Let him rule over the country and I will go to the mountains, to the Himalayas to meditate, to become a sannyasin. I have lost all interest in fighting."

Krishna tries in every way but Arjuna is a great intellectual; he goes on arguing against him. Finally seeing no other way, Krishna takes the last resort and says, "It is written in your destiny. Going away, you are going away from God. This war is predetermined by God to destroy those who are not virtuous and only let those survive who are virtuous." Now there is no argument against it because Arjuna himself believes in God and destiny.

Arjuna fought the war five thousand years ago. Krishna was responsible for destroying this country by giving a false argument, absolutely fictitious, to Arjuna. That war killed so many people. And it is not only that it killed people, it also destroyed the courage of the country; it became afraid of any small calamity.

Two thousand years of slavery… I want it absolutely clear that the people who are responsible for these two thousand years of slavery are the greatest people of India. The list is headed by Krishna; Arjuna is just his shadow. Then came Mahavira, who taught people to be nonviolent to such an extreme that his followers cannot even cultivate because plants have life; if you cultivate then you will have to kill the plants when you reap the crop. Gautam Buddha comes third, he taught people to accept, to be contented wherever and with whatever they are – poor, hungry, starving, enslaved – and remain utterly contented.

Their teachings were great. This is something to be remembered; otherwise I will be misunderstood by everyone. Their teachings were great, but they never thought about all the implications of their teachings. They never thought that if you teach a country nonviolence, if you teach a country to drop all weapons when the whole world is not doing that, then you are putting that country in a state of being victimized, exploited by anyone.

And for two thousand years invader after invader came to India, exploited it and went back. Finally Mohammedans came and they thought, "What is the need to go back? We can not only exploit people, but rule them and remain here." And then came the British and the French and the Portuguese, and they all tried to exploit the country. They all had their small pockets. Britain proved to be far more clever. But the Portuguese had their small islands of Diu, Daman and Goa, and the French had a small portion of the country, Pondicherry. Britain had the whole country.

People have remained starving and people remained hungry. And people have gone on dying from hunger. No one has ever thought that these great principles in some way are responsible for this unfortunate situation that for thousands of years India has had to pass through. Even today no one is trying to see all the implications. Every great principle has its own black cloud behind it. Unless you understand the black cloud also, you are soon going to be absorbed by the black cloud. If you understand it, you can avoid it.

God seems to be the greatest principle preached to man down the ages, but no one has looked at its implications. If God created man, then man has no individuality of his own, then he cannot claim any dignity, any freedom. There is no question of a puppet declaring, "I want to be free." If God created the universe, then whatever has happened in the universe has had to happen. It was God's will. No effort on our part was going to change anything.

Finally you can see, if God created the world, and if he is behind nuclear weapons and the people who are creating them, then no effort on man's part can prevent the destruction of the whole planet. To give the creation of the world into the hands of a fictitious God is very dangerous. It makes us absolutely impotent. We cannot do anything.

Hence, my simple understanding of consciousness is that if God did not die with Friedrich Nietzsche's declaration, then we have to kill him! Wherever you meet him, there is no need even to say hello. First kill him and then you can say hello; just to fulfill the formality. But God is not needed at all. With God above in the sky, man will always remain a slave, always remain unconscious, and will never strive to reach the peaks of his potential. With God removed you may feel a little fear – just out of old habit – but that fear will disappear.

Once you recognize that you are standing on your own feet and you have to do something to create a better consciousness in you, to create a more loving heart in you, and that prayers are useless, and there is no one to answer them… Yes, sometimes they have been answered. At least once, certainly…

A poor man asked God continually for months, "Give me fifty dollars. I don't want much, just fifty dollars." First he prayed, but then he thought, "Millions of people are praying, and there is one God and there are millions of prayers. Whether my poor prayer ever reaches him… And there must be so much noise around him – prayers from all the churches, mosques, synagogues, temples – who is going to take care of me? It is better that I write a letter."

He wrote a letter saying, "This is to remind you that for months I have been praying, but the answer has not come. It seems my prayer has not reached you. I can understand because of the noise around you of so many prayers. And great people are praying – the pope and the archbishop and the *shankaracharya* – so who is going to take care of my small prayer? And I am not asking much: no paradise, no heaven, nothing, just fifty dollars. Finally I decided to write the letter." And he wrote in big letters, "FIFTY DOLLARS! Remember, it is urgent."

But then he was very disturbed because he didn't know the address, who to address it to. He thought, "The best way is to address it to: God, c/o The Postmaster General. If the postmaster general cannot find his address, who else can?" The letter reached the postmaster general. He looked, he laughed, and then he felt sad also. He thought, "The man must be in desperate need; no one writes letters to God. And he is not asking much."

So he said to all his friends, "Please look at this poor man's letter. You all contribute, and we will send those fifty dollars to him. At least for once let a prayer be answered." They collected the money, but they collected only forty-five dollars. The postmaster general said, "No harm, at least we should send this much."

When forty-five dollars reached the man he counted the dollars, and he looked above his head and shouted, "God, remember one thing. Next time you send any money to me, never send it through the post office! Those cunning fellows have taken out their commission. I have received only forty-five dollars!"

Except this, I have not come across any prayer which has been answered, and that too not fully. There is no one to answer. Existence has to be approached in a different way. God has to be worshipped. Existence has to be loved. God has to be prayed to. Existence has to be contacted in meditation.

There are only two kinds of religions in the world: the religions of prayer and the religions of meditation. You can see my point. The religions of prayer all believe in God and the religions of meditation don't believe in any god. Because meditation takes you inward, and fulfills you, there is no need to pray, there is no need for any consolation. You are in such a rejoicing, in such a blissful state, you can bless the whole world.

I teach you existence, and the entry to existence is through your own being; hence meditation is not prayer. Remember, it is against prayer. Prayer is part of that phony jargon about God, heaven, hell. Prayer is part and parcel of that whole rubbish. Meditation is simply the only pure way of coming in contact with existence. And this contact immediately becomes a merger and a melting. You become existence yourself. Then you are in the clouds, the stars, the flowers, the rains. You are everywhere. You are no longer a drop, you have become the ocean.

Remember the clear-cut distinction between existence and God. God is a condemnation of our intelligence. It is accepting humiliation, it is accepting that, "We are only puppets; you are the power. Whatever you want to do with us you will do. All that we can do is to pray." It makes you so crippled. The very idea of God is nauseating. But existence has a freshness, a beauty, a truth. Never get mixed up with these two words. One is reality, one is simply fiction.

> Osho,
> We have heard your comments about jazz music. This question comes from two jazz musicians: Is our love of jazz music an obstacle on the path to enlightenment?

My comments about jazz music were made in a totally different context. Compared to classical music, jazz music is in the lowest category because rather than creating a spirituality in you it simply activates your sexuality. The great classical music takes you higher, beyond your mind, to silences which can give you a taste of meditation, a taste of existence.

Always remember that a certain reference in a certain context does not mean my whole approach to something. You are saying, "This question comes from two jazz musicians: Is our love of jazz music an obstacle on the path to enlightenment?" – it depends on you. You can make your jazz music free from the lower gravitation of sexuality. You can make it connected with your higher centers of being, and then it will not be an obstacle on the path to enlightenment. In fact, as far as my people are concerned, they are going to enter enlightenment with jazz music! It has never been tried; hence it is a great challenge and must be tried.

Nothing in the world is wrong if it is used in the right direction – with awareness, with clarity. You can purify anything, just as you can make anything impure. It is wholly a question of your clear understanding. If your meditation goes on growing side by side with your music, soon you will find that even jazz music starts having some quality of meditativeness. If the distinction between music and meditation drops, then whatever classical music was capable in doing, you can also do it. And you can do it more rejoicingly, more dancingly, with greater celebration.

So I don't say that there is any obstacle, but meditation must become part of your music; otherwise just your music cannot help you to go beyond the lower instincts, the biological drives. It will keep you closer to the earth, but far away from the stars.

Pope the Polack and Ronald Reagan meet in the middle of the Sahara Desert. The pope is carrying a telephone booth, while Ronald Reagan has a car engine strapped to his back.

"What are you doing with that telephone booth?" asks Reagan.

"You see," says Pope the Polack, "if a lion comes along, I put it down, go inside and lock the door. But why are you carrying a car engine with you?"

"Well," replies Reagan, "for just the same reason. When a lion comes I drop the engine and then I can run faster."

Hymie Goldberg is trying to hold a small mirror in his hand while he adjusts his tie. The mirror slips and shatters on the ground.

"Oh, no!" he complains to Becky. "Now I am going to have seven years' bad luck."

"Nonsense," replies Becky. "My uncle Sollie once broke a mirror, and he didn't have seven years' bad luck."

"Really?" says Hymie, encouraged.

"Really," repeats Becky. "He died the same day."

It all depends how you understand things…

Miss Goodbody, the teacher, is too shy to conduct the sex education class in school, so she asks her class to make this a homework project.

Little Ernie asks his father, who tells him some story about a stork. Grandma says that she was found under a gooseberry bush. Great-grandma blushes deep red and whispers that children come from God.

The next day, little Ernie gets called to report on his homework.

"Well," says Ernie, "I am afraid my family has been a little abnormal. Apparently there has been no sex at all for three generations."

Paddy Murphy is on his way home, when he comes across a woman crying hysterically.

"What is the matter, lady?" he asks.

"MacTavish is dead!" she sobs. "MacTavish is dead!"

A few minutes later he comes across another woman sobbing, "MacTavish is dead! MacTavish is dead!"

Soon he finds another woman crying the same thing, and then as he approaches the railway crossing he sees a ghastly sight.

A train has run over a man and cut him in pieces. And there on the street next to the body is lying his foot-and-a-half long prick. Several women are standing around crying, "MacTavish is dead! MacTavish is dead!"

When Paddy arrives home, he says to Maureen, "I just saw a terrible thing. A train ran over a guy and cut off his pecker. And would you believe it? His prick was eighteen inches long!"

"My God!" cries Maureen. "MacTavish is dead!"

# 10

# You Can Feel at Home Anywhere

Osho,

I have been here for two weeks, and every day I feel more and more stupid and helpless. You say that only intelligent people who understand can be with you. Listening to you, enjoying every word you say, I wonder: Do I really understand, or am I just happy to be in your presence? The same thing happened to me last time I was with you. Is there a way out of feeling stupid?

The madman never realizes that he is mad. The same is the case with the stupid – the stupid person never realizes that he is stupid. To realize that you are mad is the beginning of sanity; to realize that you are stupid is the beginning of intelligence. There is nothing wrong in being stupid. But to be stubborn and to insist that your stupidity is wisdom, that is a problem. I am happy that is not your problem. You are relaxed, sensitive, understanding. This is one of the greatest understandings: to feel one's stupidity. There is no need to go out of this circle.

I have told you about Socrates…

In his old age, he used to say that when he was young he thought he knew all. As he became a little more mature, he started feeling that he did not know all, he only knew a little; there was much more which was unknown to him. A few years later, he started realizing that even the little he used to think he knew, he really did not know. It was only information; it was not his own knowing.

Finally, his ultimate statement came in a certain situation. The oracle of Delphi had declared Socrates to be the wisest man of the world. Obviously the people who loved Socrates were very happy. They ran to Socrates to inform him, "The oracle of Delphi has declared you the wisest man."

Socrates said, "I used to think that the oracle never commits mistakes, but this time the oracle has committed a mistake. Go back and tell them that Socrates denies it. He says, 'I know nothing. How can I be the wisest man?'"

The people were very shocked, but out of curiosity they went back to find out what answer would come from the oracle. They said, "We are very unhappy. We delivered your great message to Socrates, but his response was very strange. He says he knows nothing, how can he be the wisest man in the world?"

There was laughter and the oracle said, "That's why. Because he has come to the point of realizing that he knows nothing, that makes him the wisest man in the world."

What do we know? Life remains a mystery. Our not knowing simply indicates the mysteriousness of life. Our knowing is so superficial; it is not worth calling knowing. So if every day you feel that you are more and more stupid, it is a good sign. You are moving toward the state of Socrates. One day the miracle will happen when you will be able to say that you know nothing.

Just try to experience the feel of the freshness and the innocence of not knowing anything. The mind is unburdened. You are light, so light it seems that, if you want, you can fly into the sky. And while experiencing this great not knowing you have entered the temple of the mysterious universe.

What we are doing here is not trying to make you more knowledgeable. We are trying to make you more innocent, utterly not knowing anything. When it happens to you spontaneously, from your heart, that you know nothing, all the doors of existence suddenly start opening for you; not that you will become knowledgeable, but you will become mysterious.

That's why I call this path, the path of the mystic. The mystic is not a learned man, the mystic is an innocent man, who can dance in the rain, who can love beautiful rainbows, who can fall in tune with the universe, whose life becomes a constant rejoicing. So whatever is happening to you is perfectly right. Rejoice and be grateful to existence.

Osho,
If Zen is the path and you are the gate, then who lives in the house?

Zen is the path and I am the gate and *you* live in the house. You have completely forgotten; that's what makes the possibility of making a path, to remind you. The path is only a reminder. You have completely forgotten that you are in the house. You think you are out of the house; hence a gate is needed to bring you in.

I have told you the beautiful story of Chuang Tzu…

One early morning he is sitting in his bed, covered with his blanket, very sad. His disciples have never seen him looking sad. They are worried. Is he sick, ill or something? They inquire.

Chuang Tzu said, "It is much more difficult than you think. Last night I dreamed that I had become a butterfly."

The students, the disciples started laughing. They said, "That is not much of a problem. Everyone thinks many things in his dreams."

Chuang Tzu said, "I don't know about everyone, I know only this much, that it has created a very existential question in me: if Chuang Tzu can dream that he has become a butterfly, why can a butterfly not go to sleep and dream that she has become a Chuang Tzu? Now the problem is whether I am the butterfly who is dreaming she is Chuang Tzu or I am really Chuang Tzu."

The disciples were at a loss how to figure out the problem. And then came Lieh Tzu, who had gone to another village for some work. He heard the situation: "Chuang Tzu is still sitting in his bed. He does not want to get out of his bed until the problem is solved. And we are all trying to solve it, but there seems to be no solution. It seems to be perfectly right, that if Chuang Tzu can dream he is a butterfly then why can the butterfly not dream she is Chuang Tzu? Now we are also puzzled."

Lieh Tzu said, "Wait, I will solve the problem." He went to the water well, pulled up a bucket of ice-cold water, went in and poured it over the head of Chuang Tzu. Chuang Tzu laughed and said, "You came at the right time; otherwise, the whole day I would have been sitting here, sad. You solved the problem."

Lieh Tzu said, "Do you need another bucket?"

He said, "No! The water is so cold. I am Chuang Tzu, because if I was a butterfly your bucket of ice-cold water would have killed me."

Your question is beautiful. "If Zen is the path and you are the gate, then who lives in the house?" You live in the house, but you have forgotten. And to remind you, a path has to be created; to remind you, a gate has to be created. To remind you, you have to be taken on the path and given help to enter the house, which in fact you have never left. Just an imaginary game – getting out on the path, doing great disciplines, meditations, the master… Finally the gate comes and you say, "Aha! I have arrived." And this is the house which you have never left.

Osho,
I don't know. Can you tell me a joke?

Your question is very beautiful. To be in the state of not knowing... What is left? Then to have a good laughter or sit in absolute silence and listen to the birds and their sounds... Not knowing is the ultimate knowing.

You have asked for a joke...

Hymie Goldberg has been told by the doctor that he is dying. Becky is sitting by the bedside.

"Listen Becky," says Hymie. "Soon I will be dead and I don't want you to be living alone. I want you to get married again."

"Darling," weeps Becky, "don't talk like that. I will never find another man like you."

Holding her hand, Hymie continues, "Look sweetheart, in a few weeks you will see things differently. I leave everything to you – the house, the cars, the money in the bank. You will have no worries in your next marriage."

"No, Hymie," wails Becky, "I will never look at another man."

"And you know," says Hymie, "those expensive hand-tailored suits I had made? I want your future man to wear them."

"What!" cries Becky. "Your suits? But Sollie is at least two inches taller than you."

You have asked for one joke, but it would be very miserly of me. I will have to tell you at least two more jokes.

The Goldbergs are touring India and one day Hymie finds that he has left his watch in the hotel. He had been photographing an elephant with his trainer, so he asks the trainer what the time is.

The man slowly reaches out, takes hold of the elephant's balls, shifts them slightly and says, "It is five to one."

"My God!" gasps Hymie. "That's incredible. Wait, I want to fetch my wife." A few minutes later, Hymie comes racing back with Becky and again he asks the time. The man reaches out, cups the elephant's balls as though weighing them, then moves them to one side and declares, "It is three minutes past one."

"Fantastic!" cries Becky checking her watch. Hymie digs a hundred-dollar bill out of his pocket and offers it to the Indian if he will show them how he tells the time. The man shrugs and folds the money in his dhoti. He motions to the Goldbergs to kneel beside him. They hold their breath as the man once again cups the elephant's balls in his hands. Moving them to one side, he says, "Now, do you see that clock over there?"

For five years in a row, the Annual International Joke Contest, held in New York, has been won by Rabbi Finkelstein. But amazingly enough, this year his joke only comes second. And the organizers are forced to phone him to break the bad news.

"My God!" says Rabbi Fink. "I refuse to accept the verdict until I hear the joke that beats me."

"Well," says the man, "the winning joke this year was submitted by Osho and I am afraid that it may be a bit much for your ears. But I'll tell you what I can do. I will read you the joke, and when I come to a part that is too much for you, I will substitute it with 'la-di-da-di-da.'"

"Okay," says the rabbi, "fire away."

The man clears his throat and then begins to read: "La-di-da. La-da-di-da. La-di-da. Fuck."

> Osho,
> This is the very first time in my life I have the feeling of being "at home." My heart is strongly beating and I feel a deep gratitude. Why, beloved master, do I lose this feeling of being at home when I am not physically with you, or even when you stop talking?

To feel at home is one of the most spiritual experiences. Ordinarily, no one feels at home anywhere. People go around the world in search of a place where they can feel at home, but wherever they go, they are the same person – they carry all their worries, their tensions, their anguishes. And because of their anguish and anxiety, they continue to feel a certain unease; otherwise, you can feel at home anywhere.

This whole existence is our home. It is the anxiety, worry, tension, anguish, misery, suffering, desires... They create many, many curtains around you, and you cannot feel at ease because of them. Here you feel at ease, at home, but your problem is – you say, "My heart is strongly beating and I feel a deep gratitude. Why, beloved master, do I lose this feeling of being at home when I am not physically with you, or even when you stop talking?" – there is nothing mysterious in it, it is a very simple thing. When I am talking you have to stop chattering within yourself. That's the whole purpose of my talking, so that you stop the inner chatter, at least for a few moments.

The moment there is no inner chatter in you, you are at home. That chattering disturbs the peace, the joy, the blissfulness. So when you are away from me, your mind goes on like crazy and you miss the feeling of being at home. And even here when I am not talking, the same happens. So you can understand. It is not a question of space, it is not a question of whether you are here or somewhere else. When I stop talking, you start chattering.

What is your chatter? – rubbish, crap. Naturally you start feeling not at home. But when you are silent – and you are silent only when I am speaking. Slowly you have to learn to be silent even when I am not speaking, even when I am not present, even when you are not physically close to me. Can't you feel the sunrise and the birds and the trees? Everything is at ease.

Except man, no one commits suicide – no tree, no bird. Except man, no one needs a psychiatrist. Except man, everything is exactly where it should be: perfectly happy. In these sounds of the birds, do you hear anywhere any sadness? Just overflowing joy. Not that they are talking about great philosophical ideologies, not that they are praying in their churches, not that they are specifically saying something; just the joy of overflowing energy makes them feel at home.

And they don't have anything: no money, no power, no prestige. They don't suffer from any inferiority complex, nor from a superiority complex. They never become schizophrenic. One has to learn much from the trees, the birds, the animals. And your problem is absolutely clear.

These meetings with you, these talks with you are not sermons in a church, where a certain belief system is being delivered to you. These are a special device, never used before by anyone. I speak so that you can be silent. I do your chattering, you do my silence. A simple bargain! The whole day I am sitting in silence; I also get tired. So twice a day I take revenge. You are chattering the whole day. Twice a day, take revenge – be silent. And you will be at home anywhere.

Hymie Goldberg has a little trouble with the police and he goes to see his lawyer. "If I win the case," says Hymie, "I will give you five hundred dollars."

"Okay," says the lawyer, "get some witnesses."

Hymie rounds up a few witnesses and wins his case.

"Now," says the lawyer, "you won your case. What about my five hundred dollars?"

"Okay," says Hymie, "get some witnesses."

Just a simple arithmetic. It is not a difficult job to be silent; it is immensely blissful. Suddenly you find yourself in tune with the heartbeat of the universe. And that is the greatest ecstasy that can happen to anyone. This very moment can become a momentous revolution in your life, if you can taste the silence of it.

It was the usual practice of Gautam Buddha, he had made it a permanent practice, that whenever someone came to him – and every day great philosophers, thinkers, theologians were coming to him to ask questions. Maulingaputta, one of the great philosophers of Gautam Buddha's time, had debated with many other great saints and defeated them. Now his only desire was to defeat Gautam Buddha.

He came to Gautam Buddha with his five hundred great scholars and he asked, with humbleness, "I want an open discussion with you, with the condition that if I win, you and your disciples will have to become my disciples; if you win, I and my disciples will all become your disciples."

Gautam Buddha said, "Settled. But there is one thing you have to remember. You will not start your discussion right now. My routine is that for two years you and your disciples have to sit silently among my ten thousand disciples. You are not to ask a single question in these two years, you have just to listen. And after two years I will remind you that the time has come, you can start the discussion."

The condition was accepted. Maulingaputta was not just an egoistic scholar, he was a sincere inquirer. He was debating with all these saints for the simple reason that perhaps someone can defeat him – defeat his mind, defeat his inner chattering. Someone may question everything that he believes, take away all his thoughts, destroy them completely by his arguments. Because of this reason, he agreed with Gautam Buddha, "I will wait for two years." And he sat by the side of Buddha.

As he was agreeing, laughter was heard from a faraway corner. A strange fellow was sitting under a tree. He was a follower of Gautam Buddha, but very strange. He rarely spoke; except for this laughter, nothing is mentioned about that man in all the great scriptures of Buddhism. And it has a tremendously vast literature; it is a whole world of literature on its own. No religion's literature can even be compared to it; they are very poor. This man's name was Mahakashyapa and his laughter became the beginning of Zen.

He had not spoken anything, but Maulingaputta was shocked. "Why should this person laugh?"

Gautam Buddha said, "You can ask him. He ordinarily never speaks, never laughs. He is not a man who belongs to ordinary humanity. He is a very silent fellow. You can ask him."

Maulingaputta asked Mahakashyapa, "Why have you laughed?"

He replied, "There is not much in it. Just beware of the strategy of this guy Gautam Buddha. He deceived me, and in the same way he is going to deceive you too. I laughed because again he is at his game. Two years ago I had come here, and he made me sit under this tree silently for two years. I even forgot the calendar.

"Two years of silence is such a long time. For a few days I remembered that one day had passed, two days have passed, one week has passed… Then slowly, slowly I forgot all about it. One day he suddenly said, 'Mahakashyapa, this is the day two years ago that you had come to have a discussion with me. Now stand up and start your discussion. What do you want to say?'"

Mahakashyapa had said to Buddha, "You have destroyed everything that I could have said two years ago. This silence has been such a cleansing. It has taken away all the nonsense that I have carried, thinking that it is scholarship, it is knowledge. This silence has transformed me. I don't have anything to ask, just please allow me to touch your feet in deep gratitude. Your compassion is infinite: you did not allow me to discuss with you. Rather than that you made a condition of two years' silence.

"At first I was angry. This is strange. But then I thought, it is a beautiful place, a mango grove; beautiful faces, so silent, as if they are statues. And Gautam Buddha so beautiful, so graceful. There is no harm just to sit silently and watch what is going on here, what this man is continuously saying to his people. Just listening to you, you have taken everything away."

He said to Maulingaputta, "The same is going to happen to you. If you really want a discussion, don't accept the condition, have the discussion today. We have never been entertained by Gautam Buddha in all these years; it will be a great joy."

But Maulingaputta had agreed. And he could understand the point, that unless you are utterly silent you cannot absorb the presence, the grace, the beauty of the master. He sat by his side for two years, and after two years when Buddha said, "Now two years are over. You can start your discussion,"

He said, "Mahakashyapa was right. I have nothing to say, everything has dropped. Just allow me first to touch the feet of Mahakashyapa and then I will touch your feet. He had provoked me and I had felt humiliated by his laughter. I have to ask his forgiveness." He went to Mahakashyapa and touched his feet.

This is the only incident related about Mahakashyapa. But this is the source from where the river of Zen started. Mahakashyapa laughing was the beginning of a tremendous force, and it has been continuously improved by each Zen master.

Bodhidharma was the sixth Zen master who improved much upon Mahakashyapa's laughter. And in these twenty-five centuries much has been improved, much has been added, many new dimensions have opened. But when I think about it, I look at it, I find that Mahakashyapa's laughter is still the greatest contribution. Everything else that has been added is good, but Mahakashyapa's laughter was complete in itself. He has said everything worth saying in his laughter.

It happened in the past that many masters slowly, slowly became deaf because their only function was to talk to the disciples. The disciple's sensitivity in listening became more and more clear, but the master had nothing to listen to. There was no one to say anything to him. Many times masters have become deaf because their ears are not used at all.

The experience of being at home has to be spread slowly so that for twenty-four hours you are at home – waking, sleeping. But this is possible only if you learn the greatest art of being silent. Then you are settled in yourself. Then your whole energy is turned into a silent pool without any ripples. If you can attain this state...

Existence does not want you to fulfill any other condition. This is enough. You will be accepted, welcomed by all the mysteries and all the splendor of existence. Right now, it is a small taste. But I have made it clear to you why it is happening.

You have to try it on your own. Just go into the forest and sit silently, or by the side of the river and just sit silently. Or just here in the ashram, anywhere, sit silently; just being alert of whatever is happening all around, not thinking about what this bird is saying. They are not saying anything, they are just feeling so joyous in the early morning with the new life that the sun has brought again – one more day to dance, to sing, to enjoy the whole expanse of the sky.

Just listen to them the way you listen to me, and you will feel at home. And slowly, slowly you have to learn that it is not a question of listening, it is a question of the inner chatter stopping. Then whenever you find the inner chattering is starting, simply say, "Shut up!" and you will suddenly be at home. Once the mind understands that you have found something greater, something better, something higher, slowly it recedes into the darkness. Its function is fulfilled. It is no longer needed; it is an unwelcome guest.

# 11

# Life Is for Living, Not Questioning

Osho,
Why don't you answer my questions? Is there a certain selection before they reach you? If so, then these are the wrong people at the right place, because they choose the stupid ones instead of mine, which have some quality. It's not only an ego-satisfaction-comparison state.

Amrita Jayesh, it is a miracle that your question has already been answered. The people who select the questions are certainly intelligent. Even you will have to realize their intelligence now – they have chosen your question. But still, I would like to say a few things about your question because it is not only you, many may be feeling the same way.

So many questions come and I can answer only a few questions. Naturally, many must be feeling hurt that their question is not chosen. But they are not listening perfectly well. Their question may not have been chosen, but their question is certainly answered. Answering one question I am answering hundreds of other questions too. It doesn't matter whether it is your question. The very idea that "my question should be answered" means that you are less concerned with the question and more concerned that it is *your* question. If you listen silently, you will find somewhere or other that the question is being answered, just your name is not mentioned. And that is immaterial.

My experience is that when I mention someone's name and answer the question, he is the one who is going to understand it the least. The reason is obvious. He becomes tense – it is his question – and a little worried, a little afraid. I may say something which is shocking; I may hit him, I may slap him. By asking the question he has become vulnerable; hence the moment it is your question you are listening with a tense mind. It won't reach your heart.

Others are listening with absolute relaxedness. It is not their question. In this state of relaxedness they may be able to hear much more than the person whose question is being answered. But I take every care that all the questions that reach me are answered; if not today, then tomorrow. And you are saying, "Why don't you answer my questions?" I have answered them all. Just because your name was not mentioned, you could not get them.

You are saying, "Is there a certain selection before they reach you?" – there is no selection. All the questions reach me. You are asking, "If so, then these are the wrong people at the right place..." There are no people. All the questions that come are sent to me without any selection. I go through them all, but take out four or five. And I try in every way that those other questions which have not been taken are also answered.

You are saying that these people who choose, "...choose the stupid ones instead of mine, which have some quality." But these people have chosen your question. No one is choosing; otherwise, certainly this question would not have been chosen. That can be said with absolute certainty. If someone was choosing, this question would have been thrown away; it would not have reached me.

And as far as stupid questions... All questions are stupid. The wise ones never ask, only the other-wise. Those who are silent and intelligent simply try to understand existence, rather than making a question. A question is a wrong direction. It takes you into the world of philosophy, where thousands of questions exist and each question has been answered millions of times by different people in different ages; yet not a single question has come to be answered. They are still standing unanswered.

There are two possibilities. If you make life, existence, love, a question you will always remain unanswered. But if you make love, life, celebration an experience, your questions will be dissolved. I am using the word *dissolved*, not *solved*. The word *solution* comes from the philosophical dimension. No solution is a solution because it creates new questions. Your authentic question does not need to be answered, it needs to be dissolved. And no solution is going to dissolve it, only your own experience. It is a natural and normal phenomenon that the questions that others ask will look stupid to you. And the questions that you are asking will look very intelligent to you, but to others they will look stupid, utterly stupid. What makes it valuable is your ego. The moment your ego is not there, suddenly the question loses all significance.

But I repeat again that all questions are stupid because those who have attained wisdom don't ask any questions at all. It is not that they have found the answers. On the contrary, they have lost together, all questions, all answers. The questions and answers remain together, they go together. When you are without questions and without answers, your innocence knows the deepest mysteries, the secrets, without making it knowledge. It tastes it, it becomes your blood, your bones, your marrow. It becomes your very being, your dance, but not an answer to a question.

I don't make any distinction between the intelligent and the stupid questions. But if you want me to make a distinction, the intelligent ones are more stupid than the stupid ones, because the stupid ones at least are innocent. The intelligent ones are certainly coming from the ego. They are projections of a mind that thinks, "I know."

Questions come from many different sources. Some questions come from your innocence; they may look stupid. Some questions come from your knowledgeability; they may look very clever. Some questions arise in you from your existential experiences, but they are the questions you cannot ask because you cannot bring them to language. You will have to wait. When the time is right and the season is ripe, something will blossom within you and your question will disappear. Not that there will be an answer left but a purity undisturbed by question or by answer. Both are disturbances.

I go on answering your questions, not to make you more knowledgeable, but to help you to see that knowledge is not authentic wisdom. And the moment you see that knowledge is not authentic wisdom, it drops away. The very seeing is enough. You need not do anything to get rid of your knowledge. In the very seeing it is burned, and what remains behind is utter silence, a purity undisturbed by any questions, by any answers. This undisturbed purity and silence is authentic wisdom. It knows without knowing; it is utterly innocent. It is exactly a rebirth.

You think your questions have some quality. Don't you think the stupid question also has some quality? You may call it stupid, but it has a quality. You may not like that quality, but likings differ. What seems to you significant may not seem so significant to someone else. Please stop comparing. And in the end, because you must have become aware that your question is bound to be felt by anyone as a projection of the ego… You yourself have felt it. Just to cancel that, your question ends with, "It is not only an ego-satisfaction-comparison state." If it is not "…an ego-satisfaction-comparison state," why are you stating it? Why are you denying it? Your very denial shows that deep down you are aware of what it is.

Before I take your other question – this is only an introduction to your question – I would like to tell something which has no quality, because before entering a very deeply qualified, distinguished, significant question, a good, hearty laugh is needed.

Mrs. Ivan the Terrible is having lunch with Mrs. Attila the Hun and Nancy Reagan. The three women get down to some serious gossiping.

Mrs. Ivan the Terrible says, "When I want Ivan to make love to me, I send out for half a dozen naked virgins and have them ride around the bedroom bareback on ponies for an hour or two. It never fails to make Ivan excited."

"Mmm," says Mrs. Attila the Hun, "my method is to have four pairs of women sumo wrestlers fighting in a large pool of mud in our bedroom. That usually works well to keep Attila awake long enough to make love to me."

Nancy says, "I must be luckier with my Ronnie in that way. You girls have such a mess in your bedrooms with all that mud and horse shit. If I want to keep Ronnie awake all I have to do is whisper in his ear, 'Darling, Osho is back in America,' and he immediately screams, 'Get Ed Meese on the phone. Call the FBI. Call the CIA. Call the Army. And for God's sake, give me my heart attack pills!'"

•

Now comes Amrita Jayesh's serious question.

> Osho,
> If there is no certain meaning in life, why this intrinsic logic of living thousands of lives until understanding transforms one toward enlightenment, and then into a nonphysical existence and then…and then… There seems to be no end – eternity? If there is no one or nothing who or which creates the world of a thousand mystic colors, why am I here? I did not ask to join in this game, or did I? Can't there be only a nonexistential nothingness without anything and within nothing?

It is exactly what you are saying. It is a nonexistential nothingness, without anything, within or without. I am a dream, you are a dream; don't take it too seriously. We arise out of nothing, just like soap bubbles, and out of nothing we disappear. You cannot ask me the question because I have nothing to do with this business. I am in the same boat as you are. You ask me why you are here, and I want to know why I am here!

And you call it an intelligent question…

Jesus and Saint Peter come down to earth to see how things are going. After traveling all day through the universe they arrive near an old farmhouse after dark. Not wanting to freak out the farmer, they decide to sleep in the barn.

Jesus says to Peter, "I am going to sleep upstairs in the hayloft and you stay down here. And when you are comfortable, sing me a lullaby to help me go to sleep." Peter agrees and starts singing softly.

"Sing louder!" calls out Jesus.

"But my Lord," says Peter, "the farmer may wake up."

"Peter!" says Jesus, "do you trust me?"

So Peter sings louder until the farmer wakes up, comes running into the barn and gives Peter a good beating.

"Peter," says Jesus, "do you still trust me?"

"Of course," says Peter. "A little beating can't shake me." So Jesus tells him to continue singing. After a few minutes the farmer runs out again, really furious, picks up a stick and beats Peter with it.

When he has gone Jesus says, "Peter, do you still trust me?"

"Well," says Peter, "maybe we could change places for a little while."

"Okay," says Jesus, "if you think it will help your trust."

So they change places and this time Peter sings really loudly, thinking to himself, "This will show him!"

Sure enough, a minute later the farmer, purple with rage, comes into the barn and grabs Jesus. Then he stops and says, "No, you have had enough. Now I will give it to the idiot upstairs."

It is a very playful existence, very dramatic. It is not for questioning, it is for living intensely, joyfully; without bothering at all about what the meaning is or why we are here. All these questions appear to be significant but are really stupid. Existence is as it is. And there is no one you can inquire about it, no complaint office, no inquiry office. We simply are here – no one knows why. So let us make this time as good as we can. Why bother about unnecessary things? Just enjoy, and don't be disturbed by your chattering mind.

Every question is stupid because there is no one to answer it. Who are you going to ask? Even if there was a God sitting just here among you, even he could not answer why he is sitting here. And you could not ask him, "Why have you created the world?" He would say, "Why not?" Remember, God is a Jew and Jews have a habit: you ask a question and they will answer it with another question. You ask, "Why did you create the world?" and he will ask, "Why are you asking? Who are you? Why not...?"

It is impossible to find anyone authoritative who can answer you about why you are here. Everything seems to be perfectly good. There is no need to be unnecessarily fussy about why I am here, why you are here. Just think of those who are not here, have never been here, will never be here. Those poor fellows, they will not even have a chance to ask!

Osho,
Sitting silently the other morning, I felt an incredible energy inside me. And suddenly a big fear arose before I had been able to accept or realize this energy. Could you help me to understand this fear? I am so afraid of my fire burning me totally: I had a glimpse of that and my mind has stopped this process. How to become free of this fear?

Life is a tremendous energy phenomenon. You are not aware of how much energy you have. Do you think atoms know how much energy they have? If a single atom which is invisible to the eyes explodes, it can destroy a city as big as Hiroshima or Nagasaki. Within minutes everything is burned. If an atom of matter has that much energy... Your consciousness is a far higher phenomenon. Your being must be carrying universes of energies – dormant of course, because you are not aware. But those who have become aware, their descriptions indicate similar things.

Kabir says that in his experience of inner being, he sees as if thousands of suns have suddenly arisen. All around him suns are dancing; the light is so dazzling that it makes him almost blind. But this is not only Kabir's experience. Many mystics have described it the same way.

Your experience is just a beginning. You felt as if you would be burned. Don't be worried, no one has ever burned in his own inner energy. This energy is creative, not destructive. Any energy that comes out of meditative silence is creative. There is not a single instance of it destroying anything, it has only created. It has created a beautiful space within; it has created beautiful art, music, sculpture, poetry, painting, outside. This fire is not even hot, it is very cool.

I am reminded of Moses on Mount Sinai…

Moses had gone there in search of God and he saw a very strange phenomenon, which Jewish scholars are unable to explain because it looks fictitious. He saw a fire and within the fire a green unburned bush. He could not believe his eyes. The flames were rising high and the bush inside the flames was green, and its flowers were blossoming as if a cool breeze was passing through, not a fire.

Attracted toward this majestic experience, he comes closer to the bush and suddenly he hears a voice, "Moses, take your shoes off! You are on holy ground." The voice is coming from the bush. As he comes closer, leaving his shoes behind, he does not feel any heat; on the contrary he feels very cool. And the dialogue that happened and culminated in the Ten Commandments was not with a person but an invisible voice coming from that green bush.

Theologians have been at work trying to figure it out. As far as I am concerned, I am not a theologian, but I can understand a little bit of poetry and I think it is a poetic statement, not a theological statement. Once you see it is a poetic statement all confusion disappears. What is being said is that life, or God, is a cool energy; so creative, so nondestructive that even within its fire, a bush will remain green and will grow and blossom.

Accept this life energy. This is what Bergson, a great philosopher, used to call élan vital. This life force is not something to be afraid of. You have to create a communion, a dialogue with this life energy, and you will be immensely enriched, not burned. For the first time your spring will come and your flowers will blossom.

Many ancient parables, stories, are in fact poetic statements, but the theologians have destroyed their beauty and their poetry by dragging them down and trying to prove that they are actual historical facts. They are not facts, they are far above facts; they are poetic realizations and poetic expressions.

Don't be afraid of what happened to you. There is no need for any fear. Rejoice with the flames of the energy, dance with those flames, have a communion with those flames and you will find a dialogue with existence itself. If you are afraid that you may be burned, then this very fear will stop the process, will become a barrier to entering inward to deeper realms of your consciousness. Drop this fear. No one has ever been burned by life energy.

One has to learn to drop fear as one enters inward because there is no one except your own energy, and your own energy cannot be your enemy. In fact even to say "your energy" is not right. It is because of the poverty of language that we have to use expressions like that. It is better to say you *are* the energy. Who is there to be burned? You are the fire itself, those dancing flames are your very being. Who is going to be burned? You are not a separate entity. It is language that always divides and creates trouble.

Drop all fear. The moment you enter meditation, put your fear where Moses had to leave his shoes. It is sacred ground. You are entering a temple of love, life, peace. There is no need of any fear. Go dancing in and it is absolutely certain that if you can be unafraid, a bridge will be created between you and the energy that is also you, but it is dormant; it has been asleep and unconscious, so it appears as if it is separate from you. But once it awakens, soon you will see your small flame of life has disappeared into the vast energy that has arisen. You have entered the cosmic, the universal.

And the vaster the energy, the greater the ecstasy, the more joy, the more blessings, the more laughter.

Little Ernie is sitting at the back of the class, a can of beer in one hand and a cigarette in the other, when Miss Goodbody says, "Okay children, today we are going to play a game. I'm going to say a few words about something, and you try to tell me what I'm thinking about. Okay, here we go! The first thing is a fruit. It's round and it's red."

Little Billy raises his hand and says, "An apple."

Miss Goodbody says, "No, it's a tomato, but I'm glad to see you're thinking. The next one is round and it's a green vegetable."

Little Mary says, "It's a lettuce."

"No," says Miss Goodbody, "it's a pea. But I'm glad to see you're thinking."

Just then Ernie raises his hand and says, "Hey, teach! Mind if I ask you one?"

"Go right ahead," says Miss Goodbody.

"Okay," says Ernie, "I've got something in my pocket, and it's long and it's hard and it's got a pink tip."

"Ernie!" shouts Miss Goodbody, "that's disgusting."

"It's a pencil," says Ernie, "but I'm glad to see you're thinking."

> Osho,
> This silence, this moment: so precious, so beautiful. To keep avoiding it and missing it seems so absurd. Beloved master, why? What is so difficult about dropping this whole game and just being?

The question you have asked is beautiful. "This silence, this moment: so precious, so beautiful. To keep avoiding it and missing it seems so absurd. Beloved master, why? What is so difficult about dropping this whole game and just being?" If the whole game is dropped, and you remain just being… Soon you will get tired of it, bored with it. The game also has its significance. Its whole significance is that it makes your being just silent, a beauty. Without this game, this crowd, this noise, without this marketplace your temple will not have the beauty that it has. Life is a dialectics.

During the night you see the whole sky full of stars. Do you think that in the day the stars hide somewhere? They are still where you see them during the night, but it is difficult to see them in the light of the sun. You can see them if you go into a deep well, where it is almost as dark as night.

Nearby my house I used to have a deep well. My family used to keep me away from it and finally they closed it, because it had chains and you could climb down deep into it. Whenever I could get a chance, when no one was looking at the well, I would simply go and climb down into it. There was a place in the well where it was so dark that for the first time I became aware that from that darkness you can see stars in the sky. To see the stars you need the darkness. And stars are so beautiful, but they will not be there without darkness. You have to understand the beauty of darkness too.

Life is so beautiful, but it would not be so beautiful if there was no death. Just think, if you go on and on and on living, a point will come where you would like to die. You have lived enough; now life itself has become a boring experience because it is the same round every day, and the wheel has moved for too many years, again and again.

When I say life is a dialectics I mean it exists between two polarities, and the two polarities help each other. You cannot take one polarity away; if you take one away, the other will also disappear. The silence is beautiful – no one will disagree with you – but the great moment is when you understand that the noise of the marketplace is also beautiful because the beautiful silence and the beautiful noise are part of one whole. The day and the night, summer and winter, childhood and old age, all have tremendous beauty. The moment you see the beauty of both together you have transcended them.

You can call this transcendental experience enlightenment, awakening, realization, the truth – these are only different names for the same experience. But our minds always go on trying to keep one and avoid the other. You are saying, "This silence, this moment: so precious, so beautiful." Then why do we go on "avoiding it," "missing it?" That too is beautiful. That makes the contrast. It is just a silver line on a black cloud. You can write with white chalk only on a blackboard. If you take away the blackboard, the writing will also disappear. To see this contradictoriness as complementary is to become mature. Then you don't want to drop anything, then you don't want to escape from the world; then whatever happens, you love it. The noise has its own place and the silence has its own place, and they both enrich each other.

There is no need to get out of the game. The game is tremendously beautiful. Just understand that this is the game, and because of the game we have divided it into two parts; otherwise no one is the enemy, not even death. In this absolute acceptance of everything, you have already gone beyond.

Grandma Feigenbaum takes her grandchildren shopping and leaves the house empty, except for her parrot standing on its perch by the door. The plumber arrives to fix something in the house and knocks on the door.

"Who is it?" asks the parrot.

"It's the plumber," replies the man. Nothing happens. The plumber knocks again.

"Who is it?" asks the parrot.

"The plumber," he replies.

There is silence. The plumber, who has a heart condition, is getting impatient. He knocks again.

"Who is it?" squawks the parrot.

"It's the *plumber*!" he yells and collapses in a faint.

Half an hour later, grandma returns with the kids. The little girl points at the body on the ground.

"Who is that?" she asks.
The parrot squawks, "It's the plumber!"

It is a game. Let it continue. Just go on laughing and enjoying – it is the plumber!

# 12

# Reaction Comes from the Past, Response Is Moment to Moment

Osho,
Are all jokes irrational?

Not only are all jokes not irrational – you cannot even find one joke that is irrational – but jokes have their own psychology and rationality. The psychology of jokes has to be understood and then the rationality will be clear. Man is so repressed that he cannot even speak certain words; he is utterly inhibited. A joke starts with ordinary words, but takes a sudden turn and catches you unawares. And that sudden turn you could not have expected; that's why all your repressed mind, your inhibitions suddenly explode.

No one has used jokes for cleaning your mind. It is a catharsis. The moment you see the point, suddenly you say, "My God, I was going toward a certain rational conclusion…" The joke turns at a point where you would not have expected it. That sudden turn makes you forget all your rationality, logic, language. In a split moment you are suddenly like a child.

You must have noted that jokes are only concerned with the repressed parts of your being. It is a revenge – revenge by the powerless against the powerful. They kill you, they destroy you, but you can do it better without weapons, just by a single joke! Jokes have a beauty of their own because they bring you laughter. And to me laughter is the moment when the mind stops, time stops and you are suddenly overwhelmed by a new energy, a new delight. These are simple glimpses to prepare you for the ultimate laughter.

It is said about Bodhidharma that the first thing he did after his enlightenment was he laughed loudly. Again and again it was asked of him why he laughed; there was no visible reason for it.

He said, "I laughed because I was searching for myself, and I was going round and round everywhere except within myself. Existence has played a great joke on me."

Certainly jokes are not irrational. Just look at the rationality of the jokes…

Bridget, the Irish prostitute, has just finished "servicing" her client, an English gentleman.

She asks him, "Hey, you don't have that terrible AIDS disease, do you?"

"No," replies the gentleman, doing up his shoelaces, "I get a medical check each week. I'm definitely clean."

"Oh good," replies Bridget. "Thank God for that, I wouldn't like to be getting *that* again!"

What did the hurricane say to the palm tree? – "Hang on to your nuts, this is no ordinary blow job!"

While waiting for Ronald Reagan's press conference to start, a reporter approaches a man standing in the corner of the hall.

"Hey," he says, "have you heard the latest Ronald Reagan joke?"

The man gives him an icy stare. "Before you tell it," he says, "I must inform you that I work in the White House as his personal secretary."

"Thanks for the warning," says the reporter, "I will tell it very, very, very slowly."

On an Italian airplane flying over the ocean, the pilot tells the passengers to enjoy the flight and that they can expect to reach their destination in four hours.

Three hours later the captain has another announcement. "Folks," he says, "I have got-a good-a news and-a bad-a news. First the bad-a news: We are-a lost. Now the good-a news: We are-a making hella-va good-a time!"

I have never come across any joke – and perhaps I have come across many more jokes than any living or dead man… There is a certain strange turning at the end, but it is not irrational. It is how human beings function, how their minds function. Every joke has a great reason. It is connected with your unconscious and the society's torture of humanity. It brings it out in the open and you can be unburdened. In no other way can it be released. This unburdening, this relief is the very reason of every joke.

Osho,
Many of us who have been with you for some time are experiencing a deepening of silence, stillness and joy within. With a tremendous gratitude to you, there also comes a sense of responsibility to existence to preserve this gift of life and consciousness.

To realize your vision of global transformation and the New Man, it seems that meditation, love, commitment and action are all necessary. Sometimes it feels difficult to move into activity while still remaining silent and meditative.

Would you speak to us about wuwei, action from inaction?

You have brought many significant points in your question. First you say, "Many of us who have been with you for some time are experiencing a deepening of silence, stillness and joy within. With a tremendous gratitude to you also comes a sense of responsibility to existence to preserve this gift of life and consciousness." The word *responsibility* has been continually used in a wrong way. It gives a feeling of burden: you have to do it, it is a duty; if you don't do it you will feel guilty. I want to remind you that the word *responsibility* has none of those connotations. Break the word in two – *response-ability* – and in a different direction, you enter a totally different meaning of the word. Response-ability is not a burden. It is not a duty; it is not something you *have* to do in spite of yourself.

Response-ability simply means spontaneous response. Whatever situation arises, you respond joyously to it, with your totality, with your intensity. And this response will not only change the situation, it will also change you.

There are two words to be remembered: one is *reaction* and one is *response-ability*. Most people react, they don't respond. Reaction comes from your memory, your past experiences, your knowledge; it is always inadequate in a fresh, new situation. And existence is continuously fresh. So if you act according to your past, that is reaction. But that reaction is not going to change the situation, it is not going to change you, and you will be in utter failure.

Response is moment to moment. It has nothing to do with memory, it has something to do with your awareness. You see the situation with clarity; you are clean, silent, serene. Out of this serenity, you act spontaneously. It is not reaction, it is action. You have never done it before, but the beauty of it is that it will suit the situation, and it will be a joy to you to know that you are capable of being spontaneous.

There are very few joys in life greater than spontaneity. Spontaneity means to be in the moment; it means acting out of your awareness, not acting according to your old conditionings. Those days are gone; those conditions, conceptions are absolutely invalid.

In my university days, when I was a postgraduate student, for one year I had to share a room with a very stupid student. His problem was: "Everybody is saying that they have fallen in love with some girl and they are enjoying it. But no girl looks at me – neither do I know how to fall in love."

I said, "The first thing you do is to start saying many girls are after you. They have all fallen in love with you, but you have not yet found the right girl with whom you would like to commune, to be with, to love."

He said, "But this is all incorrect, because it is not happening."

I said, "Those people who are talking, it is not happening to them either. They are just talking and making others feel they are missing the most precious experience."

He said, "I will try."

He started talking and soon he became a hero. No girl was chasing him, he had no idea what love was, but people started asking him for recipes for how to fall in love.

He would come to me saying, "You have put me in a very difficult situation. I don't know what love is, how can I give them recipes? They say, 'So many girls are chasing you and you are not interested in them. At least introduce one girl to me.' But no one is chasing me."

I said to him, "Don't be worried, from tomorrow morning a girl will start chasing you. The most beautiful girl in the university."

He said, "Is it a prediction?"

I said, "Yes, it is a prediction. Tomorrow appear in your best clothes, perfumed, smiling. And don't look sad, smile"

There was one beautiful girl in my class. I said to her, "This man is desperate. You have not to do anything, just hold his hand and tell him, 'I love you.'"

She said, "But it may create some trouble."

I said, "Don't be worried, I will take care. The man is so stupid, he cannot create any trouble."

The girl said, "Let us see."

After the philosophy period was over she took him aside. Trembling, perspiring, she took his hand in her hand and said, "You are the most charming fellow in the university! I have wanted to say it for almost one year. I am deeply in love with you."

He came running to me and said, "It has happened!"

I said, "What has happened?"

He said, "The girl took my hand, and she was so nervous to say it, but she told it beautifully: 'You are a charming man,' and that for one year she has been waiting to find an occasion to tell me that she is in love with me."

I said, "Now you know the whole strategy. Hold their hand, tell the person, 'You are charming and I have been in love with you…'"

He said, "Perfectly good. I have learned all three steps; I have been repeating them since then."

The second day he tried it on another girl and the girl slapped him. He could not believe it: How could the recipe fail? He came running to me saying, "I have been insulted before so many people. The girl slapped me – and I had done nothing, just took her hand. The only difference was that in the first case the girl was perspiring and nervous, and in this case I was perspiring and nervous. And she slapped hard. What kind of love is this?"

I said, "Remember one thing: one girl is one, another girl is another. Why should you try it on another girl? The first one would have behaved more humanly because I had told her, 'This poor guy is dying and continually thinks of love, but does not know what it means and how to start.'"

He said, "Perhaps you are right, I should not have gone to another girl. Then what do you suggest?"

I said, "Write letters to the first girl."

He said, "But I don't know how to write love letters."

I said, "Don't be worried, I will write them, and you sign."

He said, "This is great. I am immensely grateful to you."

Almost twice or thrice a week I would write a letter, and he would take the letter and hand it over to the girl. She smiled, because this was becoming a strange drama. And she knew *my* handwriting.

I told her, "It is very unkind not to answer his letters."

But she said, "You are getting me into more and more of a mess."

I said, "Don't be worried, I will take you out any moment. The day you want to get out, just slap him and that will do."

So it continued for a few months. She started writing beautiful letters to him, and he would come running and show everyone what a great love was flowering. Finally the moment came – the girl slapped him.

But he said, "This is very irrational. I will go to my master, who has been teaching me how to love, and ask him what has happened."

He came back and I said to him, "I was just giving you a chance – perhaps you can learn something – but you seem to be incapable of learning anything. It is finished."

He said, "My God, and what about the letters that I have written?"

I said, "What will you do with those letters?"

He said, "I can't write those letters, so I'm going to take them and try them on another girl." And he was rejected from everywhere because by and by everyone came to know that the handwriting was mine, the letter was mine, and this fool was not even aware what love is!

Response is not out of the past. You don't have to learn it, you don't have to be taught it; it comes out of your silence, your serenity, on its own accord. Hence I say that many of your acts are not acts because they are coming from the memory; they are reactions. The authentic act comes from your consciousness. So the first thing is to change the wrong connotation of responsibility. The mother says, "You have a responsibility to take care of me." The father says, "You have a responsibility to take care of me." The whole family says, "You have a responsibility, a duty..."

I had a very deep, intimate contact with my father. He was a rare man because whatever I said would have irritated any father, but he always pondered over it, contemplated it. I said, "Listen, I don't have any responsibility for you. You never asked if you could give birth to me. That was the point when we could have made a contract: 'This is going to be my responsibility...' You have brought me into existence without even asking me. It is your responsibility, not mine. If something goes wrong, you will be responsible for it."

He said, "I never looked at it from that angle; perhaps you are right. What kind of contact and intimacy do you have with me?"

I said, "I am response-able, not responsible. I will act out of my love for you, not because you are my father. And I will act in the moment, without referring to my memory system, because the memory is always of the past and existence is always new; they never meet."

So the first thing I want you to understand is, don't make the whole word *responsibility*; break it into two: *response* – hyphen – *ability*. And it changes the whole color.

"With a tremendous gratitude to you also comes a sense of responsibility to existence, to preserve this gift of life and consciousness." You will become burdened with these ideas! You will become almost a torture to yourself.

And I can see it as I go on. "To realize your vision of global transformation and the New Man it seems that meditation, love, commitment and action are all necessary." Commitment is not necessary because commitment is bound to become old; it will not correspond to the fresh moment. Commitment is a slavery to the past. And action, you don't have to do. If your heart is full of love, full of compassion, full of meditation, action will happen. When action happens on its own accord it is such a beautiful flower. Instead, you force yourself with unnecessary burdens – responsibility, commitment, action – and you don't understand that the global crisis is so big and you are so small, what action can you take?

I don't have any responsibility, I don't have any commitment, and I don't have any action to do to save this beautiful planet;

these are unnecessary burdens. Enjoy the moment, grow into your consciousness, be more spontaneous, more compassionate, more loving – no commitment, no great megalomania of saving the whole planet. Rejoice in it, and out of this rejoicing, action comes; again, as spontaneous. You don't have to act.

"Sometimes it feels difficult to move into activity." Not just sometimes, you will always feel difficulty in moving into activity. But a pure action, uncontemplated, suddenly grips you... And you are not doing any charitable work, you are simply enjoying it. If we can make more people lovable, celebrating, more spontaneous, the global crisis can be avoided. But don't take it seriously, be playful about it. If existence wants this planet not to exist, who are we to prevent it?

Every day stars disappear into black holes and every day new stars are born from white holes. One thing has to be remembered: anything that is born is going to die. This planet has been here for nearabout four billion years. Perhaps it has become old, perhaps nothing can be done to save it. It needs rest, and death is a rest.

But I'm not saying that you should work to destroy, I am saying that while things are alive, enjoy, dance, sing, love. Perhaps even the old existence may feel to let the planet live a little more. Make it as beautiful as possible so existence itself feels that it has to be protected. You cannot protect it, but you can create the condition in which existence will feel sad to destroy the beautiful flowers, the beautiful people, the beautiful trees, great heights of consciousness.

So my way is totally different. I am not a pacifist like Bertrand Russell who thought that by protesting, creating pacifists we can save the universe. No protest can save it, no pacifist can save it. Only one thing is possible: your making this universe more and more beautiful, so beautiful that existence becomes absolutely incapable of thinking to destroy it. It is not a burden, it is not a commitment. And as long as existence lets this planet continue, enjoy it, make it more juicy... Each act of your life. According to me that is the only way to avoid a global suicide.

You are asking, "Sometimes it feels difficult to move into activity while still remaining silent and meditative." You don't need *any* activity. Silence and being meditative are enough; they are far greater forces than your small activity. And out of your silence perhaps some action may arise which will be helpful in making the planet more glorious, more splendorous. What I am trying to say is: prove to existence that this planet is so precious that to allow it to be destroyed will be sheer nonsense. Existence will have to wait again for fifty million years to bring such people, such consciousnesses as Buddha, Lao Tzu...

Do you see my point? Make it so valuable that even existence withdraws, and destroys all that is being prepared for a global suicide. You don't have to act! You have simply to meditate, be silent, be loving and fill the whole world with laughter. I say unto you that laughter is far more powerful than any nuclear weapon. Fill the whole universe with love. And I say unto you that a world filled with love is not going to decide for war. No action is needed.

I have been condemned by people who don't understand the intrinsic mysteries of life. They think that I am making people inactive, telling them to meditate, to be silent. They don't know that I am making people spontaneously active: out of love, beauty, blissfulness. That will create the greatest barrier to the destruction of the planet.

You are asking, "Would you speak to us about wuwei, action without inaction?" That's what I am speaking about. Don't do anything; become so utterly silent that out of that silence things start happening around you – that is action without inaction. A man of silence is not inactive; his energies have moved into a totally new dimension of spontaneity, of response-ability, of love, of joy, of creativity, and his whole being is so precious that he creates a contagious preciousness around him.

If we have a few million people in the world who are playful, who are not burdened, it doesn't matter – if existence wants this planet to disappear, perhaps there is some significance in it. We will try to enjoy while we are here, while this planet exists. If our joyfulness, playfulness, our flutes, guitars, our sensitivity changes the intelligence of the universe and cancels the decision – this is not the planet to be destroyed, this is the planet to be nourished more – if it happens, good; if it does not happen then that too is perfectly good.

Do you remember when you were not – were you angry, sad? Before your birth, do you remember any problem, any trouble? After your death you will be in the same position as you were before your birth. Existence is beautiful, but if it disappears, if the whole cosmos decides for it to disappear, you will not miss it; you will not be there at all. So don't make it a fear, a duty, a responsibility to be done. Don't feel guilty that you are so small. What can you do? However small you are, you can love, you can dance, you can celebrate whatever moments are available. And this will be action without inaction.

The doctor compliments the young girl lying on his examination table.

"Go home," he says, "and tell your husband to prepare for a baby."

"But I don't have a husband," the girl replies.

"Then go home," says the doctor, "and tell your lover."

"But I don't have a lover," says the girl. "I have never had a lover."

"In that case," says the doctor, "go home and tell your mother to prepare for the second coming of Jesus Christ!"

My attitude is simple: this day is enough unto itself. Who bothers if you don't wake up tomorrow? You will not know. And an eternal sleep is such a peaceful, blissful, silence; you are not losing anything. But don't waste your today in thinking about your tomorrow. Be a little more intelligent, alert and aware.

A Polack goes into the doctor's surgery with both his ears burned.

"I have never seen such a case," exclaims the doctor. "What on earth happened?"

"I was ironing my clothes," explains the Polack, "when the phone rang."

"But what about the other ear?" asks the doctor.

"Well," replies the Polack, "I had to phone for the ambulance."

Pope the Polack puts on civilian clothes so that he can walk around the streets without being recognized.

While he is out walking, a woman comes up to him and says, "Want a blow job?"

The pope says, "A blow job? What's that?"

The woman replies, "Ten dollars."

The pope is mystified, but he continues his walk through the streets. Everywhere he goes, he is met by women saying, "Blow job, blow job!" all day long.

Finally, when he returns to the Vatican and the papal palace, he sees one of the nuns.

"Tell me, sister," asks Pope the Polack, "what's a blow job?"

The nun replies, "Ten dollars."

# 13

# Learn to See the Joyous Side of Life

Osho,
Why is it that apart from sitting with you twice a day, I only find myself meditating when I am down or confused? Why is that I rarely meditate out of my joyousness?

Your question touches the human heart and its workings very deeply. In the old way, people used to pray only when they were in misery, suffering some trouble. When they were happy, joyous, successful they never bothered God. It can make you aware of an intense involvement of all the religions with suffering, because only those who are suffering become victims in the hands of the priests. Otherwise, who cares about priests, who cares about the holy books?

When you are happy, contented, joyful, you want to enjoy your life. You don't want to waste your time praying in a church or a temple. This must have been discovered by the priests long, long ago. All religions are based on the exploitation of this discovery. Bertrand Russell is right when he says, "If we can destroy poverty, sickness, old age, inequality and make people happy and joyous, religions will die on their own accord." He is perfectly right in his analysis because the joyous man has never been in any way concerned with so-called religions. But Bertrand Russell was an agnostic.

My standpoint is totally different. To me it is natural that when you are sick you go to the doctor and when you are sick you need medicine. You don't go to the doctor when you are healthy. You don't go to the druggist for some medicine when you are perfectly healthy. And it is not that the so-called religions have in any way helped you to get out of misery; that would destroy their whole business. They want you to remain in misery, hoping that in the next life you will enjoy the blessings of God because you suffered so contentedly, you suffered without revolt against the vested interests.

The politicians became interested in religion, and the kings were very supportive of organized religion because they could see a simple arithmetic: religion provides opium to the people, a consolation, and if this opium is not provided, revolt is going to happen. So those who are in power are deeply interested that you should remain sad, miserable, in anxiety, because your anxiety and your sadness will take you to the priests and they will give you the opium called hope. "Don't be worried, pray. If you pray with a pure heart and if you pray with absolute belief, your prayer will be answered."

Now, it is a very tricky game. No one can have absolute belief. Belief as such is borrowed from someone else; you don't know anything about it. How can you be absolute in your belief? At the most you can repress your doubt with the belief, but the doubt is there. So when your prayers are not heard, you know it is not the fault of God or the fault of prayer: your belief is not total, your trust has doubt underneath it. Although you are praying, you know deep within you, "Who knows whether there is a God who is listening or going to answer?" This helps the priest to keep you in your miserable situation.

If your prayer is not heard, then fast, purify yourself, do all kinds of disciplines and certainly your prayer will be answered. No one's prayer has ever been answered. But because of this strategy, they have planted the idea in you that when your prayer is not answered, you are at fault. So you have to be absolutely pure.

They demand perfectionism. And because of their demand of perfectionism they have driven the whole of humanity neurotic. No one can be perfect. Perfection is simply out of the question; perfection means death. You have to go on trying to be perfect – in this way evolution moves. You will be coming closer and closer to perfection, but you will never be perfect. The moment you are perfect you are finished, evolution has come to an end. The ideas of evolution and perfection are antagonistic.

All over the world, through all the ages, civilizations and cultures, every child has been forced to be perfect. And once this cancer of being perfect enters your mind, you will always feel you are not perfect, you will always feel guilty. You will pray, but you know your prayer will not be heard. The religions have completely diverted your attention. Your suffering is being caused by the vested interests herenow and they have shifted the whole idea to the future – and not even to the near future – to after death. Different religions have tried different strategies, but the basic thing is to divert your mind from the exploitation which is going on right now. If all kinds of consolations are dropped, you will be able to see that your problem, your suffering, your misery is being created, manufactured by man. It has nothing to do with prayer.

And this is a very dangerous situation because all the religions – and almost everyone belongs to some religion – are trying to divert you from the actuality of things to dreams of paradise and heaven and all kinds of joys. These people are sellers of dreams and they fill your mind with dreams so much that you stop seeing the reality. The reality is that a few vested interests – politicians, the rich people, the priests – are the cause of your suffering, anguish, misery, and they can be removed. But who is going to remove them? Because the people who are suffering never think that these good people can be the cause of their suffering.

Secondly, you have found it very clearly in your own meditations that when you are in suffering you want to meditate, but when you are happy you don't even think about it. You are using meditation again as a new hope, as a new consolation. You are not really a meditator. You are also using meditation as medicine. It will give you some relief, but it cannot transform you to a state where ecstasy becomes your moment-to-moment experience.

You will have to learn something which has been forcibly killed by all the religions, politicians and all the powers; it was in their favor. In fact, we have forgotten completely that to be joyous is the basic condition of meditation. When you are joyous, that is the right moment to meditate. Then you can ride on the wave of joy to higher realms. When you are suffering, meditation may help to bring you out of your suffering, but that is not much. When you are feeling a well-being, when you are feeling ready to dance, that is the moment to meditate. Then you can ride on higher waves of dancing, music, into meditation.

Meditation has to be taken out of the hands of the religions. They are using it for wrong reasons, for exploitation. And they have done it for so many centuries that it has become almost an inbuilt program in us.

In China a strange experiment was done…

The emperor was very much impressed by Lao Tzu, Chuang Tzu, Lieh Tzu. He lived long enough to be in contact with the master Lao Tzu, then his disciple Chuang Tzu, then his disciple Lieh Tzu. These three people impressed on the emperor a very novel, original idea, but it has not been followed. The moment the emperor died the old vested interests came back and destroyed something of tremendous value.

Lieh Tzu, Chuang Tzu and Lao Tzu had a strange idea: that no doctor should be paid by his patients, because if the patient has to pay the doctor, knowingly or unknowingly the doctor would like the patient to remain sick as long as possible; that is his business. If he cures him quickly he cannot earn much.

A famous story Chuang Tzu used to tell was about an old doctor. His three sons were studying medicine. The first son came back from the university and said, "Now you are too old, you rest. I will take care of your patients." So the father allowed him to take care of his patients. After two days the young man came to the old father and said, "It is very strange. You are such an experienced doctor and I have cured a woman you have been treating for thirty years, in two days. And I am fresh from the college, I don't know much."

The father said, "You idiot, it is that woman who has paid all your expenses in medical college. She was going to pay for your two other brothers. She was rich enough, there was no need for her to be healthy. And she was my main source of income."

Lao Tzu and Chuang Tzu impressed on the emperor that if the patient has to pay the doctor, you are creating a very dangerous situation. The doctor's interest will be that the patient remains a patient as long as possible. And he will apparently show concern that he wants to cure you. He will be in a dilemma himself.

The emperor asked Lao Tzu, "Then what is your suggestion? Because this has been always the case."

He said, "The solution is very simple. All doctors should be paid by the government, and the whole population should pay the government – nothing to do with the doctor. The doctor has not to be paid because he has cured a patient, he has to be paid if his patient has remained healthy. Every month the patient has to report, 'I am healthy, you can pay my doctor.' If the patient falls sick, then the doctor cannot be paid: 'What business are you doing here? If people are falling sick, then what use is your medicine, your knowledge, your experience?'"

So a very strange system… But the emperor was impressed, it was absolutely logical. And in my understanding, one day it is going to be the system in the whole world because its logic is very clear. The doctor should be paid for health, not for sickness. If his patients are sick, then his salary should be cut. His interest should be in the health of the patient, not in his disease. The patient has not to pay him, the patient has to pay the government a certain fee to be kept healthy. The government pays the doctor to keep people healthy, and if they are not healthy, he misses his salary.

But once the emperor was dead, the system disappeared, the old idea came in again; which is absolutely foolish.

The priest, the religions have learned the strategy perhaps from people suffering from diseases, that they are the most vulnerable sources for exploitation. Just give them hope; all that they need is consolation. This has corrupted the whole human psychology. So when you are sick you think of meditation, when you are suffering you start meditating. But when you are down and confused, it is very difficult to meditate; it is going against the current.

So, on the one hand you have chosen a wrong situation in which to meditate. At the most meditation can pull you out, somehow from your down-going, your suffering, but it cannot give you joy or ecstasy. It is enough if it can take you out of your misery. The real situation is a healthy, happy, joyous state of mind. But at that time you think of playing football, going to the movies, watching television, going to a discotheque. In fact that is the time to meditate.

When you are suffering you can go to hell: any discotheque, any restaurant, any game – boyfriend, girlfriend game. When you are suffering, these are the things to do. But when you are happy, feeling good, in tune, surrounded with a certain well-being, don't miss it by doing stupid things. This is the right springboard from where you can take a jump into higher realms of consciousness, blissfulness, peace, ecstasy. This way of being is just an old conditioning, forced upon you by those who were immensely profited by it. You have to understand it and change the situation.

In my childhood it was a constant conflict between me and my father: whenever I was feeling good, that meant a holiday from school. He said, "You are a strange fellow. When you are sick, have a fever, suffering from a cold, then you go to school. You have an upside-down mind!"

I said, "Whether the mind is upside down or not, when I am feeling good I go to the river" – where I loved to swim for miles or to boat. In a beautiful full-moon night, the river looked almost like silver. And I told him, "I am not going to waste my time in school. When I have a fever and I cannot go to the river, school is good. School to me is a kind of hospital."

He said, "Do whatever you want to do. There is some truth in what you are saying because you cannot enjoy the river and swimming when you are sick."

I said, "You have understood my point. Whether I am sick or I am not sick, I don't enjoy your history, your geography anyway. So when I am sick it is perfectly good, I can waste my sickness on your school and your education. For the remaining part of my life I am going to enjoy nature, enjoy the stars, play the flute, sing songs, go to the forest and to dance there among the dancing trees. I have made a clear-cut distinction."

In my childhood I was rarely sick, so rarely present in the school. But you will be surprised, I was not present in school, but they gave me seventy-five percent attendance every year. They were very happy that I was somewhere else! Every principal of every school, college, every vice-chancellor of every university I was taught in, told me once or twice, "If you can go somewhere else – to the library, to the botanical garden… Or the whole world is there. Just don't go to your classroom because it creates so much trouble for us. And I promise you that we will not prevent you from entering the examination because you have not attended enough." Seventy-five percent was the right percentage of attendance, only then could you enter the examination. "Even if you don't come at all, just appear at the examination hall and every paper will be ready and you will be allowed."

I said, "This is such a good arrangement. I am happy outside, you are happy inside. But once in a while when I am not feeling well, I want to make it clear to you, I will not allow you or your college either to be in a state of well-being. If I am not feeling well, I am going to come. So pray to God that I never fall sick. That is your only protection!"

When you are feeling joyous, this is the time to come in tune with existence. This is the time when you can love the trees, the moon, the sky. This is the time you can enter yourself very easily, with no hindrance. Meditation is not for the suffering type.

There are types… There are a few people who are born with English faces. Seriousness is an inbuilt program in them. Leave those few people for the churches because after all, priests also need to feed themselves, to clothe themselves. I don't want to destroy their business completely. But ninety percent of their business has to be completely destroyed. And I will suggest to you also that whenever you are sick, go to the church, go to the synagogue. Spread all kinds of infections there, weep and cry. But when you are happy and joyous it is better to go to the mountains, it is better to climb a high tree and sit there silently.

Sometimes one falls… I have many marks on my feet because so many times I have fallen from trees. But in my experience the farther away you are from gravitation, the easier it is to meditate. But the trouble is, the easier it is also to fall asleep. So just make a good arrangement, tie down… I learned slowly that after falling again and again, I was going to have fractures. So I would tie myself to the tree, so that if I fell asleep at least I would be hanging, but I would not fall. But even hanging from a tree, with the beautiful fresh wind blowing is such a joy.

Use your joyful moments in discovering the truth, in discovering yourself, and it will be a very easy thing. People have been discovering at wrong times, in wrong seasons, and against the current. My whole approach is to go with the current – no effort, just floating, not even swimming. There is no need.

The gravitation of the earth is less in water because water functions under a different law – levitation. That's why you can pick up a big rock in water without any effort because the gravitation is not the same, but the moment you come out of the water you cannot hold that rock. You will be amazed how much difference it makes. The water takes much of the gravitation. Even on the earth, meditation is very easy if you are joyful, in a mood for dancing. So it is up to you to make your meditation easy and successful, or difficult and unsuccessful.

Paddy's at the bar and he's drunk so much that the bartender asks him to leave. Paddy insists that he is not drunk, and he will prove it.

"See that cat coming in the door?" he says. "Well that cat has only one eye and that proves I am not drunk."

"You are drunker than I thought!" says the bartender. "That cat is not coming in, it's going out."

A rich young girl finds that she has developed a passion for the smell of burning rubber. So she buys herself a sports car and satisfies her passion racing around country lanes. One day she passes a young man who is hitchhiking and stops to pick him up. The hitchhiker settles back in his seat, thinking that his luck has really changed.

Suddenly the girl stamps her foot on the accelerator and drives full speed toward a steep cliff. At the last minute she puts her foot on the brakes and the car stops inches from the edge.

"Can you smell that?" she asks her passenger enthusiastically.

"Smell it?" sobs the man. "I'm sitting in it!"

A pretty young farm girl has been to the market one day and is walking home to her farm after dark. Soon she meets one of the lads from the neighboring farm walking in the same direction. They walk together for a little while and the girl says, "You know, I'm not sure a weak and defenseless girl like me should be walking with a big strong chap like you after dark."

The farm lad says nothing.

A few minutes later she starts again, "I'm almost afraid to be alone in the dark with you like this. You might take advantage of me."

The boy laughs and says, "Here am I carrying a pitchfork and a chicken in one hand, a washtub in the other, and leading a goat. And you think I'm going to get ideas? No chance."

The girl thinks for a few seconds and says, "Well, I only thought that if you were to stick the pitchfork in the ground, tie the goat to it and put the chicken under the washtub, I would be in trouble."

A woman is on the fifth floor of a burning apartment building, screaming, "Help, save me!"

The fire truck drives up to the building and a burly fireman is soon climbing up the extension ladder. As he approaches the woman he says, "It gives me great pleasure to save a pregnant woman."

Indignantly the woman replies, "But I'm not pregnant!"

"Well lady," replies the fireman, "you're not saved yet!"

Just be joyful. All around, life is so hilarious. You have just to look joyfully and you will not find time for suffering and agony. In this beautiful life there is every possibility for you to become a great meditator. But you have to learn to see the joyous side of life. It is full of juice, full of laughter, and if you can also laugh with it, no one can prevent your meditativeness. Meditativeness will come on its own accord, following your joy like a shadow.

What is meditativeness? – just a silence, a dancing silence.

Ruthie Finkelstein is lying on her deathbed. "Moishe," she murmurs to her husband sitting beside the bed, "I must make a confession before I go. The fact is, I have been unfaithful to you."

"I know," says Moishe quietly.

"I don't think you understand," pleads Ruthie. "What I mean is that I have been with another man."

"Yes, I know that," Moishe murmurs.

"Not just once," continues Ruthie, "but lots of times – in his office, in his house..."

"Yes, I know that, dear," says Moishe soothingly.

"Even in this house, in this very bed!" cries Ruthie.

"Yes, I know," whispers Moishe. "That's why I put rat poison in your tea."

Hymie Goldberg walks into an appliance store and asks the price of a remote-controlled TV.

"One dollar," replies the clerk.

"You've got to be kidding," says Hymie.

"Listen," says the clerk, "do you want it or not?" Of course, Hymie gives him a dollar.

On his way out of the store, he sees a big refrigerator. "How much for that?" asks Hymie.

"Fifty cents," replies the clerk.

Hymie pulls out fifty cents and gives it to the clerk. "What the hell is going on here?" he asks.

"Nothing is going on here," replies the clerk. "But my boss is at my house with my wife and what he is doing to her, I am doing to his business."

# 14

# Love Loves You, Not Your Masks

Osho,
When you look at me in discourse – whether or not you actually see me – I feel your love pouring out of you and penetrating my heart. At first it feels a little scary because I feel very exposed, and then I love the feeling inside my heart. Can you talk about exposing oneself?

You have raised one of the most fundamental questions. Each human being has to face it. The majority face it in a cowardly way by escaping from it, by forgetting it, by not looking at it. The very few spirits who are rebellious, courageous, and want to know their own essential being, the meaning and significance of their life – who don't want to be here accidentally, but want to be a significant, creative participant in existence – have to go through the agony of exposure. They cannot escape.

Why has it become such an agony, such a suffering to expose oneself as one is? – because you have been told again and again that you are unworthy, that you are not acceptable, that you are not of any worth at all as you are. You will have to attain respectability by following certain rules and regulations made by others. If you want some kind of dignity, you have to become a puppet in the hands of others. Because they decide what you should be, how you should act, and how not.

And this ugly education starts from the very first moment a child is born. I was present at one of my friends' first childbirth. The woman had been a long acquaintance – she had studied with me, she had become a teacher with me – and this was going to be her first child. Even though the husband was against my presence – why should another person be present there? – she insisted. I had no idea that there had been a quarrel and a fight. Finally the doctors interfered and said, "There is no harm. If her feeling is that she has found a man of grace and she would like her child to be seen by the same man whom she has respected..."

On the surface everything looks beautiful, but as you go deeper into analysis things start changing their colors. The mother is even deciding what the child should see first, who he is going to have his first human encounter with. The mother is deciding that. And our whole education starts from such decisions.

Naturally, a strange calamity falls over the whole humanity. No one seems to be the right person. Everyone seems to be in the wrong place. Someone else may be in the right place, but you are never in the right place. The person you think is in the right place is not in the right place either; he is thinking someone else is in the right place.

This whole madness is the ultimate result of a wrong educational system, which does not accept you as you are in your naturalness, in your simplicity. You may not be a great leader... In fact there is no need of great leaders. What have they done except made history to torture small children with? They have to remember the names of all the great leaders, do homework. What have all your great men done?

Who are these great men? – mostly criminals. Either they themselves committed the crimes: people like Genghis Khan and Nadir Shah and Tamerlane. Just these three people killed nearabout one hundred and twenty million people. And you don't call them criminals; they are great leaders, great conquerors. There are others who have not committed crimes themselves, but have created the very source from which crimes arise.

I have heard an ancient story…

God had made the world. On the sixth day everything was complete, just one thing was missing – a moral code. So he went around to the Babylonians, the Egyptians, the people who lived on the drowned continent of Atlantis and asked them, "Do you want a commandment?"

Everyone asked, "What is a commandment?"

Someone said, "Thou shalt not commit adultery."

The Egyptians said, "Then what shall we do? The whole of life will lose interest! We don't want any such commandment."

God was getting tired when he found Moses. He asked, "Do you want a commandment?"

Just like a fundamentalist Jew, Moses asked, "How much?"

God said, "Free!"

He said, "Then I will have ten."

Those ten commandments are torturing Jews, Mohammedans, Christians. Although these people Moses, Jesus, are not criminals, they are sources of certain criminality. For example, all the religious leaders of the world have made celibacy one of the most moral acts. And it is one of the most immoral acts because it is unnatural. That which is unnatural cannot be moral.

Amrito, my sannyasin is here… I was in Greece, and she told me that the Greek Orthodox Church believes very fanatically in virginity. I said, "That means all the girls that are not married in Greece are virgins?" She laughed. She herself had been a beautiful girl, and had been chosen as a beauty queen in Greece; she had also worked as a model. She said, "Don't ask that. If you want to know, you cannot find a single virgin. This is simply a principle. And no one ever inquires how many virgins there are."

Now, to make virginity a moral precept, unknowingly you are creating criminals, guilty people, psychopaths, perverted people.

In Europe, during the nineteenth century, it was absolutely necessary that you married a virgin girl. But sometimes a girl was a virgin, but the certificate that made her a virgin may have been lost. It is a very small certificate! Just riding on a horse, you can lose your virginity. Even riding on a bicycle you can lose your virginity, because it is a small, thin skin which prevents the male sperm from reaching the female eggs. It is such a small, thin layer of skin that it can be broken in any accident: you fall from a tree and you lose your virginity. That's why… I was always wondering why no one allows girls to climb trees. Finally I found out myself that the real reason is – no one talks about it, perhaps no one knows about it – that climbing a tree is very dangerous for virginity. And once lost, it is lost forever.

In Europe, during the nineteenth century, there were doctors who were selling virginity. They prepared thin pieces of skin and planted them in the right place. And it was a great profession because almost every girl is going to lose it; it is not simple to protect it. Just swimming in a pool you may lose it! Now, this made the girl feel unnecessarily immoral, unworthy, afraid that sooner or later she is going to be found out. How can she prove that she lost it when she was swimming? She has not done anything and her virginity is gone. It created guilt and it created criminals. Those doctors who provided the virginity for a certain fee were the criminals. They were absolutely exploiting innocent women.

You will not believe that not only does her virginity have to be there, but after the first night of marriage the young husband has to show the bed sheet to his family and to his friends with blood on it. It is not necessarily true, even if the girl is a virgin and has not lost her virginity, that making love to her is going to bring blood. So she has even to supply the blood, too. Those doctors who were implanting virginity also gave the woman a small tube of blood, so she could just spill it over the bed. And this was a show, an exhibition; the neighborhood would see that yes, that girl was a virgin.

What is your business in it? In what way are you concerned with it? But because certain idiots have made virginity a moral concept, many more things are bound to develop by the side. Similarly, celibacy has created even more crime. It has created all kinds of perversions: homosexuality, sodomy. And the reason is not in the homosexuals, the reason is in your religions. They are preaching something which is unnatural. I challenge all the religions of the world, all their *shankaracharyas*, imams, popes, rabbis, to come to a medical college and prove that they are celibate. Only a medical examination can give you a certificate saying whether you are celibate or not. You cannot be a celibate; it is such a stupid thing.

It is as if a religion arises and makes it a point that to urinate is against God. It looks to be against God! It is not a very nice thing to do. But if some religion arises and says it is against God, there will immediately be people who will say, "We will never urinate." And we see these people drinking water… Then where is the water going?

We don't need to worry about their urination, but where is their water going? Once you have drunk water it has to find a way out of your organism. You cannot go on accumulating it; you will become a reservoir! It will be a very strange, funny situation: reservoirs all around, carrying such a load. And anyone with a sense of humor can put a knife into them and the whole city will be flooded, people will be swimming!

You eat food, you drink water, you breathe air; you do everything just as any other animal does. Whether you are celibate or not, you do the same things. You cannot be separate just on the question of celibacy. You don't even know what is happening inside you, how your sexual energy is created. It is created by your intake of air, oxygen, by your food, by your milk.

Strangely, it happened…

I was staying in a rest house with a *shankaracharya*. I said to him, "Celibacy is an absolutely unnatural idea. Only an impotent person can be celibate. If you are potent then you cannot be celibate. Tell me what you are, potent or impotent?"

He said, "I am celibate."

I said, "Then I will take you to a medical hospital this very moment."

He said, "You seem to be a strange man. It is a question of ideology. Where does the medical hospital come into it?"

I said, "It is not a question of ideology. Do you know how your sexual energy is created? Do you have any scripture in which it is described? Do you have any control over it – not to create it, to prevent it? You don't have any control over it, just as you don't have any control over your blood, you don't have any control over your hair. Your organism has not left anything essential in the hands of your mind. And celibacy is part of your organism; the most important part. Biology cannot leave it in your hands."

He said, "I don't want to be in unnecessary trouble."

I said, "Trouble or not, I can bring a doctor here."

He said, "But I don't want to argue with you."

I said, "You *are* arguing because you are saying that you are celibate."

Not a single religious person – there are thousands of monks: Catholic, Hindu, Buddhist, Jaina – not a single monk has been to the people who can check whether he is celibate or not. But this ideal of celibacy has been created by very good people. They have not committed any crime: Mahavira, Gautam Buddha. They have not committed any crime, but they have created something which goes on creating immense crime.

According to me, they have to take the responsibility for it. With absolute respect and humbleness I want to say that all your religious leaders are responsible for your perversions, your pathologies, your mind going berserk. They are the people who have condemned you. They won't allow you to accept yourself. That's why you are afraid to expose yourself: no one should know that you urinate, hide it. You are hiding yourself because everything in you has been condemned. I have been looking… Is there anything in man which has not been condemned by one or other of the religions? I have not found a single thing. Everything is condemned.

As long as my grandmother was alive, poor tomatoes were not allowed in the house because Jainas believe in eating only vegetables; they are vegetarians. The tomato is also a vegetarian, but it looks like a meat eater. The color looks to be of the nonvegetarian food.

I had not eaten anything during the night up to the age of eighteen because for Jainas it is a sin to eat at night, it is a crime. The first time I went on a picnic with my school friends to a nearby beautiful old castle… They were all Hindus, so for them food was not a problem. And they were so very interested in exploring the whole castle, and it had so many beautiful points to explore. I was feeling hungry and tired, but I could not say anything. Finally, at night they all prepared food.

Now a great question was before me: to commit the sin or not. The whole traditional education of my family was not to commit the sin; just one night's hunger is not going to kill you. It takes thirty days even for the sickliest person to die if he remains hungry. For the healthy person it takes ninety days, just by starvation. So just one night and you are going to lose your paradise and all the beauties of paradise and fall into hellfire. It was not a simple question of eating or not eating, it was a great metaphysical question. My whole existence was in turmoil.

I said to the boys, "I am feeling hungry, but it is against my understanding, I cannot eat. I will have to suffer the whole night."

They said, "Are you mad? We won't tell anyone. Your family will never know, no one will ever know."

I said, "That is not the question. Their knowing is not the question. I will know, and I will feel always guilty that I have committed a sin. Then I cannot expose myself, I cannot be read as a book – open, no secret."

But the hunger was there. The whole day being on the mountain was tiring, and the food they had prepared was so inviting.

And they were all persuading me, "You will not be able to sleep the whole night."

I said, "That I know. Either way I am not going to sleep the whole night."

They said, "Why either way? Eat well and sleep! We eat every night and we sleep." And they were right; that was their experience.

Finally I got persuaded by my hunger, by their arguments. I did not eat much; to be safe I took just a small amount of food. I was not committing a very great sin – even God will forgive a boy of eighteen years committing a small sin. But that small sin could not allow me to sleep the whole night. I had to vomit continuously. By the morning, when I had thrown everything out, I could go to sleep just for two or three hours.

Those boys could not understand it: "What kind of man are you? We all slept. We were so tired that we could not even dream. One needs some energy to dream too. And we were so utterly tired and so well fed that we slept. What were you doing?" They could not understand it. But I could understand that my psychology had been polluted, that my mind had been corrupted by those whom I loved.

This corruption goes back to Mahavira. Mahavira is responsible for my whole night's suffering on that mountain. He created the idea that eating during the night is a sin. And perhaps in his situation it was right because there was no light, no electricity, no kerosene oil. So to eat during the night was not only irreligious, it was unhygienic too. You can understand that with so many mosquitoes and all kinds of animals, to eat in the night, in the dark, was dangerous. Anything could fall into your food. But Mahavira was not aware that a situation was going to come when man would be able to create ways of having more light at night than there is in the day. Now there is no need to be worried. But habits die hard, and habits which have been followed for thousands of years…

I used to stay in the house of one of the richest men in the world, Sohanlal Dugar. He was a rare man, and just because of his rarity he fell in love with me. I was speaking in Jaipur. Jaipur was his home, but his business was in Kolkata. So most of the time he used to live in Kolkata and for a few days in his home in Jaipur.

I was speaking in Jaipur and as I finished, an old man with a great turban… And I could not think that this man was one of the richest men in the world. He gave me a bundle of one-hundred-rupee notes.

I said, "What are you doing?"

He said, "I want to offer this to you."

But I said, "I don't need it. If sometimes I need… Just give me your address."

He said, "I will give you my address on the condition that you accept this money."

I said, "But I have never accepted money from anyone." When I was saying this, tears started coming to the old man eyes. I asked, "Why are you crying? You should be happy, this much money is saved. I should be crying. Why are you crying?"

He said, "Listen, I am a rich man as far as money is concerned, but I am a very poor man as far as the heart is concerned. I don't know how to give love except by giving money. If you reject my money, you are rejecting me and my heart and I will never forgive you." He continued, "Take it and burn it – that is not my concern – but don't reject it."

And that's exactly what I did. I took it from his hands – it must have been ten thousand rupees – and burned it then and there.

He was very happy. He said, "You have followed your principle, I have followed my principle, we both are happy. But now remember, whenever you come to Kolkata you have to be my guest."

So since then, for almost ten years, I used to be his guest three or four times a year. His whole house was centrally air-conditioned, but he would sit with me at the dining table with a small bamboo hand fan. I would be eating and he would be moving the bamboo fan.

I said to him, "What are you doing? You know perfectly well that the house is absolutely air-conditioned; there is not even a single mosquito here. It is so clean. There is no need."

He said, "But it is traditional for the host to sit and fan the guest while he is eating."

I said, "It may be traditional, but it should not be stupid. In these conditions it is becoming stupid."

He said, "You don't understand. This air-conditioning, this house, everything can collapse because I am a gambler. Today I am the richest man, tomorrow I might be a beggar. It has happened many times – up and down. But this bamboo fan will always be with me. I cannot depend on something which I can lose; I can depend on this fan."

I said, "You are giving a beautiful argument, but deep down you know and I know that it is just an old habit. In the whole of Rajasthan this is the habit, everywhere."

That night I became aware that you can corrupt the mind in any way. In fact any kind of ideals given to the mind are corrupting. You are telling the person, "This is right and this is wrong." This is not love and this is not education.

According to me, you have to tell your children, "Be alert, be aware. To be alert, to be aware, to be more conscious – of the consequences, of the implications – is the only morality. We don't give you particulars, what is right and what is wrong, because situations change. What is right in one situation may be wrong in another situation. We give you only awareness, so you can find with the light of awareness what is wrong in a situation and what is right. But you should remain the center of your decision. The decision should not come from outside." If the decision comes from outside, that has created the problem.

Everyone is afraid of exposing himself. What will people say? Everyone is trying to pose according to people's ideals: what they want, what they like. If you want their respect you have to be a puppet, but then you cannot be real and authentic; you will be a hypocrite. And the hypocrite is certainly afraid of being exposed. If someone takes away the curtain that you were putting over your reality, you are going to be afraid. This is the situation. Not only are you in this situation, every human being is in this situation because up to now the right human atmosphere has not been created on this planet.

One of my friends was the oldest member of parliament. He was a member of the parliament for sixty years, without any discontinuity. His name was Dr. Govindas. He was second only to Winston Churchill; Winston Churchill had been in the parliament two years longer.

I used to stay with him in New Delhi. He was a fanatic about cows – the Hindu fanatic mind… And you cannot believe that a man of intelligence, a man who has a doctorate, a man who has been a member of the parliament for sixty years, was so fanatic that he would only drink the milk of a white cow.

I said, "This is strange. Up to the cow I can understand, but a white cow?"

He said, "Black is a symbol of evil and bad things."

I said, "A symbol is one thing, but just a patch of black on the cow will not make the milk black."

He said, "Don't disturb my mind. I have followed this idea my whole life."

He used to take a cow everywhere he went, because who knows? Somewhere you may not find a purely white cow. Some spots on the cow – finished, religion is finished! And Hindus think that cow's milk is the purest food.

The reality is that the more milk you drink, the more milk you take in, the less is the possibility of your being celibate. No one even points out the fact that the milk of the cow is not produced by nature for man. It is produced for bulls, and certainly it has a thousandfold more sexuality in it than a woman's milk.

And you can see that no animal in the whole of existence goes on drinking milk their whole life. Only for a few weeks when the animal is small and cannot digest solid food does it depend on the mother, and then it is free. It is strange that man is the only person on the whole planet who goes on drinking milk even when he can digest solid food. It is thought in India that if someone lives only on milk he becomes a saint. To me he becomes a bull! He is dangerous, he should be kept in chains. But people worship him.

But perhaps worship is, in a very psychological way, chains. When you worship someone, when so many people give you so much respect because you just drink milk – a great creative act! – the crowd and its respect become chains. This man will still have to find some perversion to release his sexuality. So every day newspapers are full of stories: some great saint has been found sexually misusing small children, somewhere a bishop is found…

In America, the man who was most against me in Portland was the bishop of Portland. He was continually saying, in every sermon, that my presence in America would corrupt people. And just recently he was caught, and has confessed before the court that he has been using small boys and girls sexually, in the name of teaching them the Holy Bible. These are the people…

Now, I have been looking at these things because the question has become very prominent. Even the person below the archbishop of England – only one step more and he can become the archbishop – is saying, "Celibacy does not include homosexuality. You can be celibate and you can be homosexual; they do not in any way contradict each other. Celibacy is only against heterosexuality. Men should not contact women and women should not contact men, but it has no implications…"

In a way he is right because in no Christian books, scriptures, has anyone ever thought that about homosexuality. Then there are other kinds of sexuality; there is sodomy. In faraway places – in deserts, in mountains – when you cannot have a woman or a man, people start making love to animals. That is sodomy. Certainly celibacy cannot include sodomy. *Sodomy* is such a saintly word! And these people are coming up with these ideas now because they have to prove that they are really celibate.

Monasteries are full of homosexuals. In one monastery in Athos there are one thousand people, and they have divided the monastery in two because five hundred people are homosexual – not a small number. Half of the monastery is homosexual. And who knows about the other half, what they are doing?

These people are made unnecessarily criminal, unnecessarily unnatural, guilty, condemned. Then everyone starts having a mask: don't show your face, just show the face people want to see. And that's how everyone is functioning. But there are moments when one would like to drop the face, the mask, and in these moments the problem arises.

You are asking, "When you look at me in discourse – whether or not you actually see me – I feel your love pouring out of you and penetrating my heart. At first it feels a little scary because I feel very exposed, and then I love the feeling inside my heart." Love is one of the things that forces you to expose yourself. You cannot cheat love; that is sacrilegious. That is the only authentic spirituality: not to cheat love. If you can cheat love then there is no hope for you because love is the opportunity to expose yourself. Whatever garbage the society has poured on you, throw it away and be utterly nude in yourself, in total acceptance, respect and dignity. Love loves you, not your clothes. Love loves you, not your masks.

And love certainly creates a great question: whether to choose the mask or to choose love. The mask is a miserable life. It has not given you any joy, it has led you more and more toward the false. Love is the beginning of a new journey toward blissfulness. Don't miss that moment. When love calls, say yes. When love calls, move. Move beyond your so-called personality.

So your problem is simple. First you will feel scared, afraid. You have been hiding behind this mask so long that you yourself have started believing in it. You have forgotten your own face; the mask has been there so long.

It happens...

In the Second World War, ration cards were issued for the first time. One great American scientist, Edison, had to go to register his name; everyone, family members, dependents had to go personally to get a ration card. He had never been in such a situation. He was not a social being; otherwise he, a single man, would not have been able to give humanity one thousand inventions. No one else has done that much. Everything that you use – you don't know – Thomas Alva Edison is behind it. Electricity, radio, anything that you are using; your whole life is filled with his contributions. But that meant the whole day he was hidden in his lab.

This was the first time he was standing outside in a queue under the sky. When his number came, as the queue became smaller and smaller and the clerk was facing him, the clerk said, "Thomas Alva Edison." He looked here and there; perhaps he is searching for someone called Thomas Alva Edison. The clerk was also at a loss – certainly this man who is standing in the front cannot be Thomas Alva Edison. He was supposed to be because that was the order of the queue. He shouted, "Thomas Alva Edison, your number has come!" No reply. The whole queue stood silent.

One man looked at Thomas Alva Edison and said, "I think the first man who is standing in the queue is Thomas Alva Edison because he lives just near my house."

The clerk said, "You seem to be a very strange man."

Edison said, "Strange? In fact for sixty years no one has used my name. And do you think for sixty years you can remember? My colleagues call me professor, my students call me professor, and there is no one who ever calls me Thomas Alva Edison. It seems this gentleman may be right because far away, sixty years back... I can hear a small murmur, 'Yes, Thomas Alva Edison. I have heard this name before.'"

There is a limit. You can forget, your own falseness can become your reality. So when love strikes you like lightning it exposes your reality for a moment. Then the fear, "Should I throw away all the falseness and be myself and risk, whether I am respected or disrespected, condemned, blamed? Whatever happens, without thinking of these consequences, should I expose myself?" When love strikes you, it fills you with fear and also underneath with joy, and with a feeling of love because a moment has come into your life when you can change from the false to the real.

As for the beginning part of your question, it is a little difficult for me to say. You are asking, "When you look at me in discourse – whether or not you actually see me – I feel your love pouring out of you." When I am looking at you, I am simply looking. I am not seeing you. And particularly when I am speaking and I look at you, it is not possible for me because I am no longer there, just a great emptiness responding to your heart, responding to your being. Yes, love is there showering on you.

It has nothing to do with seeing you or not seeing you. Even when I am exactly seeing you, if you look into my eyes it is utter emptiness. Only out of that utter emptiness love flows. Then it flows without any address. Then it simply flows for whoever is ready, receptive. It is available, it comes close to you; you can be filled with it or you can remain standing on the riverbank, thirsty.

An Indian mystic, Kabir, used to sing a song. The title of the song is, *The Fish in the Sea Is Thirsty.* That describes you. But there is no need, it is an unnecessary misery imposed upon yourself. Drop it!

A little priest, a minister and a rabbi get together and talk about the issue of "When life begins." The priest opens by saying, "I think that life begins at the precise moment the sperm fertilizes the egg."

The minister says, "Well, I think life begins at the moment the baby draws its first breath."

Then they both look at the rabbi, who says, "Well, I think life begins when the dog has died and the children have moved out of the house."

It all depends on you when life begins. It can begin right now: the dog need not die, the children need not move out. And what kind of life will that be when the dog has died and the children have moved out?

I have heard about a court case – a divorce. A man of ninety and a woman of eighty-five wanted a divorce. The magistrate asked, "But how long have you been married?"

They said, "Nearabout sixty years."

The magistrate said, "If you managed for sixty years, then what great crisis has come into your life that you want a divorce?"

The man said, "There is no question of crisis. We were waiting for all of our children to die. Now we are free – no burden, no responsibility – so please help us to go on our own ways. Up to now whenever we raised the question of divorce, everyone said, 'Think of the children!' So for sixty years we have been thinking about the children. And those idiots went on living, went on living, went on living… Just yesterday the last one died. Now we want to live our own lives. Enough thinking about children!"

It is not a question of when that great moment of transformation will come into your life; it can come this very moment. The whole existence is ready, except you. You go on finding excuses, and then you become so expert in finding excuses that it becomes almost impossible for life, love, beauty, existence to penetrate you. You see and yet you don't see. It is all around. It touches you, it comes with the wind, but it does not enter you; your doors, your windows are closed.

This has nothing to do with your question… I am as irrelevant as the existence. What is the point of a roseflower? Or what is the point of a deer or an elephant? Was God thinking of a circus? Elephants and camels… These are all jokes!

Paddy nearly has an accident at work, and he is so shocked that he decides to become a reformed Christian. He tells Maureen that he is going to give up sex for a month.

With only a few days to go before the end of the month, Paddy and Maureen are shopping together in the local supermarket. Maureen leans over a tray of apples and Paddy gets a good look at her chest and nearly goes mad. A few minutes later, Paddy sees her thigh when her dress gets tangled in another customer's shopping cart. In the confusion, he loses all control of himself, forgetting his one-month vow of celibacy completely.

A few days later, Paddy goes to confession and tells Father Murphy that he has broken his vow. The priest tries to console him, saying that after all the days and nights of his great effort, God and the church would forgive him.

"I'm not worried about God and the church," replies Paddy, "but Maureen and I feel terrible because they won't let us back in the supermarket!"

# 15

# Love Does Not Dominate

Osho,

I feel a new kind of authority and love growing in me, a clarity about myself and love for myself and others. It feels like everyone is equal for me and I don't have a special affection toward anyone. I feel free and beautiful. And all these gifts are just given to me. I don't do anything to get them. Everything just happens. Can you say something about this?

Your question is a little complicated. Perhaps you are not conscious of its implications. To say the truth hurts a little – and I cannot say anything else than the truth – so be prepared. These are the games the mind goes on playing within itself. And slowly, slowly it starts believing in them as if they are real. You say, "I feel a new kind of authority and love growing in me…" The remainder of the question will reveal that you don't understand the difference between authority and authoritativeness. The reason for me to take it for granted that you don't understand is because you are putting authority and love together. Love knows no authority.

It *is* authority, but it knows no authority. It never feels any authority. It is just a roseflower dancing in the sun, in the rain, in the wind. What does a poor flower think about authority? Again, it is the ego from the back door that gives you the sense of authority.

Only one can be true: either your love can be true or your authority can be true. But these words have never been disassociated from each other. For the simple reason that the love and authority come from the same people: the mother is the authority and love, the father is the authority and love, the priest is the authority and love. They get entangled with each other. You have never entered deep enough to see that they are not only two absolutely separate phenomena, they are absolutely contradictory.

The second thing: love does not grow. It is not grass! It is born suddenly, out of nowhere. You feel the song, the dance of love, and you are amazed. It does not come with any indication: "I am coming." It simply comes whenever you are ready, whenever your meditation is ready, whenever your being is silent; it suddenly comes, and all your being dances. It has an authority, but not authority over others. It has an authority in the sense that it is your own experience. You can say, "I am not quoting scriptures, I *am* the scripture." Ordinarily, authority is always a kind of domination. And authority is always derived from someone else.

Jesus derives his authority from God; otherwise he has no argument for what he is saying – just a villager's statements. He gets the authority because these are the words coming to him from his father who is above in heaven. And then the whole train starts; pope after pope. This Polack pope seems to have forgotten to die. Polacks are Polacks; you can't depend on their intelligence. Down through twenty centuries, popes have lived one year, six months, two years, at the most three years, but to get rid of this Polack is very difficult. From where does their authority come? – from Jesus Christ. And all down the line: the cardinals, the bishops, the priests; they all derive their authority from above. It is not their own experience.

I used to live in a neighborhood in Raipur, and a Catholic priest also lived there. We used to go for a walk early in the morning. I was very new; he had no idea who I was. I suddenly took hold of his collar and asked him, "Tell me truly: Do you know God?"

He said, "My God! This is a strange situation. So early in the morning, in the darkness, and I can't even see your face, who you are. I don't know, but those who know, they have taught me."

I asked him, "Have you asked them if they know? The same reply would have been given to you. 'Those who know have taught us.'"

That is the authority derived from others. And when you derive your authority from others, you start being authoritative over others. You have to take revenge. If you have to believe in others, you will force others to believe in you. It is simply a question of who is more powerful.

A beautiful story is related by a great Indian emperor, Akbar, in his autobiography, *Akbarnamma*…

One day in the court – and he had the wisest men of the land in his court… He was always in search of wise people. And certainly he had great poets, painters, musicians, philosophers, all kinds of geniuses. Just by his side the court joker was standing. Every court used to have a joker; just to keep things from becoming too hard, and to bring them down once in a while to a human level, to laughter. It was a very basic insight into psychology.

The name of the joker was Birbal. Akbar, just being playful and also wanting to know what Birbal's response was going to be – he was a very responsive person, immediate – Akbar slapped him hard. Not waiting even for a moment to think what to do, Birbal slapped the person who was standing by his side. While this was going on, people were watching… It went all over the capital; everyone was slapping everyone else. In the night, Akbar asked Birbal, "Why did you act in this way?"

He said, "Wait, in the morning you will know the answer." And in the morning he knew the answer. In the night when he entered the chambers of his queen, she slapped him.

He said, "My God! You are also in this game? Who told you?"

She said, "No one tells anyone. Things are moving, the whole city is in a deeply hilarious mood. The only question is that you should hit the person who is weaker than you. I was waiting for you."

Then Akbar remembered that Birbal had said, "In the morning you will know." Of course Birbal could not hit Akbar, the emperor – he was too powerful. Birbal was just a beautiful man, a wise man, but not powerful. He could hit only the next one down in rank. And once it was understood, who is to hit and who is to get the hit, the game started. It ended with the queen hitting Akbar. Akbar was a very honest man to write in his autobiography, "That moment I understood the great intelligence of Birbal. He had hit me, but in a very roundabout way."

Authority has two sides. One side is to be dominated by those who have power; they are authoritative over you. And the other side is to take revenge with those who are below you, who cannot react, who have to take your hit and still smile. The husband comes home and hits the wife because the boss was very angry, and it was nasty but still he had to smile, falsely. He wanted to hit him, but that would be dangerous, and the job would be lost.

The Italian consul who was here...

When he was asked, "Why are you afraid of meeting Osho with someone present, taking notes or recording – whatever you prefer?"

He said, "Do you want me to lose my job?"

I laughed when I heard this and said, "I will make certain that he loses his job." Now it is all over the world in the newspapers, in Italy and everywhere. It would have been better if he had come and met me. His job is gone.

People are living in a hierarchy. Someone is higher than you, someone is lower than you.

An Indian saint – I should call him a so-called saint... All saints are so-called, so that does not matter. He was teaching and I was present. He was teaching that to be contented, one fundamental rule has to be remembered: "Always look down. Look how people are suffering. Look, someone is blind; look, someone is crippled; look, someone is dying. You are in a far better position. That will give you consolation and contentment."

I had to stop him. I said, "What you are saying is absolutely stupid because a man who looks down cannot avoid looking up. There are people who are in higher posts, having more money, more power, more prestige. Do you think he has to look continuously toward the blind, the beggars? The mind does not function like that. The mind looks at both sides. And this kind of contentment… What are you going to say to the man who is blind? Tell him, 'At least you are alive, you are not dead. Look, many are in their graves, but you are out of the grave'? Where will this stupid logic lead?"

Just a few days ago, a very grumpy, negative type of mind was dying. His friends were around, and of course this was the greatest chance for him to show his negativity, sadness, misery: he has been treated very badly by the world; he cannot forgive this world. If he meets God, he is going to have a good talk with him.

Then someone said, "Cool down, at least you have one thing positive – that is AIDS. Everything else is negative. Look at the positive and be happy!"

People have been told to continuously look at the positive and just ignore the negative. But by your ignoring it, it does not disappear. It is there, and any moment it can explode. So you cannot have authority in this way – looking to those who are unfortunately lower than you in any area of life – because the superior ones are also there. They will make you inferior and you will feel hurt. This is a sick kind of authoritativeness. It can even become aggressive. The politicians, criminals, generals – they become aggressive. They want to prove that they actually have authority. They can kill millions of people, but even by killing millions of people you don't become superior. You remain the same, just you become the ugliest creature on the earth.

So first you have to understand all these nuances of authority. Yes, there is an authority which is not felt. That is the authority of love. But it is not felt, it is simply there. It does not dominate anyone, it is not superior to anyone; it is just enjoying the tremendous gift of life from the very sources. This authority will give you humbleness, not turn you into an arrogant egoist. These are the checking points: if your authority makes you humble, loving, a nobody.

And you are asking, "...a clarity about myself, and love for myself and others." You are really confused. First you say, "Love is growing." It is not a crop. It is just a diamond you find in your clarity, radiating in your silence. Secondly, you are saying that the love that is growing is for "...myself and others." Love knows no division: "...myself and others." Love is an experience in which duality disappears. You simply feel one, in tune with the music of the whole.

"It feels..." you say, "...like everyone is equal for me..." Now, I suspect something is hidden in this which is sick. "It feels like everybody is equal for me..." No one is equal. Equality is one of the most wrongly conceived ideas, which has created all kinds of communisms, socialisms, anarchisms. They are all based on the foundation of equality. Even people who are not communist don't have the guts to say that equality does not exist. It has become almost ingrained in everyone's mind.

I want you to know that everyone is unique, not equal. And uniqueness gives a totally different dimension. A rosebush is not equal to the bamboos reaching to the stars. In what way is it equal? A rose is a rose, a lotus is a lotus; there is no question of equality. I am not saying that they are unequal, I am simply saying they are not equal. That is their dignity. They should rejoice because they are simply themselves, there is no one else to be compared with. These ideas of equality, inequality... Are all comparisons. In existence everything is so unique, you cannot compare. But I can see just between the lines…

You say, "It feels like everyone is equal for me…" Do you see the point? You want everyone to be equal to you. The president of a country, the prime minister of a country, the king of a country, the queen of a country – you would like them all to be equal to you.

It is not strange that two ideas have gripped the human heart more deeply than anything else. The first idea is that of equality because that gives you a feeling that now there is no need to prove… All are equal. And deep down you know that you are superior because *you* know that all are equal – all are not knowing. In your knowledge of equality, in a certain way you satisfy your superiority.

Strangely, both ideas have gripped humanity. Half of the world is communist; equality has not happened. Equality cannot happen; equality is not possible. It is against nature. You are not built for it. And it is good; otherwise, just to see equal faces, equal people would be so boring. The differences create a variety and a life with color and rainbows.

The second idea is that poverty has something spiritual. Both, strangely, were created by Christianity. Jesus was not crucified because he was teaching a great philosophy or was against the tradition or was in any way dangerous. He was crucified because he consoled the poor: "You are the chosen people of God and you will enter paradise. Even a camel can enter through the eye of a needle, but a rich man cannot enter paradise." This was the reason he was crucified. It was nothing to do with religion. But this was also the reason that the poor became converted to Christianity, because he was the only messiah who was giving them a free ticket to paradise. Just being poor is enough.

Christianity has given many diseases to the world. One is enhancing poverty, making poverty something spiritual. It is *not* spiritual. It is simply our stupidity that we are poor; otherwise everything can be comfortably settled, without any poverty, without any beggars. But rather than looking at the roots, they started talking about equality. Have you seen two people who are equal? – in any way? Even twins are not exactly equal. Their parents recognize one from the other.

A man married a woman who was a twin. A friend asked him, "It must be a very difficult job to figure out who is your wife."

He said, "This is giving me such great joy because there is no need to bother about who is my wife. I have two wives, and a clear-cut excuse that it is very difficult to distinguish who is who. And neither do they speak because it would look awkward – 'Why didn't you stop him?'"

Even one-egg twins have small differences. About others the differences are great. And the greater the differences are, the more unique you are, but not equal. I am not saying you are unequal, remember, I am simply denying the whole philosophy of equality. Instead I am giving you a new idea of uniqueness which is far more beautiful. It accepts everyone. Equality is something idiotic.

In Greek mythology there is a story…

A king was a little crazy. He had made a beautiful guesthouse with a golden bed, but only a few guests ever stayed in his guesthouse. And they never came out alive because his principle was that the guest had to fit with the bed. Now, this is a strange idea. He was a powerful man; people were standing there with swords to fit the guest. If his head was too long, it was cut; what is the need of it? If you were too short, then traction… Pull him from both sides. Sometimes their legs would come off. Until the guest was completely comfortable, the king remained in the room.

Naturally, the guest disappeared. Slowly, slowly people became suspicious. What happens? Whoever becomes a guest never comes out of the palace. Some servant leaked the message, "No one should ever come because that bed is not made for man. That bed is made as a piece of art, and man has to fit to it." Guests stopped coming to the palace; otherwise they used to enjoy the palatial pleasures. But by the first night everything was finished!

Equality is something similar. Do you think you are equal in intelligence to Albert Einstein? Or even with the man who proclaimed the philosophy of equality, Karl Marx? Do you think you are equal to him? I have met many communists, and I have asked them, "Have you read Karl Marx's great contribution, *Das Kapital*?" But it is so complicated and so voluminous that they have a copy of it, just as every Christian has a Bible, every Hindu a Gita, every Mohammedan a Koran. It is the holy *Das Kapital*, but no one reads it.

You cannot read it. The argumentation is very complicated. And the man worked his whole life doing nothing but sitting in the British Museum consulting books. Before the museum opened, he was always present before the door. When the museum closed, he was physically forced to leave. Sometimes while reading or writing complicated philosophical questions he became unconscious, so an ambulance was called.

Do you think you are equal to Gautam Buddha? Drop the idea of being equal. That simply shows deep down you are feeling the inequality. To cover it, you have come with a beautiful mask of equality. Learn a new language, a new grammar, a new manifesto, of uniqueness. That gives credit and dignity to every human being, whatever he is doing. He may be making shoes, he may be a carpenter, he may be a scientist, he may be anyone; it does not matter. But what he is doing has his own touch, his own individual flavor, his own creativity, his own signature.

But your feeling does not look right. "It feels like everyone is equal for me and I don't have a special affection toward anyone." It would have been better to say, "I have a special affection for everyone." Why fall into the negative? – it is a protective mask; you are afraid of love. A special affection for anyone means trouble. It is better to keep out of trouble and convince yourself that you don't have any special love for anyone. But this will shrink you. And just a moment before you were saying, "My love is growing toward myself and toward others."

Love need not be more or less. It is just a rain cloud. It showers on mountains, trees, streets, people, not because these are its special favorites, but because it is too full of rain power, too full of rainwater. It has to unburden itself, so it does not matter who helps it to be unburdened.

You are saying, "I am free and beautiful." Free from what? You are not even free from the idea of beautiful. And who gives you this idea of beautiful? – your mirror? Because you don't have any special affection toward anyone? I don't think such a person will get special affection from anyone else either; only a mirror. You can purchase a good mirror, and whenever you are feeling a little suspicious…

Women keep small mirrors in their bags. The moment they start feeling suspicious about whether they are beautiful or not, immediately they look into the mirror and they say, "Everything is good."

"And all these gifts are just given to me." They must be given by the mirror. "I don't do anything to get them." Obviously – just standing before a mirror is enough. You don't have to do anything. You don't have to persuade the mirror and you don't have to tell the mirror, "I love you very much. I really, really love you."

"Everything just happens. Can you say something about this?" I can say only one thing: that you are not grateful. If everything happens and if it is authentic, following it will come a deep gratitude. That gratitude is not in your question anywhere. And gratitude is religiousness, gratitude is the only prayer. All prayers are just man-made. Gratitude is not a word, it is a deep feeling in the very center of your being. If that gratitude is felt, everything is right; then whatever I have said, don't take any note of it. But if gratitude is not there, then ponder over what I have said. Meditate more and don't get into such stupid ideas.

To me, gratitude is the greatest experience that you can have – not to God, not to me, not to anyone in particular; just simple gratitude for this whole existence. These birds, these beautiful trees, this whole existence is so beautiful that not to feel gratitude about it is to remain blind, ignorant, unaware. The function of meditation is to pull you out of your blindness and make you aware of this tremendous splendor that is spread all over.

A shy young man with a fine voice is asked to take part in the local play. But he tries to refuse, saying that he always gets embarrassed under such circumstances.

He is assured it will be very simple, and he will only have one line to say: "I come to snatch a kiss, and dart into the fray. Hark! I hear a pistol shot." And then walk offstage.

At the performance, he comes onstage, very embarrassed already by the bright green tights he has been forced to put on at the last minute, and becomes completely flustered at the sight of the beautiful heroine lying on the garden seat, in a white gown, awaiting him.

He clears his throat and announces, "I come here to kiss your snatch, no! snatch a kiss, and fart into the fray – I mean, dart into the fray! Hark! I hear a shistol pot, no! oh shit! Yes shit! Shit on you all! I never wanted to be in this damned play anyway!"

Don't take it seriously. To live is to be playful, and with this playfulness, prayer is bound to happen. And particularly in Pune you should be very alert, calm and quiet…

A sannyasin asks an Indian in a chai shop for information. He says, "Excuse me, where can I buy some shampoo?"

The chai wallah says, "You are from which country?"

"Australia," says the sannyasin.

"America?" queries the Indian.

"Not America – Australia!"

"England? Germany…? Good. You are married?"

"Not married," says the swami. "But where can I buy some shampoo?"

"What you want?" asks the Indian.

"Shampoo!" cries the sannyasin.

"For what you want this?" inquires the Indian.

"To wash my balls!" snaps the sannyasin. "What do you think?"

"Oh yes," says the Indian, "you are a tourist or you are coming for study?"

"I want to buy some shampoo. Do you know where I can buy some?"

"What? What you want?" says the Indian casually.

"Shampoo!" screams the sannyasin.

"Oh yes, you can buy," replies the Indian.

"But where can I buy it?" the sannyasin asks hopefully.

"In shop you can buy," answers the Indian.

"Yes, but which shop?" pleads the sannyasin.

"What you want?" asks the Indian.

In desperation the sannyasin screams, "I want some fucking shampoo!"

"No!" shouts the Indian, standing up, "no fucking here!"

# 16

# Become Master of Yourself

Osho,

To the Western world the terms "freedom" and "the master" are virtually mutually exclusive; for those who have met you this is wildly inaccurate. How do you redefine "freedom" and "the master" for the Western understanding?

The Western world has not come in contact with the tremendous reality that happens in the meeting of a master and a disciple. Of course, it is not visible. It is just like love, but far greater, far deeper, far more mysterious.

The West has known saints and followers. The saints demand surrender, the saints demand faith. And the moment you become faithful, you are no more; your whole individuality has been erased. Then you are a Christian, you are a Jew, but you are not *you*. The phenomenon of the master and the disciple happened in the East in its golden days, when there were people like Lao Tzu, Zarathustra, Gautam Buddha. They created a totally new kind of relationship.

Not everyone can paint a Picasso; neither can everyone be a Michelangelo. The West has missed having a Gautam Buddha. Jesus is not at all comparable to him. Jesus is simply a Jew, believing in all the Jewish dogmas. He is faithful – in fact, a little too much.

Gautam Buddha is a rebel; he is not a follower of anyone. Neither is Lao Tzu a follower of anyone.

They don't have any scriptures, they don't have any belief systems. They have searched on their own, alone – risking. They are moving away from the crowd on the lonely path, not knowing where this journey is going to end, but trusting their hearts; experiencing small symbolic indications that peace is growing, that love is flowering, that a new fragrance has come to their being, that their eyes are no longer full of dust, of the past. A tremendous clarity, transparency, and they know they are on the right path. There is no guide. And you will not meet anyone on the path to inquire how far the destination is.

It is a flight from the alone to the alone. But once a man finds a truth on his own, naturally he becomes aware that no organized religion is needed – it is a hindrance – that no priest, no mediators are needed; they will not allow you to reach the truth. Such a man, who has found the truth, becomes a master. The difference is subtle and has to be understood. The disciple is not a follower; the disciple has simply fallen in love. You don't call lovers followers. Something has clicked in his being, in the presence of someone.

It is not a question of the disciple being convinced about his ideas. It is not a conviction, it is not a conversion; it is a transformation. The moment a seeker comes in contact with one who has found, a great synchronicity happens. Looking into each other's eyes, without saying a word, something that they have never dreamed of suddenly becomes the greatest reality.

It is not belief because belief is always in the philosophies, in the ideologies. It is not faith because faith is about fictions for which no one can find an argument or evidence; it is trust. What relates the master to the disciple is trust. Trust is the highest flowering of love. And how can love make anyone a slave? The very fact that it is love that joins the master and the disciple is enough indication that the master will prepare every possibility for your freedom; otherwise he will be betraying love, and no master can betray love.

Love is the ultimate reality. The master has to fulfill it in his actions, his words, his relations, his silences. Whatever he does, he has to fulfill only one thing: that is his love. And a person groping in the dark, a disciple, has come to him. Only a priest, a politician can exploit him. Both the priest and the politician are in search of followers. The politician and the priest are agreed on one point, that they need followers; only then can they become someone. They have divided their territories: the politician has taken the mundane world and the priest the spiritual. Between the two of them, they have made the whole of humanity slaves. They have destroyed everyone's freedom.

The greatest contribution has come from a few masters who managed not only their own freedom but also the freedom of those who loved them. It is simply inconceivable: If you love me, how can I enslave you? If you love me, I will rejoice only in your freedom. When I see you opening your wings into the sky toward the unknown, the far away, the mysterious... That will be my joy; not that you are tethered to a certain dogma, creed, cult, religion, philosophy. These are all different names of chains, manufactured by different kinds of people. But their purpose is the same.

The West has not known masters, it has known popes, prophets, saviors, saints. It is absolutely unaware that there is a dimension it has missed; that dimension is the most valuable dimension. And because the West has missed it, a great misunderstanding has arisen out of it.

It happens...

You know the beautiful parable of Aesop: a fox is trying, jumping as hard as possible, to reach the beautiful, ripe grapes hanging just above his head. But his jump is smaller than the height of the grapes. Tired, perspiring, having fallen many times, he looks around to see if anyone is watching.

A small rabbit, hiding in a small bush, was watching. This was dangerous; this rabbit would spread the news all over. The fox walked away from the grapes. The rabbit followed and asked, "Uncle, just one question. What happened? Why couldn't you reach the grapes?"

The fox was very angry. He said, "I suspected, the moment I saw you, that you were going to create rumors about me. I have not chosen to take those grapes because they are not ripe. And if I hear anyone talking about those grapes, I will kill you, because you are the only witness."

It is a small parable, but it contains immense meaning: that which you cannot reach you start condemning – the grapes are not ripe.

You are asking, "To the Western world the terms 'freedom' and 'the master' are virtually mutually exclusive; for those who have met you this is wildly inaccurate. How do you redefine 'freedom' and 'the master' for the Western understanding?" The word *master* creates confusion. It gives you the idea that you have become a slave and someone has become a master of you. In the East, the word is used in the sense that you have become master of yourself, that you are no longer a slave, that you have attained freedom. Different languages, grown in different climates by different people, different experiences, are bound to create such kinds of confusion.

To be master of oneself has never been a goal in the Western consciousness; it has always been how to conquer others, how to be a master of others. It is difficult to translate many Eastern words into the Western language. The same difficulty is there if you want to translate quantum physics into Eastern languages; you will not find the words because before language comes in, the experience has to be there. Experience creates language.

If you try, very funny things are bound to happen. The Eastern word for master is *acharya*. The word *acharya* means one who lives his life authentically, according to his own consciousness and awareness. And if you come close to such a person, what can he give you? – being with him, you will learn only one thing: how to live in freedom, awareness, in deep integrity and dignity. We are using the word *master* for acharya.

The word *disciple* is more fortunate because the Eastern word *shishya* and the word *disciple* have exactly the same meaning – for different reasons, but the meanings are the same. The disciple is one who is trying to learn something. The root meaning of the word *disciple* is the same as the root meaning of the word *discipline*. It means, preparing yourself to learn, to understand. It is perfectly good as it is; it can be used.

As far as the word *master* is concerned: the disciple has just fallen in love with the man and wants to learn the same freedom, the same sincerity, the same integrity, the same height of consciousness. The question of surrender does not arise and the question of belief does not arise. In the presence of the master, in the climate of the master, disciples start growing into new dimensions; which they did not know they were carrying within themselves as potential.

The master does not give them anything except his love. And that too it cannot be said that he gives. It is simply showering, just the way the sun showers its rays on all the flowers, the birds, the animals; whoever comes close to the master is showered with love.

If you are searching, if you are ready to learn, if you are not already learned, if you are not already prejudiced; if you are not already faithful, if you have not sold your soul already to some theology, to some religion, to some ideology, then just being close to the master, something starts transpiring. It is a transmission of the lamp. That's how it has been known in the East: a transmission of light from one heart, which has come to its own fire, to another heart which is groping in darkness.

Just coming closer… Think of two candles, one lit and one unlit, coming closer and closer. A moment comes when you will be suddenly amazed – both candles are lit. The flame has jumped to the other candle. Just a certain proximity… Love creates that proximity, and the flame jumps from one heart to another heart. There is no question of anyone surrendering, there is no question of anyone believing.

But your question is significant because even in the East you will not ordinarily find the master I am defining. The East has fallen deep into darkness. The days of Gautam Buddha are no longer a reality but just a beautiful memory, a dream that perhaps happened or perhaps someone dreamed.

One morning a great king, Prasenjita, came to Gautam Buddha. He had in one of his hands a beautiful lotus flower and in the other hand one of the most precious diamonds of those days. He had come because his wife was persistent: "When Gautam Buddha is here, you waste your time with idiots, talking about unnecessary things."

She had been going to Gautam Buddha from her very childhood; then she got married. Prasenjita had no inclination of that kind but because she was so insistent he said, "It is worth at least one visit to go and see what kind of man this is." But he was a man of very great ego, so he took out the most precious diamond from his treasure to present to Gautam Buddha. He did not want to go there just as an ordinary man. Everyone had to know… In fact he wanted everyone to know: "Who is greater – Gautam Buddha or Prasenjita?" That diamond was so precious that many fights had happened, wars had happened over it.

His wife laughed and she said, "You are absolutely unaware of the man I'm taking you to. It is better that you take a flower rather than a stone to present to him."

He could not understand, but he said, "There is no harm, I can take both. Let us see."

When he reached there, he offered his diamond, which he was carrying in one of his hands. Buddha said simply, "Drop it!" Naturally, what can you do? He dropped it. He thought that perhaps his wife was right. In the other hand he was carrying the lotus, and as he tried to offer the lotus, Buddha said, "Drop it!"

He dropped that too and became a little afraid. The man seems to be insane, but ten thousand disciples… And he stood there thinking that the people must be thinking he is stupid. Buddha said the third time, "Don't you listen to me? Drop it!!"

Prasenjita said, "He is really gone. Now I have dropped the diamond, I have dropped the lotus; now I don't have anything."

And at that very moment, Sariputta, an old disciple of Gautam Buddha, started laughing. His laughter turned Prasenjita toward him, and he asked him, "Why are you laughing?"

He said, "You don't understand the language. He is not saying drop the diamond, he is not saying drop the lotus. He is saying drop yourself, drop the ego. You can have the diamond and you can have the lotus but drop the ego. Don't take it back."

Those were beautiful days. Suddenly a new sky opened to Prasenjita. He dropped himself at Gautam Buddha's feet in utter humbleness, and he never left. He became part of the great caravan that used to follow Gautam Buddha. He forgot all about his kingdom, forgot about everything. The only thing that remained was this beautiful man, this tremendous grace, this invisible magnetism, these eyes and this silence. And he was gripped by all this.

It is not a question of belief. It is not a question of conversion, argumentation, it is a question of the highest quality of love. It is rare to find a master today, and there are many pretenders. One of the things that can be said about the pretenders is that you can recognize them immediately. The moment they ask you to believe in anything, the moment they ask you to follow a certain rule, regulation, the moment they ask you to have faith in them, to never doubt, never question, have indubitable faith – these are the indications of the pretenders. Wherever you find these pretenders, escape from the place as fast as you can.

But these people are all over the world, not only in the West but in the East too. It is very rare that you come across a master who gives you dignity, who gives you love, who gives you freedom; who does not create any bondage for you, and who does not make any contract, and who does not want you to be a shadow of him.

He wants you to be yourself. The moment you find a man like this, the greatest moment of your life has arrived. Don't miss it. Pretenders are many, but authentic masters are immensely rare.

It is unfortunate of our age, of our times, that we have forgotten a certain dimension completely, and not only in the West. In the West they never discovered it, but in the East we discovered it and lost it. And if there are no more masters who have attained their ultimate potential, who have become a god unto themselves, then it is very difficult for disciples who are groping in darkness, in blindness, in all kinds of diversions, to find their own dignity, their own self.

My effort here is not to create disciples – that is just the preface – but to create masters, as many masters as possible. The world immensely, urgently, needs many people of awareness, of love, of freedom, of sincerity. Only these people can create a certain spiritual atmosphere that can prevent this world from being destroyed by the suicidal forces; those forces are very powerful, but not more powerful than love.

> Osho,
> Is it possible for a master to take the pain of his disciples in helping them to understand their enlightenment, and in the process cause his body to become sick?

It *is* "...possible for a master to take the pain of his disciples in helping them to understand their enlightenment, and in the process cause his body to become sick." Theoretically it is possible, but practically it is not. When I say, theoretically it is possible, I mean, there is no barrier to its happening. But the problem is that the moment the master becomes enlightened, his grip over his own body comes to the minimum. Most of the people who have become enlightened have died either immediately or within a few minutes or a few hours. The experience is so great, and the shock to the system of the body is unabsorbable. Out of thousands, perhaps a few have survived. And there are reasons why they survived.

But they suffered tremendously from sicknesses. These are not sicknesses taken from disciples, these are sicknesses intrinsic to the experience of enlightenment. Enlightenment means suddenly becoming aware that you are not the body, and a distance is created. The old identity that, "I am the body," was keeping you together. You start falling apart. Mostly, the shock is so much that people have died.

But it has not been discussed because to discuss it... People have thought, "Rarely does someone become interested in enlightenment. And if you tell them that enlightenment means that you will have to suffer afterward, then anyone will simply say, 'Then why should we become enlightened? We are good as we are.'" That part has not been disclosed. But I don't want to keep anything secret because I know my people can die celebrating, laughing, rejoicing. Death is not a fear to them.

Just today, Anubuddha was massaging me, because my hand has been in terrible pain for many weeks. He said, "You seem to be aware of every pain point, wherever I touch. I have never seen anyone..." And he is our best bodyworker – very sensitive, very alert, very loving, and very successful.

His work is that ordinary people, who are identified with the body, should become more aware, if there is some pain or not. "But you are not identified with the body. Then how do you become aware? And so minutely?" Because I go on telling him, "This is the right point, this is where you should work." No one may have told him before, because you don't tell the bodyworker – he is the expert, not you. And I go on telling him, "You missed a point just now." He has to go back and he finds it. So he was asking... I told him, "After the massage." But then I forgot, so I said, "It is better to tell it now."

Once you are enlightened, a distance starts creating itself between you and your identity with the body. That does not mean that death is inevitable. It only means that now you will not be able to control the body in the same way you used to control it in the past. But it does not prevent your awareness; it gives you more awareness. You become a witness. Just as he is working on my body… For him it is only guesswork, whether some point is a pain point or not. To me it is not guesswork; I am watching from within that it is a pain point.

Awareness comes with enlightenment, but awareness brings its own problems. Ramakrishna died of cancer, Maharishi Raman died of cancer, J. Krishnamurti suffered with a terrific migraine for forty years continuously. The migraine was so much, twenty-four hours a day, that he said, "Sometimes I feel like hitting my head against the wall and crushing it. The pain is unbearable."

Your question is created by the disciples because disciples cannot understand: "J. Krishnamurti suffering from migraine? No, it cannot be. There must be some hidden reason. He must have taken the migraines of many, many disciples." And then they feel satisfied – a right explanation has been found.

Ramakrishna suffered from cancer, and his disciples go on writing that he had taken the cancer of some disciple. But even if you take the cancer of some disciple, that disciple is not going to become enlightened, so what is the point? The poor fellow was suffering with cancer. At least there was something – you have taken even that.

In fact, if your body sicknesses can be taken by enlightened people, you will not think of becoming enlightened. It is better to be unenlightened and let the enlightened people take care of your sicknesses, and meanwhile enjoy – unless accidentally you become enlightened because then you cannot go back. That's what I mean when I say that theoretically it is possible. That needs some explanation.

You have two words in English, *sympathy* and *empathy*. Sympathy is when you feel superficially: someone is miserable, someone is sick and you feel sympathetic. You sit by their side, cry a little and then go on to the movies. What else to do? Your eyes are cleaner, and now… Empathy means that you become so one with the person that sicknesses or anything can be transferred.

It happened in Ramakrishna's life…

And I take Ramakrishna's story because others are very ancient, maybe just parables. Ramakrishna's was just in the last century. And there were hundreds of eye-witness reports and not a single denial of the fact, what had happened.

Ramakrishna was travelling in a boat on the Ganges crossing to the other side; a few disciples were with him. Suddenly he started saying, "Don't beat me, don't beat me, it hurts! I say don't beat me!" And tears started coming to his eyes.

The disciples said, "But no one is beating you. Is this a new game you are playing? We have seen many things you have done, but this is absolutely new."

But he was really crying and weeping and shouting, "Help me, save me! They will kill me!"

The disciples said, "But what should we do? Because no one is beating you, no one is killing you."

When they reached the other shore, they found a sudra – one of the untouchables, the lowest Hindu category of people, who are not treated like human beings – was being beaten by his master, his owner because he had made some mistake. That man was half naked, and there was blood on his back and lines from the lashes.

Ramakrishna's people suddenly took away his shirt, and they could not believe it – the back of the sudra and Ramakrishna's back were both exactly the same: blood oozing… Ramakrishna said, "I was telling you, but you did not listen. They were beating me."

Then they looked at that man who was lying almost unconscious. He was a sudra, but for Ramakrishna this stupid and criminal categorization of society did not exist. That sudra used to come to Ramakrishna, he was one of his devotees. Even Ramakrishna's own people used to say, "This sudra should not be allowed."

Ramakrishna said, "Then I should not be allowed either because I don't see any difference. Everyone is born a sudra. Then if he becomes enlightened he can be a brahmin. If he becomes a warrior, he can be a kshatriya. If he becomes a businessman, he can be a vaishya. And if he remains in the lower kind of work – shoemaker, butcher, fisherman – then he should be a sudra. But as far as birth is concerned, everyone is born a sudra. It is the lifestyle and the raising of consciousness that can make a difference."

But this is not the definition of the Hindus, it is not the definition of the *Manusmriti*, the Hindu holy scripture that divides society into four classes. According to the scripture, everyone is born as a brahmin or as a kshatriya or as a sudra or as a vaishya. It is not action, it is birth that decides. Neither Mahavira, nor Gautam Buddha, nor Ramakrishna believed it.

There was so much disturbance that Ramakrishna said to the sudra, "When no one is here… By the evening all these people go away" – he used to live outside Kolkata, near the Ganges – "and you can come then. You live on the other side, so if you cannot come, I can come. We can have a little chit-chat. And you play the flute so beautifully; you can play the flute."

The man was immensely in love with Ramakrishna and Ramakrishna showered his whole heart on him. What happened on that day was empathy: so much at-one-ment that the same experience starts happening to both people. That's why I say that theoretically it is possible. And once in a while it has happened, not because consciously enlightened people take other people's sicknesses and diseases on themselves, but accidentally, just like in the case of Ramakrishna.

The reality is that the enlightened person is somehow pulling together his body. He has lost all desires, all ambitions. He has no impetus for tomorrow. He has no reason even to breathe one more breath. So suddenly a great gap starts growing. Awareness becomes more and more clean and clear, he can witness his own body from inside, but a witness is only a witness; he cannot do anything.

So all these stories that are being spread around, that some master took away a disease, are just an explanation to protect the so-called master. But how can a master fall sick? In fact, the master can fall sick more than anyone else because he has separated himself from his body. The old clinging, the old grip is gone. Now it is a miracle that he goes on living for a few days. Hence he lives in a very calculated way.

You can see me: I live in such a calculated way that all that I do is speak to you. I have saved all my breath just to give you a sense of the eternal and an experience of the ultimate. And mostly I am asleep. You cannot find a more lazy man in the world. Just today my secretary, Hasya, was saying, "I am sending the information to *The Guinness Book of Records* that my master has four hundred books to his name." And she was asking me other things also. I wanted to tell her, but I thought it was better not to say, that the miracle is that this man sleeps almost twenty hours a day and has managed four hundred books. And he is the laziest man in the world – about that you can be certain; no one can compete with me. You can send a challenge, to see if there is anyone.

Just a few days ago, a sannyasin had asked, that when I look at her she feels so loved, can I wink my eye? I said, "In my whole life I have not winked my eye. I can close both my eyes or I can open both." In fact, I am not doing the opening and closing, it happens on its own. But I don't think that it can happen on its own that one remains closed and one open. That is not possible. I tried, sitting in my dark room, that perhaps… But each time either both are open or both are closed. And I am not doing anything, they are going on their own!

Then she said, "At least you can move your big toe." I said, "It is possible – theoretically possible, but practically impossible. I have never done such a thing in my life. At this stage, now, to start moving the toe will be too childish. You know perfectly well, I don't move my leg." That is the difficulty poor Anubuddha has while massaging, because I don't move. I have told him, "You can do anything you want, but don't ask me… Just don't say, 'Do this, do that.' That I cannot do. If you can exercise for me, good."

My grandfather was very interested in all kinds of gymnastics and he was always telling me to exercise. I said, "For what? Everyone dies, whether you exercise or not. And unnecessarily getting tired before entering your grave… Why not rest fully? Slip into your grave!"

He said, "You talk nonsense. If you exercise, you can live a few years longer."

I said, "For what? To exercise more?" It is a strange idea: live a few years more, and for what? – to exercise. I dropped it.

He said, "You are incurable."

Before he was dying I said to him, "Look, I have told you: exercise or no exercise, everyone has to die. When the ultimate destiny comes on its own, why unnecessarily walk to it?"

He said, "At least at the time of my death don't disturb me!"

Now something nonserious…

A drunk is hauled in off the street and taken before the magistrate, who asks him to explain his drunken behavior.

"Well," says the drunk, "I had ten bottles of whiskey in my cellar and was told by my wife to empty the contents of each and every bottle down the sink, or I'd be in trouble.

"So I withdrew the cork from the first bottle and poured the contents down the sink, with the exception of one glass, which I drank.

"I took the cork from the second bottle and did likewise with it, except for one glass, which I drank.

"I then withdrew the cork from the third bottle and poured the whiskey down the sink, which I drank.

"I pulled the cork from the fourth bottle down the sink, and poured the bottle from the cork of the next and drank one sink out of it and threw the rest down the glass.

"I pulled the sink out of the next glass and poured the cork down the bottle. Then I corked the sink with the glasses, bottled the drink and drank the pour.

"When I had everything emptied, I steadied the house with my hand, counted the glasses, corks, bottles and sinks with the other hand, which were twenty-nine, and as the house came by, I counted them again and finally had all the houses in one bottle, which I drank.

"I'm not under the affluence of alcohol, as some tinkle peep I am. I'm not half as thunk as you might drink.

"I fool so feelish, I don't know who is me, and the drunker I stand here, the longer I get."

# 17

# Buddhas Trying to Be Buddhas

Osho,
The other day, when you said we look like Gautam Buddhas when we laugh, a big let-go happened deep inside me and I cried for a long time. Today I feel very fragile and the crying often comes back. I cannot even meditate. Also there is some fear. Can you tell me what is happening? Also, is there an Australian joke?

When anyone has realized his buddhahood, his enlightenment, his immortality, the first thing that has happened is laughter. Laughter at himself because he was seeking and searching for millions of years for something that he himself was.

You can seek the other, but you cannot seek yourself. You can separate from the other, but you cannot separate from yourself. There is a possibility of distance between you and the other, but there is no possibility of distance between you and you. This is one part: one realizes the hilarious situation that buddhas are trying to be buddhas. Naturally a great laughter arises.

It is also true from the other side: if a great laughter arises for any reason or no reason, suddenly your mind stops, your time stops. Those are the basic preconditions needed to experience your buddha nature – of course, only for a moment because it is not through awareness that you have attained buddhahood, but through laughter. Laughter gives you both keys, as if for a single moment in the middle of the night the sun rises and all is light.

Laughter has a tremendous spiritual value. No religion has accepted it. In fact, all religions have condemned it. I can understand their condemnation: they don't want you all to be buddhas. They don't want you even to have a glimpse of who you are because once the glimpse has happened you cannot remain in the old, miserable agony, anguish. You know that if time and the mind stop, you are more than you can ask for. Utter serenity, peacefulness, blissfulness, love, sensitivity and a sense of belonging to the universe; not just as an accident, but as an essential part. The religions have taught people to be serious. It is a very cunning strategy. It is preventing you from having glimpses which ultimately culminate in the realization of your own self.

The moment you are a buddha, you are free from all religions, all scriptures, all dogmas. Sheer freedom and love; a fresh breeze that never goes stale, a fragrance that goes on and on and on from eternity to eternity; a dance in which you are not alone, and the whole existence participates: the birds sing on their instruments, the trees bring flowers of different colors. That is their way of contributing. Poor trees, but their flowers are more precious than any stones, than even the Kohinoor, because the Kohinoor is a dead stone and a roseflower is a living reality. The whole existence in some way or other contributes to your dance.

Your question is, "The other day when you said we look like Gautam Buddhas when we laugh..." I did not say you *look* like Gautam Buddhas, I said you *are* Gautam Buddhas when you laugh. Just look at the cunningness of the mind, its cowardliness. It cannot roar like a lion and say, "I am the buddha!" At the most it can say, "I think, perhaps...I may be a buddha, in some future life."

You are saying, "...a big let-go happened deep inside me and I cried for a long time." That was beautiful. Some window opened, perhaps for a split second, and you realized what you can be and what you have become. You can be a buddha, which is your reality and you have become a beggar, which is not your reality. Gautam Buddha used to say to his disciples, "I will take away all that you are not and I will give you all that you are, and the whole transformation is complete."

Tears came. Tears have a beauty if they come out of a joyful moment, out of a let-go. Then they are almost like flowers, dewdrops shining in the morning sun. They cleanse you of all the rubbish, of all the garbage, of all the crap that your so-called religions, professors, preachers – and there are all kinds of peddlers around – have imposed on you. For a moment you slipped out of their prison and you saw the full-moon night – just for a moment.

The experience was so precious, you could give your whole life for that experience. You don't have anything else to give. Life already belongs to the eternal life; it is not yours. But you can shower your gratitude, your prayer, your thankfulness with tears. Words are very small; they cannot say what tears can say. Tears are silent, but still say something immense. If they come out of joy, they are the most precious experience. They will cleanse not only your outer eyes, they will cleanse your inner eye too. They will give you a clarity.

You also felt "...fragile and the crying often comes back." Certainly it is a great shock to realize, even for a moment, that you are a buddha. It is a shock because you cannot believe it yourself. You a buddha, smoking cigarettes and a buddha? But I don't see there is any problem. And certainly a buddha can smoke cigarettes in a totally different way than you smoke. You smoke because of your tensions. He can smoke just out of playfulness. But he avoids it mostly because it contains poison – and why poison the air when it is free and available? That poison in cigarettes, nicotine, is not free; it has to be paid for. It is a simple understanding.

Theoretically there is no problem, but practically no buddha is going to smoke cigarettes. It doesn't look right. Just visualize the statue of Gautam Buddha with a cigarette in his hand, smoke coming out of his nose... No, practically it is not possible. But even if theoretically it is possible, then a buddha will do anything with the grace of a buddha, in an enlightened way. You may be doing the same thing, but it is the same only on the surface. Inside, between the buddha and you there is an unbridgeable distance.

A king went to see a master; the master lived in a deep forest. The king met a man and asked him, "Where can I find the way to the master's place?" The man simply showed him with his finger, did not say anything, and went on chopping wood. The king went to the master's place and he was surprised – it was the same man who had been chopping wood, sitting on his throne wearing the robe of a master.

For a moment the king hesitated, but then he said, "I had come for other questions. This question I have never thought about, but it has become the most important one now: Are you the same man who was chopping wood?"

He said, "I am the same man, and now I am going to chop you! But I chop only that part which is false, pseudo, and leave your reality – pure, simple, natural. Are you ready?"

The king said, "I have not come to be chopped. I have some questions."

The master said, "All those questions are futile. First say it – are you ready? You see my axe?"

The king thought, "The man seems to be mad." He said, "I will think about it."

The master said, "These things are not to be thought about. Either you get it or you don't; it is just a 'click'. You have not looked into my eyes. You are so afraid, shrunken, closed, you have not allowed my love to enter you; otherwise you would have thought, 'This idea of chopping is a great idea. A man of such love, understanding and such realization is not going to kill me. And if he wants to kill me, it is better to be killed by such a man than by an unknown, dark death.'"

The king said, "I will come again. You are making me afraid." He never went back again.

When such moments happen in your life they make you fragile because it is a turning point. The old way is at risk. All that you have been is finished and you don't know what is ahead, what is going to happen. That is the fragileness, the hesitation: to choose the past or to choose the future. Those who choose the past choose their graves. Those who choose the future are the adventurers, the seekers. They also feel fragile, but in spite of their fragileness one thing is certain, that going back is simply stupid. You have not found anything, what is the point of going back? Going ahead there may be some new realization, a new light, a new being.

And you are saying that tears are coming back again and again. Those tears are coming again and again because you have missed a great opportunity. The first tears had a different quality; they were flowers of joy. The second layer of tears is just a deep hurt, a wound that you missed.

You are saying, "I cannot even meditate." For the same reason, because in meditation what I said may become clear to you, and again the fragileness… "Also there is some fear." You are asking, "Can you tell me what is happening? Also, is there an Australian joke?" Much is happening. You have just to become accustomed to such moments. No harm is going to happen to you. You are doing all the harm that you can do. You will not be wounded; on the contrary, all your wounds will become roses. You will not die; on the contrary, you will enter the life stream of eternal being. It is a tremendous opportunity, the doors are open. Don't hesitate.

There is a Sufi story…

There have not been more than five or six enlightened women because women have been engaged in forcing the man to become enlightened. They completely forgot that they also have to become enlightened. But out of those five or six women, one of the most beautiful is Rabiya al-Adabiya, a Sufi woman. She was very courageous, of the quality of Bodhidharma – almost dangerously ferocious for those who used to come to her as disciples.

For the master it is a question of urgency. For you, you can postpone: Tomorrow, the day after tomorrow, what is the hurry? But for the master it is a question of absolute urgency because this is his last life. He will not be coming back again. Once you have become enlightened, you start losing grip of the body; slowly, slowly all ties with the body are broken. You will be here in the trees, in the sunrays, in the ocean waves, in the stars, but not as an entity. Unlimited, you will become oceanic.

The master is in a hurry because no one knows, tomorrow the master may have to leave the body. All attachment with the body which was keeping it alive is gone, and there is not going to be another life. For you there are many lives ahead, you can go on postponing.

Another seeker who finally became a master in his own right was Hassan. He used to sit before the mosque and pray for hours, and the prayer was always the same. The prayer was, "God, open your doors. I have been waiting long and I have been praying long. Open the doors so I can enter you and dissolve into you." The whole city was aware: "This man is a little crazy. Mohammedans do prayer five times a day, but this man seems to be doing prayer almost the whole day. And the prayer is not much, just one: 'Open the door.'"

One day Rabiya was passing, and she hit on Hassan's head. She said, "You idiot! The door is open, but you are so engaged in your prayer that you cannot see it. Stop praying and enter, the door is open!"

The hit… A silent moment… He looked and certainly the door was open. The same mystic became a great master. He used to tell this story again and again, saying: "A single hit from Rabiya brought me home. But my God, that woman is really strong! She stopped my mind, my prayer and then I laughed and thanked her, 'Your grace is great, your compassion is great because thousands of people pass here, but no one has said to me that the door is open.'"

You know, Jesus had the same fallacy. He needed a Rabiya al-Adabiya. His statement is, "Knock and the door shall be opened unto you. Ask and you shall be answered. Seek and you shall find." Rabiya would have given him some good slaps, "What kind of nonsense are you involved in? The doors are open, there is no need to knock. Just enter." Once you have entered, questions and answers all disappear. And once you have entered, you have found what was always yours; there is no question of searching and finding.

If you go on allowing yourself, relaxing in these silent moments, in these gaps which are really the doors, much, so much is going to happen. What has happened to you is just the beginning. But you are caught. You cannot go back; you have to explore what is ahead. What did you have in the past except misery, agony, anxiety, anguish, fear? – all kinds of dark forces. You don't have anything in your past. Realize it with totality, so that you can move when a new door opens. And every day the window opens to someone or other or sometimes to many.

And finally you are asking, "Also, is there an Australian joke?" Never heard of it. Jokes need a little intelligence. That land of kangaroos is itself a joke! But I inquired of all my Australian sannyasins – many are here. "Manage something. Create, be inventive." Many jokes came, but they were just wishy-washy. Just one joke I liked…

Swampy Marsh, the young Australian father-to-be, is waiting anxiously outside the maternity ward where his wife is having their first baby.

He is pacing the floor when the nurse comes out and says, "You have a little boy, Mr. Marsh, but you had better go and have a cup of coffee because there might be another one."

Swampy turns a little pale and leaves. Sometime later he phones the hospital and is told that he is the father of twins, but the nurse cautions, "There is another on the way, so call back later."

At that Swampy decides that coffee is not strong enough so he goes to a bar and has some beer. When he phones the hospital again he is told that the third baby has arrived and a fourth is on the way. White-faced, he stumbles to the bar and orders a double scotch.

Twenty minutes later, he tries to phone again, but he is so drunk that he dials the wrong number and gets the recorded cricket score. When they pick him off the floor the recording is still going strong: "The score is ninety-six all out," says the voice, "and the last one was a duck."

> Osho,
> Although I'm not yet one of your sannyasins officially, perhaps you might still answer this question. The other morning you told us we needed only to stop the chattering within us to come home. My experience is different: I can drop into silence, but then I still feel some layers separating me from "home." Could you talk about these layers and how to get through them? Twice in my life I "came home" accidentally. But whenever I look for home, my effort is in vain.

The first part of your question is also important – not only for you but for others too. You are saying, "Although I am not yet one of your sannyasins officially, perhaps you might still answer this question." A sannyasin need not be one officially. Any seeker, anyone in search of truth is a sannyasin. And a sannyasin need not be *mine*. A sannyasin is not a follower, but at the most a fellow traveler. If you are seeking and searching for the truth, the meaning and significance of life, it is enough.

You are saying, "The other morning you told us we needed only to stop the chattering within us to come home. My experience is different: I can drop into silence, but then I still feel some layers separating me from 'home.'" That does not mean your experience is different, it only means you can fall into silence superficially, so the chattering mind – the thing that is on the very surface – stops. But there are the subconscious mind, the unconscious mind, the collective unconscious mind, the cosmic unconscious mind, about which you are not aware. When I say silence I mean all four. When you say silence you think only about the first, because you are aware only of the first.

But it is good. People even find it difficult to stop the first layer of the mind. You are fortunate, the first layer is happening on its own. But your trouble is that you have taken it for granted that the first chattering layer is the whole mind. It is not. There is the subconscious mind…

Just a few years ago scientists were trying a very strange experiment. They succeeded, but the experiment was stopped because it was dangerous. The experiment was that you are watching a movie; that is on the first layer. And just in between, very quick flashes and a whisper – unless you are absolutely aware you will not see or hear them – are put on the screen: "You are very thirsty. You need a Coke."

Strangely, no one read them. People were watching the picture. It was such a subtle penetration into their subconscious, but the result was clear. On that day no other drink was sold in the movie house other than Coke. Everyone was feeling thirsty and wanted Coke.

Many other experiments were done, and they were all successful in reaching the subconscious layer. But then a problem arose: if this method falls into the hands of the politicians, just as atomic energy and nuclear weapons have fallen, this can prove even more dangerous. A whole country can be sold things which are useless or dangerous. They can be given ideas and they will think they are *theirs*, but they are from the Communist Party or some other party which is in power. And then it will be difficult to remove that party from power because it has infiltrated the minds of people continuously for five years through all the movies, television, radio with only one thing: "This is the right party. This is my party."

It can have even more dangerous implications; hence it was stopped, as far as it is officially known. But I don't think that it has been stopped; it cannot be. It is such a significant weapon that each political party, each religion will try to poison you through your subconscious. And you will believe that this is your idea.

I have done experiments on my own – more simple, not that sophisticated; I had no instruments. I used to live with a friend and he had a very intelligent younger brother who became very loving toward me. We used to go for walks. At that time that experiment was being done in Soviet Russia, in America. I thought, "Why not do it and see whether it works?" I hypnotized the boy.

To hypnotize anyone is very simple. Just tell the person to gaze at some light – a light bulb – so that his eyes become tired, and tell him, "Do not close your eyes until you cannot manage to keep them open." And the hypnotist goes on saying to the person, "Your eyes are becoming very tired, sleep seems to be coming." The person has been told, "Fight as long as you can fight. Don't close your eyes."

On the one hand he is fighting – that is making him more tired – and on the other hand the hypnotist is saying to him, "Your eyes feel very tired, very, very tired. Your face feels sleepy. Your body is relaxed. I don't think you can remain awake for more than one minute. I will count up to sixty seconds and then you will be deeply asleep. Just remember one thing: you will be able to listen to me even in your deep sleep, and to no one else. So close the doors and keep just a single communication line." Within sixty seconds, after two or three minutes of gazing, the person falls into a very strange sleep.

Hypnosis, the very word means sleep, but with a difference: not ordinary sleep, but deliberate sleep, created sleep. And because there is only one line of communication, the birds may go on singing and the person will not hear. If someone else wants to talk to him, he will not hear. Only the hypnotist has the approach. He has kept a line open for himself.

I said to the boy, "I am going to mark a cross on the corner of the pillow you sleep on. And tomorrow at twelve o'clock you have to kiss that cross." Absolutely irrational – no one kisses his pillow!

The next day I and his brother waited to see what would happen. As the time came close – 11:00, 11:50 – I took the pillow and locked it in my suitcase. And the boy was becoming very fidgety, very nervous, going again and again close to the suitcase, but it was locked. Finally, he fell to my feet and said, "Please open that suitcase."

I said, "For what?"

He said, "I don't know for what, but open it, otherwise I will die! I am suffocating. Something strange… I don't know."

I said, "Okay, I will open it."

It was just one minute before twelve. I opened the lock; he pulled the pillow out and kissed the pillow. No lover may have ever kissed it with such romance. And he felt very ashamed and embarrassed because two people were watching.

We asked him, "What is the matter?"

He said, "I don't know. Something in me was forcing me to kiss the pillow at the point of the cross."

Now, if your subconscious mind goes on working – and you know it goes on working. When you are asleep it is not chattering, it is dreaming. That's why in the morning you cannot relate all your dreams, only the last ones, the tail end of the dreams. You may be amazed to know that in eight hours sleep you dream for six hours. Not continuously – one or two minutes' sleep, then again you dream – but all together six hours of dreaming. How much do you remember in the morning? That too only for a few seconds.

As you are coming out of the subconscious to the conscious, there is just a faint remembrance that you were dreaming. And within three minutes, exactly three minutes, you will forget all about it; otherwise life would become very difficult. The whole day the mind chatters. That is one part of the mind; it needs rest. In the night it rests, then the other part starts dreaming. If you remembered those six hours in the morning too, you would go mad. Psychoanalysts have not yet reached the collective unconscious, neither to the unconscious, nor the cosmic unconscious – that is far away. So you have a four-layer system.

It is possible that you have come to silences which you feel are your home; they are not. Chattering has stopped, and the difficulty is that there is no communication between the conscious mind and the subconscious or the unconscious. There is no communication at all. Only in deep meditation, slowly, slowly does communication happen.

It is the experience of thousands of my meditators that first they come with a great smile, a Jimmy Carter smile, saying that they have been able to be silent, no chattering. And I have said, "Just continue. Soon another deeper layer will surface."

Then they start dreaming – awake. Now a certain communication can be made. And when dreaming disappears, the unconscious, the dreamless sleep, is also not without its own seed thoughts. It is just like seeds under the earth. You don't see them, but they are working. Soon there will be sprouts and flowers and trees. The unconscious is your underworld, underground.

It has happened in many courts that murderers have simply denied that they have murdered. No court listens to them because all the evidence is there – the witnesses are there, the person has been murdered. But I have a different attitude. My opinion is that they murdered the person in an unconscious state. You are asking them questions in a conscious state and there is no communication between the two states. They are not lying – as it is taken in all the courts of the world that they are lying – but they are saying authentically that they have not murdered. Certainly they have not murdered consciously, but unconsciously. They cannot remember it.

The final stage is the cosmic unconscious, which becomes clear to you only when your awareness reaches the very depth of your being, the very center of your being.

So don't think that your experience is different. And don't think that this experience is coming home because once you come home you cannot go out of the home again. In fact, you are in the home already, you don't "come." It is only a question of deepening awareness, so that you start feeling, "My God, I have been searching for my home and my home is within me." Just don't get mistaken that homes are outside you, and that you go in and you come out. The home we are talking about is inside you, so wherever you go the home goes with you. You cannot leave it anywhere because you are not separate from it.

So coming home means only a glimpse, and a very superficial glimpse. If you meditate – and intensively – on awareness, you will not come home, you will find you are at home. And a little laughter at yourself will arise, "I have always been here and I have been searching all over the world."

There is no need of any search and there is no need to go anywhere – to Mecca, Jerusalem, Kashi, Moscow. You have to close your eyes and intensify and sharpen your awareness. As you go more and more inside, it sharpens by itself.

Something serious…

Shimon Peres, the prime minister of Israel, Rajiv Gandhi, the prime minister of India, and Ronald Reagan from America are driving together to a conference when their car breaks down and they are forced to spend the night at a small motel.

"I'm sorry," says the clerk, "but we have only one room left and it's a double. But one of you can sleep in the barn. We will make it comfortable."

"No problem," says Rajiv Gandhi, "I will sleep there."

A short while later, the other two men are getting ready for bed, when there is a knock on the door. Gandhi is standing in the hallway.

"I'm sorry," he says, "but I can't sleep with a holy cow."

"So, I will sleep in the barn," says Shimon Peres and off he goes. A few minutes later, he is back.

"I'm sorry," he says, "but being Jewish, I can't sleep with a pig."

Ronald Reagan shrugs and says, "I guess I will sleep in the barn."

He leaves. Gandhi and Peres are just getting into bed, when they hear a knock at the door. They open it and standing there are the pig and the cow.

# 18

# Waiting Is a Great Meditation

Osho,
In the old days in Mumbai, even though I felt physically so close to you, you were so far away. Now sitting here with you in Buddha Hall with thousands of us, I feel you so intimately and personally, like I never did before. Have you dropped serious political talks and become more intimate and juicy? Your smile is happening more often than ever. Please comment.

In a very simple question and you have touched many implications. I would like to go into those implications because without understanding them your question cannot be answered sincerely and authentically. In those days in Mumbai you were certainly physically close, but that very physical closeness destroyed the possibility of a deeper closeness, where the heart meets the heart, and where the spirit dances with the spirit. It happens because if you are physically close, people start taking you for granted.

Now, no one can take me for granted, not even the prime minister of India. I live in seclusion, in isolation. It was possible in the old days for anyone to come to me at any time to ask any stupid question. You will be amazed if I tell you about all the incidents that used to happen.

I was traveling from Udaipur to Chittorgarh in Rajasthan. I was alone in the first-class compartment. Suddenly I felt someone massaging my feet.

I said, "Who are you and why are you unnecessarily disturbing my sleep?"

He said, "Keep quiet!"

I said, "This is strange. These are *my* feet."

He said, "Simply keep quiet. I am very angry and I am very frustrated because I am also coming from the Udaipur meditation camp. They did not allow me to massage your feet and those guys were always surrounding you, so I thought, 'Let us wait, because he will pass through Chittorgarh.' So I left ahead of you and I have been waiting here. Now no one can prevent me. And certainly I know that you are so loving, you will not prevent me."

I said, "I am loving and I don't want to prevent you, but you should also be compassionate toward me – tired after a seven-day camp. I had just fallen asleep."

But he wouldn't listen. For two hours continuously… I had to persuade him, "If you don't listen to me then I will have to pull the chain and call the conductor."

He said, "My God, I had never thought about that. You can do that?"

I said, "I have every birthright to protect myself, at least from people like you who can't see a simple thing: that I am tired and I don't want to talk, I want to sleep."

Just with this threat, he got off at a small station somewhere. But from the window he said, "At least touch my head."

I said, "You have tired me for two hours continuously massaging my feet, and now I have to massage your head!"

He said, "Do it, otherwise I will enter the compartment again."

I had to do it. He was very happy.

I was staying in a university campus, taking a meditation camp. In the afternoon when I was sleeping, I suddenly became aware that someone was walking on the roof. I opened my eyes and I saw a professor had removed a tile and was looking at me.

I said, "Hello! Why can't you come through the front door? Are you going to jump on me?"

He said, "They don't allow me entrance at the front door. They say you are asleep, and in fact you are not asleep, you are talking with me."

When people think they can approach, ask, inquire of me at any time… I will be available tomorrow, what is the hurry today? This taking me for granted creates the problem. You remain physically close but spiritually far away. It is difficult for me to make an effort for thousands of people separately to be spiritually close to me. And man's mind functions in a very strange way. If you get closer to him, he becomes afraid, he becomes more closed. If you want to open his heart, he becomes hard, he resists. The only thing possible was to tour around the world inviting my would-be people, and when they started arriving I closed myself in a dark cell, where there was no possibility of anyone reaching me.

Strangely enough, this has opened thousands of hearts. And because I am not making any effort to open their hearts, am not interested in opening their hearts, they have suddenly become open. There is nothing to be afraid of. Twice a day I am with you, you wait for me. Waiting in itself is a great meditation. Waiting in itself is the whole religiousness. Waiting for the unknown, waiting for the guest, waiting for the master – whatever form it takes, but waiting for the right season when you will also be blossoming is the whole inquiry and the search of man.

I could have come into the ashram as many times as possible – it is not far away. But I have not been in the office since 1974. I have never seen anything in the ashram except my room and the meeting place where I see you, where I talk. It is not a sermon, it is not a discourse, it is simply an outpouring of a heart who loves you and wants to reach you; who trusts you and wants to enter your deepest core, who wants to help you on the way.

And I don't come knowingly, because I don't want you to take me for granted. I want you to wait for me. Sometimes I disappear, I don't come. But even then you wait lovingly – perhaps tomorrow I will be coming, or the day after tomorrow. And those days of waiting are not without significance. They are as significant as the days when I am with you. I want you to be absolutely free of me, absolutely independent.

I don't impose any doctrine, cult, philosophy. I don't want followers. I simply want people who know freedom, who know love, who know the dignity of man, who know the peaks of awareness. Only those who know the peaks of awareness will be my friends, only those who go to the depths of love will be my friends.

I talk to give you hints, not forcing anything on you, but simply whispering in your ear. It is said that if you want a woman to hear you, you have to whisper to someone else. Don't talk directly, no one is going to hear you, but whisper to someone else. And it will be more perfect if you can find another woman. Whisper anything and your wife will hear it. I am simply whispering things to you which cannot be managed in words, in language, things which need to be understood only in the silences of the heart. Perhaps I come to you in a gesture or perhaps in the depths of the eyes.

Anand Murti, I have known you for almost twenty-five years. You were here in the ashram when I was away, you are here in the ashram now. I have never talked to you because I don't want to destroy the silence that is growing between me and you. I have not even said hello to you. And this is the same about everyone who is here.

There are a few more things. In the Mumbai days I was surrounded by Indians. Now, to be with Indians you have to be serious; otherwise they don't think you are a religious man. You will not believe me, that in the whole Indian history of ten thousand years there has not been a single Indian joke. Laughter is simply a foreigner. India does not even allow laughter a tourist visa.

You are saying, "In the old days in Mumbai, even though I felt physically so close to you, you were so far away. Now, sitting here with you in Buddha Hall with thousands of us, I feel you so intimately and personally." The reason is simply that now I am surrounded by my own people. They are not Indians, they are not Germans, they are not Americans. They don't have a religion, they don't have a race, they don't have a nation; they are purely individuals. It is a gathering of friends. It is because of this that you can feel me intimately and personally, although I don't know where you live in the ashram. I have never invited you even for a cup of tea.

In this way I am showing you what a spiritual relationship is. It does not depend on anything visible. It is purely invisible, an energy that transpires in hearts, that makes them aflame. And my people know in the deepest of their depths that they are part of this commune, part of me, and part of this universe. They have thrown away all limitations and have become citizens of the universe.

You say, "Osho, have you dropped serious political talks and become more intimate and juicy?" I am the same but the people around me have changed many times. In these past thirty-five years I have been working to raise the consciousness of humanity. Many people have come and left, and it has been always good because they emptied some space for better people. It is a strange experience, that those who have left me have always left places for a better quality of people. I have never been a loser.

There was a time... Because, accidentally, I was born into a Jaina family. Now, it is not my fault; you can call it unfortunate. But naturally because I was born into a certain religious group, they were the first people to surround me. When people started looking at me, asking me questions, feeling that something has happened in me, the first ones were bound to be Jainas because they were my relatives, they were my neighbors. It was obvious that they would be the first. Naturally their questions were concerned with Jainism, with Mahavira. You could not ask their questions; it would never occur to you that this also can be a relevant question.

I was staying with a Jaina family...

The father of the family was almost eighty years old and he had retired; according to the tradition that after seventy-five years you should retire. He had retired to a small hut outside the city. The family provided food, care, but he lived alone there chanting Jaina mantras, reading Jaina scriptures.

Someone gave him my first book, *The Path*. He was so impressed by the book that he could not believe it: "All my learning of the scriptures was futile, only this small book is enough. And the man who has written this book must be a saint; otherwise, how can he write such great truths?" When he heard that I was staying with his family – his son was very interested in me – he came to see me.

I said, "You unnecessarily walked for miles in your old age. You could have given a message, a phone call. I could have come to you; your son has a car, there is no problem."

He said, "No, I wanted... To me this is a pilgrimage."

In Jainism, only twenty-four masters are accepted in one circle of creation. Those twenty-four masters have happened – Mahavira was the last. That was twenty-five centuries ago and now there still are thousands of years which will remain empty; there will not be another Jaina master they call the tirthankara: "the man who makes the path."

The old man was very learned and he said, "If it was in my power, I would have declared you the twenty-fifth tirthankara, but it is not according to the scriptures and it is not in my power. But I respect you exactly as the twenty-fifth tirthankara."

I said, "You should wait a little, you should watch a little. You may have to change your idea."

He said, "Never! I will never change my idea. I have come to a definite conclusion. I have seen all the Jaina scriptures – you go miles and you find such small nourishment. Your small book is enough for a man who really wants to find the truth. It is enough, more than that is nonessential."

It was evening time and the sun was setting. The woman of the house came and said to me, "It is time for your supper. The sun is setting." In a Jaina family, you have to eat before the sun sets; otherwise you have to remain hungry.

But I said to the woman, "Don't be worried. Your father-in-law has come from miles away to see me. It doesn't matter to me, I will eat a little later. Let me first converse with him because he has been waiting for me for years."

The moment the old man heard that I was going to eat in the night, he was so shocked. He said, "What am I hearing? I called you the twenty-fifth tirthankara and you are going to eat in the night! I have been thinking that your book is the essential for all those who are seekers of the path – and the reality is, you don't know even the *ABC* of religion." This is the *ABC* of religion, that eating in the night is preparing your path toward hell!

I said, "I told you just to wait, not to make decisions, but you didn't listen, you said you were determined. In fact just to show you how determined you were, I told the woman that I would eat after one hour."

He said, "Really? Then forgive me. I touch your feet, just forgive me."

I said, "Wait, you are making decisions too quickly."

He said, "No, I am absolutely determined. This time I am not going to change." And he touched my feet, asked for my forgiveness.

I said, "There is no difficulty in forgiving because you have not committed any crime, but one thing you should understand: the twenty-fifth tirthankara eats in the night."

He said, "You eat in the night?"

I said, "I am saying it myself, and if you want, you can wait. Let the sun set and things will be clear."

He said, "My God! Then how could you manage to write such a book?"

I said, "Eating in the night or not has nothing to do with religion."

But he was very frustrated. He left and told me while he was leaving, "I am going to burn your book."

I said, "That's the right thing. But think before you burn it. You seem to be a very quick, decisive man. And each decision is absolute. I may not eat… And I was just joking when I said that I eat in the night."

He said, "Really?"

Now, what can you do with such people? When I was surrounded by Jainas I had to talk with these people about things which have no importance, nothing. But those were the people and these were their questions. Slowly, slowly others started moving toward me, and Jainas became a minority. Out of that minority a few are still here – very few, their percentage has fallen to one percent at the most.

The second group that followed, which was certainly the closest group to the Jainas… Mahatma Gandhi had adopted a Jaina doctrine of nonviolence, so all the Jainas became Gandhians, and all the Gandhians came close to the Jainas. At least on one point they were in agreement. So when Jainas were becoming alert that I am a dangerous man, Gandhians followed. Their great leaders: Vinoba Bhave wanted to meet me; Shankar Rao Dev attended a meditation camp; Dada Dharmadhikari attended many meditation camps; Acharya Bhagwat attended many meditation camps. And because these were the thinkers of Gandhism, all over India Gandhians started becoming interested in me.

Again I was surrounded by a certain group with a fixed ideology. The day I criticized Mahatma Gandhi… I was simply stating the facts, not even criticizing him. Someone had asked, "What do you think about Mahatma Gandhi and his philosophy of nonviolence?" Now, *you* would not ask that kind of question.

I said that Mahatma Gandhi was simply a cunning politician. By adopting nonviolence he was managing many things. All the Jainas became his followers. They found a certain man who was in tune with them; although he was not a Jaina, he was at least nine percent Jaina. I have the percentages about Gandhi: he was born a Hindu, but he was only one percent Hindu; he was born in Gujarat, an area very dominated by Jaina philosophy, he was nine percent a Jaina. And ninety percent he was a Christian. Thrice in his life he was just on the verge of being converted to Christianity.

I said to them that he managed the Jainas by nonviolence. He also managed the upper-class Hindus who are nonviolent people, and he also managed to influence Christians and Christian missionaries, because Jesus Christ's message is of love, and nonviolence is another name of love. These were not all the benefits of accepting nonviolence. The most important thing is that India has been an enslaved country for two thousand years. It has forgotten what it means to be independent. It is not yet independent, its mind has become that of a slave.

Two thousand years is not a small amount of time. In these two thousand years a certain slave psychology has penetrated the Indian mind. They have become cowards. India has never invaded anyone. Small invaders, uncultured, uneducated – Mongols, Turks, Hunas, very small tribes from Central Asia – simply came, and they were not even given any resistance. India has lost the nerve to fight. So when Gandhi said nonviolence, the whole of India was absolutely convinced by him, because there was no question of fighting.

Firstly, Indians are very afraid of fighting. They have never fought. A small group could manage to keep this vast continent in slavery. The ownership changed from one group to another, but India remained in slavery. Secondly, Gandhi was intelligent enough to see that on the one hand Indians are not people who will fight, and on the other hand they don't have any weapons to fight with. Thirdly, the British empire of that day was the greatest power in the world. It was impossible to fight violently with the British empire: you don't have weapons, you don't have trained people to fight, you don't know anything about fighting.

Nonviolence was a political policy. It served many purposes and served well. It shocked the British empire and it destroyed the British empire too. Britain was absolutely ready if the Indians were going to fight. But the Indians would not fight; even if there were British soldiers killing them, they would simply stand and be killed. All over the world the British empire was condemned: "This is absolutely stupid. People who are not fighting, who are not terrorists, who are not revolutionaries, who are simply asking for their freedom… And instead of giving them freedom you give them a bullet in the chest – unarmed people!"

Britain was in a very awkward situation. You can arrest the people who are following Gandhi – and they were ready to be arrested – you can put them in jail, but how many can you put in jail? And what is the point? Sooner or later you will have to release them because feeding them, clothing them is an unnecessary burden on you. And thousands more were coming every day to be arrested. People were standing, waiting to be arrested outside every jail, outside every court, shouting, "We want freedom or arrest us."

Nowhere in the world had such a situation ever happened. Britain became puzzled. It looked inhuman to kill these people, it looked inhuman to jail these people, and a worldwide condemnation… Finally the whole empire collapsed because India was the central beam. Once India was free, other smaller countries started becoming free. And with India out of the British empire, Britain itself had become such a small power that it is not counted at all as far as great powers are concerned. It was the topmost.

So I said that Gandhi's nonviolence was not a spiritual philosophy but a political policy. And it is proved by the facts. He had promised before independence that the moment India became free, all armies would be dissolved, all arms would be thrown into the ocean. When asked, "If you do this and someone attacks, what are you going to do?" he said, "We will receive them as our guest and we will say to them, 'We stay here; you also can stay.'"

After independence everything was forgotten. Neither the armies were dissolved, nor the arms were thrown into the ocean; on the contrary, Gandhi himself blessed the first attack on Pakistan. Three Indian Air Force planes came to receive his blessings and he came out of his house and blessed the planes. All nonviolence and all that bullshit talk that he was doing his whole life was forgotten.

The moment I criticized Gandhi... And this was only on one point. I am a man who loves to go deep into everything. If I don't go, I don't go at all. Once I started, I had to condemn Mahatma Gandhi on a thousand and one grounds; on each point Gandhians disappeared. Now I don't think even one percent of those present are Gandhians – not here, even in India, because they cannot be Gandhians if I am right. I have condemned him point by point.

I have not changed, just the people around me went on changing. When Gandhians disappeared then the people who were communists, socialists, who were against Gandhism thought, "This is a great chance. If he can support us..." But I had not condemned Gandhi to support communism. I had never thought that this would become an opportunity for socialists and communists. And then I had to condemn them. There is no other way to get rid of such people.

So all those political talks were a necessity to find out exactly who my people are: who are without any prejudice, who have come to me, who have not come to me to hear about Christ, Buddha, Gandhi, Mahavira; who have come directly to listen to me. I have my own message, I have my own manifesto to the world. The people who are here have a totally different quality. I can talk to you without ever thinking that it can hurt you, without ever thinking that I have to somehow say things which you like. Now I can say things which are my own experience, which my own existential being is ready to express.

I have never been a serious person. But I was surrounded by serious people for many years, and it is very difficult not to be serious among those serious people. It is almost like being in a hospital.

You have at least to pretend that you are serious. For years I was surrounded by sick people and I had at least to pretend that I was serious. I am not serious at all because existence is not serious. It is so playful, so full of song, music, subtle laughter. It has no purpose; it is not businesslike. It is pure joy, sheer dance, out of overflowing energy. Now I can talk to you as if I am talking to myself. There is no problem.

Just the other day Chaitanya Keerti was translating a few of my talks into Hindi, and he was puzzled about how to translate the jokes because the Indians will not be able to swallow them. Those jokes will get stuck in their throats. I told Chaitanya Keerti, "You are an Indian and you know perfectly well what will be troublesome – drop it. You are not only translating into the Indian language, you are also translating for the Indians. Keep in mind that they cannot understand jokes. You are in a totally different climate, in a different atmosphere. They are not in the same situation. They are afraid to enter the door."

I had an ear infection and Dr. Jog a specialist was called. He could not believe that such a beautiful ashram exists in Pune. And he lives in Pune and is the topmost expert here. He had passed, looked at the door, looked at the people, but he had never dared to enter. He said, "When I told my wife that it is a beautiful place and there are beautiful people, full of laughter and joy – it is nothing like what the third-rate yellow newspapers go on printing about it, lies, absolute lies – she wanted to come."

They both came one Sunday when he was free. And when he came to see me again, he said, "My wife wants to come whenever she can manage. I cannot come every Sunday because that is the only free time for conferences, meetings, this and that. But whenever I can come, I will come. Can she come alone?"

I said, "There is no problem. Here men are afraid of women, women are not afraid of men! This is a totally different world. You can see the scene: the swami is running away, and not one, but many mas are trying to catch hold of him, saying, 'Where are you going? Come back!'"

He said, "One more thing, she wants to see you for five minutes alone."

I said, "There is no problem. Whenever you want, inform me and she can see me."

He himself wondered, "What does she want to see you alone for?"

I said, "That is your problem, that is not my problem. She may have some trouble with you. You may be torturing her or you must be doing something."

Even that day I had seen, as the car stopped, that his wife seemed to be intelligent, educated. They were sitting just here, and his wife showed him the thumbs-up sign. Perhaps he does not know that I have seen it. I never miss anything that is worth seeing!

Now something serious…

Prince Edward, the queen's youngest son, takes a horse ride every morning in Hyde Park. Every day he sees the same beautiful girl sitting on a park bench. He soon falls madly in love with her, but is too shy to introduce himself. Not knowing what to do, he consults his elder brother Charles who is more experienced in such matters.

"Simple," says Charles. "Just paint your horse green."

"Green?" exclaims Edward.

"Yes, green," says Charles. "Then next time you see her, she will say, 'Your horse is green?' and you can say, 'That's right, and my name is Prince Edward.' Then you can take her for a drink and you can invite her for a weekend in Scotland, and if you play your cards right, you may end up with a romp in the heather."

"Great!" says Edward. The next morning he arrives in the park with a green horse.

The girl looks up, sees him and cries, "My God, your horse is green!"

"Yes," says Edward, and then he stammers, "well, er, well, well… I wanna fuck you!"

Continuing their tour of India, Hymie Goldberg and Becky Goldberg go trekking in the Himalayas. Walking along the path, gazing at the mountain scenery, Hymie bumps straight into a yeti, one of the legendary abominable snowmen. The yeti picks up Hymie and runs off into the hills, leaving Becky wailing and crying that she will never see her Hymie again.

Sure enough, a few minutes later there is a piercing shriek that echoes around the mountains and Becky fears the worst. But a short while later, Hymie comes limping down the path into Becky's arms.

"What happened?" she cries in relief. "How did you escape?"

"Well," says Hymie reluctantly, "I thought I was finished, all twisted up in the creature's arms until I could not breathe. And then I saw this pair of balls hanging in front of my nose, so with my last energy I bit the balls as hard as I could. You have no idea how much strength a man gets when he bites his own balls!"

# 19

# From India to Japan: The Journey of Zen

Osho,

The other day you said it was easier for one to meditate when one was elevated from the earth, such as on a tree. In aikido, one of the fundamental principles is to feel the body connected with the gravity of the earth. Is there any contradiction in it? Aikido also teaches one to be always aware of the point a few centimeters below the navel. What is the relation between this point and our being?

It raises a very historical question. Zen was born in India in the absurd laughter of Mahakashyapa, a close disciple of Gautam Buddha. He had many disciples even closer than Mahakashyapa. And Mahakashyapa is mentioned only once: when he had laughed. Mahakashyapa's laughter is the beginning of Zen. So first you have to understand why Mahakashyapa laughed. Why had he laughed?

One such beautiful morning as this, and with such beautiful, silent people as these, Gautam Buddha was expected to come and give his morning talk. Unexpectedly, he came with a beautiful roseflower in his hand. Everyone wondered – he had never come before with anything in his hand. The situation was more mysterious because he sat on the podium looking at the roseflower. Seconds passed, minutes passed and people became fidgety. "Isn't he going to talk today? And what is the meaning of Gautam Buddha just watching a roseflower?"

After half an hour it became almost a tension. Something had to be done – he did not look at people, he was looking at the roseflower. At that moment, Mahakashyapa laughed. Gautam Buddha raised his eyes and called Mahakashyapa close to him and gave him the flower. And he told the people, ten thousand sannyasins, "Whatever could be said through words I have said to you, and whatever could not be said through words I have transferred to Mahakashyapa."

This is the only mention of Mahakashyapa in the whole Buddhist canon. It is a vast literature, and for twenty-five centuries, inquirers have been asking the question, "Why did Mahakashyapa laugh? And why was his laughter accepted? Not only accepted, but raised to the highest point of communication." Something transpired in that silent giving of the roseflower to Mahakashyapa. Since then Zen has been mysterious. It is the purest mysticism that has existed on the earth.

In India, it was called *zan*. Buddha used the people's language; it was a revolutionary step. Pali was the people's language. In the people's language, words become simple, rounded, easy. In Sanskrit the same word is *dhyana*. But for the people, *dhyana* seems to be a little difficult. Buddha never used Sanskrit.

You may not be aware that Sanskrit has never been a living language; it was only a language for scholars. They kept a separate system of communication among themselves. Buddha was the first man in India who revolted against this ugliness. Everything should be said in the people's language. It should not become the monopoly of scholars, it should not give the scholar a great ego. He used the lowest language that is used in the marketplace, where things change. The words may not be accurate grammatically, but become more rounded, more usable, more simple. *Dhyana* became *zan*.

In India, for example, in the villages, station – railway station – is not called *station*. It is called only *tation*. Why bother about *railway station*? That is too big a word for poor people. They simply use *tation*. And the same is true about many words. Sanskrit is very polished – perhaps the most polished language – because only scholars used it and they were very fussy about its accuracy, grammar. Buddha simply dropped that.

*Zan* became a new stream, flowing from Gautam Buddha to Mahakashyapa. You will know what was transferred between your master and you when something happens in silence, because Buddha said, "What could be said, I have said to you and what could not be said, I have given to Mahakashyapa. This roseflower is only a symbol of recognition that Mahakashyapa will represent the unsayable." After Mahakashyapa, it was bound to be a very small stream of seekers because of its mysteriousness.

The next great name is Bodhidharma. His master told him to go to China, not to convert China to Buddhism: "But in China there is already a fragrance existing, created by Lao Tzu, Chuang Tzu, Lieh Tzu. Truth is no one's monopoly. It will be good if you take the treasure that Mahakashyapa has given, from generation to generation, to China. And let these two beautiful streams of mystics meet." Just as in crossbreeding the child is stronger, the same happens when two streams of thought, or of no-thought, meet, merge. And something new, far deeper than either arises, far greater than either arises.

It took Bodhidharma three years to reach China. But when the master had said it, there was no question. The relationship between the master and the disciple is of such deep love that it is always YES – in capital letters. He did not even ask why; the master must know. He went to China and the crossbreeding happened. What was *zan* in Buddhism was made even more simple, so that the Chinese could understand and use it. It became *chan*. It flourished in China, and great masters arose out of the mystic experience.

From China it was taken to Japan. Again a new crossbreeding... From *chan* the word became *zen*. And in Japan it is manifested in many dimensions.

Your question is very fundamental. There are two ways to disappear as a personality: one we can call "grounding" and one we can call "centering." Mahakashyapa and Bodhidharma both used centering: going within to the point where nothing remains, just a pure presence, no person. The same became even more beautiful with the great heritage of Chuang Tzu, Lieh Tzu and Lao Tzu. They were also people of centering. They were exploring their interiority to find themselves, and what they found was an absolute absence of anyone – even the finder disappeared. Out of that state came neither the found nor the finder, neither the seeker nor the sought, but an absolute silence, alive, full of its own music, full of its own dance. Seeing this, Mahakashyapa laughed, "Buddha goes on saying to people 'Seek yourself, find yourself' and he is tricking them."

It is a perfectly legitimate statement, to seek yourself. But Mahakashyapa knew that when you find yourself, you are no longer there. It is a very strange situation; nothing can express it except laughter.

There is an old definition of a philosopher: in the darkest night, in a dark house where there is no light – and moreover, the philosopher is blind – he is looking for a black cat which is not there. But the search continues. And if suddenly light comes in and his eyes are cured and he thinks of all the trouble that he was taking to find the cat which does not exist, what else to do except to laugh at himself? Fools laugh at others. Wisdom laughs at itself.

But in Japan the crossbreeding had a tremendous manifestation. It has gone very far away from Mahakashyapa's laughter – a long journey. On the journey it gathered many new manifestations, many new revelations, many new methods. Finally, in Japan it turned out to be the peak. And the peak was that anything can be used to find the truth. Even a warrior can use his sword, fighting with another warrior; there is no need for him to sit and meditate. The archer can find it in his archery, the painter can find it in his painting, the sculptor can find it in his sculpture.

What in India was only pure meditation, in Japan grew into many branches. Indians cannot even conceive how a warrior, a fighter with a sword can be meditative, or how archery can be a meditative method, because Indians have never tried. It needed Mahakashyapa's laughter to travel from India to China and from China to Japan. And it gathered much insight on this long journey of a thousand years.

A German professor, Herrigel, was reading about Zen. And he could not believe how the art of archery can be meditation. There seems to be no relationship. It seems to be perfect that Gautam Buddha sitting in the lotus posture is meditating. But to conceive that an archer or a swordsman, whose effort is to kill the other, can be meditative.

Herrigel went to Japan. He was in Japan for three years and there he found the secret. He learned archery. He himself was an archer, a master archer; he was a hundred percent successful in hitting the target. But his Zen master said, "This is not the point. The point is not there in the target; the point is within you. Are you grounded?"

He said, "In the West we have practiced archery for hundreds of years and no one has thought about grounding. What is this grounding?"

The master said, "Grounding means you become almost part of the earth and allow the gravitation to flow in you, to flood you – particularly below the navel, two inches below to be exact. The gravitation comes from all around and settles two inches below your navel."

But Herrigel asked, "What has it to do with archery? I have to concentrate on the target."

The master said, "Forget about the target, first be grounded. And when you shoot your arrow, be relaxed, so that that gravitation shoots it, not you."

He said, "You are making strange statements. I will have to shoot, how can the gravitation shoot it?"

In three years, he never missed a single target; he was a master archer. But his master would say, "No, you have still missed. I am not watching your target – who cares about your target? I am watching you; you are the target."

And why two inches below the navel? – that is the center of life. It was from there that you were connected with your mother. It was from there that for nine months you were supplied with everything that you needed, and you didn't have to do anything, you were simply relaxed.

Grounding means, bringing this life center within you in contact with the gravitational force, so that the gravitational force starts filling it. And a moment comes when you don't shoot at the target. Certainly you aim, but it is as if the arrow shoots itself. The gravitational force is enough to take it to the target.

Three years, and a German mind… Finally, Herrigel gave up. He said, "You are driving me crazy. Day and night I am thinking about how to do it."

And the master said, "That's what I have been telling you. Don't think about how to do it, let it happen. Just have enough energy so it happens."

Finally, he decided to go back. Three years are enough, and not even a single time had the master said, "Good." He always said, "You missed again." Every day Herrigel would come and every day he would be a failure.

He said to the master, "I am sorry, but I could not get the point. Tomorrow I am leaving, so tomorrow I will come to say good-bye."

He came the next day. The master was teaching another disciple, and Herrigel was sitting on the bench, simply watching because it was not his business, he was finished with it. If he cannot get it in three years, he cannot get it in three lives. What the master is saying is beyond any logic.

He was sitting relaxed, watching – watching the master because the master was showing the new disciple. Suddenly he saw the point. The master was so relaxed, it was not his hands which were shooting the arrow; it was so clear that some inner force was at work. Spontaneously he stood up, went to the master, took the bow and arrow and shot the arrow.

For the first time the master said, "I can certify that you have achieved. You were tense, trying with your mind. Today it was just accidental; you were sitting relaxed, it was not your business, you were finished with it. And because you were finished with it, your eyes were clear, your heart was silent, you were watching in deep peace and silence, and you could see. I was trying to show it to you for three years, but because you were in a hurry to learn quickly and go to Germany… Just now there was no hurry – you were going to Germany.

"I can certify that you have achieved not only the art of archery, but simultaneously the art of grounding. And the moment you are grounded, as the trees are grounded – with deep roots in the earth – when your body is receiving forces from the earth and you are available, relaxed, allowing them to fill your life center, the mind stops functioning, time stops."

So just by the side, meditation happens. People around the world have wondered, "What has meditation to do with archery?" But it happens. It can happen with anything. The question is that the mind should stop, time should stop; you should be relaxed and allow life to take possession of you.

You are asking, "The other day you said it was easier for one to meditate when one was elevated from the earth, such as on a tree. In aikido, one of the fundamental principles is to feel the body connected with the gravity of the earth. Is there any contradiction in it?" – no, only variety. Either you are connected with the earth or you are connected with the sky. You have heard the word *gravitation*; perhaps you have not heard the word *levitation*. Just as the earth pulls you toward itself, the sky pulls you toward itself. The pull of the earth is called gravitation and the pull of the sky is called levitation; either way, you can manage. The earth is your life – so is the sky.

In fact, my suggestion is that the sky is far vaster than the earth. Its energy sources are inexhaustible, more than the energy of the earth. It is enough for a small human being to be filled with the energy of the earth. But if you really want to know the universal force, it is better if you go farther away from the earth.

The first astronauts were very much puzzled… They had not thought about it. Later on they were trained, but the first astronauts had no idea: as they moved out of the gravitational field of the earth, they started floating inside their spacecraft. They could not believe it, they became weightless. Their weight on the earth was of gravitation. You don't have any weight. The moment you become weightless, if you are aware that this weightlessness can be associated with meditation, then exactly what happens in grounding will have happened, and far more tremendously. You will be flooded with the universal energy.

But because the astronauts were Western people, they had no idea of energy. They became even more tense, more afraid, "What is happening?" Somehow, they tried to grab their seat belts, tied themselves to their seats. It was such a shocking experience. Just think if you start floating, going to the disco, or just on a visit to MG market… No one has heard of it; hence it has no name.

It was my experience that in water, in a river, gravitation is nullified. You think you have to learn how to swim – it is not true; someone has just to push you into the river and you will swim. First you will shout, "Save me, help!" And when no help is coming, then you will throw your arms about. They will be haphazard, not coordinated; you may drink a little water…

And you know perfectly well that if you float a dead body in the water, it does not drown. It doesn't know about swimming; it has no idea. People drown because they thought that they don't know how to swim, and they have made so much fuss and created trouble for themselves. First, they will go under water while they are alive; the moment they are dead, they are swimming perfectly well on the surface. It seems dead people know something which we don't know.

A Japanese scientist has been proving that children need not learn how to swim; they are born with the capacity. He started with one-year-old children, then six-month-old children. Now he has come to three-month-old children; they swim perfectly well. No one has told them, "You don't know how to swim. Don't go near the water." And now the Japanese scientist is trying to go back even more, toward the first day the child is born. His hypothesis is – and I agree that it will prove right – the child will swim. He has been floating for nine months in the mother's womb. Why do you think the mother's belly becomes so big? Do you think there is that big a child inside? It is a small pond.

And mothers know: they start drinking more water, they become interested in eating salty things because the water the child needs has to be exactly like ocean water. The first man was born as a fish, and man is still born as a fish. Even after you are born, don't think you have gone far away from the fish. Eighty percent of your body is water – ocean water. No one has worked it out.

It happened to me accidentally…

I was in my postgraduate class. Just behind my hostel, there was a small hillock with three trees. And it was difficult to find any place where you would not be disturbed – particularly if you were meditating. Then someone would come and shake you: "What has happened to you? Why are you sitting here with closed eyes? Some sad news?" With thousands of students, hundreds of professors… Someone was bound to come. If you closed your doors, they would knock. If you didn't open the doors they would call the fire brigade, "Something has gone wrong."

I found those trees were good. I used to climb the tallest and strongest tree and sit there. It had a very beautiful place where two branches separated, and I used to meditate there early in the morning at three o'clock because there was no possibility of any disturbance. I was amazed: I would sit under the tree, then I would sit on top, high on the tree and the silence would immediately deepen; the mind would stop, the time would stop.

Aikido is perfectly right and what I said is not against it. Just like aikido, another science is needed. Perhaps this academy of meditation may be able to develop it. And my experience is that not only gravitation helps you to be filled with life, the tree also helps you to be filled with life – it is life.

Aikido was developed in Japan for warriors, archery for archers. I don't think that you want to be a warrior or an archer or a boxer. You want to be a silent, joyful, loving awareness; a presence but not a person. What I am saying will help you much more than aikido. Aikido will also be introduced soon. We will be having aikido classes because there are a few fools and they have to be satisfied. We are going to have archery. One of my sannyasins is a master archer. She is French, she is ready to come any day if we want archery. But she is not meditative, she is just technically perfect. I will have to send her to Japan to learn the combination of meditation and archery. But what is the point? We are not going to kill the birds, we are not going to kill each other. And if you want a perfect archer, the simplest is...

I have always loved the story of a king who was passing through a village. He loved archery; he himself was a master archer. He could not believe that in that small village there lived someone who was certainly a greater archer than himself. He himself had not been one hundred percent; once in a while the target was missed. But there in that village he saw circles on many trees with an arrow exactly in the middle.

He said, "This is... Even the best archer cannot manage this. It seems so perfect. I want to meet the man."

So he called the people and asked, "Who is the archer?"

They all laughed. They said, "Forget about him. He is the village idiot."

He said, "You don't understand. Bring him, his archery is perfect."

The villagers said, "You don't understand his archery. First, he shoots the arrow and then he makes a circle around it. Naturally, he is perfect, always perfect. And we have told him, 'This is not the right way. First you should make the circle on the tree and then shoot. In that way one can miss. This is a simple way, you never miss.'"

Japan has been a warrior race, so naturally when Zen reached Japan it became associated with all kinds of swordsmanship, the art of archery and other things. But they have retained the essential of Zen in it. Even Mahakashyapa would not be successful in archery, but that does not mean that he is not the originator.

I don't think Gautam Buddha will be able to pass the aikido examinations. He is bound to fail. But that does not mean that this whole aikido is just a faraway echo of Gautam Buddha's experience of his own being. There is no contradiction. Just remember, whatever you are doing – chopping wood or carrying water from the well – you can be a meditator. Meditation is simply a silent thread inside you. You can do anything, just that silent thread should not be disturbed. Be careful that your awareness remains and then you can do anything.

Meditation is not something separate from life. It was a great mistake of the past that people thought meditation is separate from life. So when you are finished with life, one foot in the grave, then it is time to meditate – that's how the Hindu conception is. Up until twenty-five years old you should be a celibate and a scholar. Then up until fifty you should get married, do business and all kinds of things of life – children… And when you are fifty, turn your face toward the forest. Don't go yet, just turn your face because your children may be small. So just start preparing; it is called *vanaprastha*. Just a preparation of twenty-five years for going to the forest.

At seventy-five you leave. Your children will be almost forty, forty-five. They are also getting ready and preparing to look toward the forest. At seventy-five you go into the forest. And those twenty-five years, the last part of your life, are for meditation.

This is a very wrong conception. I condemn it forcefully because it destroyed this country. Firstly, it keeps meditation as the last thing on your laundry list; it is not a priority. Secondly, it creates a division between meditation and life, which is not right. Life can be meditative; meditation can be a joyful life. And thirdly, very few people live after seventy-five – particularly in India.

Forty years is the average age. Now, how to divide it? Ten years for a scholarship? The other ten for marriage? The other ten for preparation to go to the forest? And by the age of thirty your ticket is given to you to go to the forest. The idea of a hundred years is absolutely imaginative. Nowhere has a hundred years been the average time of life. Even in the most developed countries – technically, medically, scientifically – a hundred is not the average length of life. And when we are thinking about such an important thing as meditation, it should not be missed. A man who has missed meditation has missed the most beautiful experience of his life.

Now a few moments for prayer...

For years, the Goldberg family have been trying to persuade Hymie to buy a hearing aid. But all he says is, "Nonsense. You people should talk louder."

But one day Hymie is walking down the street when he sees a sign in a shop window: Hearing aids – sixty percent off. Hymie rushes in and within ten minutes, he has been fitted with a hearing aid.

Stepping out into the street with a broad smile on his face, a voice calls him, "Hymie, hey Hymie!" It is his friend Moishe Finkelstein. "What are you doing in this part of town?" asks Moishe.

"This," replies Hymie pointing to his ear. "It is wonderful. My kids were right, I can hear like a seventeen-year-old."

"That's great," says Moishe. "What kind is it?"

Hymie glances at his watch and says, "It's a quarter to five."

And the last…

An American from Texas goes to England for a holiday, and when he walks into a cafe, he asks the waiter for a cup of black coffee.

The waiter replies, "In England, we serve tea. We have three types of tea: we have orange pekoe tea, which is eighty percent aroma and twenty percent substance; we have herbal tea, which is twenty percent aroma and eighty percent substance. And we have English tea, which is preferred."

Then the Texan says, "I don't want tea, I want black coffee. But in Texas, we also have three teas: we have shi-*t*, which has eighty percent substance and twenty percent aroma; we have far-*t*, which has eighty percent aroma and twenty percent substance. And we have cun-*t*, which is preferred."

# 20

# We Have to Make Our World More Beautiful

Osho,
A friend told us that she once heard you say that you want us to become enlightened in the most aesthetic way possible. Will you speak on the aesthetics of consciousness? Have you ever spoken of anything else?

You have raised a very significant question. All the religions that have existed on the earth have been very unaesthetic because they denied life, they denied all the beauties, all the flowers, all creativity, sensitivity. They killed the possibility of millions of people attaining enlightenment through aesthetic creativity. They simply closed the door, and for centuries no one has even asked the question, "Is it possible that just to be a musician is enough to become enlightened?" I say yes.

No one will agree with me: neither Mahavira, Gautam Buddha, Mohammed, Jesus. Knowing it well that the whole history will stand against me, I am absolutely certain that music, sculpture, dancing, painting can become meditation. Simply, these doors have been closed. It is one of the greatest crimes committed against man.

And people who are uncreative are praised as saints. All that they may have done is fasting. But being hungry is not a great quality, and it does not enhance humanity in any way. They may have lived naked, but that does not mean they are making life more beautiful. Most of these naked saints are so ugly that it would have been better… They should be praised if they stop being naked. But their nakedness has been praised; it is thought to be a great discipline.

Sometimes stupid ideas that are carried for a long time almost start looking like ultimate truths. All the animals are naked. I don't see any saintliness in being naked. I am not saying that to be naked is criminal, I am simply saying that if the time is right and the climate is beautiful and you have a body worth to be seen… First stand naked in front of the mirror before you disturb other people. But on a sea beach, of course, in a good climate; in the home you can be naked. But there is nothing saintly in it, it is simply natural. Every animal, every bird is naked – except for a few dogs.

In the Victorian age in England, where morality became hilarious, even dogs were covered with clothes. This was thought to be very Christian. You will not believe it, even the legs of the chairs and tables were covered – because they are called legs and legs should not be left naked. Except for those few idiots, the whole world of the animals has remained natural.

Perhaps for man it is now difficult to be naked in all the seasons. His body is no longer capable, is no longer so strong as it was in the age of the primitive man who lived naked. For thousands of years we have protected our bodies. But remember, whenever anything is protected it becomes weaker. The more you protect, the weaker it becomes. A primitive man in the jungles of India still lives naked – in the winter, in the rain, in the hot sun – but he has the stamina and he has the body. He is not a saint, he is simply uncultured, uneducated, uncivilized, primitive. There is nothing that can be said in praise of him.

But religions have been preaching very uncreative disciplines to people, which are sometimes so funny that even to believe that thousands of people live under those beliefs seems impossible. In India, Jainism is a religion whose monks, step by step, finally become naked. In five stages of discipline, the last stage of their discipline is to be naked. And because of this stage, Jainism has to deny women direct entry into their paradise. First, they will have to become men because they cannot attain the final stage of discipline, of nakedness.

And the people who became naked... Throughout twenty-five centuries continuously, thousands of people have become naked, and they have not contributed anything to the world; have not painted, have not written poetry. In fact, these are mundane affairs, worldly things, which they have renounced. In every way their disciplines have made them ugly.

For example, the Jaina monk eats standing. Now, if you eat standing, soon you will have a big belly. Your chest will sink and your belly will become bigger. You will be pregnant without pregnancy! They have to eat food in their cupped hands because they cannot use any kind of instruments. What nonsense! To use a plate is not great technology. But they are praised because they are using only their hands and that creates many problems.

They cannot use a razor blade to shave their beards or their hair. The problem becomes more complicated because they are not allowed to have a bath at all. Their discipline does not even allow them to have a mouthwash. They don't brush their teeth because the brush is a great technology, and toothpaste is certainly manufactured in great factories. They have disowned the whole world – how can they use a brush? And why should they use one?

Their logic is worth understanding because that will explain many other things in other religions. They are the extreme and the extreme is always good to understand, because things have come to the very climax where even a blind man can see that it is stupid.

Every year, they pull out their hairs with their own hands; that is celebrated as a great religious ceremony. Thousands gather to see the naked monk pulling out his hairs. He cannot use a razor blade –

the razor blade belongs to the materialist world. It is worth seeing the scene when a Jaina monk pulls out his hairs. Thousands of Jainas gather and women are crying, a few have fainted. The great saint is going through so much suffering.

And who has told him to go through so much suffering? Anyone can give him a free shave. Now, he has imposed a stupid thing upon himself and people are praising him for his great disciplined life. This is not discipline, this is self-torture. The reason is that he is not the body, so why should he take a bath? Now, without you, the body cannot take a bath, that is certain. The body cannot have a good mouthwash without you.

The reasoning goes that people try to decorate their body. Your brushing the teeth – you may have never thought – is condemned by the Jainas because it is beautifying your body, which is really part of your sexuality. Having a bath, having a beautiful body, a good hairstyle, is certainly indicative that you are interested in bodies. If you are interested in your own body, you are certainly interested in other people's bodies also. And a man who has renounced the material world has also renounced his own body.

In fact these people are not saints. Looked at without any prejudice they are psychologically sick, masochists who enjoy torturing themselves. There are many in mad asylums, but people don't know that they are Jaina saints. You are putting them into a madhouse unnecessarily. They torture themselves and they enjoy it.

There are two pathological categories: one is of the masochists, who enjoy being tortured, and the other is of the sadists, who enjoy torturing others. And it is said that the only perfect marriage is between a sadist and a masochist. Certainly it will be perfect. The husband beats and the wife enjoys it; the husband enjoys it because he is beating, or vice versa.

I used to be a student of a professor whose every lecture started with the description of how that morning he had been misbehaved with, mistreated by his wife. One day I heard it, the next day I heard it, the third day I had to stand up. I said, "This is too much. I can say from the symptoms that you are a masochist."

He said, "What do you mean?"

I said, "I mean, you enjoy being tortured. Otherwise, what is the point? Here you teach economics – what relationship does it have with your wife? And I have inquired about everything before standing up. I have been to your wife too because I never question anything without proper homework."

His wife was really dangerous. The one who chose her… And it was a love marriage! She was bigger than the professor, stronger than the professor, uglier than the professor, in every way ahead of him. I inquired of the people in the neighborhood. They said, "They are a strange couple. The wife beats the professor."

I said, "It is not news to me because every day the professor himself begins his lecture with it. Half of the lecture is about how he has been mistreated, misbehaved with by his wife. He is not hiding it. And I have seen the joy on his face when he relates it. Both need to be in psychiatric hospitals."

But the neighbors said, "Whatever you may say, they are both happy."

I said, "That's true. That's the perfect marriage. The wife is perfectly happy; she beats the husband, tortures him in every way. Even with the doors open – the neighbors are looking in and she is sitting on the chest of her husband."

I have never again come across such a perfect couple. And it was a love marriage. I don't think that even before they got married things would have been different. In fact, this relationship of torture had brought them together.

My understanding is that the people who are weeping and crying when a Jaina monk is pulling out his hairs… He is a masochist and the crowd is made up of sadists. They are also enjoying; those tears should not mislead you. They have come from long distances just to see a madman pulling out his hairs. But what is spiritual in it?

I started asking my parents, "What is spiritual in it?" A man may be naked… It is no one's business, let him be naked. If he pulls out his hairs, perhaps he enjoys the exercise. Let him enjoy, just take care that he does not start pulling out other people's hairs. And that's what the Jaina saint is doing. He is pulling out his hairs and he is teaching others to be initiated, so finally they will have to pull out their hairs. It is done in a very indirect way, but in fact he is torturing himself and teaching others, "Torture yourself. Without torturing your body, how can you attain the spiritual?" The division between the body and the spirit has destroyed all religions. Rather than becoming a blessing to the world, they prove to be a great calamity.

I teach an aesthetic consciousness. You should learn to appreciate beauty, you should learn to create beauty, you should behave in a beautiful way. Your life should be a long story of beauty, grace, love, peace. Whatever you are doing, there is no need to renounce the world; there is nowhere to go. This is our world. We have to make it more beautiful, more graceful, more lovable. And whatever you are doing, it is possible to do it meditatively.

There have been mystics like Kabir, who was a weaver. He remained a weaver, although he had kings as his followers, thousands of followers. And he was a poor man. Very few poor people have attained the same grace and radiance as Kabir. All his disciples prayed: "Stop weaving. You don't have to, we are all here to support you, give you anything you need."

Kabir said, "But my meditation and my weaving have grown so together that neither can I meditate without weaving, nor can I weave without meditation. So please don't disturb me, just let me do whatever I have been doing." Another mystic was Gora. He was a potter and he continued to make beautiful pottery after his realization. His pottery also became of a different quality. Something of his beauty became part of what he was making.

His disciples said, "Stop, we feel ashamed. People say, 'You go to a potter?'" – in India a potter is counted as an untouchable – "'And you touch the feet of that man?'" But still, thousands of people became illuminated by Gora's experience. And he remained a potter to the very end.

Whatever you are doing, my approach is, make your doing your meditation. Don't think in terms that you have to leave something and then you will meditate. Those are tricks of the mind of postponing, and you will end up in some ugly situation.

To me, religion can only be aesthetic and nothing else. A religious man will be in every way graceful. His very being will be surrounded by an aura of beauty. His words will be poetry itself, his silences will touch your heart, and his very being will become a dance and celebration for you. What he does is not the question. What he *is* is the question. Whether he is a potter or a weaver or a shoemaker…

There was a shoemaker who was also a mystic, Raidas. If a shoemaker can be as realized as a Gautam Buddha, then there is no need to go anywhere. Just be wherever you are, create more beauty, create more grace in your life, in your actions. Everything should be a prayer, a gratitude to existence. Then a totally different kind of religion will prevail in the world, which will be bringing great treasures to the world.

Up to now all the religions have been escapist – escape from the world. I teach you to remain in the world; just remember, don't be worldly. There is no need to renounce the world, just don't let the world enter your consciousness. You can sit in the Himalayas and still go on thinking about Sophia Loren. The Himalayas cannot prevent you.

Once a man came to Ramakrishna with ten thousand golden pieces. At that time the rupee was pure gold. The very word *rupee* is from Sanskrit; it means gold. He came with ten thousand gold pieces in a big bag and told Ramakrishna, "I have been collecting and waiting – when they became ten thousand, I was going to offer them to you."

Ramakrishna said, "But I don't have any place to keep them. And anyway, I don't think I need them. But I cannot refuse you either. Do one thing..." Just behind Ramakrishna's temple the beautiful Ganges was flowing. He said to the man, "Go and throw the whole load into the Ganges."

Now, Ramakrishna was saying it. And in the first place he had offered the rupees to Ramakrishna, so they belonged to him, and he was saying it. So very reluctantly he went. His heart was sinking. His whole life he had been collecting those rupees. "And that fellow seems to be absolutely insane. What will the Ganges do with them? If he does not need them, he could have told me so. I could have taken them back. If he does not need, the Ganges does not need either. But what to do, how to argue with the man? That man is mad!"

One hour passed. Ramakrishna inquired, "What happened? That man has not returned."

Someone was sent and he informed Ramakrishna, "That man is doing a great job. He has created a big crowd. Many are swimming in the Ganges, many are standing on the bank. He takes one rupee at a time, shows the whole crowd that it is pure gold by throwing it on a stone – the sound of the gold – and then he throws it into the Ganges.

"So it is a very long process. Ten thousand rupees, and the crowd is gathering and those who can swim, those who can catch the thrown rupees, they are all enjoying."

Ramakrishna said, "This is strange. I had told him to throw the whole lot."

He himself went to see. It was really a great festival there. Ramakrishna tapped the man on the shoulder and said, "What are you doing?"

He said, "Nothing. Just I check whether the gold is real or not and then I count: three hundred thirty-nine, three hundred forty, three hundred forty-one..."

Ramakrishna said, "You idiot. When someone is collecting money, certainly he checks whether it is real gold or not and he also counts. But when you are throwing it away, why bother? Just throw the whole bag in one go."

He had to do that, but very sadly. He was enjoying his life's greatest moment because so many people were appreciating him, that this is great renunciation, throwing away wealth.

All the religions have been teaching you to throw away wealth. And then all around the world millions of people are starving, dying in poverty. No religion has taught to create wealth. Wealth is not something that comes from the sky; it has to be created. Not everyone is a Henry Ford. It needs intelligence, it needs inventiveness, it needs many qualities; only then can man create wealth. If all the religions had taught the people, "Create wealth and we will respect the wealthiest as the saints," the world would not be poor. There is no reason for the world to be poor.

Even today, although the population has got to five billion, the scientists say that if we put all our intelligence and scientific and technological understanding together, we can make not only five billion people healthy, wealthy, comfortable, we can make twenty-five billion people live perfectly happily on this earth. But all the religions have been teaching poverty. Jesus says, "Blessed are the poor." And everyone knows who is blessed! But these consoling lies have helped the poor to remain poor. Jesus says that those who are rich don't have any hope. "Even a camel can pass through the eye of the needle, but not a rich man through the gates of heaven."

Now, if this kind of teaching has been rampant all over the world, you see the ultimate result. Thousands of people are dying every day just because there is not enough food. Just by the end of this century, only in India alone five hundred million people will die, if the situation remains the same. And there seems to be no possibility that this situation will change.

India does not produce food, it only produces children. It is a very productive land! When it became independent in 1947, its population was only four hundred million. Today its population is nine hundred million. Just in forty years the population has increased by five hundred million, and within the coming ten years India will pass beyond one billion. For the first time, India will be the leading nation in the world as far as poverty, hunger, starvation, population is concerned. Up to now China has been the leader, but in the coming ten years China is going to lose its permanent position. It has been the leading nation up to now – no more.

A man was saying to his wife, "In this newspaper is a report about population. It says that in every five children born on the earth, one is Chinese." This will not be the case after ten years – in every five children born on the earth, one will be an Indian.

The wife was very worried. She said, "My God. I am pregnant and this is my fifth child, and I don't want a Chinese in the house!"

Religions have been teaching wrong values. Man would have been in a totally different position… People have not been taught how to live in tune with nature, in tune with ecology; they have not taught how to live with each other without continuous killing, massacre, rape. In three thousand years there have been five thousand wars – as if man's only profession is to fight. For whom are you fighting?

If religions had taught, "Instead of being destructive, be creative. Rather than renouncing the world, renounce the nation, renounce the race; renounce all discriminations between black and white; renounce all limitations, boundaries that divide humanity. It is one humanity. This planet is our home, and we are all responsible for making it more beautiful, more livable." But they were teaching, "Renounce this world, escape from this world." And where will these people escape to? They don't escape anywhere, they simply live here. They become parasites.

Now there are thousands of monasteries in China, Japan, India, Europe. In these monasteries there are thousands of monks. Who feeds them? They don't create anything. All that they have created in the whole of history is the disease AIDS, nothing else. That is their only positive contribution! Homosexuality, sodomy… But their highest point is the disease AIDS. And they had renounced the world. Then why do they go on sitting on our necks? They should go and jump into the ocean. They have renounced the world; we can tell them good-bye. But they live here, they torture us, and they go on preaching all those ugly teachings which have made this earth so suicidal, so meaningless, so utterly poor in every dimension of life.

My basic interest is in bringing religiousness to life, to the marketplace, and in destroying the antagonism that has been created by all the religions between religiousness and the world. There is no antagonism. Religiousness is a beautiful flower; it can blossom in the marketplace. There is no problem, because religiousness can be reduced to a simple principle of meditation. There is no need of any other discipline.

Just as you deepen your meditativeness, your awareness becomes more and more crystal-clear, your life starts becoming more moral. Not according to any scripture because they are all old and dead, and the situation in which they were written does not exist anymore. According to me a moral person is one who is capable of responding to the real situation directly, not according to any principle.

I am reminded of a Chinese story…

There was a fair. And in old China the wells, water wells, were not protected by any walls around them. They were open holes. In the night, in darkness, you could fall into a water well.

A man had fallen into a water well, but there was a fair – so much noise, so many people, who would hear his… He was shouting with his whole energy, "Help, I am dying!"

Just by chance a Buddhist monk passing by heard the man and looked down into the well. The man said, "Thank God you have heard; otherwise in this fair people are so mad, all kinds of noises are going on – music, dance, singing – who is going to hear me?"

The Buddhist monk said, "Don't be worried, I will listen to you."

He said, "It is not a question of listening! You have to take me out of the well."

The Buddhist monk said, "That I cannot do because according to my scripture, everyone has to suffer for his own evil acts done in past lives. You must have done evil acts. Suffer silently, be peaceful so that in the next life you don't have to suffer. Take care of the next life. What has happened has happened."

The man said, "I am still alive! All has not happened. I am young, my wife is there, my children are there, and you are saying all that has happened has happened. Do something!"

He said, "I cannot go against my scripture." And he went away.

He was followed by a Confucian monk. The monk said, "Confucius was right."

The man said, "I agree, but first get me out!"

He said, "That will happen, but it will take time. A great revolution is needed."

The man said, "But by that time... What revolution are you talking about?"

The monk said, "Confucius has written that every well should have a protective wall. I will go all over the country for your sake, for your children's sake, saying that every well should be protected with a wall."

The man said, "But, what about me?"

He said, "As for you...I cannot do anything. No one listened to Confucius – what can I do? But as for your children, certainly no one will fall in."

The man said, "This is a strange place. A living man is dying and these idiots are talking about great revolutions."

Then came a Christian with a bag, and inside was a rope attached to a bucket; he immediately threw the rope in with the bucket and told the man, "Sit in the bucket and I will pull you out, don't be worried."

The man said, "This seems to be the only real religion. All those others are very cunning people talking about scriptures."

He said to the Christian missionary, "Your religion is the only true religion. But by the way, I want to ask, why were you carrying a rope and a bucket?"

"Because," the missionary said, "I am always on the safe side. Who knows? Someone may have fallen, and this is the only way I can enter paradise. I am going to oppose that Confucian monk who is trying to make walls around every well. Then no one will fall, and if no one falls there will be no need of saviors. The door of paradise will be closed."

The man understood for the first time that he was not being saved. The missionary was making his own account, his bank balance in paradise.

All these scriptures, all these religions, all these moralities may have been useful, may have been useful in certain circumstances, but life goes on changing. Every moment is new. So there are two ways of receiving the new moment that is knocking on your door. One is reaction: reaction comes from your principles, scriptures, knowledge, your church. And the other is response: response comes from your awareness. Except response there is no morality. Without response, whatever you do is going to lead you into some stupidity.

You see in Pune there are so many nonvegetarian mosquitoes. I have not heard of any species of mosquito which are nonvegetarian. You may not believe that in Kolkata the rich vegetarians have many cots in their gardens. Anyone who is ready to lie down on those cots, naked, the whole night, is paid. It happens even today.

They are so compassionate about the mosquitoes because what will happen to those mosquitoes? Their scriptures say to save people, help people. They are saving people, helping people. Those people are the mosquitoes! And just giving five rupees to a man... He suffers the whole night, but it is worth five rupees. He will fight with the mosquitoes, but he will remain on the bed. And the people who are paying him are doing a virtuous act of paying the hungry.

Now, this net around the Buddha Auditorium is very against the scriptures because it is preventing the hungry. It is very immoral – so much good food and hungry people all around, but barriers… That's why people are against me; I teach against the scriptures.

Now a few religious things. You force me to talk about irreligion, but I don't forget the real religious things.

A young Arab returns to his tent late one night, very hungry. He lights a candle and starts to look through his bag for some food until he finds four dates. Taking out his knife, he cuts open a date to find it full of worms. He cuts open a second date, but it too has worms. The third date also has worms.

He sighs deeply, blows out the candle, and eats the last date.

A Canadian farmer is chopping wood to store it for the winter when an old Indian comes out of the forest and says, "Cold winter this year."

Hearing this, the farmer decides to chop more wood than usual. The following day he is still chopping when the old Indian appears again and says, "Very cold winter this year."

So the farmer keeps chopping late into the night. The following day he is at it again and by now he has a huge pile of wood when the old Indian comes by and says, "Very, very cold winter this year."

The farmer stops chopping and says, "Hey chief, how do you know that?"

"Well," says the Indian, "in my tribe we have a maxim which says: Cold weather comes to the neighborhood when you see the white man chopping wood."

Moishe Finkelstein gets a nasty letter from the tax office and he has to go for an interview. He phones his son, Fagin the lawyer, for some advice, and Fagin suggests that he wears old clothes so that he does not look too prosperous.

On the way to the tax office, Moishe bumps into Mendel Kravitz who tells him that dressed in this way he looks like a rascal and that the tax officer would immediately suspect something.

Moishe is very confused so he goes to visit Rabbi Nussbaum. The rabbi is out, but his wife lets Moishe into the house.

"What is your trouble?" she asks. And Moishe tells her his story.

"Aha!" she replies at the end of the tale. "This reminds me of when I was about to get married. I could not decide whether to wear a white nightdress and look like a virgin, or a black one and look experienced and seductive, so I asked my grandmother for advice."

"Oy!" cries Moishe. "And what did she say?"

"Well," says the rabbi's wife, "she told me, 'It doesn't matter what you wear – you'll get fucked anyway.'"

# 21

# Logic Creates Contradictions

Osho,

The other night I heard you say that you are as irrelevant as existence. However, as far as I am concerned, you are totally relevant and essential. Are we in contradiction with each other?

I am in absolute agreement with you. Do you see the contradiction? Logic has interpreted that which is complementary as contradictory. And logic rules our education, our minds, so whenever we see two complementary things, immediately the idea of contradiction arises. Otherwise, in one interrelated existence, how can there be contradiction?

Complementariness is essential. For example, the day and the night are not contradictory; they are complementary to each other. Nor are life and death contradictory; they are complementary to each other. They make one whole, one circle, complete and entire. But seen through the eyes of logic, it is hard to believe that life and death are not contradictory.

It seems obvious that death is the end of life; that is not true. Death is only a beginning of a new life – a refreshment, a rejuvenation. The old body is tired. You need more experiences to become mature. You have to move through many other forms of life, and there are millions of forms of life.

Moving through all these forms of life, learning by and by, step by step, inch by inch, you arrive at humanity. Humanity gives you a new opportunity of transformation, to jump out of the circle of life and death and to become part of the eternal. Those who achieve it have really lived. Those who have missed may have to learn the old route again. Who knows how many lives it takes to recognize that humanity is a point of departure, not only from death, but also from life – life as you know it – to a new immortality, to a life which can be equivalent to godliness. Logic has created many misunderstandings. It goes on insisting on the duality of things without seeing the interconnecting link.

I am reminded of one incident…

Mahatma Gandhi and Muhammad Ali Jinnah were both fighting for the freedom of India. There was only one difference between them: Muhammad Ali Jinnah wanted Pakistan as a separate country, only for Mohammedans – a Muslim state – and Gandhi wanted the whole of India to remain one, big and vast. They fought continuously, and the British Empire depended on their agreement. Unless they agreed… The British Empire went on saying: "You are not in agreement yourselves, and we don't want to leave the country in a chaos. If we leave it in a chaos, without any decisive guidelines, there will be tremendous massacres, and the whole responsibility will be ours."

This was their politics. Jinnah was very stubborn. Finally, seeing the situation – either you have to remain slaves or you have to divide the country – Gandhi agreed on the division. India became two countries.

What I want to point out is that they had both become so attached in fighting with each other, and they were almost intimate friends. In Karachi, the capital of Pakistan in those days, Jinnah felt very lonely without Gandhi; he lost all interest. And here in New Delhi, Gandhi, who used to say that he was going to live to one hundred and twenty-five years, dropped the idea and said, "I want to die as soon as possible. There is no joy."

On the surface, logic will say that these two people were contradictory to each other, enemies to each other. But deep down there seems to be an intimacy. Jinnah was the head of his government in Pakistan. Gandhi was no one; his disciples were running the government. Just one year after, he was shot by a Hindu, which no one could have ever thought. It was possible that he might be shot by a Mohammedan, but he was shot by a Hindu. Life has its own way.

It looks strange, but deep down there is a certain connectedness. With Gandhi being alive, the Hindus in India would not be the only power because there were Mohammedans, Jews, Christians, Jainas, Buddhists. And Gandhi wanted to make an absolutely secular state. Jinnah did a good job; he got rid of almost all the Hindus in Pakistan and made a Mohammedan state, a religious state.

Gandhi could not do that. If Gandhi were alive, he would have prevented anything along those lines. And the strangest thing is that India has the greatest Mohammedan population in the whole world. No other country has… Even today, after the division of Pakistan on one side, Bangladesh on another side, India has the biggest Mohammedan population. It is the biggest Mohammedan nation.

The fear of the Hindus was: "Soon these Mohammedans, who produce children more efficiently and are allowed by the constitution to have religious freedom – each Mohammedan can marry four women – soon they will be the majority in the country. Again, Hindus will be living under Mohammedan rule."

Gandhi had to be removed. And the moment the news reached all over India that Gandhi had been shot, everyone, without any exception, thought that he must have been killed by a Mohammedan. I said to my father, "I don't think so because the Mohammedans have achieved what they wanted. They wanted a separate country – they have got a separate country. Whatever their demands were, they have been fulfilled. Why should they kill

Mahatma Gandhi, who is not in their way at all? He was certainly killed by a Hindu."

Unfortunately, that Hindu came from Pune. But the day Gandhi was killed and the news reached Karachi… That whole year Muhammad Ali Jinnah had not had guards, security, because he could not think that any Mohammedan would kill him. He had given them a whole country which did not belong to them.

He was sitting in the garden talking to his secretary when the news came on the radio that Gandhi had been assassinated by a Hindu. Suddenly Muhammad Ali stood up, and his secretary had to support him because he was staggering. He was so shocked by the very idea: a Hindu killing Mahatma Gandhi! Then what was possible became clear to him – he could also be killed by a Mohammedan.

And actually, he was killed by Mohammedans, but in such a slow way that it did not look like an assassination. He was old and sick, and since Mahatma Gandhi had died he never left his bed.

Everyone said, "You should be happy that Gandhi is dead."

He said, "I feel very hollow without him. He was my joy, we were party to a game. Now I am alone. Now there is no one with whom I can play the old game. Now there is no one who is exactly my contemporary. My only contemporary was Mahatma Gandhi; he is dead."

He became sick and he gave the position of acting head of the country to his closest disciple, Liyakat Ali Khan because he was not able to work. And what Liyakat Ali Khan did… Just now the diary of the doctor who looked after Muhammad Ali Jinnah has been published. Liyakat Ali Khan moved Muhammad Ali Jinnah to a remote part of Pakistan where there was no medicine, no hospital – if you asked for any medicine it would take three weeks to reach there – no railway lines, no airport, nothing, with the argument that the climate would suit him. Now he was in power.

And Jinnah was only given a doctor, not even a nurse or a servant to look after him. The doctor's remembrance is, "It was a political murder done in a very diplomatic way." There would be periods of three weeks when there was no medicine. The doctor would go on giving information that medicine was needed absolutely immediately, and after three weeks the urgent medicine would arrive.

My own feeling is that Jinnah was also killed. The doctor reports in his book, "Jinnah confided a strange secret to me: 'I have committed a mistake by dividing India and Pakistan.'" This is a very strange thing. His whole life he fought for Pakistan, and at the end he says, "I committed a great mistake, and now there is no going back. I am too old and Gandhi is not alive. If I had a little health left, I would have flown to New Delhi, to Jawaharlal, and said to him, 'Drop this idea of two countries. It is foolish.'" But he could never agree with Gandhi.

Were they enemies or complementaries? Ordinary historians will say they were enemies; they were not. Jinnah had immense respect for Gandhi, and so was the case with Gandhi. Agreement or nonagreement on political matters was one affair, but love for each other was a totally different thing.

You will not believe what Gandhi had offered Jinnah: "I will make you the first prime minister of India, but let India remain undivided. And you can choose your cabinet. I will not interfere, and I will withdraw Jawaharlal and others who are contenders. They are my people; I can tell them to withdraw, let Jinnah have his government. I trust you; the country will not suffer in your hands, it will prosper in your hands. Your intelligence, your caliber, your character – everything makes it reasonable that you should be the first prime minister of the whole country. Why be the head of a small section of the country when I am offering you the whole continent of India?"

But Jinnah refused. He said, "I never accept anything. I fight for it and I win it. Your idea is good, but it is your idea." They fought their whole lives and both suffered. Gandhi was continually inquiring about Muhammad Ali Jinnah's health: "How is he? Is he still the same warrior, with the same sharp intelligence?" And the same was true on the other side.

I am just giving you an example from human reality. When your enemy dies, something in you dies too; you are no longer the same. The enemy was also part of your being. You may not have thought about it in that way, that he was complementary to you. On a wider scale the whole existence is complementary. But Aristotle, who created Western logic, could not understand this complementariness. He is thought to be the father of logic – he is not even the uncle because by and by his whole logic is proving to be wrong.

In the East, we have a totally different logical approach. It is in tune with life. Those who are not accustomed to it will say it is contradictory, it is inconsistent. But those who understand, they can see the underlying connectedness.

One morning a man asked Gautam Buddha, "Do you believe in God?" Buddha said, "God? God does not exist. The question of belief does not arise." And he said it so strongly.

In the afternoon, another man came and asked, "Does God exist?"

And Buddha said, "Yes, absolutely yes. Without God, life would be just dead, unconscious. God is the intelligence of existence."

In the evening another man came and said, "I don't know from where to begin. I am not a thinker; I don't know whether God exists or does not exist. I have not yet taken a partisan view. Would you help me to see the reality?"

Listening to him, Gautam Buddha did not answer, but closed his eyes and went into deep meditation. The man, seeing the beauty and the grace of Buddha meditating, himself fell… You know that kind of experience: if you are sitting with a few people and one man goes on yawning, soon you start feeling sleepy also. We are not islands, we are connected, so things enter each of us. And a man of the quality of Buddha, with such tremendous silence, created such an atmosphere that the man fell into that silence; he also closed his eyes.

After one hour, Buddha shook him and asked him, "Have you received the answer?"

The man touched Gautam Buddha's feet and said, "I am grateful. There is no question and there is no answer. There is only pure silence in the inner being of man, and that silence goes on spreading into the innermost core of the universe. But there is no question, no answer. Life is very innocent. I am grateful that you showed me the way."

Ananda, who remained always by Gautam Buddha's side to take care of him, was very puzzled because he had heard all three answers. In one God does not exist, in one God exists; in another, the question does not arise. When everyone had left, Ananda asked Gautam Buddha, "Don't disturb my sleep. I will not be able to sleep with such kinds of contradictory answers. One expects you to be consistent. If you say yes then go on saying yes, if you say no then that is your answer. But what kind of answer is this?"

Buddha said, "Ananda, I have told you many times: those were not your questions and I was not answering you."

Ananda said, "I know, I have also heard you saying all kinds of things to me. But one thing is certain, I have ears and they hear. I cannot close my ears when you are answering someone. I have heard all three answers and they are contradictory."

Gautam Buddha said, "Just for your sleep's sake… I would like to say to you, the first man who came to me was an atheist – a confirmed atheist, a well-known atheist. He wanted me to say something that supported him. He was not a seeker, he was not really on a quest. I had to shatter his ego. The same was the case with the other man. He had come with a prejudice and he wanted to be supported in his prejudice. And that would be very unkind, to support anyone's prejudice. I destroyed his prejudice. You simply heard those answers, you did not see what the undercurrent was.

"The undercurrent was the same: to destroy the prejudice, to destroy the belief and to bring those people to real, authentic experience. That's why I did not answer the third man because he had no prejudice. He was so innocent that to tell him something would have been a crime. So all I could do was to go into meditation, and around me in the deep silence of the night... And he was an innocent man; he also fell into silence. He experienced his own inner peace for the first time – no question, no answer. He was grateful. He touched my feet, saying that I had solved his trouble."

The work of a master is very complex because he is working with so many people of different prejudices, different conditionings. And he has to shatter them all and make them absolutely clean, just as they were born, knowing nothing. But that knowing nothing was such a beautiful flower in the child. It filled him with wonder. Knowledge kills wonder. Not knowing fills you with mysterious experience.

When the child opens his eyes and sees the birds, the sun rays, the trees, the greenery, and so many colors... He cannot describe them; he does not know even their names. But he lives almost in paradise. In his innocence is paradise.

My effort here is to make you as innocent as a child. I am teaching no belief system, so the question of contradiction does not arise. I am preaching no philosophy, so contradiction does not arise. My effort is to demolish all the rubbish that you have collected down the ages. If I can remove all that rubbish from your mind and can give you a clean sky, my work is done. Without knowing, you will know. The mystery, the mysterious, the poetry of life, the music and the dance, all will become available to you.

A truck driver is racing down the freeway at seventy miles per hour when suddenly a face appears level with his left-hand cab window. The driver leans over and sees that a man is standing on the saddle of his motorbike, steering with one foot on the handlebar.

The truck driver rolls down his window, and the biker holds up a cigarette and says, "Have you got a light?"

"I have," says the driver holding out his lighter, "but you'd better be careful or you'll kill yourself."

"No, I won't," replies the biker, "I only smoke three a day."

Logic is not the way to life – it leads away. The path that leads to life consists of a clarity just like that of a mirror: it reflects everything but holds on to nothing.

Aristotle, although considered to be the father of Western logic, was not much of a logician. He has written in his books that women have less teeth than men. And he had two wives; any night he could have counted his wives' teeth. But no, in Greece it was just as in other lands: a prejudice against women, that they must have something less than men; they cannot be first-class citizens on any grounds – even about teeth.

This man Aristotle gave many ideas which worked up to a point and then flopped because they were not coming from an enlightened being, they were not coming from a deep meditation. They were just superficial thinking. Today a new logic has come into existence: non-Aristotelian logic. Following logic, Euclid made his geometry. Now, because the father figure is falling, Euclid has been losing ground every day. A non-Euclidean geometry has come into existence.

You can enforce stupid ideas on small children. For example, that two parallel lines never meet. But no one asks, "Can you draw two parallel lines – exactly parallel?" It is impossible. Whatever you create is going to meet; maybe miles away, but parallel lines meet because parallel lines are created by human beings, who cannot do anything with absolute perfection.

Euclid goes on saying, "The definition of a line is that it has length, only length." But can you draw a line which has only length? However thin it is, it will have something more than length. He defines a point as that which has no length, no breadth; can you make a point without length or breadth, however small it is? Now every concept of Euclid is being questioned. And Euclid is only a logical extension of Aristotle. Aristotle is not a sage; he is simply a thinker. A thinker cannot come to conclusions which can be true – only in appearance. Only the sage can see reality as it is. It is Aristotle who divided the world into two: the material and the spiritual.

It is such a coincidence, interesting coincidence, that the spiritual world is called the metaphysical. And the reason is only that in Aristotle's book he has chapters, and after the chapter on physics comes the chapter… He does not call it metaphysics, he simply says that there are things which are not confined to the physical world. But because the chapter comes after the one on physics – *meta* means after, *metaphysics* means after physics – it has taken a strange meaning.

Existence is one. You may divide it arbitrarily for certain purposes, but never for a moment forget that your division is arbitrary. Existence is one solid whole. Matter is nothing but spirit condensed; spirit is matter which has come to blossom. The difference between the seed and the flower.

It is not a difference because the seed contains the flower and the flower contains many seeds. So it is a circle, it is not a division. All divisionary ideas are dangerous. The East also has grown its own logic, but it is not Aristotelian. Buddha's logic is a fourfold logic. If you ask him, "Is there God?" he may say, "Perhaps." Perhaps is not an answer. If you ask, "Is there any doubt?" he will say, "Perhaps." "Are you not certain?" he will say, "Perhaps."

Mahavira extended the idea of "perhaps" to the very extreme. His logic is sevenfold. It is one of the most complicated ideas, but very representative of reality, because he says, "Whatever you say contains only one aspect of reality. What about other aspects? You have to make other statements." According to him, unless you make seven statements you will not be able to cover the whole reality. But those seven statements are going to be contradictory to each other.

Ask him, "What about God?" and he says, "God is." Immediately he says, "God is not." And following that, "God is both: is, is not." He continues, "God is both not: neither is, nor is not." He finalizes, "God is indefinable."

Mahavira could not gather many followers for the simple reason that only very crazy people will accept such a thing. People want definite answers. But existence is a flux, it is not definite; it is changing, it is moving. It has all aspects possible. In some way you can say, "Yes, it is true." And in some way, you can say, "It is not true."

A man was on the witness stand in a court. There had been a murder. Another witness had said that the murder had happened inside the house, and this witness said that the murder happened under the open sky.

The judge was a little puzzled. Both men were trustworthy, of integrity. Then his clerk told him, "Don't be puzzled, both are right. The house was being built, but the roof had not been put on it. So the murder happened in the house, but it happened under the open sky."

If you watch life, you will find so many things which logically don't fit. But that simply means you have not gone deep enough; otherwise they *have* to fit. They are part of this existence.

Paddy is called as the prime witness in an assault case, but gets things a little mixed up in his account of the affair.

"It was Dennis who started it all, your honor," begins Paddy. "He trod on my foot. So I pushed him off and smacked him on the jaw. Just then, his dog ran up and I hit him again."

"Hit the dog?" asks the judge.

"No, your honor, I hit Dennis. Then I picked up a stone and threw it at him and it rolled him over and over."

"Threw a stone at Dennis?" asks the judge.

"At the dog, your honor. Then he got up and hit me again."

"The dog?" asks the judge.

"No, Dennis. And with that he stuck his tail between his legs and ran off."

"Dennis?" asks the judge.

"No, the dog," says Paddy. "And when he came back at me, he got me down and pounded me, your honor."

"The dog came back at you?" asks the judge.

"No, Dennis, your honor. And he was not hurt at all."

"Who was not hurt?" asks the judge.

"The dog, your honor," says Paddy.

The judge scratches his head and fines the dog ten dollars.

After an unfruitful evening at the village dance, Ned begins his long, lonely walk back to the farmhouse. When he is halfway home the rounded, moonlit shapes of the big pumpkins in the fields remind the horny young fellow of so many shapely female asses. Settling down next to one of the pumpkins, he cuts a whole in the side and begins to get physical with it.

Suddenly a voice cries out, "Hey, you! What the hell are you doing with that pumpkin?"

Ned bolts upright, sees the policeman's badge glinting in the moonlight, and thinking quickly blurts out, "Pumpkin? What pumpkin? Oh, Christ, is it midnight already?"

Paddy decides to try life in the army and gets sent to a training camp. One night, he comes back from an exercise covered in cow shit.

"Why are you late back in camp?" snaps the sergeant major.

"Sorry, sir," says Paddy, "but as we crossed that field full of cows my hat blew off, and I had to try on thirty before I found it again."

# 22

# Drop Comparison and Feel Light and Joyous

Osho,
A lot came up for me in the discourse when you said that Anubuddha was so loving, so caring, so successful. The line that got me the most was, "our best bodyworker." My need for praise and fear of rejection was hit by a strong punch in the stomach. I feel like I'm drowning; you look like the lifeguard, so I scream out for help, but you just smile and tell a joke. How deep is the water?

Deva Satyarthi, I knew, as everyone else did, whose question this was! I was waiting for it; in fact it arrived almost the same day. But I waited so that you could cool down a little. You don't seem to understand the language of this commune. Here *everyone* is the best! I have never come across another category. This is not the ordinary world that you are in. Here things have a different meaning. And you need to be understanding enough; otherwise you will go on missing the basic points of inner growth.

Just the other day, when Anubuddha was working on my hand it was hurting so much, and I had to decide whether to say to him, "Do your worst, don't be worried," or, "Do your best, don't be worried." For the first time I came to understand that the worst and the best can be the same. But it is our whole upbringing which teaches competition, jealousy, which teaches comparison and continuously keeps us in a despair.

These are the foundations of despair and anguish. If you are continually comparing… Maybe someone has a little longer nose than yours, and you will feel very hurt and be against God saying, "What kind of miserliness… Just a little bit longer nose and I would have been a beautiful person. And he has given me a nose which looks as if he has punched it. Is it a nose or a joke? – punch line!"

You are always looking all around – thousands of people. There are people who have beautiful bodies, there are people who have great intelligence, and there are people who have money. And they all keep you in misery. They don't do anything to you, you do everything yourself; it is a self-created hell. But by continually comparing yourself with everyone you come across, you will never be without misery; you are following all the rules which create misery. One has to learn not to compare, not to be competitive.

Satyarthi has been working on my body almost for one month and he is my *best* bodyworker. There is no question and no doubt about it. But he is a best bodyworker in his own way; Anubuddha is in his own way. Leela was working on my body… My body is a kind of test for my bodyworkers. So many people… They enjoy working. I say, "Okay, torture me as much as you can. Anyway, I have nothing else to do. You are doing the whole work, I am simply witnessing how much people can torture each other."

Satyarthi is one of the best body torturers. If you are feeling in the dumps, feeling down, go to Satyarthi because there is only one way to get out of misery: to invite greater misery. Lying down, I have nothing to do, but I go on watching what their method of torture is. Satyarthi has a very clear-cut method. First, he does such a deep massage that your whole body hurts – naturally. And slowly he starts doing less deep massage and you start improving. Finally, he is doing a soft massage and your whole body is healthy. It was healthy in the first place! The day I understood his trick, I told him, "Now give someone else a chance."

But remember, the moment you drop comparison, competition, all jealousy disappears. You are yourself, perfectly beautiful; as an individual, incomparable. But even the greatest people suffer from such stupid things.

The man who created the greatest revolution in the world, Vladimir Ilyich Lenin, had small legs, disproportionate to his body. His feet never reached the ground when he was sitting. Special chairs were made for him; otherwise he was dangling in the air. Naturally he was feeling very inferior. The greatest revolutionary of the world... But what to do? Existence goes on joking with people. He was always very conscious that no one mentioned his legs. And in such situations the ordinary thing is that everyone will mention his legs: "What happened?"

A guest was coming to Hymie Goldberg's family and he was a great politician, very powerful. And Hymie Goldberg and his wife Becky were telling their son, Herschel, the whole day, "Remember, don't mention his nose!"

The boy was very much puzzled, "Why so much concern about his nose? Many guests have come, but no one has told me, 'Never mention his...' Why should I mention his nose?"

Then the guest came and there was great silence. Herschel said, "My God, he has no nose! The whole day I have been tortured: don't talk about his nose. And Jews know what a nose is! This you call a nose?"

Hymie Goldberg hit his head. He said, "I wasted the whole day telling him, 'Herschel, you can go out and either play or meet someone or go to your grandmother's house. But if you remain here, a guest is coming – don't mention his nose.'"

Herschel had said, "I am not leaving this place because if something strange is coming..."

Naturally, the thing that you don't want anyone to know, everyone will know. Your very hiding will indicate that something is wrong. It is a very strange atmosphere, created by the whole world. It has a certain background behind it. It wanted to destroy the individual, take away his dignity. It wanted to destroy the joyfulness and give him misery because only miserable people are controllable, only miserable people are able to be exploited. Miserable people are always ready to play into the hands of others, the vested interests.

The vested interests don't want individuals because an individual, just by the very definition, is a rebel. He does not belong to any crowd, religion, nation, race; he simply is himself. It is very difficult to exploit a world which consists of individuals. If the world consists of individuals, it is very difficult to create unnecessary wars, destruction. Because if the world consists of miserable people, you can force them to do anything. They are always looking upward, for someone to order them. It comes to the extreme point in the army. All the trainings in all the armies of the world are basically the same. The structure is how to destroy the individual, but in such a way that you will never think that it is destroying the individual. They call it discipline, they call it obedience, they call it courage. They call it many beautiful names. And what is the training?

In the Second World War when there was a shortage of people in the army; a professor in England had to be compulsorily enrolled. He resisted. He said, "Listen, I am a professor of philosophy. I cannot do anything without thinking about it. I cannot even shoot without first contemplating about the consequences."

But they did not listen. They thought, "We will manage." They had their training.

The first day he was standing in the line in the morning for parade and the commander said, "Left turn." Everyone turned except the professor.

He was thinking, "I don't see any point, why should I turn left? There is no reason at all. I am perfectly good as I am."

The commander looked very angrily at him, but remained silent, thinking that he would take him to task afterward. Then he ordered everyone to turn to the left, to the right; to go backward, to go forward. And then finally to stand in the same place where they had started the whole exercise. He then came to the professor who was standing and asked him, "Why don't you move?"

He said, "Why should I move? And what have all these people gained by moving? These are all idiots! For no reason: move left, move right, go forward, go backward. I am not an idiot."

The commander said, "This is a strange fellow. No one has ever raised the question." He said to the general, "This man is absolutely uncontrollable. Whatever you say, he asks why. If you say, 'Your shoes are not shining as they should be shining,' he says, 'I am perfectly happy with them as they are. And what has it to do with the training and the discipline?' If you say, 'Your clothes are not perfectly well ironed,' he says, 'It is not your problem. I like loose clothes.'"

Finally, he went to the general and said, "You take over this man. He may spoil the others because the others laugh. And the others have also started thinking, 'Perhaps the professor is right. What is wrong in loose clothes, if he likes loose clothes? What is wrong if the shoes are not shining? In what way are shining shoes going to win the war?'"

The commander said, "He raises such questions that I cannot manage. Take him away."

The general called the professor and said, "You'd better work in the mess." And he gave him a pile of peas and told him to sort out the bigger peas from the smaller peas: "Make two piles, and after one hour I will come to see the result."

After one hour he came and saw the result. The professor was waiting, looking at the peas. The peas were sitting in the same place. The general asked, "What is the matter with you? Can't you sort out bigger peas from smaller ones?"

He replied, "The problem is, where to put the middle ones? And I never do anything unless I have planned it completely. I have not been able to figure out where to put the middle ones. Not all are big and not all are small – there are middle ones too. Tell me, where should I put the middle ones? And if you tell me with the big ones, then why? Explain! If you tell me with the smaller ones, an explanation is needed."

He was released from the army, with honor. This type of man is not needed in the army. The army wants obedient people. Whatever is said has to be done; there is no question of why. This obedience is nothing but another name of slavery, creating a slave psychology. First, "Left, right, backward, forward" – innocent things because you are not destroying anything, not killing anyone. But they have developed certain tactics down the ages.

Once you become obedient and start doing things you are told, and you don't ask why, then when one day you are marching with guns, the moment you are ordered to shoot you don't think even for a moment, "Why?" That man is absolutely innocent. He has not done any wrong to you. He also has a wife, he also has children, he also has old parents waiting for him, just as your parents are waiting and praying that you will come back home soon. If the soldiers start thinking this, both soldiers will throw away their guns and will hug each other and say, "It is time to go home. What is the point?"

If the politicians cannot agree on certain points, that is *their* business. They should wrestle with each other. Gorbachev and Ronald Reagan can have a boxing match and decide – whoever wins. But why waste millions of people's lives? Millions of people are in the army wasting their lives. Just "Left, right, left, right." And finally comes the loaded gun, "Shoot!" Or the bomb.

The man who dropped the bombs, atom bombs, on Hiroshima and Nagasaki did not think for a single moment about what he was doing. His mind was completely brainwashed, completely mechanical. He had been ordered; he was obeying. Obedience is the greatest religion, not only in the army, but also in the church; not only in the politician's world, but also in the priest's conception of existence – obedience, just obey. And he obeyed.

A man of *small* intelligence and individuality would have thought at least twice, "What am I going to do? One hundred thousand people will be destroyed within three minutes." But he dropped atom bombs on two cities. Two hundred thousand people... He came back to his camp, and in the morning when asked, "Did you have any rest?" he said, "Why not? I followed the order, I rested well. I am an obedient person."

Obedience is the greatest value in a world of slaves. And this is not only the case with the ordinary politician and the priest; it begins with your God himself. He was against Adam and Eve because they disobeyed. What kind of God have people been worshipping? A God who prevents his own children from eating the fruit of the tree of knowledge and the tree of eternal life does not seem to be a very loving father. He seems to be the most dangerous, a despot. That's what the Devil managed to convince Eve of. And the Devil was absolutely right.

You will be surprised to know, there are thousands of Devil worshippers in the world. I can see the point, why they worship the Devil. He was the first revolutionary, and he suggested the right thing. He said "These are the two most important trees in the whole garden of Eden. If you know and if you experience eternal life, what else is needed? Wisdom is enlightenment and eternal life is deathlessness: you have attained everything. God has prohibited the two most important things in life. And the reason why he has prevented you is that he is afraid that if you eat these two fruits, you will also become like God. He is jealous! He is afraid that he will lose his power and everyone will be as powerful as he is."

Now, this fascist has been worshipped as God and the poor fellow, the Devil, has been condemned. He who has been the greatest benefactor of humanity. He has not harmed anyone, he has simply suggested that these are the two things worth achieving: the wisdom of the truth, and the life which knows no death. Then it takes a totally new aroma, a beauty and a blessing.

God has prevented you so that you can remain slaves, afraid of death, afraid of disease, and always a worshipper. He has destroyed your dignity by preventing you. I have always loved that, for some reason which is lost far back in the historical records, the word *devil*... It comes from the Sanskrit word *divine*. It exactly means God. In its origin, God means nothing; it doesn't have any meaning in any language. It is just Godot.

When I was reading *Waiting for Godot* I thought, Godot seems to be like a German word. The very sound of the word... One of my old sannyasins, Haridas, was with me. I asked Haridas, "What is German for God?" He said, "The German for God is *Gott*!" It seems only Germans have *Gott* it! God does not mean anything. It is a meaningless word and you can manage to give any image to it.

So I cannot condemn Devil worshippers. They are growing. Just a few days ago there were reports from Australia that Devil worshippers are not only worshipping the Devil, they won't allow the Christian church to continue their Sunday ritual. They throw stones at the churches, at the windows, disturb the meetings. And they are all Christians – they are not my sannyasins!

Deva Satyarthi, your question is good for everyone. From this moment start learning that we don't have any other category than the best. Everyone is the best in his own way. There is no one else to be compared to. And once you drop this comparison business, you will feel so light and so full of joy. The same energy that goes on becoming jealousy, competition, comparison turns into blissfulness, and becomes a shower of ecstasy in the deepest core of your being.

That day after I talked about Anubuddha I remembered Satyarthi, and I knew that he was going to be very disturbed. While passing him I had smiled at him – just to give a finish, the last touch. But he could not laugh. If he had laughed, he would have become enlightened!

Little Herschel Goldberg is causing his parents much heartache by his behavior. He has already been kicked out of two state schools, so in desperation they send him to a Roman Catholic school.

When Herschel gets home from his first day at school, he goes straight to his room to do his homework. Hymie comes home from work and says to Becky, "Well, how did Herschel get on at his new school?"

"Fine," says Becky, "he is upstairs now doing his homework."

"Homework?" cries Hymie. "He has never done any homework in his life!"

So Hymie runs upstairs and says to Herschel, "Well, son, how come you are doing homework? Why this big change?"

"Well," says Herschel, "I am the only Jewish boy in the school and up on the wall they have a picture of the last one who went there. And, Oy! you should see what they did to him. They nailed him to a lamppost!"

Man is living in fear. He is doing everything out of fear. If he does not do it, he will lose respectability; if he does not do it according to the idea of others, he will not be thought to be someone special. It is all fear, and nothing great ever comes out of fear. Anything great is born only out of love, meditation, silence, understanding. If you create out of fear, it is not creation. Your fear will be there, just like a shadow, destroying the beauty of your creation. If your creation comes out of joy, then whatever you do has a beauty, a beauty that you can be proud of. Whether anyone understands it or not does not matter.

I am reminded of Van Gogh…

He painted – perhaps the first painter – with his own blood. He was a poor coal miner's son. The family was not able to send him to an arts school. The family could not conceive what crazy kind of idea he had got, that he had to become a painter. He left the family, but he had no other kind of education, qualification. Every week his brother used to send him exactly seven days' money for food, clothes, absolute necessities. And Van Gogh was fasting for four days and saving the money to purchase paints and canvases and brushes. One day he would eat, one day he would fast.

Perhaps no man has fasted so spiritually. This I call a spiritual fast because it is in the service of creativity. It is not out of greed where you fast because you want heavenly pleasures after death. Where it will be counted how many fasts you did. That is sheer greed; it is not spirituality. You give to beggars just as a way of opening an account in God's bank. And these beggars go on saying that if you give one rupee here, there you will get a thousand in return. It is not even business; it is sheer gambling. It is not spirituality. I can say that only a man like Van Gogh fasting is spiritual.

He would paint, and he was so far ahead of his contemporaries that no one ever understood what he was painting. Not even painters could understand his paintings. He could not sell a single painting his whole life. And now a single painting is sold for ten million dollars, twelve million dollars. There are only two hundred left, and he had painted thousands. He had given them just to friends because what else to do? He had no place to store them.

One day, a man came to purchase a painting. Van Gogh was very happy. He started showing him all the paintings that he thought were his best creations.

The man said, "Don't worry. Give me anything, just this is the price."

This was so insulting. He immediately threw the money out on the street and pushed the man out and told him, "Tell my brother never to send any other man to purchase my paintings. You are not the man… You don't even have an eye for the beauty, for creativity. You don't even want to see… Certainly I can say that this money has been given to you by my brother, just to give me a little satisfaction that at least one painting has been sold."

It was a very strange life – fasting, continuously painting, he was becoming weaker and weaker. Finally, he wanted to paint the sun, so day after day he was just watching the sun – painting, but then rejecting the paintings; they were not coming up to his standard. He went crazy. He was forced to enter a mental asylum. He remained in that madhouse for one year.

That was the only peaceful time, where the medical and the psychiatric doctors were sympathetic to him and his whole misery. He had done no harm. And they allowed him to have paints and everything that he wanted, from the institution's money. For the first time he had everything he needed to paint without being hungry. His best paintings are those which he painted in the madhouse.

But still he was thought mad because the paintings were not created for selling; the paintings were not competitive, had no ambition; the paintings contained no desires and greed to become someone special. The paintings were the children of his love. And he painted as an individual; his society could not understand them because he did not follow the society's symbols. For example, his trees all reach higher than his stars. Now, anyone can point out, "This is not factual. Stars are far higher, and your trees are going beyond the stars." He said, "What can I do? Whenever I listen to the trees I feel that they are the desires of the earth to reach the stars. I am simply painting what I am experiencing."

He painted his stars as spirals. Everyone laughed because stars are not spirals. Just a few days ago, physicists have come to the idea that stars are spirals – just because of their distance we cannot see that they are spirals. And for the first time Van Gogh was validated by science. Just a hundred years before, with naked eyes, with no scientific instruments... Van Gogh's clarity must have been immense. His love must have been so enormous, his silence so penetrating, that it reached the farthest stars without any instruments, without any support. Everyone was against him, but he painted stars as spirals.

A man should live according to his heart. Even if he remains a beggar, he will have a dignity which even a king cannot have. A king can lose his dignity within minutes. A man shouldn't work out of fear and comparison to defeat someone, but to express his own genius. And everyone has a genius of some kind.

Now something for Deva Satyarthi to laugh. I don't want anyone to be serious here. It is a temple of love, a temple of laughter. Seriousness is considered sickness by me.

A woman is out riding one day when she falls off her horse and shoots straight through a hedge, where her jeans and sweater are torn off. She is lying naked and unconscious in the field when Father Murphy comes by on his bicycle.

Seeing the naked girl, he runs over to see what has happened, but not knowing what to do, he places his black priest's hat over her pussy and jumps on his bicycle to go and get help.

Just then, Paddy and Sean stagger out of the pub and go over to the hedge to take a piss.

Seeing the girl lying there, Paddy turns to Sean and says, "Look, that girl seems to be in trouble."

"She is," says Sean, "and the first thing we've got to do is to get Father Murphy out of there."

A young cowboy, in the Wild West for the first time, finds himself in a town without women. At the local saloon, he asks the other cowboys how they manage without women, and they tell him to find a sheep or a cow for a companion.

A few days later, the young man walks in with a pig. He sits her down at a table and then walks over to the bar and says, "I will have a large whiskey for myself and a root beer for the young lady."

The bartender reaches below the bar and brings out his shotgun. He points it at the young man, who starts to back away.

"I don't understand," he says. "You told me I could find a companion."

"I know," replies the bartender, taking aim.

"Then why are you pointing that gun at me?" cries the cowboy.

"We told you to find a companion," says the bartender, "but not the sheriff's wife."

# 23

# Woman's Greatness, Woman's Freedom

Osho,

Theoretically speaking, enlightenment and women are just great. But what about practically speaking?

Without women there would not have been any enlightenment. That's the reason why women themselves don't become enlightened; they are continuously engaged in making men enlightened. They don't have time enough for themselves. Their sacrifice is great.

There is an incident in Gautam Buddha's life. When he was born, he was born the son of an old man. The father was praying to the gods; otherwise, who was going to inherit the kingdom? Finally, Gautam Buddha was born. There was great celebration. But in the whole celebration, the most important thing that happened was…

A great enlightened sage used to live in the Himalayas, and people used to go to him just to feel his presence; just to look into his eyes, just to hear his words which indicated toward the wordless, for his silence, his music. His very being was music. His very presence was an invisible dance. He was very old. The sage suddenly got up and rushed toward Gautam Buddha's house. It was a long journey from the Himalayas, but he said to his disciples that he had to do it, he would not be born again. Enlightenment means ultimate death. You will not have another imprisonment in a body, in desires, in jealousies, in all kinds of uglinesses. You will be here, but just a pure breeze, merged into the whole.

The sage said, "I am not going to be born again, and Gautam Buddha has just been born. One day, he will become the greatest enlightened one. I want to touch his feet because our meeting can happen only now."

The king was very impressed. He could not believe it; he wanted the old sage to bless the child. He said, "Bring the child." Rather than blessing him, the sage touched his feet. And tears rolled down from his eyes.

The king said, "What is the matter? Is there something wrong? Is there some fatality, some danger?"

He said, "No, I am crying because I will not see this beautiful being blossoming in its utter beauty. But I am happy that at least I have touched his feet."

This created great trouble in the mind of Buddha's father. "It means he is going to become enlightened, a sage. Then who is going to take care of the kingdom? He will renounce the world."

He called all the astrologers of his kingdom and asked them to find out the future of the boy. They all looked at his birth chart and remained silent. Each looked at the other: "You say it, because the old man may have a heart attack." But a young man, Konda, was not very concerned about anything except the truth.

Konda said, "Listen, all these old astrologers are silent because they don't want to say something which may hurt you. But I have to say it. Whether it hurts you or not is not my business; you have called me, the chart is before me. This boy has two possibilities. Either he will become a world conqueror, a chakravartin, or he will become one of the greatest enlightened people."

A new problem arose: how to prevent his enlightenment. All the astrologers made a suggestion. What they suggested, in fact became the cause of his enlightenment. They knew astrology, but they did not know anything about enlightenment. They said, "Give him all the luxury, all the pleasures, never allow him to see anything miserable, old, dead. Not even a dead leaf should be left in his garden. All the dead leaves should be removed in the night. And surround him with all the beautiful girls of the kingdom. Let life be just a playfulness to him. Then there is no need to renounce it. Obviously, one renounces life because it is not all playfulness; it is just the opposite – a long, long agony."

Gautam Buddha's father arranged everything: beautiful palaces for him, for different seasons in different places, far away from people. He was not allowed to move among the people. No old men, no old women, no dead people were allowed in his palaces. And the most beautiful girls were his playmates. He grew up in immense luxury; perhaps no one has grown up the way he did.

The astrologers said, "As soon as he is old enough, mature enough, get him tied in a marriage." One of the most beautiful women, Yashodara, was chosen to be his wife. His whole life was just pleasure. The whole night was dance, song, music, women, wine, and the whole day was for rest, sleep. But this whole situation created the impetus for enlightenment.

Every year, he had to go to inaugurate the youth festival of the kingdom; it was a special occasion. The story is beautiful. At this point, I think it becomes mythological, but it does not lose significance, it gains more significance. The gods in heaven became very worried. Twenty-nine years had passed and they are waiting and waiting that this man is going to become a buddha. Now he is married, has a child, born just a day before. They managed a small strategy: an old man, coughing, with an utterly sick appearance passed by the golden chariot.

Buddha asked his charioteer, "Channa, what has happened to this man?"

The story is that Channa would not have said the truth, so a god spoke from inside Channa: "This happens to everyone. This life is nothing but a death every moment, and he has reached the last stage. Ahead of it is the graveyard."

Buddha said, "No one told me anything about death. I have never heard about it." And the gods had managed for a small funeral procession to pass by the side of the chariot.

Buddha again asked, "What has happened to this man? Why are people carrying him?"

And the gods within Channa spoke, "My lord, this happens to everyone. Everyone is here to die. Life is only a prelude, a preface to death."

A great transformation was happening in the mind of Buddha. And then suddenly he saw a sannyasin. He said, "Why is he wearing orange clothes? I have never seen anyone wearing orange clothes."

The gods spoke again, "This man is in search of something deathless before death comes. This man wants to avoid death. This man wants to know not this ephemeral life but the real life, the authentic life which has no beginning, no end. He wants to know the existential, not this life which is made of the same stuff as dreams are made of."

A great turning point. Buddha said to Channa, "Turn back, I am not going to inaugurate the youth festival. I am no longer young. If youth is going, old age is coming, and death is the only certainty in life. Then before time is lost, I want to seek and search for the truth."

That very night he escaped. And while he was escaping, he saw beautiful women sleeping: someone's saliva was flowing from his mouth, someone had one eye open... For the first time he saw that these women and men were just bags of skin; behind them were hidden only skeletons.

If instead of Konda, I had been there and if the king wanted his son not to be enlightened, I would not have suggested that solution. He became fed up with women, bored and tired; he became fed up with luxury. One becomes accustomed to everything. And the moment you are accustomed it loses all juice.

He had nothing to live for in that palace; he never looked back. In the Buddhist scriptures this sentence comes so beautifully: "He never looked back." Because he had seen everything: all luxury, comfort, women, food, beautiful gardens, palaces. What is there to look back for? The point is to find something ahead – totally different from what he had been living up to now. He was asleep; a certain awakening had come to him, and now he wanted this awakening to reach its ultimate peak. Enlightenment is not something outside you. It is your own consciousness, growing to ultimate potentiality. It is your own lotus flower that blossoms in the silences of your heart.

Women have really supported men very much by nagging them, by torturing them, by harassing them.

In a small school, the teacher was asking, "Can you name an animal which goes out of the house as a lion and comes back as a rat?"

A small hand was raised. The boy said, "I know him, he is my father. Outside he is a lion; inside he is just a rat."

And man has to be a rat inside. In fact, every husband is a henpecked husband. It is just a way of adjusting. The whole day he is tired – so many things, so many ambitions, so many desires, so many conflicts – and when he comes home, the wife is ready, full of energy.

Hymie Goldberg comes home wearing a new hat.

"My God!" says Becky, "where did you get that hat?"

"At a clearance sale," replies Hymie.

"No wonder they wanted to clear it," says Becky, "it makes you look like an idiot."

"I know," says Hymie.

"Then why the hell," snaps Becky, "did you buy it?"

"I will tell you," replies Hymie. "When I put it on and looked at myself in the mirror, I looked so stupid that to argue with the salesclerk was impossible."

In fact, women should be given every honor for all the great awakened people. But to awaken someone else is charity. Men have not allowed women to become enlightened. Men have not allowed women to be anything that is their potential. In the whole of history, at the most ten women have become enlightened. The fact is very sad and miserable. These women must have been very rebellious.

In the Vedas, there is one woman, Gargi, and you can see her courage… The king of those days, Janak, used to have a great conference of the wise ones every year, to argue and discuss about the ultimate truth. He was himself very much a seeker. He wanted to listen to all the aspects, all the different pathways.

Yagnavalkya was one of the most important wise people. He had thousands of followers. And there was also a great prize: whoever won that great contest would get one thousand cows, which were standing outside the palace with their horns covered with thick gold.

It was getting hot. Yagnavalkya said to his disciples, "Take these cows to the ashram."

But they said, "You have not won the debate."

He said, "That I will do later on." He was so confident and everyone knew he would win, so no one objected, not even the king – but this was absolutely not right, to take the prize before you have even entered the discussion. You have accepted yourself as victorious already.

His disciples took away those one thousand cows. And Yagnavalkya was winning against other learned people; one by one, whoever stood against him was defeated immediately. But then for the first time he encountered a woman, Gargi.

Gargi said, "You will have to bring those cows back. You have not won the debate – I am here. I will ask a few questions and you will be finished." Even Yagnavalkya became afraid. No one had behaved like this, and a woman…

Gargi said, "Do you think God exists? Then give the evidence."

There is no argument that can prove God's existence – either you believe or you don't believe, but belief is not an argument. It is simply failure of your nerve. Yagnavalkya remained silent.

She asked, "Can you tell me if anyone created the world?"

He said, "Yes, God created the world."

Gargi laughed. On that beautiful, auspicious occasion, her laughter was immensely beautiful. She said, "Are you sure? Were you a witness? Or have you any other witness, who has seen you seeing God creating the world?"

Now, this was difficult. No one had ever witnessed it. The problem was, if Yagnavalkya said, "I witnessed," that meant the world was already created. What were you witnessing? You are the world. Certainly, the beginning cannot be witnessed. And if it cannot be witnessed, it cannot be proved.

Gargi said, "Neither is there God, nor is there any beginning, nor is there any end. These are all things which the parasite priests have invented, imagined, propagated. All kinds of nonsense and superstitions."

Yagnavalkya was known to be a silent, peaceful man. He forgot all about silence and peace, and said, "Gargi, if you speak any other word your head will fall on the earth."

Now, the sword is not an argument. Yagnavalkya had to return those one thousand cows in deep shame. When they were returned, Gargi said, "You can keep them. I am not interested in cows and gold. I was interested to see how much understanding you had."

There have been a few women… Yagnavalkya had two wives. Before leaving the world to go to the forest to meditate, he said to them, "You can divide all my possessions" – which were big and huge. But one wife, Katyayani, said, "If these possessions have not given you peace, do you think they will give me peace? If these possessions have not given you the truth, do you think they will give me the truth? I refuse. If you are going to meditate, I am going to meditate. Your going away proves that whatever we have been doing is futile. It does not create a connection with existence, it does not fill your heart with love, truth, celebration." And as Yagnavalkya went to the mountains, Katyayani also went in another direction to the mountains.

A few women have been of tremendous courage, but most women have been crippled by men. They have not been educated. They have not been allowed to read religious scriptures, they have not been allowed any social contact. Half of the world has been cut away from the other half completely. This is the greatest slavery that has happened on this earth; all other slaveries are very small. But even with this slavery, once in a while, women have asserted themselves. That shows the possibility.

In Arabia, Rabiya al-Adabiya was one such woman. One day people saw her running through the marketplace with a pot full of water in one hand and a burning torch in the other. They asked, "Where are you going?"

She said, "I am going to burn your paradise and I am going to drown your hell. These are all inventions of the priests, with which they have managed to enslave the whole humanity."

A mystic, Hassan, was staying with Rabiya. In the morning, he asked Rabiya's for her copy of Koran Sharif, and he was shocked to see that Rabiya had corrected many places in the Koran. "That is not done. The Koran is God's word, from God's only and final prophet, Mohammed. You cannot improve upon it." That's why there are no commentaries on the Koran.

Many times, many Mohammedan friends have sent me the Koran, beautifully printed, and asked me if I can comment on it. I said, "You have not commented on it for a different reason: Mohammedans will not tolerate anyone commenting on the Koran. My reason is different: there is nothing in it to comment on.

But al-Adabiya changed many words in the Koran. Hassan was very shaken. He said, "Adabiya, someone has destroyed your Koran."

She said, "No one can even touch my Koran. I have corrected it wherever it was wrong."

Hassan said, "You think the Koran can be wrong?"

Rabiya said, "The line you are reading is: when you meet the Devil, hate him, curse him. I have crossed it out because when I became myself, when my own flame became a great light around me, I could see one thing: I can only love, I cannot hate. Even if the Devil comes, stands before me, I will be loving, just the same as I will be loving if God is there. It is my own experience and I have not to follow the Koran; I have to correct the Koran according to my experience. A man is not made by books – books are made by men."

Now, such women indicate that if man had not repressed them… My own understanding is that more women would have become enlightened than men because man's mind is full of rubbish. And man's mind is much more outgoing. He may go to the Everest… Just think of Edmund Hillary standing on the Everest, how stupid he must have looked. And he risked his life on Everest for just two minutes.

Now people are going to the moon. The earth is in a mess and people are thinking of going to Mars. You cannot put your home right and people are trying to approach some other planet where living beings exist. Here in this world there is no dialogue, there is no love.

And because the woman is heart-oriented there is more possibility of her being awakened. Man is more logical, more arithmetical. Perhaps he can become a great scientist, but a woman is more poetic – potentially, but we have not allowed her. She can be a beautiful dancer, she can be a musician. She will open new avenues of enlightenment through the heart. Love will become her God.

You know Jesus said, "God is love." If it had been written by a woman she would have written, "Love is God." God must be secondary; it is a mental hypothesis. But love is a reality throbbing in every heart.

We have seen people like Meera… But only very courageous women could manage to come out of the repressive social system. She could manage because she was a queen; although her own family tried to kill her because she was dancing on the streets, singing songs. The family could not tolerate it; particularly in India and in Rajasthan, where the woman is very repressed. And a woman of the beauty of Meera, dancing in the streets, singing songs of joy…

There was a temple in Vrindavan, where Krishna had resided. In his memory a great temple was made, and the priest of the temple had to be a celibate. Now, celibacy is absolutely unnatural. It can drive you crazy, into unnatural perversions. No woman was allowed to enter that temple. Women were allowed only on the outside, to touch the steps of the temple. They never saw the statue of Krishna inside because the priest was adamant. When Meera came, the priest became afraid that she would come into the temple.

Two men with swords, naked swords, were placed before the gate to prevent Meera from coming in. But when Meera came – and such people are so rare, such a fragrant breeze, such a beautiful dance, such a song that brings into words that which cannot be brought into words – those two swordsmen forgot what they were standing there for and Meera danced into the temple. It was the time for the priest to worship Krishna. His plate, full of flowers, fell onto the ground as he saw Meera.

He was utterly angry and he said to Meera, "You have broken a rule of hundreds of years."

She said, "What rule?"

The priest said, "No woman can enter here."

And can you believe the answer? This is the courage… Meera said, "Then how have you entered here? Except one, the ultimate, the beloved, everyone is a woman. Do you think there are two men in the world – you and the ultimate? Forget all this nonsense." Certainly she was right. A woman full of heart looks at existence as a beloved. And existence is one.

There have been a few other women – Sahajo… But they are very few. It is a condemnation of men that you did not allow a woman to become a Gautam Buddha, that you did not allow a woman to become a Lao Tzu. The crime is so big that it is incalculable.

You are asking, "Theoretically speaking, enlightenment and women are just great. But what about practically speaking?" Practically speaking, they are great also. And the day that woman's greatness is accepted, her uniqueness is accepted, her freedom, her individuality are respected, the world will be filled with more love, more flowers, with more fragrance.

What has man been doing down the ages except fighting? And what has man's genius been doing except creating more and more dangerous, destructive weapons? They are not satisfied with the nuclear weapons which exist today; they are enough to kill the whole earth seven times. I don't understand: What is the point, now, of piling up more and more nuclear weapons? There is only one incidence – Jesus – of someone who resurrected and may have needed a second killing. But ordinarily people die only once.

The fact is that Jesus was not resurrected; he never died on the cross. He was taken off the cross before he could have died. The Jewish cross is such that it takes forty-eight hours to kill a person, because blood flows out of the body slowly, slowly. And Jesus was young – only thirty-three years old, healthy.

He was taken off the cross after six hours. It was a conspiracy between his disciples and the Roman governor of Judea; Judea was in slavery. The governor was not interested in killing an innocent man who had not done anything wrong. If he believes that he is the son of God, why prevent him? – let him believe. You can believe you are the father of God! Just a little imagination. He had not done anything wrong, he was just a little crazy and took things literally, but he was not a criminal.

So, this arrangement was made: Jesus was brought down after six hours – and in six hours, no one can die on a Jewish cross – and he was put into a cave; the guards were Romans. He was removed in the night. As he started to heal, he escaped. He died in India, in Kashmir. And Kashmir was one of the parts where Jews had been living for hundreds of years.

When Moses was looking for God's city, God's land, Israel, a tribe of the Jews got lost. In fact, Moses reached the wrong place; Israel is not worth anything. The lost tribe reached Kashmir. Kashmir is certainly the most beautiful place in the world. If anything can be said to be God's land, then Kashmir is it. Moses himself came to look for the lost tribe and he died in Kashmir. It is strange that Moses and Jesus both died in Kashmir. And there is every evidence; I have been to their graves.

In India, no one writes Hebrew. And those graves are not Mohammedan graves because Mohammedan graves have to be made in a way so that the head is always pointing toward Mecca. Those two graves are not Mohammedan graves. The Mohammedans have allowed the person who takes care of those graves to remain a Jew; otherwise, Mohammedans converted the whole of Kashmir. You can convert people's religion, but you cannot convert their noses. Their noses show that they are Jews. Just look at the nose of Jawaharlal Nehru or Indira Gandhi – these are Kashmiris.

And you will not believe it: they are brahmins but they eat meat. No brahmin eats meat in India, but because they were basically Jews and then became Mohammedans or Hindus, the basic nonvegetarian food continued.

A very detailed analysis is needed, which Christianity prevents because if it is known that they are certainly Jesus' and Moses' graves then it will become a holy place for both Christians and for Jews. And you should remember that Jesus was never a Christian. He was born a Jew, lived as a Jew, died a Jew. He never heard anything about these idiot Polack popes.

In this beautiful morning, in this silence, in these beautiful sounds of the birds, it is out of place to talk about serious things. So now a few really nonserious things, in tune with this beautiful morning. Don't destroy it with sermons.

Somewhere in a little shack in the middle of Australia, Bruce, Edna and their daughter, Shirley, have finished their kangaroo stew dinner, and are arguing about who is going to do the washing up.

There's a big fight, and finally Bruce suggests that they all lie down on the floor and the first person to move does the dishes.

The same night, Hamish MacTavish is driving his old pickup nearby, when the radiator overheats. He sees the shack and walks over there to get some water.

Going into the shack, he finds everyone lying on the floor, so he decides to help himself to water. On his way to the kitchen, he steps over Shirley, and in a moment of passion, jumps on her and fucks her.

He gets up from Shirley and finds Edna on the kitchen floor. The temptation is too great for Hamish and he jumps on Edna too.

Then he takes some water back to his car, but while he is filling the radiator, he burns his arm.

Hamish rushes into the shack and cries out, "Have you got any Vaseline?"

Hearing this, Bruce jumps up and yells, "Okay, okay! I will do the dishes!"

Paddy and Sean are deep in the mountains on a hunting trip, when they stop to rest. Paddy gazes at Sean and says, "You know, I'm a pretty big fellow. If I had a heart attack or broke a leg, how would you get me out?"

"Don't worry," replies Sean. "Last year I shot a sixteen-hundred-pound elk, way back in the hills, and got it out all right."

"How did you manage that?" asks Paddy.

"Simple," says Sean, "it took me twelve trips."

Paddy goes to the horse races in Dublin. In the evening, he walks into a pub and orders a large brandy for himself and drinks for everyone in the bar.

"And have one yourself," he tells the bartender, generously.

Half an hour later, the order is repeated, and this goes on all evening until at closing time when the bartender taps Paddy on the shoulder.

"I hope you don't mind my mentioning it," he says, "but your bill comes to two hundred pounds."

"Does it?" asks Paddy. "Well, I am sorry to hear that because I've not got a penny."

The bartender leaps over the bar and starts to beat Paddy and eventually kicks him out of the door, into the street.

The next evening, the pub is just opening when Paddy walks in.

"A large brandy for me," he announces, "and drinks for everyone in the bar. But I am not giving *you* one," he says to the barman. "After a couple of drinks, you get very nasty!"

# 24

# The Computer Is Part of Man's Creativity

Osho,

Some scientists are concerned that man will someday relinquish his intellectual supremacy to computers – monster artificial super-brains with an intellectual power far beyond anything we can now comprehend. Another fear is that through genetic engineering, man will be capable of growing artificial intelligence to order. Or there could be a combination of both, where super-grown organic brains can "plug in" to a super-computer; or computer super-chips can be implanted into brains. Would such super-computers or super-brains be capable of taking man on a quantum leap, cutting our deadly connections with the past, or would they too be unable to escape man's idiotic conditionings?

Anando, the question may not appear very serious, but it is one of the most serious questions possible. The first thing to remember is that it is going to happen. There is no possibility to avoid it; neither is there any necessity to avoid it. Perhaps I am the only one in the world who is in absolute support of mechanical brains taking over the work of human intelligence. The reasons why I am in support of such a strange thing are very clear. First, what we call the human mind is itself a biocomputer. Just because you are born with it does not make much difference. A better computer can be implanted in your mind – far more efficient, far more intelligent, far more comprehensive.

There are always people who are afraid of every new thing. Every new thing has been opposed vehemently by religions, by churches because every new thing changes the whole structure of human life. For example, the computer can change all the stupidity that man has shown through the whole of history. I don't think that computers would like to create war, or computers would exploit people, or discriminate between black and white, between man and woman.

Moreover, you are always the master, not the computer. You can always change the program of the computer. The computer is simply a tremendous instrument, which gives you immense possibilities that are not available to you biologically. You can do things which man has never dreamed of. The computer can be a thousand times more superior than Albert Einstein. Naturally the computer can produce a science far more fundamental, far more real; not changing every day because new discoveries go on happening and the old discovery becomes out of date. The computer can reach the very center of reality. It is an instrument in your hands; it can reveal to you whatever you want. It is not a danger.

And because it will be doing all the intelligent, intellectual, mental work, no one has seen the possibility that I am telling you: that you are left very simply to relax into meditation. The computer can be put to the side. The computer can do all the thinking; you need not go on continually chattering unnecessarily. The computer is not Christian, Hindu, Mohammedan. It is simply a mechanical device created by human consciousness. In return, it can help human consciousness to reach its highest potential.

But every new thing will be opposed because every new thing will make old things out of date. Old factories will close, old industries will close. There are many inventions which are never marketed in the world because the people whose business will be affected by them purchase their patents. And the scientist hasn't the money to make his own conception into a reality.

For example, in Japan there are a few scientists who have discovered that railway trains need not go at sixty miles per hour. They can go at four hundred miles per hour. And the significant is that if they go at four hundred miles per hour, just the speed alone will take them up four inches above the rails. But it is dangerous to all the old owners of the railways, small stations because the trains can't stop there. And particularly in Japan they have only the departing station and the terminal station – it is a small land.

They will not have accidents the way accidents happen today. They will never be late. They may even be ahead of time. And people sitting in them will never feel any bumps. The trains can go according to the whim of the driver, and can take thousands of passengers. But they are not being marketed. No country is interested in the invention because so much money is involved in the old railway trains, old railway stations. If these new trains are accepted, that whole business will go bankrupt.

It is just an example. There are at least a thousand inventions which can help humanity to be more comfortable, to be more joyous, to have better clothes, better food. But they will not ever come to light because there are people who are going to be ruined if those new things come onto the market. And naturally new things create fear. Now, sitting in a train for the first time, which is then going to take off, do you think you will not be afraid?

The situation was the same when the first railway train started in London – just ten or twelve miles of track. And all the churches were denouncing and condemning: "God never created the train, so this must be an invention of the Devil." And the old trains and their engines looked like the Devil! They were saying to people to be aware, "Don't get into them." The organizers were not asking for anyone to buy a ticket. On the contrary, they were offering free breakfast, lunch, to whoever was ready to go for the first ride in a railway train. In the whole of England only eight people were courageous enough.

The fear was created by the churches: "It is true that these trains will start, but what is the guarantee that they will stop? Once you are in, finished, the train never stops. And do you think just one breakfast and one lunch will do – forever? Can you give the guarantee that they will stop? Now, no one could guarantee it because the train had never even started. It was not a question of stopping.

The families of those eight people who entered were crying and weeping and their children were trying to pull them out, saying, "Dad, don't go." Wives were crying, "Are you mad? Don't you see? All the wise people of the land, the archbishops, bishops, ministers, priests, were all against it. Have you gone mad, staking your life on a free breakfast and lunch? I will give you the money, just get out!"

But those eight people said, "We are not going to get out. We have seen enough of the world, now let us see what happens if the train does not stop – something is bound to happen. And the driver will also be concerned about stopping it; otherwise he will be killed – we will kill him."

All the passengers had come with their guns so that if the driver did not stop, they could shoot the driver or force the driver to stop the train. But there was no need because there were no tracks longer than twelve miles. It had to stop after twelve miles and come back. And people could not believe it when the train came back and those eight people, smiling, with their guns, got off. They said, "Never in life has such a beautiful thing happened. Such speed!" Now, no one ever asks the driver, "Give me a guarantee that the train will stop." No one travels with a gun. The train is accepted.

But a train that goes at four hundred miles an hour is dangerous. All the churches will join together, all the religious people will join in, and will protest, "The government should stop it. This is very dangerous. These trains can run into cities, over people; no one can prevent them. Once they have taken off, they can destroy the whole earth; no need of any nuclear energy." And the people inside can enjoy all kinds of scenes. But it will be very difficult to persuade people: first to make those trains, and then to become passengers in them.

Now robots are working; they have already come into existence. And particularly in Japan, which is far more advanced in technology than any other country today, and where many factories are run by robots. They never tire, they never retire; they don't ask for a salary or for a raise. They don't make unions, they don't go on strike. They are the nicest people you can find. They work twenty-four hours, day in, day out. Their efficiency is perfect, a hundred percent.

But it is a danger because people will become unemployed. Now, the unemployed people are going to create trouble; they don't want robots. But I am all in favor of robots. Everyone should be unemployed *and* paid – paid for being unemployed. Robots are doing the work, you get the pay. And then life becomes sheer joy.

Then you can meditate, you can dance, you can sing, you can go on world trips. The problem arises because we cannot think of the solution. The solution is simple. You were paid because you were producing. Now the robot is producing more, many times more, and he is not being paid. There is no need for you to remain unemployed, hungry, poor. It is such simple arithmetic: you should be paid, paid more, because now you have vacated the place for a robot which produces a hundred times more. So, if your salary is doubled there is no loss.

And if the whole world is unemployed and has enough money to enjoy, do you think anyone is going to join the army? People will join carnivals, circuses... All kinds of celebrations will happen, but there is no need for war. Even if war is an absolute necessity, there are robots, just let them fight. No one is going to win. Both sides are robots; no one is going to be killed. Just, every day they come back with a few parts missing; repair them and send them back. Even war can become a great joy – no question of defeat or victory.

But people are afraid because they cannot conceive a certain possibility in which people don't suffer. Anando's question is that these computers are going to take the place of intelligence. They will be far superior in intelligence. But remember, those computers which are far superior in intelligence are in your hands. You are not in their hands, so there is no problem.

Up to now you have lived according to memory, which is an unnecessary burden, carrying it in your head. Twenty-five years of teaching in the schools, colleges, universities; PhDs, DLitts… What are you doing? – you are creating a computer, but with an old, out-of-date method which you are forcing small children to memorize. There is no need. The computer can do everything, the computer just has to be given information.

You can buy a computer which knows everything about medical science. You need not go to a medical college; you simply ask the computer and immediately the answer is there. Your memory is not so reliable. And the computer can always be fed with new memory because new discoveries are being made every day. The computer can be plugged into the main computer of the university, so without your even bothering, every new discovery concerning your subject is immediately fed into your computer. It waits there; you inquire, and the computer tells you.

You can have a multidimensional computer which has all kinds of memory, or a one-dimensional computer which has only history: the whole history of mankind. Now, *you* cannot have the whole history of mankind. Do you know on what date Socrates was married to Xanthippe? The computer can tell you immediately. That unfortunate date… I have always suspected that Socrates accepted the poison so easily because of his wife, because life was so torturous – death cannot be worse than that.

How much can you memorize? Your memory has a limitation. But the computer can memorize almost unlimitedly. And there are many more possibilities: one computer can join together with another computer and manage to figure out new inventions, new medicines, new ways of health, new ways of living. Computers should not be taken as monsters.

It is a great blessing. And what man's intellect has done is very small. Once the computer takes over, so much can be done that there will be no need for anyone to be hungry, no need for anyone to be poor; no need for anyone to be a thief, no need for anyone to be a judge because these all belong to the same profession – judges and thieves, criminals and law makers. There is no need for anyone to be poor and no need for anyone to be rich. Everyone can be affluent.

But perhaps no government will allow this to happen. No religion will allow this to happen because it will go against their scriptures, it will go against their doctrines. Hindus believe that you have to suffer because in your past life you committed evil acts. No one knows about past lives. They cannot accept an invention which can remove misery, poverty, sickness because then what will happen to the theory of reincarnation, and rewards and punishments of good and bad deeds? The whole doctrine of Hinduism will be simply meaningless.

If the computer can make your life as long as you want, if a computer can manage that you are always young – no need for old age unless you want – then who cares about... So many people will be affected. The medical profession will be affected, pharmacies will be affected, people who are living on your sickness will be affected.

A young man came from the university with an MD degree. His old father was waiting for him because he was tired, working his whole life. Three of his sons were studying at medical college – if at least one comes back, he can take his place and support the other two. And the young man immediately said, "Don't be worried. Rest and relax, I will take care."

On the third day he approached his father and said, "Dad, I have cured the woman you have been treating for thirty years."

The father said, "You idiot! That is the woman who has paid for your education and was paying for your two other brothers. I was keeping her in this condition. She was so rich she could afford to be sick. She was not poor."

To be rich and to be sick is very dangerous. To be poor and to be sick is not very dangerous. You will be cured very soon because you cannot pay much. On the contrary, you may ask the doctor, "What about the medicine, what about the food you have prescribed? I don't have any money." The doctor will think, "It is better to cure him and get rid of him." But when a rich man is sick it becomes professionally a very strange dilemma in the mind of the physician: to cure him or to have him linger on because the more he lingers on, the more money you get. If you cure him, you don't get that money.

But if computers can manage, then many professions will be affected. And these will be the professions that prevent it; they will make a thousand and one excuses: God never created a computer; computers are dangerous because they will take all intelligence away from you. What are you doing with your intelligence? – being miserable, being jealous? At least computers will not be jealous and will not be miserable. What are you doing with your intelligence? – destructiveness, all kinds of wars, all kinds of violence.

Computers can give you a complete holiday for your whole life. You can relax. You will have to learn how to relax because you have all become workaholics. For thousands of years, work, work, work hard! Computers will go against your whole conditioning about work. For the first time laziness will become a spiritual quality: Blessed are the laziest, for theirs is the kingdom of this planet. And if they want, in their laziness they can make beautiful gardens. Just out of joy, for no purpose. They can paint, not to sell, but just to rejoice in the colors, the mixing of colors, the dance of colors. They can play music, not for any monetary reason, not as a business, but simply as a playful joy.

Life can really become what man has dreamed of in paradise, here on this planet. There is no need to go that far. No one knows the way and no one has ever gone there. And those who have gone have not even dropped a card: "We have arrived!" Such miserly people – just a Christmas card… But paradise has to be created; there is no paradise in existence. It has to come out of man's awareness, consciousness.

The computer is also part of man's creativity. There is no need to become a competitor; you are the master. For the first time the computer and you are separate. That's what all the teachings of the mystics have been telling you: that your mind and you are separate. But it is difficult because the mind is inside your head and your consciousness is so close to it, so thousands of mystics have been teaching, but no one listens. The distance is not very much. But with computers, the distance will be very clear; there will be no need for any mystic to tell you.

Everyone will have his own computer in his pocket and knows that it is separate. And one is free from thinking; the computer is doing it. You want to think something, tell the computer. If your old habit of chattering arises tell the computer, "Chatter," and it will chatter. For the first time you can be what the buddhas have been saying: just be aware, silent, peaceful, a pool of consciousness.

A computer cannot be aware. A computer can be intellectual, a computer can be knowledgeable; a computer can be so knowledgeable that it can contain all the information of all the libraries in the whole world – a single computer that you can keep it in your pocket. It will relieve millions of people from memorizing unnecessary things. It will keep millions of people from teaching and torturing students. Examinations and all kinds of stupid things will disappear. The computer can be one of the greatest phenomena that has ever happened. It can become the quantum leap. It can break away from the past and all conditionings of the past.

Hymie Goldberg answers a classified advertisement in a newspaper which says, "Opportunity of a lifetime!" He is given an address and finds himself face-to-face with old man Finkelstein.

"What I am looking for," explains old man Fink, "is someone to do all my worrying for me. Your job will be to shoulder all my cares."

"That's quite a job," says Hymie. "How much do I get paid?"

"You will get twenty thousand dollars a year," says old man Fink, "to make every worry of mine your own."

"Okay," says Hymie, "when do I get paid?"

"Aha!" says Fink. "That's your first worry."

Something serious for Anando…

A flea calls up his travel agent on the phone. "Listen," he says, "I have had enough of this armpit, I need a vacation. What can you do for me?"

"Well," says the travel agent, "it's a bit late in the season, but if you are prepared for something expensive, I've got a celebrity mustache vacancy."

The flea jumps at the offer and the next week he moves into Robert Pickford's mustache. However, all is not well and he phones his travel agent again.

"I am really having a great time seeing all sorts of famous people and places," says the flea, "but it is just too busy here talking and eating and drinking all the time. Can't you fix me up with something a little quieter?"

"Well," says the agent, checking his files, "there is a last minute cancellation in the world's most famous pubic hair."

The flea jumps for joy and that evening he checks into Raquel Scotch's crotch.

The next day he is back on the phone.

"A fine holiday this has turned out to be," he tells his agent. "I went to sleep last night and this morning I am back in Robert Pickford's mustache!"

A young man home from the sea walks into the pub. He orders a large scotch whiskey and offers a hundred-pound note.

"I'm sorry sir," says Hamish MacTavish the barman, "I have only just opened and I can't change that."

"Well, it's all I have got," replies the man. "So you can either let me drink until you have got the change, or I'll have to go somewhere else."

After an intense mental struggle, Hamish agrees to let the man keep drinking until he gets the change. Soon the young man is chatting with Mrs. MacTavish and starts buying her drinks. A dozen drinks later, Hamish looks around and the man is gone.

"Where is that man with the hundred-pound note?" asks Hamish, panic stricken.

"The last time I saw him," says one of his locals, "he was going upstairs with your wife and they were both taking their clothes off."

"Thank God for that," gasps Hamish. "I thought he'd left without paying!"

Gloria rushes into Fagin Finkelstein's law office.

"I want him arrested!" she cries. "He threw me on the bed, it was terrible!"

"Now calm down," says Fagin, "and give me the full story."

"He locked the door," she sobbed.

"Aha! Kidnapping!" says Fagin, making notes. "Ten years. Then what did he do?"

"He pulled up my skirt," says Gloria.

"Indecent exposure. Two more years," says Fagin. "Then what?"

"He put his hand on my...on my...." sobs Gloria.

"I understand," says Fagin, writing fast. "Attempted assault. Five years. And then what?"

"Then, he did it to me!" she cried.

"That's rape!" shouts young Finkelstein. "Thirty years, or maybe the gas chamber. And all the time you were screaming and struggling?"

"Well," replies Gloria, "not exactly. It was late and I didn't want to disturb everybody."

"Ah, shit!" shouts Fagin, tearing up his notes. "That's just a regular screw."

# 25

# Gurdjieff Was Living Zen

Osho,

Years ago, Vimalkirti and I met Count Durkheim, who at that time was eighty and one of the most influential so-called spiritual leaders of Europe. He called us for a visit to warn us against you. He said that your picture on the *mala* reminded him of Mr. Gurdjieff whom he met in Paris. He told us how dangerous men like Gurdjieff and you are. Then he said, "I brought Zen to Europe. Have you got my books?" How is it possible that a man who claims to have done lots of Zen sittings in Japan with various Zen masters, and has written so many books of Zen, is so unable to recognize you?

Turiya, the man, Durkheim, whom you met in Europe, and you think did not recognize me… The moment he compared me with his meeting with George Gurdjieff was the moment of recognition. He absolutely recognized: I am certainly dangerous, far more dangerous than George Gurdjieff was.

But Durkheim was only a man of knowledge, learning, scholarship. He was a great intellectual. I have gone through all his works; I can see that he has heard only the words of the Zen masters, but he has not heard their silences. He has met their skeletons, but he has not encountered their presence, their existential essence. Durkheim certainly has introduced Zen to Europe, but his Zen is just like a paper boat: you call it a boat, but don't start using it as a boat.

He has been in the East. And he is right when he says that he has been sitting with many Zen masters, and he has brought Zen to Europe. He has brought only echoes. He has brought only a bird in the cage, not the bird with open wings in the sky. He has brought it very accurately – about his accuracy I have no doubt – and he has done his best to present Zen to people who have never known anything like it. As far as experience is concerned, he himself knows nothing about it. As far as knowledge is concerned, he knows much; perhaps much more than the Zen masters he is talking about.

If he had understood Zen, he would have understood George Gurdjieff. If you have seen the full moon, you have seen all the full moons that have passed and all the full moons that will appear in the future. If he could not understand George Gurdjieff, naturally, seeing my picture and seeing you as my disciples, he warned you that you were moving on a dangerous path. And if a man is afraid of moving into the path of aloneness, silence... He may understand the word *silence*, but he has not tasted it. He has not looked into the eyes of George Gurdjieff.

Durkheim may have introduced the word *zen*, but it is George Gurdjieff who introduced the East to the West, without even mentioning it, without even claiming it. Because the very claim that, "I have introduced Zen" comes from the ego. Gurdjieff never talked about Zen, and he was *living* Zen. Certainly he had his own individuality – of the same caliber as Bodhidharma, and as colorful and as unique. He was not a carbon copy of anyone else. He was himself, so much so that perhaps if Durkheim could not understand him, it is understandable.

For example, if you wanted to be initiated by Gurdjieff... The initiation used to happen in the night after a long meal of dining and wining. Gurdjieff himself was a great cook; he would cook food for his disciples. And he would go on forcing, "Eat!" He would force alcohol, drugs on the disciples, and they were shouting, "It is enough, we are going mad!" But unless you were really mad, he was not going to listen. Finally, in his congregation only he was aware, everyone had fallen: someone was shouting, someone was saying something – muttering, moaning, crying, weeping or laughing – or someone was just sitting silently, wooden… It was a scene. And Gurdjieff was watching every disciple because what you never say in your conscious state comes out when you are unconscious.

The whole Sigmund Freud psychoanalytical movement depends on your dreams. They are not worried about what you say, they are worried about what you dream. Strange people – you have come to them, they should listen to your disease, your problems, and they say, "Don't be worried about your problems, bring your dreams. Your problems are just on the surface and your dreams are your roots."

But Gurdjieff was not one to waste time like psychoanalysis does – a person can go into psychoanalysis for fifteen years. When he goes in he is a little sane; when he comes out he is absolutely insane.

A man used to think that he was a woman. Naturally his family were worried, his wife, his children were very worried. But he was completely unworried. He said, "What can I do? If I am a woman, I am a woman. I am not doing any harm to anyone."

Finally he ended up on the couch of a psychoanalyst. After three years of psychoanalysis he met a friend. The friend asked, "How is the psychoanalysis going?"

He said, "It is going perfectly."

The man was a little interested in the psychological movement. He said, "It is going perfectly? Has it helped you?"

He said, "Helped? First I had some doubts; now I don't have any doubts."

The friend said, "That's great, but what was the thing that you had doubts about?"

He said, "I am a woman. In these three years the psychoanalyst has convinced me, and I have convinced him that we both are women. And we are enjoying the company."

Psychoanalysis has not helped anyone. Gurdjieff was not interested in wasting your time and your money. What psychoanalysis can do in twenty years he was able to do in one night. If you want to be a disciple of Gurdjieff… A man who has never eaten meat – the first thing was to force him to eat meat. Now, you can conceive it. If you are a vegetarian, to eat meat goes against your whole conditioning. You are bound to vomit. You will vomit and he will bring more meat for you. This will continue till the vomiting stops. That means your conditioning about meat is erased.

If you have never drunk alcohol before, he will force you to drink so much that you are bound to start doing things you could have never conceived – but they were inside you. And before he accepted you as his disciple, he wanted to know you from your very roots because from there the work of transformation will begin.

Now, naturally people like Durkheim and almost the whole world of so-called religious people were against Gurdjieff. His methods were strange, but he transformed more people than all the so-called religions, organized churches, psychologies. A single man has done an immense service, and without using the name of Zen. What he was doing was Zen, but it was his way of doing it.

Certainly Bodhidharma will not agree, neither will Buddha agree, but they will not disagree either. They will not agree with his methods, but they will agree with the man. The man was certainly crystallized – the ultimate peak a man can reach. Now, you may not agree with what path he has followed, but he *has* reached; that you have to concede.

I am not in agreement with George Gurdjieff on many things – or with anyone else – but that does not mean that I don't recognize that there have been Himalayan peaks of consciousness. They followed a certain path which does not agree with me.

I will condemn that path and I will condemn that method, but I will respect the man. That creates a contradiction in many people's minds.

That's what happened to Durkheim. He had heard the words, beautiful words of Zen masters, but he had not seen a single unique Zen master like Bodhidharma or Mahakashyapa. And if he could not recognize George Gurdjieff's realization, naturally he would deny me and warn you not to be with me. Because Gurdjieff was using very crude methods: forcing meat, alcohol, drugs on people. I am also destroying your conditioning but in a far more refined way.

Have you heard the Zen story…

There was a competition of swordsmanship. And swordsmanship in Japan is a very refined art. Three competitors had come to the final from different provinces.

Even the emperor was present. He himself released a fly from a small box and the first swordsman immediately cut it into two. He released another fly and the second swordsman cut it into three. He released the third fly and nothing happened, the fly simply flew away. The swordsman moved his sword, but nothing happened. People laughed – just as you laughed. But you will have to laugh again because the man said, "These people laughed, and you are laughing, but that fly will not create any more children!"

Such a subtle operation… I was that swordsman! I do my work. Durkheim cannot understand my work if he cannot understand Gurdjieff, whose work is very crude and primitive, but of course absolutely right. My work is very sophisticated. That's why only very intelligent and sophisticated people, who can see what has happened to the fly, are my people. Those who have seen the first two warriors and think that they are great warriors don't understand much. Certainly they know the technique, but their technique is very primitive, very visible.

Durkheim, rather than becoming a man of Zen himself, became just a reporter, writing what Zen masters are talking about, translating it. He forgot completely that he had himself to become a master, only then could he understand what he was writing, what he was listening to.

A certain similarity of consciousness is needed to understand the deeper ways of the heart. Many people have written in the West, and the story is almost always the same – except for one man, Alan Watts. And they all have written well. A few have done almost an impossible job, writing about something they know nothing about! They have done it very accurately, but they remain the same ordinary people. They were not transformed.

Durkheim is not a buddha. And these are the people who will prevent anyone because they start thinking of themselves as an authority; they have written a few books and they have become an authority. Durkheim said to Turiya and Vimalkirti, "You should not be with this man, this is dangerous."

Turiya, if he is still alive, tell him that as far as dangerousness is concerned he is right. And because I am dangerous it is worth being with me. You will not gain anything by being with Durkheim. There is no danger, no risk; he is simply a translator, a good translator. I appreciate his capacity as a translator, but not as a man who has understood the truth. It is good that you did not listen to him and continued on the dangerous path with me.

Vimalkirti has already gone beyond. The German royal family is perhaps the oldest royal family in Europe: one thousand years old. And in all those one thousand years, Vimalkirti was the only one who was really royal. He was my personal guard, so I watched him sitting silently for hours, day in, day out. He was here against everyone – and those were not small people: against Queen Elizabeth of England, who was telling him, "This man is dangerous." All the royal families of Europe were certainly worried that the last descendant of the oldest royal family, of Germany, had fallen into the hands of a dangerous man.

But he did not listen. And he is blessed because he ignored all these idiots – they may be royal, they may be royal idiots, they may be kings and queens, princes and princesses. People like Durkheim must have been thinking that the royal descendant of the last emperor of Germany should not follow such a dangerous group, which is condemned all over the world. But for anyone who has any guts, this is the very point: that I have either friends or enemies. Enemies are many; they don't count, they are unaccountable. Friends are few, but they are the people who are going to inherit this earth. They are the people who are going to create possibilities for more consciousness, more love, more laughter, more joy.

In a strange way, a tremendously great responsibility has fallen on you. You don't have any power except your love. You don't have any atomic weapons except your laughter. You don't have any destructive forces, but you have creative hearts, creative intelligence and a tremendous secret of meditation, of entering your own mystery. And your mystery and the mystery of the universe are not two, they are the same.

If Durkheim is still alive – I even suspect that he was never alive – tell him to come here and just be here without any prejudice. He may have been with Zen masters, but he has had no possibility to be in a commune where Zen is the very breathing, the very heartbeat. We don't mention it; there is no point, it is our whole being. In this very silence it is our breath and it is our heart. And we are ready to share it with anyone who comes without any prejudice.

Lastly you say, "Finally he said, 'I have brought Zen to Europe. Have you got my books?'" Zen masters have been known to burn books. And a man who is saying, "I have brought Zen… Have you read my books?" is not able even to see the contradiction. He has brought books; he has not brought Zen. Zen is not confined to books. Zen is a flavor, a spiritual aroma, a contagious blissfulness. Have you brought that meditativeness in which thousands of roses blossom in the heart? Then you will not invite anyone to read books. You will invite them to meditate, to dance, to sing and to disappear in your dance. And perhaps after all this, those books may be useful just to understand your own experience; those books may help to give you the right words, exact expressions. Not vice versa – you don't go from books to Zen.

Zen comes first and overwhelms you. And it is so new and so unknown that you are puzzled and you don't know in what space you have entered; there a master's book can be helpful. It can give you some indications that you are not lost, can give some milestones. It can describe some qualities of which you don't have any past experience. Let me repeat this, because it is never said in this way: Zen comes first and then you can read it in books, not vice versa, that you read the books and then you understand what Zen is. That's not the way things work.

Durkheim worked hard and I have immense compassion for him. Wherever he is, in this life or in some other life, he needs a master of the quality of Gurdjieff. Only then he may be able to understand.

Gurdjieff was perhaps the first man from the East who penetrated the Western consciousness. He was a very strange man; he passed through strange experiences and learned on his own, without any master. He moved in many monasteries, in many groups, and never belonged to anyone, but collected fragments of forgotten teachings. And he was of tremendous intelligence: to join all those fragments and make a system out of them which can certainly transform man. But it is very primitive; it is a bullock-cart method. It will take you, but when you can reach there without even moving an inch, when you can reach there just sitting here... Only then have you understood the difficulty of Gurdjieff.

His father died when he was nine – a small child coming from a nomadic tribe, moving from one tribe to another tribe. And those tribes were ancient; they had their methods. Collecting fragments from everywhere and working out... But he was in a strange position. He was a Caucasian, so he had no knowledge of any contemporary language. But somehow he worked out how to indicate methods in broken language.

If he had not been found by Ouspensky, the world would not have known anything about him. He himself was not able to communicate. He knew, but just like when you have a taste on your tongue but you don't have any word for it, and you don't have the talent... Neither did life give him the opportunity to grow the talent, the intellect.

It was one of the great meetings of this century when Ouspensky discovered him in a refugee camp in Istanbul. The First World War had ended, and Russia had entered the revolutionary period which culminated in the 1917 revolution. Now, there was no possibility in Russia for a man like Gurdjieff. The country was in the possession of the materialists, who don't believe that there is any consciousness, who don't believe that there is any possibility of evolution. They were killing all kinds of mystics. Gurdjieff escaped and he was found by Ouspensky. Ouspensky was a world-renowned mathematician.

And there you will understand the difference between Durkheim and a man of Zen: a man who writes about Zen and a man who lives Zen; a man who composes poems about love and a man who loves; a man who simply contemplates and a man who experiences.

Ouspensky had written great books before meeting Gurdjieff. One of his books I love as I love no other book. His way of writing is so precise; he was a mathematician. He brought mathematics to language with such beauty that the mathematics had come to language, but the poetry of the language did not die but was enriched. And he talks with such authority that you cannot think that this man knows nothing, but that he is a great scholar. He has read much and collected teachings from different sources, polished them, refined them, gave them more beautiful words, but he himself was just an ordinary man; no one would have thought this.

It is a strange coincidence that he found Gurdjieff because he was searching... He had come to India in search of a man who really knows – not a man of knowledge, but a man who really knows. And even in India he could not find a man who really knows. Then he went back to Moscow and someone said, "You are unnecessarily wandering here and there. There was a man here in Moscow while you were gone. I am not interested, in fact I am afraid of meeting such people, but I feel that is the man you are searching for. You are searching for the man who knows, but it is a dangerous encounter."

Ouspensky went in search of where Gurdjieff had gone; he had escaped from Russia. Ouspensky met him in a refugee camp in Istanbul. It was at night, and a dozen disciples were sitting around Gurdjieff silently, doing nothing. Ouspensky became fidgety, "What is going on? No one speaks, the night is becoming darker and deeper. And I have come and the man who has brought me, he is also sitting with closed eyes. I was thinking that he would introduce me."

Finally Gurdjieff said, "Take this paper" – no introduction – "and go into the other room. Write on one side what you know and on the other side what you don't know. Bring me that paper because that which you know I will never talk to you about. That which you know already, that is finished. That which you don't know I will talk about. I will take you to those spaces which you don't know."

And in that cold night, Ouspensky, sitting alone for half an hour in the room with a small candle, could not figure out what he knew. Does he know God? Does he know himself? What does he know? And he had written so many books, with such authority, without ever thinking that this was egoistic: writing, without knowing.

"But this man is a totally different man because I was not even introduced as someone who has come to be a disciple." Perhaps a silent communication… The man who had brought him was an old disciple of Gurdjieff, a musician who used to play for him. Something must have transpired. "But suddenly he gave me this paper." And holding the paper in his hand he could not write a single thing that he knew. He returned the paper blank and said, "Seeing you, it is impossible to be insincere. Seeing the real authority, it is impossible to pretend to be authoritative. I don't know anything. Accept me or reject me, but I am an ignorant man." Ouspensky started writing about Gurdjieff's teachings; he was a profound writer. He made Gurdjieff's name world famous.

Gurdjieff's methods were strange because no one had heard that these were religious methods. But there are secret streams… There are superficial religions which exist in churches, temples, synagogues and there are religious streams underneath which you don't know about, but which continue to carry the eternal treasure.

Gurdjieff would talk, but no one was able to understand what he was talking about. Even to write a book would take twenty years. And his way of writing a book you will not believe. He would write a book in Paris in a crowded cafe, sitting in the middle of a crowd of people coming and going – many people were shouting, someone was getting drunk, and Gurdjieff was writing. Many times Ouspensky asked, "Why don't you move to a silent place?"

He said, "It does not matter. In fact in these places I have learned a few words; these people go on talking so I have learned a few words. In silent places, who is going to tell me?"

But slowly, slowly through Ouspensky, he managed to make available methods which were not known before. A very old method, called: Stop! The disciples dance; the dancing becomes more and more maddening, the music becomes more intense. It comes to a peak, where the dancer forgets himself, becomes almost a puppet in the hands of an unknown energy of music that is surrounding him. And at that moment Gurdjieff says suddenly, "Stop!" And everything has to stop: the music, the dance.

You are not even to adjust anything to make yourself comfortable because in a dancing position you may be standing on one leg. You are not to move, you have to remain… You may fall; that is another thing. You are not to do anything on your part, you simply stop. It is such a beautiful exercise. When you stop suddenly time stops, everything stops, and the whole existence becomes just pure silence, a serenity and a deep experience of yourself and of the whole. But sometimes… That's why he was called dangerous.

He was staying in Tbilisi with a few of his disciples. They were thinking to stay there for three months to meditate. He was in a camp and outside was a dry canal and people were collecting wood inside it. The winter was coming and more wood would be needed. Suddenly someone opened the canal gate, not knowing that these people were carrying wood through the canal. Gurdjieff was inside the tent, and from there he suddenly shouted, "Stop!"

Those who were cunning thought, "He is inside the tent, he does not know what the situation is. If we stop, we will be drowned. And he is not looking, so just jump out and stop there!" Everyone jumped out except one single disciple. They waited, but when they found that the water was coming up to their noses, they thought, "It is too much. Now this spiritual search is going to finish me." They jumped out. Just one disciple remained as he was. Water was flowing over his head and Gurdjieff came running out, jumped into the canal, and pulled the disciple out. He was almost unconscious, but he was transformed.

Just that moment of decisiveness created an integration in him: whatever happens, if he has agreed with the master to stop then he will stop; if it brings death then death is welcome. In that welcome of death do you think you can remain the same as you were before? You become steel. This is what Gurdjieff calls crystallization; you become an individual for the first time.

He brought the disciple to the tent, forced the water out of his body, warmed the body, wrapped it with blankets. And to the remaining disciples who had jumped out and were still standing outside, he said, "Just get lost! You are not the people to be with me. I am too dangerous for you. You are too cunning, you are not sincere."

He was giving a demonstration in New York of the stop exercise. He had a group of thirty disciples, trained for years – dancers, musicians – and he was giving a demonstration. There came a point when the dancers were coming to the edge of the stage, and even the people who had gathered to see became afraid that the dancers were going to fall from the stage. And exactly at that moment, Gurdjieff, who was standing by the side smoking his cigar, said, "Stop!"

Everything stopped. People started falling over each other, but no one moved, everything was silent. Many had fallen off the stage, many had fallen over them; the people who were in the hall were standing in awe! They could not believe what was happening. That silence and that total agreement, that contract with the master and the fulfillment of it was so beautiful, so dignified that even the people in the theater became silent. They had never seen such a thing.

Now, who is going to join such a man? He had his own ways. It was an ancient exercise of the Sufis. An ordinary man seeing him smoking a cigar will say, "What kind of enlightenment is this? This man is smoking a cigar and he goes on smoking his cigar and everyone has fallen. Someone may have got a fracture; the musicians have fallen, their instruments are broken – what kind of man is this? And he is smoking a cigar and standing there enjoying the whole scene!"

But the reason needs tremendous understanding. In the West, he never wanted to call himself enlightened because that would create a distance and people would not be able to understand. Already what he had brought was so far away that to call himself enlightened would make it more difficult.

In the East you can become enlightened, there is no problem; many people become enlightened and then become unenlightened. Just two or three days ago Nandan became enlightened, went beyond love, and just now… What to do? One falls in love again. So one puts enlightenment off for later on, postpones it for the time being. Finally one has to become enlightened, but don't miss this chance because this boyfriend is not something permanent.

Here every romance lasts not more than seven days. By the seventh day people are thinking how to get rid of each other. And when they have got rid of each other, it is very easy to become enlightened – having nothing to do, no boyfriend, no girlfriend, what do you want? One finds it easier just to become enlightened!

Now, Nandan was worried that if I came to know then I will say, "This is again a case of being German." Germany has some quality. I have more German disciples than of any other country. And the German parliament prevents me from entering Germany. But that does not matter. Even the parliament is afraid. Their fear is that anyone who goes to Pune never returns! Now, here there are so many problems: either boyfriend, girlfriend… If somehow you avoid boyfriend, girlfriend problems, then comes this enlightenment. For a few days one remains enlightened, and then one day one wakes up and says, "It is enough, now give someone else a chance."

Just a few serious things…

A Polack and a Jew are riding together in the same train and start chatting.

"How is it possible," asks the Polack, "that you Jews are so successful in business?"

"It is simple," replies the Jew. "We have good-luck charms."

"What are they?" asks the Polack.

"Well," replies the Jew, "it is something we carry with us all the time that brings us good luck." He pulls a plastic bag out of his pocket and begins to unroll it. Inside is a fish head.

"Wow!" says the Polack, poking the fish head. And he asks if the Jew is willing to sell it.

"Twenty dollars and it's yours," replies the Jew.

The Polack hands over twenty dollars and pockets the fish head. But ten minutes later he is upset. "I have just realized," says the Polack, "I could buy at least ten fishes in the market for twenty dollars."

"Aha!" says the Jew. "You see, it's working already!"

Hymie Goldberg is touring Ireland in his car when he finds Paddy hitchhiking, holding a cow.

"I can give you a lift," says Hymie, "but I can't take your cow."

"Oh, that's okay," says Paddy, "she will follow us at her own speed." So Paddy gets in and Hymie is soon driving at thirty miles per hour. The cow is trotting along behind. Hymie speeds up to forty miles per hour and the cow is still keeping pace. At fifty miles per hour Hymie sees that the cow is right behind, but he notices that she seems to be getting tired.

"I'm a bit worried about your cow," says Hymie, "her tongue is hanging out of her mouth."

"Which side of the mouth?" asks Paddy.

"On the right side," replies Hymie.

"Oh, that's all right then," says Paddy. "That just means she wants to pass you!"

# 26

# The Language of Universal Silence

Osho,
What is the "dark night of the soul"? Is it out of date? Looking inside and all around me, I only see more joy, contentment, lovingness, appreciation of life and of what is. Looking back, I see a lot of misery, heaviness, pain – but they seem to be related to wrong upbringing and unnecessary self-torture, not to any dark night of the soul. Yet, I seem to remember you also talking about having gone through deep despair yourself, related to the search for truth. So I wonder, is this relaxing more and more into the joy of being alive, with such beauty all around, with slowly growing watchfulness, just fine; or are we, am I, somehow just staying on the surface and not moving into the depth of the "search"? And why am I asking?

The question you have raised is very significant in the context of the whole human past. Every religion has been life negative. And when you negate life, you create misery for yourself; when you go against life, you are going in darkness. Life is light, but no religion in the world has existed up to now that does not teach people attitudes leading to darkness, despair, depression, guilt, sinfulness. They all reduce your dignity, your humanity; it is their vested interest.

I agree with Bertrand Russell only on one point, where he says, "If every human being becomes happy, comfortably happy, religions will disappear." No one has taken note of the significance of his statement, what the implication of it is. Its implication is that religions need misery, despair, unhappiness, for their very survival; they have a vast investment.

Now, the Catholic Church is the greatest firm, compared to any business firm in the world. Six hundred million people, almost a nation, are under the thumb of a Polack pope. So much money and power and prestige are bestowed on religions, their deities, their temples.

In India, there is a temple in the south whose daily income is such that it runs a whole university. Perhaps that is the only university in the world that is run by a temple – all the salaries and everything. And still the temple goes on becoming rich because the superstition is that if you donate to the deity of the temple, you will get a millionfold in the other world. Now, who is going to miss such a chance?

And you can see it clearly: only when you are miserable do you remember God, heaven, hell, the Bible, the Koran, the Gita. Have you ever seen someone who is happy and rejoicing carrying a Bible? He will carry a bottle of wine; this is not the time for carrying a Bible. And who reads these Bibles, Vedas? – just old people who are coming close to death and are becoming afraid – afraid there may perhaps be a God. Maybe they are going to encounter God, and if he asks any questions… Naturally he will ask any question. It is better to do some homework.

A salesman of dictionaries and encyclopedias was telling the woman, standing on her doorstep, "This is the latest encyclopedia. You and your children will be benefited by it."

But she said, "We have it already. You can see, there in the corner."

The man looked in the corner. There was a book of the same thickness. He said, "That is not an encyclopedia, that is the Holy Bible."

The woman could not believe that from that far, he could judge that the book was the Holy Bible. She said, "That amazes me. You are certainly a man of knowledge. How could you manage to see that it was a Holy Bible?"

He said, "Anyone can conclude that, just seeing the layer of dust that has gathered on the Bible."

Who opens it? People become interested in the Bible only when they are almost in their graves. I say almost, because they don't want to take any chance. To be on the safer side, look in the holy book, read something here and there. If God meets you and inquires, and you can't answer, you are bound to be in trouble.

I have never seen a man who is joyous, blissful, peaceful, and rejoicing in all that the existence offers you: its silences, its rain, its music of the wind passing through the pine trees, its people; all that it gives you. If you cannot dance, then perhaps you don't know the language. You have been forced to forget the language of dance; you have been forced to forget the language of love.

Everything valuable has been condemned; even love is sin. Even to rejoice in the world is preparing your path to hell. The only way to God and to his paradise is to torture yourself, and torture as perfectly as possible. Renounce everything that can give you joy. Escape from every place where people are happy, where people are loving. Go to the mountains, to the monasteries where other idiots have already gathered. Read the same stupid stories of the Bible every day. And naturally, if a man can read the Old Testament every day, even if he has any intelligence, he will lose it. Then begins the dark night of the soul.

You are more fortunate than I am. You are saying, "Even you have talked somewhere about having yourself gone through deep despair, related to the search for truth." I was not so fortunate to meet a man like me! I met all kinds of fools; it was sheer fortune that I never became convinced of any life negative attitude. That remained my criterion: unless I find a source which affirms love, which affirms beauty, which affirms flowers and the stars; unless I find the source from where all that is great has arisen – great poetry, great art, great painting, great architecture… I am not going to be convinced by any person whose whole contribution in life has been destructive.

It is a strange phenomenon. Politicians have been continuously destroying in wars. Religious people are destroying not others but themselves, very piously, and feeling great. But whether you commit suicide or you commit murder, you destroy life in every case. It doesn't matter whether it is suicide or murder; the politician commits murder, and your so-called saint commits suicide. This was so clear to me that I never followed any life negative approach.

I had to struggle alone, without any guide, without any friend, without any map. It is a miracle that, surrounded by all these religious teachings, I was not convinced by anyone. I remained stubborn, absolutely trusting only one thing; you can call it love, you can call it life, you can call it light. But to me, only creation can be the goal of existence, not destruction. That which creates is the only authentic religious consciousness. You can understand my problem, why all the religions are bound to be against me, and why I am going to be against them.

In a world news conference, the first question that I was asked was by a woman reporter: "Don't you believe in coexistence?" I simply said, "No." Everyone was shocked. All the reporters, all the news media people – no one was expecting such an answer. Coexistence means compromise; coexistence means, "I know you are my enemy, I am your enemy, but what to do? Neither can I destroy you, nor you can destroy me because no one wants to go to jail. So it is better to talk about a great philosophy of coexistence."

I believe in love, but I don't believe in coexistence. But unfortunately every husband and every wife are living in coexistence, not life; tolerating each other as much as possible. They can see the superstitions of religions, but again they compromise because so many people… Who is going to be against six hundred million

Catholics? And you have to live with them, you have to work with them. It is better to compromise, it is better to remain silent; it is better to ignore points where you differ. Your life is a life of compromise. And a life of compromise is a life of the dark night of the soul.

I have never compromised. Either I am right or I am wrong. There are not degrees – that I am a little right. There are not percentages; that fifty percent I am right, fifty percent you are right. Right is a hundred percent; otherwise it is not right. And a lie is a hundred percent a lie; otherwise it is not a lie.

But from the very childhood, in every sphere of your life you are told not to come in conflict, be polite. In other words, always manage some compromise. But when there are so many compromises – politically, spiritually, socially – you become a stranger to yourself. You have so many masks, you lose contact with your original face. And a mask cannot enjoy, it is dead. It cannot laugh, it cannot love. Only the original face is capable of understanding the language of the universe. Love is the language. Dance is the expression of your gratitude.

There is no question of any dark night of the soul, but I had to pass through it because no one told me. There was no reference anywhere in the whole literature of the world. I went to this saint and to that saint. And I cannot tolerate it, if I see all kinds of idiots doing all kinds of stupid things. When I see something stupid, I make it a point to make that man alert, that this is stupid.

A saint was fasting for sixty days, and thousands of people were coming every day to touch his feet – a great spiritual master. Seeing that so many people were going, I thought, "There is no harm. Perhaps this is someone in whose eyes I can see the light, in whose gestures I can see the grace." But there I saw a half-dead, utterly stupid man. I asked him, "Before you die, answer me at least, what relationship is there between spirituality and starvation? And if starvation is spiritual, then why are people trying to remove poverty from the world? People should try to remove richness from the world, so that everyone becomes spiritual."

That man looked at me and said, "You are asking me a strange question. For thousands of years fasting has been considered spiritual."

I said, "I am not worried about thousands of years. You have the experience of sixty days. What spirituality have you gained? Just give me some indication." He looked here and there; what indication could he give?

I said, "The only indication is that within a few days you will die. But there is still time if you have courage – it needs great courage to disappoint the worshippers. When you have thousands of worshippers, it needs tremendous courage." I continued, "I can bring delicious food for you. These people will be very against me, but if you are ready…"

He said, "Don't talk about such things. Don't seduce me! You are trying to drag me out of my spiritual path."

I said, "I am simply wasting some money on your food, I am not dragging you. Once you are okay, you can drag yourself anywhere you want to go. I can manage to keep you in my house for a few days. You can get well and then go on any path you want. But right now you are going into death, it is not a path."

The man thought for a moment, understood clearly that what I was saying was right. But to disappoint so many people… And it was not only a question of disappointing so many people, it was a question of losing respect in the eyes of so many people.

He said to me, "Please, don't disturb me." Because I went every day with the same proposal, with greater persuasion. And the man was getting more and more persuaded and more and more afraid of me.

Finally, he said to his disciples that if I was coming there, he did not want to see me. "Prevent this man from coming because one or two days more and he will convince me, and I cannot give any argument about why being hungry is spiritual." And if being hungry is spiritual, then why are you drinking water? Stop drinking too. That will make you more spiritual. In fact, why waste the time of so many people? Just commit hara-kiri! Why make such a circus? But these circuses have been going on around the world for ages.

What do these worshippers see in these saints? They are suffering, they are being tortured. It touches a very strange thing in human psychology. You enjoy people being tortured and you enjoy more if the people are torturing themselves. Then no one is responsible. The crowd that follows such saints are sadists; they love to see torture. And the people who are torturing themselves are suffering from another psychological disease; they are masochists. They enjoy torturing themselves and enjoy also the great respect that is coming to them.

But no religion in the world has given respect to love, to joy, to music, to dance, to any creativity that beautifies existence. They are all against it. Their whole business is to convince you that your authentic blissfulness is not in this world. Jesus says, "My Kingdom of God is not of this world." This is, in essence, the teaching of all the religions. Their kingdom is beyond death, a fiction. Torture yourself if you want to enter their fictitious paradise. And meanwhile let the priest enjoy the power, the money; let the priest enjoy the ego.

In fact, seen in the light of psychological analysis, up to now, the whole humanity has been sick. But because the sickness is so prevalent, it is very difficult to think that it is sickness. You never think that having a nose is something wrong, but if you have six fingers instead of five, you think something is wrong.

I used to work in a university, and one university teacher had twelve fingers. She used to hide them, and I said, "You are an idiot. You should make other people feel that 'You are missing. I have six – you have only five.' What is wrong in having six fingers? Why feel guilty about it? Make some use of it and let others feel that they are missing the sixth finger." But it is difficult because millions of people have only ten fingers.

That's why every language in the world has ten basic mathematical digits because in the primitive days, man started calculating on his fingers. And a person like me still counts on the fingers and still gets lost after the fourth – it becomes so complicated! You will be surprised that strangely, all the languages are in agreement and have developed ten basic digits, without even being in contact. And then it is repetition – eleven, twelve, thirteen… After ten you can go on repeating as long as you want, but ten is the base. It simply means that man has always had five fingers, so no one thinks that anything is wrong about five fingers, or anything right about five fingers. One simply takes it for granted; that's how things are.

The psychological sickness of enjoying either your own torture or someone else's torture is the very foundation of all your religions. And you will not believe how inventive these psychologically sick people have been. Just a few examples… I will have to count on my fingers, and I know I will get lost!

In Russia there was a most prominent Christian sect; prominent, because no one could do what they were doing. Every religion has been teaching celibacy, but that sect had done the ultimate: they started cutting off their sexual organs. A man who cuts off his sexual organs would become a saint – so simple. That means people who are born… A few people are born impotent; they are born spiritual people. You may not be aware of them; in the world outside India, perhaps they don't show themselves the way they do in India.

In India they have their own organizations and their only work is… They are neither man nor woman. They don't have any sexual organs. They look like men and they use women's clothes; they are very strange people. Their main center, their headquarters is in Lucknow; they have their president there. And their only work is that when someone is born, they go and dance and celebrate and get rewarded. They move from one place to another place in groups, finding out if someone has been born. They look strange, very ugly.

But in Russia, thousands of men used to cut off their sexual organs in great ceremonies. Thousands of people would come to see it – if they cannot do this, at least they can see the great saints who are renouncing sexuality completely. And they don't know that sexuality is not in the sexual organ. Sexuality has its center in your brain. That's why you can have a sexual dream, and if you start thinking of sexual images, immediately your sexual organ will be ready to act. But the source is in your mind. The soldier does not act on his own accord! Even if you cut it off, do you think you will not think of sex anymore, that your dreams will not be sexual? They will be more sexual. Of course, you cannot do anything…

And women were not going to remain behind when so many men were becoming saints so easily. Poor women, thousands of them started cutting off their breasts. Before the Russian Revolution, they made it a law that anyone doing such harm to the body will be thought a criminal. It continued for centuries. It is a crime, but it is the same kind of crime whether you fast, torture the body, or take the vow of celibacy; you are torturing the body. Or you can learn distortions of all kinds from yogis; the training, the discipline, takes a long time and all you can do is unnecessary, stupid distortions.

Someone is standing on his head… Do you think a man standing on his head becomes spiritual? All it simply says is that he is an idiot. He will lose all intelligence: man has intelligence because he is the only animal who stands on legs, against gravitation. So a very small quantity of blood reaches his head. And because of the small quantity of blood, very fine nerves have grown in the brain. If you stand on your head, all the blood rushes toward your head, destroying this delicate system. It is so clear. Have you seen any yogi who has contributed anything to life? Anything intelligible, anything understandable? In this country, for thousands of years, there have been millions of yogis. But they become great saints.

In Varanasi, which is the Hindu capital, you will still find people lying on a bed of thorns. And flowers, sweets, coconuts are showered on them. That man was a nut himself, and now you are offering him coconuts! I have been with these people and I became friendly with such a coconut, to find out his secret. He said, "Do you want to become a saint like me?"

I said, "Really, I want to become a saint like you. This is such a beautiful job, and you are the most expert here." I puffed up his ego as much as possible. I told other people also, "You are unnecessarily wasting time. The real saint is lying there in that corner." More flowers, more coconuts started coming. The man became very friendly. He said, "Come on, I will tell you the truth."

One evening when there was no one… And on the bank of the Ganges where he used to lie it was now silent. The day had ended, the sun had set, with just a little light before the night came. He showed me his back. What I suspected was the truth. On your back there are points which don't feel pain and there are points which feel much pain. You can tell a friend to take a needle and prick a few places on your back, and you will be surprised that there are a few places where you cannot feel the needle.

Those beds are made in such a way that the needles touch only the painless spots. It is simple cheating, but it is called saintliness. But if you say this, you are against religion, you are against tradition; you are destroying and corrupting people's faith.

There is a record of a certain Christian sect in the Middle Ages which used to have shoes made in such a way that needles were sticking up inside the shoe and piercing the feet. They would make wounds and the monk would walk on those shoes. They would make belts with needles entering the body, and those needles would make wounds. And people would worship the monks.

There was another sect that was very highly praised. Every morning, the saint had to stand naked under the sky and beat himself. Blood would start coming out, and people were gathering around churches to see these scenes. In Mohammedanism there is still a sect in which the person beats on his chest until he becomes unconscious. And when he becomes unconscious, then people touch his feet. Then people take the dust on which he has fallen because he is a saint. These ideologies, and similar kinds of different ways of torturing, created the dark night of the soul.

To you, to my people there is no dark night of the soul. For me it was. I had seen that it was a tradition-oriented, self-torturing ideology which dominated all over the world, in every religion. But I went on questioning, until I was satisfied that something was in tune with life. Those were the days of despair because I was trying to find and there was no answer anywhere for any question.

No one could tell me what the meaning of our being here is, what is the significance. Why should I go on living? If today has been a wastage, tomorrow is going to be a repetition. Those days were days of despair. But I went on questioning; I did not compromise. I did not get consoled with some bogus, hocus-pocus ideology. I never said to myself, "One has just to live, so don't go on digging in the roots. Just accept whatever is offered; millions of people are living without any problem, why should you create problems?"

But I never accepted any beliefs, I never accepted any ideas. Slowly, slowly the ultimate result was that a tremendous silence started happening to me. My friends, all the people of my family became afraid; it seemed I was going mad because they had seen only mad people in such situations. I would sit for hours staring at nothing. My friends would ask, "What are you staring at?"

I said, "Nothing."

They asked, "Then why are you staring?"

I said, "What else to do?"

It is a difficult world. If I sit with closed eyes, people ask, "Why are you sitting with closed eyes?" If I don't close my eyes, they think I am going mad: "Why are you staring?" If I stare at someone, he becomes fidgety. He starts becoming angry: "Why are you staring at me?" Psychologists have found that you can look at a person without making him annoyed only for three seconds. More than that and he will start becoming annoyed – why does this man go on staring at me? Just try. And I said, "I have nothing else to do. I don't see anything worth seeing here; you are worth seeing, so I am staring."

My inner world was becoming so silent that either with closed eyes or open eyes there was not a single thought moving. This silence was the beginning of my learning the language of universal silence. This is what I have called *hari om tat sat*. It has nothing to do with any religion. It simply means the divine sound: that is the only truth.

Everything else is a fiction. Everything else is ephemeral, illusory. But the music of the universe, if you can get in tune with it… There is nothing to be done. You don't have to be on a fast, because if you are on a fast you cannot get in tune with the universe; you will get in tune with your hunger. But even in this end part of the twentieth century, in the most evolved countries like America, stupidities continue.

One man, the founder of EST, Erhardt, was here. He has been earning millions of dollars, but finally people found out the trick; they have been befooled. That's why so many religions have arisen and disappeared. There was a time when they became the fashion; they appealed and everyone started saying, "This is great!" And particularly in America, any stupid thing and you will find people who will say, "This is great. Far out!"

What Erhardt was doing was such a simple strategy: a seminar for two weekends; one seminar for two hundred and fifty dollars. For two days, from morning till late at night sitting in the hall, you have to listen to all kinds of nonsense. You are not allowed to go to the toilet – that was the spiritual discipline. But the bladder is the bladder; it becomes full sooner or later. People will keep holding, they will become tense as the time passes, and they will look all around; everyone is tense, but it needs courage. You cannot be allowed to go to the toilet, otherwise you will miss it. No one asks what it is that you will miss. Finally, someone will get it. There will come a moment when you cannot control it; there is a limitation. Finally, one man proves courageous enough and urinates in the hall. And immediately others start, because everyone is ready.

You can try it alone, although it will not be so effective alone. When after a long, tense control you relax, it feels so great! It is a spiritual experience. You cannot say to anyone that it is not because you have paid two hundred and fifty dollars. So you go on spreading that "I have got it. What *it* is, is inexpressible. One has to get it, only then one understands." And spreading by word of mouth, that a few people are getting it just for two hundred and fifty dollars... Give it a try.

Women were first to get it because their bladder control is not that great. Men can control a little longer. So women became leaders, almost saints because they got it first. And when a woman is getting it, it hurts the ego of the man: "Forget all about it and get *it*." Now Erhardt has stopped that business because everyone has got it. Now no one is ready; everyone understands that they have been befooled. But for almost ten years he made thousands of people enlightened!

It is certainly a great experience, and you don't have to depend on anyone, you can try it alone. There is no need to waste two hundred and fifty dollars. Just one morning go on controlling, and soon there will come a moment when it will happen. You don't have to do it. That is how Zen has come to the West: it happens, you don't have to do it; it is effortless effort. And when it comes it brings such peace. One feels so much at ease, forgets all anxiety. One has arrived. Although tomorrow the same rut, but now you have the key. Whenever you want to arrive – a simple strategy. But in a very well-educated, sophisticated society, if people can be deceived, what about the whole past of humanity?

All the religions have been deceiving you. They have been deceiving in the name of God. They have been deceiving by telling you that you will get rewarded after death, and if you don't listen you will be punished by hellfire for eternity. And people believed it.

I have heard about Christian missionaries in the Middle Ages, who would shout and beat on the table about what will happen to the sinners. They would describe it in such detail that ladies will faint, children will start crying. Even men will start perspiring. "Hellfire. Somehow one has to save oneself from hellfire. Only God can save you. Only Jesus Christ can save you." And the strangest thing is, Jesus Christ could not save himself. Now, what stupidity! My people in America made a small sign to be put on cars: Moses earns, Jesus saves, Osho spends.

You need not be worried, there is no dark night of the soul for you. There will be only a starry night, full of light and joy, with a dawn coming closer every moment. I want to insist on it.

It appears very strange, but I cannot resist. I have to declare that you are the first religious people in this world, in the sense that you can laugh, that you can love, you can live, you can enjoy small things of life without bothering about fictions. And if you can learn to enjoy this life, this moment, then if there is any other life, you know how to enjoy it.

Learn to enjoy in this life. Discipline your senses to be more musical; discipline yourself to be more sensitive, intelligent because whatever is going to come… I don't talk about what is going to come, who cares? – because whatever will be said will be simply a fiction again. Whatever is going to come tomorrow, we will enjoy it with more intensity, more clarity, more discipline, more love.

And the same is true about after death. If there is life after death… I say there is, but I don't want you to believe it. There is no need to believe. Just live this life and if any life happens after this life, you will be able to enjoy. If nothing happens, nothing happens. There is no harm; you simply are not. What was the problem when you were not born? Everything was going perfectly well. One day you will die and everything will go perfectly well. Either you will be – then you know how to enjoy – or you will not be, so there is no problem for you. My understanding is simple and clear.

Something serious…

Paddy and Seamus are sitting in the pub, having a drink together.

"A burglar got into my house at three o'clock this morning," says Paddy, "while I was on my way home from the pub."

"Did he get anything?" asks Seamus.

"He certainly did," says Paddy. "The poor guy is in the hospital. My wife, Maureen, thought it was me!"

Hymie Goldberg walks into where the last supper is being held. He sits down at the table and says to the waiter, "Give me a scotch and soda."

"I'm sorry sir," replies the waiter, "all we are serving here is wine."

"Okay, some wine then," says Hymie, "and give me a mushroom pizza and a large salad."

"Sorry sir," says the waiter, "but all we are serving is bread."

"My God! Only bread and wine?" yells Hymie. "The guy who's giving this party should be crucified!"

A man goes into a pharmacy and buys a pound of arsenic poison. Next week he comes back and asks for a packet of sleeping pills.

"I'm sorry, sir," says the pharmacist, "but you need a prescription for them."

"My God!" says the man. "Last week you sold me a pound of arsenic poison and I did not need a prescription for that."

"I know," replies the pharmacist, "but arsenic is not addictive."

Paddy wakes up in hospital, covered in bandages, and notices Seamus sitting at his bedside.

"What happened to me?" asks Paddy.

"Well," replies Seamus, "you had a few too many drinks last night, and then you made a bet that you could jump out of the window and fly around the pub."

"Why didn't you stop me?" Paddy screams.

"Stop you?" replies Seamus. "Hell, I bet twenty-five dollars on you."

27

# Eternity Entering the World of Time

Osho,

You once said, "The moment is rare when eternity penetrates time." Can you speak more on this?

The question seems to be simple, but the answer is very complex. And the complexity becomes multidimensional because the answer can come only from your own experience, not from the outside. Just as the question is arising in you, the answer has also to be part of your interiority. But I will go into a little detail, to explain what I mean when I say that the moment is rare when eternity penetrates time.

Time is that in which we live; it is horizontal. It is from *A* to *B* to *C* to *D*; it is in a line. Eternity is vertical. It is not from *A* to *B* and from *B* to *C*. It is from *A* to more *A* to still more *A*. It goes on upward. The moment is rare because it happens only when meditation has reached a ripening, a maturity; when you have touched your innermost core. Then suddenly you become aware that you are a crossroad. One line goes horizontal; in other words, mediocre, ordinary, meaningless and leading finally to death. The horizontal line is continuously moving toward the graveyard.

I have told you the story, significant in many ways – for you to be reminded…

A great king saw a shadow in his dreams and became afraid even in the dream. He asked the shadow, "What do you want?"

The shadow said, "I have not come to ask for anything. I have come just to inform you that this evening at the right place, when the sun is setting, you will breathe your last breath. Ordinarily I don't come to inform people, but you are a great emperor; it is just to pay respect to you."

The king became so afraid that he woke up, perspiring, and could not think what to do. The only thing he could think of was to call all the wise men, astrologers, prophets and to find out the meaning of the dream. Dream analysis is thought to have originated with Sigmund Freud – that is not true. It originated with this king, one thousand years ago.

In the middle of the night, all the prophets, wise men of his capital, and all those who were concerned in some way with the future – dream readers – were told the story. The story was simple. They had brought their scriptures and they started arguing with each other: "This cannot be the meaning," or, "This is bound to be the meaning." They wasted time; the sun started rising. The king had an old servant whom he treated just as a father because his own father had died very early. The king was too young, and his father had given the guardianship to this servant and told him, "Take care that he becomes my successor and does not lose the kingdom."

And the servant managed. Now he was very old, but he was not treated as a servant. He was almost as respected as a father. He came close to the king and said, "I want to say two things to you. You have always listened to me. I am not a prophet, I am not an astrologer and I don't know what all this nonsense is that's going on. The scriptures are being consulted. One thing is certain, that once the sun has risen, the sunset is not very far away.

"These people, the so-called knowledgeable people, have never come to any conclusion in centuries. In just one day they will quarrel, argue, destroy each other's arguments, but you cannot hope that they will come to a consensus, a conclusion.

"Let them have their discussions. My suggestion is that you have the best horse in the world" – those were the days of horses. "Take the horse and escape from this palace as fast as possible. This much is certain, that you should not be here; you should be far away."

It was logical, rational, although very simple. The king left the great intelligent and wise people arguing; they did not even notice that he had left. And he certainly had a horse worth an empire. He was very proud of the horse; there was no other horse known of that strength. There was such a love between the horse and the king, such a deep affinity, a kind of synchronicity. The king said to the horse, "It seems my death is coming. That shadow was nothing but death. You have to take me as far away from this palace as you can manage."

The horse nodded his head. He fulfilled his promise. By the evening, as the sun was setting, they were hundreds of miles away from their kingdom. They had entered another kingdom in disguise. The king was very happy; he got down from his horse. He was tying the horse to a tree because neither he nor the horse had eaten anything. He said to the horse, "Thank you my friend. Now I will make arrangements for your food, for my food. We are so far away, there is no fear. But you proved the stories that were told about you: you became almost like a cloud, with such a speed."

And as he was tying the horse to the tree, the dark shadow appeared and said to the king, "I was afraid that you might not be able to make it, but your horse is great. I also thank him. This is the place and this is the time. I was worried – you were so far away, how could I manage to bring you? The horse served destiny."

It is a strange story, but it shows that wherever you are going horizontally, with whatever speed, you will end up in some graveyard. It is strange that every moment our graves are coming closer to us – even if you don't move, your grave is moving toward you. The horizontal line of time is, in other words, the mortality of man. But if you can reach the center of your being, the silences of your innermost center, you can see two roads: one horizontal, another vertical.

You will be surprised to know that the Christian cross is not Christian at all. It is an ancient, Eastern, Aryan symbol, the swastika. That's why Adolf Hitler, who was thinking that he was of the purest Aryan blood, chose the swastika as his symbol. A swastika is nothing but two lines crossing. In India, at the beginning of every year, without knowing why, business people write in their books, begin their new books with a swastika. The Christian cross is simply a part of the swastika. But it also represents the same thing: the vertical, the horizontal. Christ's hands are horizontal; his head and his being are pointing in a different direction.

In a moment of meditation, you suddenly see that you can move in two directions – either horizontal or vertical. The vertical consists of silences, blissfulness, ecstasies; the horizontal consists of hands, work, the world. Once a man has known himself as a crossroad, he cannot be disinterested, he cannot be unintrigued about the vertical. The horizontal he knows, but the vertical opens a door to eternity, where death does not exist; where one simply becomes more and more part of the cosmic whole, where one loses all bondages, even the bondage of the body.

Gautam Buddha used to say, "Birth is pain, life is pain, death is pain." What he was saying was when you move on the horizontal line, you are continuously miserable, in pain. Your life cannot be a life of dance, of joy. If this is all, then suicide is the only solution.

That's the conclusion of the contemporary, Western philosophy of existentialism – Jean-Paul Sartre, Jaspers, Heidegger, Kierkegaard and others have come to: that life is meaningless. On the horizontal plane it is because it is simply agony and pain, disease and sickness, oldness. And you are encaged in a small body while your consciousness is as vast as the whole universe.

Once the vertical is discovered, one starts moving on the vertical line. That vertical line does not mean you have to renounce the world. But it certainly means that you are no longer of the world, that the world becomes ephemeral, loses importance. It does not mean that you have to renounce the world and escape to the mountains and the monasteries. It simply means that you start – wherever you are – living an inner life which was not possible before.

Before you were an extrovert; now, suddenly you become an introvert. As far as the body is concerned, if the remembrance is there that you are not the body, you can manage very easily. But the body can be used in many ways to help you to move on the vertical line. The penetration of the vertical line, just a ray of light coming into your darkness of horizontal life, is the beginning of enlightenment.

You will look the same, but you will not be the same. Those who have a clarity of seeing, to them you will not look the same either. And at least for yourself, you will never look the same. You can never be the same. You will be in the world, but the world will not be in you.

Ambitions, desires, jealousies will start evaporating. No effort will be needed to drop them, just your movement on the vertical line and they start disappearing because they cannot exist on the vertical line. They can exist only in the darkness of the horizontal, where everyone is in competition: full of lust, full of will to power, a great desire to dominate, to become someone special.

On the vertical line all these stupidities simply disappear. You become so light, so weightless, just like a lotus flower: it is in the water, but the water does not touch it. You remain in the world, but the world has no longer any impact on you. On the contrary, you start influencing the world – not with conscious effort, but just by your sheer being, your presence, your grace, your beauty. As it grows inside it starts spreading around you.

It will touch people who have an open heart and it will make people afraid who have lived with a closed heart – with all windows, all doors closed. They will not come in contact with such a person. And to convince themselves why they are not coming in contact with such a person, they will find a thousand and one excuses, a thousand and one lies. But the basic fact is that they are afraid to be exposed.

The man who is moving vertically becomes almost a mirror. If you come close to him, you will see your real face; you will see your ugliness, you will see your continuous ambitiousness, you will see your begging bowl.

Perhaps another story will help you…

Early in the morning a man, a beggar with a begging bowl entered the king's garden. The king used to go for a morning walk in the garden; otherwise it was impossible to meet the king – particularly for the beggar, the whole bureaucracy would prevent him. So he had chosen a time when there was no bureaucracy, and when the king wanted to be alone, in silence with nature, to drink as much beauty and aliveness as nature was showering. The beggar encountered him there.

The king said, "This is not the time – I don't see anyone."

The beggar said, "I am a beggar. Your bureaucracy is so long and for a beggar it is impossible to see you. I insist that you give me an audience."

The king just thought to get rid of him and said, "What do you want? Just say and you will get it. Don't disturb my morning silence."

The beggar said, "Think twice before you offer to give me something."

The king said, "You seem to be a strange man. In the first place, you entered the garden without permission, insisting that you have to have an audience with the king. And now I am saying that whatever you want, just say it. Don't disturb my peace and don't disturb my silence."

The beggar laughed. He said, "A peace that is disturbed is not peace. And a silence that is disturbed is just a dream, not a reality."

Now the king looked at the beggar. He was saying something of tremendous importance. The king thought, "He does not seem to be an ordinary beggar, that is certain."

The beggar said again, "I want you to think it over because what I want is just for you to fill my begging bowl with anything and I will go. But it has to be full."

The king laughed. He said, "You are a madman. Do you think your begging bowl cannot be filled?"

He called his treasurer and told him, "Fill his begging bowl with diamonds, precious stones."

The treasurer had no idea what had happened. No one fills beggars' bowls with diamonds. The beggar reminded the treasurer, "Remember, unless the begging bowl is full, I am not going to move from here." It was a challenge between a beggar and a king.

Then there followed a very strange story. As diamonds were being poured into his begging bowl, the moment they were poured in they would disappear. The king was in a very embarrassed state. But he said, "Whatever happens, even if my whole treasury is gone, I cannot be defeated by a beggar. I have defeated great emperors." The whole treasury disappeared. The rumor reached the capital, and thousands of people gathered to see what was happening. And they had never seen the king in such a trembling, nervous breakdown.

Finally, when nothing was left in the treasury and the begging bowl was still as empty as it was before, he fell to the feet of the beggar and said, "You will have to forgive me, I did not understand. I have never thought about these things. I did my best, but now I don't have anything else to offer you. And I will think that you have forgiven me if you can tell me the secret of your begging bowl. It is a strange begging bowl – just a few diamonds would have filled it. It has taken the whole treasury."

The beggar laughed and said, "You need not be worried. This is not a begging bowl. I found a human skull and out of the human skull I made this begging bowl. It has not forgotten its old habit. Have you looked into begging, your own begging bowl, your own head? Give it anything and it will ask for more and more and more. It knows only one language: more. It is always empty, it is always a beggar."

Only beggars exist on the horizontal line because they are all rushing for more, and because the more cannot be fulfilled – not that you cannot get to a position you want, but the moment you get it, there are higher positions. For a moment maybe a flicker of happiness, and the next moment, again the same despair and the same race for more. You cannot fulfill the idea of more. It is intrinsically unfulfillable. This is the horizontal line, the line of more and more and more.

What is the vertical line? – it is of being less and less and less, to the point of utter emptiness, to the point of being no one. Just a signature – not even on sand, but on water. You have not even made it and it has disappeared. The man of the vertical line is the authentic sannyasin: one who is immensely happy in being no one, immensely happy with his inner purity of emptiness because only emptiness can be pure; one who is absolutely contented with his nothingness because only nothingness can be in tune with the universe.

Once this being in tune with the universe happens, you are in a sense no more. In the old sense, you are no more. But for the first time you are the whole universe. Even the faraway stars are within you, your nothingness can contain them: the flowers, the sun, the moon, the whole music of existence. You are no longer an ego, your "I" has disappeared. But that does not mean that you have disappeared. On the contrary, the moment your "I" has disappeared, you have appeared.

It is such a great ecstasy to be without the feeling of "I," without the feeling of any ego, without asking for anything more. What more can you ask? You have nothingness. In this nothingness you have become, without conquering, the whole universe. Then the singing birds are not only singing outside you. They appear outside because this body creates the barrier.

On the vertical line you become more and more consciousness and less and less body. The whole identification with the body disappears. In nothingness, these birds will be within you; these flowers, these trees and this beautiful morning will be within you. In fact, then there is no without. Everything has become your vision. And you cannot have a richer life than when everything has become your within. When the sun and the moon and the stars and the whole infinity of time and space is within you – what more do you want?

This is exactly the meaning of enlightenment: to become so nonexistent as an ego that the whole oceanic existence becomes part of you.

Kabir, a great Indian mystic was uneducated but has written such tremendously significant statements. They may not be grammatical. One of his statements he corrected before he died. He had written a beautiful statement when he was young. It was, "Just a dewdrop slips from the lotus leaf in the early morning sun, shining like a pearl, into the ocean." He said, "The same has happened to me."

His words are, "I have been searching, my friend. Rather than finding myself, I got lost in the cosmos. The dewdrop disappeared into the ocean." Just before dying, as he was closing his eyes, he asked his son, Kamal – who himself proved of the same caliber and of the same status. And sometimes one thinks that he was a man of more courage than Kabir.

Kabir was very courageous against all traditions, orthodoxy, everything. But Kamal even criticized Kabir when he found something wrong in his statements. Kabir said to Kamal, "Please change my statement, which has been praised all over, that 'My friend, I have been searching for myself, but rather than finding myself, I got lost, just as the dewdrop disappears into the ocean.' Change it."

Kamal said, "I had always suspected that there was something wrong in it." And he showed him his own writing, in which he had already corrected it. The correction – even before Kabir realized – had been done already. That's why Kabir called him Kamal: "You are a miracle." *Kamal* means miracle. And the man *was* a miracle. He had changed the line that Kabir wanted: "My friend, I was seeking and searching myself. Rather than finding myself I have found the whole world, the whole universe. The dewdrop has not disappeared into the ocean, but the ocean has disappeared into the dewdrop."

When the ocean disappears into the dewdrop, the dewdrop is simply losing its boundaries, nothing else.

On the vertical line, you become less and less and less and less. And one day, you are no more.

A Zen master, Rinzai, had a very absurd habit, but beautiful. Every morning, when he woke up, before opening his eyes he would say, "Rinzai, are you still here?"

His disciples said, "What kind of nonsense is this? You ask 'Rinzai, are you still here?'"

He said, "I am waiting for the moment when the answer will be, 'No. Existence is, but Rinzai is not.'"

This is the ultimate peak that human consciousness can reach. This is the ultimate benediction. And unless one reaches this peak, one will remain wandering in dark pathways, blind, suffering, miserable. He may accumulate much knowledge, he may become a great scholar, but that does not help. Only one thing, a very simple thing, is the essence of the whole religious experience, and that is meditation.

Go inward. It will be difficult to get out from the crowd of your thoughts, but you are not a thought. You can get out of the crowd, you can create a distance between you and your thoughts. And as the distance grows bigger, the thoughts start falling like leaves which have died. Because it is you and your identity with the thoughts that gives them nourishment. When you are not giving them nourishment, thoughts cannot exist. Have you met any thought standing somewhere by itself?

Just try to be indifferent. The word of Gautam Buddha is *upeksha*. Just be indifferent to the whole mind and a distance will be created. And then you will come to a point from where all nourishment to the thoughts is stopped. They simply disappear; they are soap bubbles. The moment all thoughts disappear, you will find yourself in the same situation, asking, "Rinzai, are you still here?" And you will wait for that great moment, that great, rare opportunity when the answer will be, "No. Who is this guy Rinzai?"

This silence is meditation. It is not a talent. Everyone cannot be a Picasso, a Rabindranath, a Michelangelo. Those are talents. But everyone can be enlightened because it is not a talent; it is your intrinsic nature, of which you are unaware. And you will remain unaware if you remain surrounded by thoughts. The awareness of your ultimate reality arises only when there is nothing to prevent it, when there is nothingness surrounding you.

The vertical line is rare. It is perhaps the only rare thing in existence because it takes you on the journey of eternity and immortality. The flowers that blossom on those paths are inconceivable by the mind. And the experiences that happen are unexplainable. But in a very strange way the man himself becomes the expression. His eyes show the depths of his heart, his gestures show the grace of the vertical movement. His whole life radiates, pulsates, and creates a field of energy.

Those who are prejudiced, those who are not already determined and concluded – I feel sorry for them. But those who are open, unprejudiced, who have not concluded yet, they will immediately start feeling the pulsation, the radiation, and a certain synchronicity between the heart of the man of the vertical, and the heart of the man who is not yet vertical. The moment the synchronicity happens, in that same moment you also start moving vertically. These are words simply to explain things which are not explainable through words. But those who are intelligent enough, not intellectuals because those people are full of rubbish. Never get mixed up between being intellectual and intelligence. Intelligence is a pure clarity of seeing, a perceptivity. The intellectual is a computer; he is a memory. Intelligence is not memory. Intelligence is a sharp sword which penetrates directly into reality, once it sees it.

It is said that Mahakashyapa, himself a prince, had gone to see Gautam Buddha. But he was very simple, innocent, unprejudiced, having no belief systems, no philosophy, no theology. He simply touched the feet of Buddha, looked into the eyes of Buddha, and everything happened: some transfer of light, something invisible, some meeting of the heart, some merging. He never asked Gautam Buddha a single question.

Even others became aware of the fact: "All the disciples ask questions. This Mahakashyapa is strange. He simply sits under a tree; he has almost monopolized the tree. Everyone knows, 'Don't sit there, Mahakashyapa will sit there.' He sits there – if Buddha speaks, good; if Buddha does not speak, good."

Slowly, slowly older disciples approached Mahakashyapa, particularly Sariputta who was a very close disciple of Gautam Buddha. He asked Mahakashyapa, "Don't you have a question?"

Mahakashyapa said, "All my questions were answered the moment he looked into my eyes. Since the moment I touched his feet, I have not been a body. I am just a consciousness and the body is my house. All identity with the body was broken in a single, split moment."

He is described in the Buddhist scriptures only once, when another king was offering Gautam Buddha a great, valuable diamond and Buddha said, "Drop it!" Reluctantly, because it was a very valuable diamond, but before ten thousand people if you have offered it and Buddha says, "Drop it!" He dropped it. He had also brought a very rare flower: a lotus which had blossomed out of season. It was not the time for lotuses. He offered Buddha that flower and Buddha again said, "Drop it!" He dropped it but he felt very strange, hurt: "My gifts are not being accepted."

And Buddha said, "Drop it!" Now he had nothing to drop, so he looked all around, "What to make of it? Is this man mad? I dropped the diamond, I dropped the flower. And those two things were in both my hands. Now I don't have anything to drop." This is the moment where Mahakashyapa is mentioned – once only.

Ten thousand sannyasins were utterly silent because it was a strange thing, Buddha had never done that. He had always accepted from anyone who had brought a flower or a gift. But Mahakashyapa sitting under his monopolized tree laughed loudly. He had not spoken to anyone; he had been there for four years. This was the first time he had made some kind of expression. He laughed. And this was even more hurtful.

The king said, "Why are you laughing?"

He said, "I am laughing because you are not dropping yourself. He is not concerned about your flower and about your diamond, drop yourself! And I say it with my own experience – before he said anything, I had dropped myself. He had to lean and hold me up, and our eyes met and everything happened."

Mahakashyapa is perhaps the most mysterious disciple of Gautam Buddha, but the most perceptive. That was a rare moment, when Buddha looked into Mahakashyapa's eyes. That was the moment when eternity penetrated time, when the vertical penetrated the horizontal. And just a single moment can be such a radical change. Beautiful were those days, golden are their memories. It looks very far away and faint now.

My effort here is to make this small island a part of eternity, where those innocent moments, those innocent experiences are still possible. Nothing is said, nothing is heard, and yet the heart starts dancing in tune with the master. The universal and the eternal are the same, only man has become more and more drowned in darkness. In India, the seers have named this part of time Kaliyuga – the age of darkness. They were certainly very perceptive.

Just a few days ago, the editor of *Illustrated Weekly* wrote an article about me in which he said a few significant things. He is not a religious person, neither does he believe in any spirituality. But what he saw and felt in our commune, was his closest experience of spirituality.

Someone from England wrote him a very angry letter which was published. The man said, "What has happened to you? Either you have been bribed or you have been hypnotized." Looking at his letter, it became something more important. Because if anyone tells any lies about me, if anyone is against me, no one will say to him,

"You have been bribed by the enemies of Osho." And no one will say or even conceive that, "You have been hypnotized by the people who are against Osho."

Many people have told me, "We want to come, we want to understand. But then people start saying, 'You are being hypnotized. If you are not saying anything against Osho, then certainly you are being hypnotized.'" Just twenty-five centuries ago, do you think Mahakashyapa was hypnotized? Do you think anyone would have said to him, "Either you have been bribed or hypnotized"? Those were days when people were not so closed and allowed some fresh breeze to pass through them.

Now everyone seems to be completely closed. Someone is a Christian, a Hindu, a Mohammedan. Before experiencing anything, they have decided what is true and what is false. Before coming in contact with a living source, they have covered themselves completely, defensively. They are afraid that if they open up, all their prejudices will look stupid and all their belief systems will fall down.

I am here in my own land, but I consider myself a foreigner. People are afraid to enter the gate of the commune. The fear is of hypnosis. And they don't understand what hypnosis is. The fact is, they have been hypnotized from their very childhood to worship a monkey god because no intelligent man will do that. They have been hypnotized to worship an elephant god. This is possible only through constant repetition, from the very childhood, by the whole society around them; so that it becomes a conditioning in them. Otherwise, they will also think – what are they doing?

But they never think. Thinking is one of the greatest crimes. So no one thinks, everyone believes. But if you want to reach the heights of a Buddha, to the heights of a Chuang Tzu, then you will have to drop all belief systems. You will have to drop all thoughts which have been given to you by others, and which are borrowed.

A man came to Chuang Tzu one day and was arguing. Chuang Tzu said, "Wait. I just want to know one thing: Would you like to use someone else's shoes?"

He said, "Why should I use someone else's shoes?"

Chuang Tzu said, "You are so alert about your legs, about your feet, but you are not so aware about your head, because every thought that you have is someone else's. It is not yours. You have heard it, you have read it, you have been told; you have gathered it from the atmosphere, and you have never thought that you don't have a single thought of your own."

In fact, there is no thought which is your own. There is only clarity, perceptivity, silence, understanding, intelligence which are your own. And with these you can be ready for eternity to enter the world of time. It is the greatest moment. I cannot conceive of anything more valuable or more precious. It makes you the whole universe; it takes away all your boundaries which are really an imprisonment. It makes you a bird on the wing in the open sky.

Now something serious, because we have been in a nonserious world so long...

A man goes into a bar and orders a beer. When he is served, he reaches into his breast pocket and lifts out a perfectly formed little figure, four inches tall. Then he pulls out a thimble and places it on the bar. "A beer for my friend here too," he requests. "And go easy on the head."

"Is he for real?" asks the bartender.

"He is," says the man.

"Can he talk?" persists the bartender.

"He can," replies the man.

"Arnold," he goes on, "tell this guy about the time we were on safari and you called the witch doctor a black son-of-a-bitch."

Silverman is killed in an accident and Mendel Kravitz is sent to break the news to his wife.

"Be careful how you tell her," advises a friend. "She is a very delicate woman."

Mendel knocks on the door and Mrs. Silverman comes out. "Are you the widow of Silverman?" he asks.

"Certainly not," she replies.

"Wanna bet?" asks Mendel.

An African tribe is living through a famine and having a bad time with its crops. The chief calls a meeting and says, "We will send a telegram to the Russians, telling them that we are having agricultural problems and need their help. They will send seeds, tractors and one hundred young technicians to help us.

"Then we will send a telegram to the Americans, telling them that the Russians are helping us. And the Americans will send us seeds and tractors and one hundred technicians. When all the technicians arrive, we will eat them."

# 28

# Meditation Is More than Vipassana

Osho,
Over the past five years I've spent many weeks in isolation at Dhamma Giri, practicing *vipassana* meditation as taught by S. N. Goenka. I've never experienced such pain, suffering and doubt ever before. Presently I feel very exhausted, tired, yearning deeply to connect with my heart. My interest in the meditation practice is passing away. Is this type of meditation practice necessary? Is it helpful? Can awareness and celebration alone pierce the depth of the mind and dissolve the darkest nights?

The *vipassana* meditation was invented by Gautam Buddha and for twenty-five centuries Buddhists have been torturing themselves. Now, who told you to go to Dhamma Giri to S. N. Goenka, to learn a meditation for which the whole context is missing? The meditation was perfectly right for a man like Gautam Buddha. Always remember, everything is related, interdependent, and with a certain context.

A German poet, Heine, was lost for days in a forest. Utterly tired, exhausted, hungry, he could not find the way; neither could he find anyone who could show him the way. In the night he was resting up in the trees; otherwise wild animals would destroy him.

And then came the full-moon night. He had written many poems... The moon had been one of his most loved objects and he had written beautiful songs about it. But that night, tired and hungry and afraid, he looked at the full moon and he could not believe it – what he saw in the full moon he had never seen before. And he had been a lifelong moon gazer. That night he saw a loaf of bread!

What you see depends on you. People see the faces of their loved ones, people see their dream girls in the moon, but no one has ever seen a loaf of bread. But his experience was absolutely authentic – but only in *his* context.

I am reminding you of this because people tend to forget that life is a very interwoven, interdependent, cosmic whole. You cannot take a part out of it and keep it alive, meaningful. I will not tell you to do *vipassana* unless I can also give you the experience of Gautam Buddha. Poor Goenka cannot understand this. He is just a businessman. What does he understand about the context in which *vipassana* arose?

Gautam Buddha had lived in tremendous luxury, surrounded by beautiful girls, beautiful palaces. The whole night was a celebration; the day was for rest, the night for dances and drinking. Out of this experience he became tired. He had seen all the beautiful girls; there was nothing more to be seen. He had seen that every man and woman is just a skeleton, covered with a thin skin. Just think for a moment: here all of you are skeletons covered with thin skin! This body and its beauty fades very soon.

He had seen all that was possible in those days for a man of power and riches to see, but he could not find peace, contentment, silence. He could not find himself. Utterly frustrated, one night he moved out of the palace – because this life is going to end in a few days, or in a few years. It is not something to cling to. Each moment death is coming closer; before death grabs you, you have to figure out something which is eternal, which is immortal.

All that you see around you is made of the same stuff as dreams are. Do you think you are on the earth for the first time? Millions of people have come on the same earth and simply disappeared into thin air. Scientists have calculated that the place you are occupying has been occupied by at least ten people before you. You are sitting on ten corpses! And don't think too much of yourself because you cannot get out – you will be the eleventh. Remember, it is not a laughing matter for you. Those ten corpses will laugh at you: "Look, the poor fellow was thinking of great things and finally he is flat on the pile of corpses."

Gautam Buddha's search for truth, for himself, for the source of life which is eternal, cannot be the search of a poor man who is hungry, who is searching for a loaf of bread. But people have completely forgotten Gautam Buddha. They have taken his meditation out of context. He could meditate because there was nothing else in the world to think about, to desire, to be ambitious for. The world was, in a way, finished the day he left his house; he never looked back.

I am reminded of a beautiful story…

Buddha was afraid that if he went into the mountains of his own kingdom, his father's armies would find him; he would not be able to escape. He was the only son of an old king, who was hoping that he would succeed him. And the old king had made a big kingdom for him. So he immediately passed beyond the boundaries of his kingdom to the neighboring kingdom. The old king was furious. He ordered the armies not to leave even a single inch unsearched: "Look around, all over the country."

Gautam Buddha was not found, but he was not aware that the kingdom he had entered belonged to a friend of his father. His father informed this king and the other kings surrounding his kingdom, "You have to find my son. In my old age, at least you can do this much for me; we have been friends."

The neighboring king found Gautam Buddha and said, "If you are angry, if you have fought with your father… It happens. It is not something strange or unfamiliar; fathers and sons have always been fighting. Don't be worried. I have only one daughter and no son, if you get married to my daughter, you will have two kingdoms together. Your father is old; he cannot live long. And my kingdom is far bigger than your father's. He is my friend and I have come with a request. You have everything to gain, nothing to lose. You get a beautiful wife, a great kingdom, and of course your own kingdom is there. You will be a greater king than me or your father because your kingdom will be bigger than the kingdoms we have. You will have two kingdoms together."

Gautam Buddha said, "You don't understand the point. I have not fought with my father, I have not been angry with him and I have not come here in search of a girl. I am not interested in a kingdom, however big it is. But I would like to ask you a few questions; you are my father's friend. First tell me, you say your girl is very beautiful – is this beauty going to remain forever? Will she not be old one day?"

The king said, "You ask strange questions. Everyone becomes old."

"And do you think," Gautam Buddha asked, "she will never die?"

The king laughed. He said, "You are hilarious. Everyone dies."

Gautam Buddha said, "I don't want to get married with someone who is going to die."

The king said, "She is not going to die tomorrow."

Gautam Buddha said, "You cannot give any guarantee. Are you sure *you* will be alive tomorrow?"

The king said, "I have never thought about it. I hope that I will be alive, but I cannot be certain. But you are creating anxieties in my mind. I had come to take you to the palace and it seems you are trying to convince me to follow you to the mountains."

Gautam Buddha said, "It is better; there is still time, it is still light. Maybe you have a few days more to live. Devote these few days to a search for something which cannot be taken away from you. Your youth will disappear, your beauty will disappear, your kingdom will one day belong to someone else. And what does it matter to whom your kingdom belongs when you are dead; whether he is your son or someone else's son?"

The king said, "You are a dangerous fellow. I don't want to talk to you."

He informed Gautam Buddha's father, "I have met your son; he is in the mountains in my kingdom. I tried hard, but he is very convincing. And he has created such anxiety in me that I have not slept since. I am continuously thinking of death – what is going to happen after death? What have I gained by having this big kingdom? I am a poor man inside. I have never looked into my own being; I am not even acquainted with myself. I request you not to try to prevent him, let him go and let him search. What we have missed, perhaps we can hope he will find."

Gautam Buddha could sit silently, desireless, thoughtless, moving inward because for him the outside had lost all interest. He had seen that it is just a phenomenon, the way you see a film. But there are idiots who even seeing a film will cry, will weep, will laugh because they will become identified and they will forget that there is nothing on the screen, it is just a projected film. Our whole life is not much more than that, but to know it you have to go through it. Gautam Buddha had a great chance to experience life and see its futility. This gave him the opportunity to sit in deep silence, undisturbed. *Vipassana* was discovered in these moments.

My own effort here is not to give you any meditation like *vipassana* directly. This place is not a place of ascetics; here people are enjoying everything. I want you to enjoy and to see the futility of it. I want to see how many times you become enlightened and how many times you become unenlightened. I know one day you will simply get tired and you will say, "Finished!"

Not finished like Nandan – she has started again. But she is going to be finished one day. When she says good-bye to her last boyfriend it will be possible for her to meditate; particularly a meditation like *vipassana*. Otherwise, you can sit with closed eyes and beautiful girls will harass you.

That has been the experience of thousands of meditators down the ages. It is strange, the moment you sit to meditate, suddenly, from nowhere, such beautiful girls start coming. And you open your eyes and there is no one. Not only girls. If you have not known money, thoughts of money; if you have not known power, thoughts of power; if you have not known what it means to be a celebrity, then a deep desire to become famous. The mind will go on weaving a thousand and one thoughts and desires.

The so-called teachers like Goenka will go on teaching you, "Don't allow these thoughts in your mind." And the more you push them away, the more they will come close to you. You will throw away one girl and you will find there is a queue of girls, and at the end of the queue is standing Sophia Loren. Now, naturally you think, "*Vipassana* can be done later on."

A man said to his friend, "Last night was just the greatest experience of my life."

The other asked, "What happened?"

He said, "I went fishing and I caught such big fish that I could not believe it. Even to carry one fish to the shore was difficult. And the whole night I was fishing."

The other said, "This is nothing. You are saying you had the greatest experience – the greatest experience happened to me. Last night when I dreamed, what I saw I could not believe. On one side was Marilyn Monroe, utterly nude; on the other side was Sophia Loren, utterly nude."

The other man could not contain himself. He said, "Stop. Why didn't you call me? At such a moment! And what were you going to do with two such women? One is enough for you, and one you should have thought of your best friend. You call me your best friend? This is great friendship!"

The man said, "You haven't heard the whole thing. I had gone to your home to find you, but your wife said you had gone fishing!"

If life has not been a rich experience – if it has been a repressive, religion-dominated, conditioned phenomenon – you cannot do *vipassana*. In twenty-five centuries, millions of people have been doing *vipassana*. How many have become Gautam Buddhas? My own analysis is very simple, but very significant: you should not repress anything in your life. Live a nonrepressive, joyous life. Soon you will find all those joys and all those pleasures are empty.

Unless you have found through your own experience that pleasures are not pleasures, but simply toys to keep you ignorant, to keep you engaged… Once you have found that through your own experience – remember that is most fundamental; it has to be your own experience; then *vipassana* is the simplest meditation. You don't have to go to any businessman to learn it. Buddha had never gone to S. N. Goenka. This kind of people existed at that time too: businessmen who were ready to teach you at a certain price.

I have never met or seen Goenka, but I saw one of his interviews. He says that he met me in Chennai. I have only been to Chennai once in my whole life, and I remember it perfectly. I have not met any Goenka. He is simply lying. And his Dhamma Giri is not very far away from here. If he wants to meet me, he can come any day. It is perhaps a five-hour drive. But he does not have the guts because I am very merciless. When I see a fox pretending to be a lion, then I do what needs to be done: expose the fox, take away the hypocrisy. He has not lived a life of love; he has not lived a life of pleasures; he has not lived at all that which can create the context in which *vipassana* is possible.

He is simply a refugee from Myanmar. And because Myanmar is a Buddhist country, everyone knows what *vipassana* is; just as every Christian knows the Christian prayer, every Buddhist knows *vipassana*. Coming from Myanmar he knew the structure, intellectually, of what *vipassana* is. Here he found many people searching for meditation.

He does not create a situation in which to be associated with him becomes dangerous for you. He is a noncontroversial businessman;

you will not offend anyone if you go to Dhamma Giri. But if you come here, you don't see many Indians. The reason is clear: to be associated with me in any way is to be condemned by the outside society. People start saying that you have also been hypnotized, you have also become corrupt.

Dhamma Giri is safe because he does not say to you, "You have to drop tradition, you have to drop your conditioning, you have to get out of all the knowledge that has been forced upon you. Unless you are so clean, unconditioned, unorthodox – neither Hindu nor Mohammedan nor Christian – you will not be able to enter the world of meditation." He does not say anything like that. You just enter *vipassana* as you are. Nothing is demanded from you, that first you go through a fire to be purified, that you have to get rid of the society which is utterly polluted.

I was surprised when I was in America: almost every week someone would phone from San Francisco, someone from New York, saying, "We are coming from Mumbai," or, "We are coming from Pune and we want to meet Osho." I told my secretary to tell those people, "Osho has been there in Pune for seven years – couldn't you manage to see him then? He will come back to Pune again, you can see him then."

Strangely enough, not a single one has turned up. I have been here for two years. Those people who phoned – from Mumbai, from Pune – they have not dared to enter the door. In America they were happy that no one would know that they had been to see a dangerous man. Here the wife will start crying, the children will say, "Papa, where are you going?" The neighbors will crowd around saying, "Don't do this. Just look at your old parents." It will become a scene.

And deep down you yourself are such a coward that you believe in all the lies that have been spread. You never come here to check who is being hypnotized. But the trouble is, people say, "Once you are there, you will become hypnotized, you will start saying the same things." It is a very strange world.

A German sannyasin is here. He is an old, experienced journalist. He had come from *Stern* magazine to write on what was happening here. But he was a man of integrity; he reported exactly what was happening. They refused his report. They said, "You have been hypnotized." If you lie you are not hypnotized, if you say the truth you are hypnotized. They did not publish his article. He insisted and finally they published it, but he had to change much in it. But he became so disgusted that he resigned and came back. Since then he has been here, he has been in America; he is again here.

There are many writers who have had a strange experience: if they write just a positive account, factual, neither for nor against, no one is ready to publish their books. They say, "These books won't sell because they don't have any sensation. Make them sensational." But how to make them sensational? – lie, create fictions which do not exist, and publishers are ready, magazines are ready to publish them. And these books, these publishers, these magazines spread unfounded things all around the world. So that people are so afraid that even to mention my name is dangerous.

One of my sannyasins who is a Nobel Prize winner asked the president of the Nobel Prize committee, the King of Norway, "A man has written five hundred books and you have not taken any note of it."

The king suggested, "Remember never to mention his name. This time you did because you were not aware, but next time it will be dangerous for your job" – he has a big post – "it will be dangerous for your reputation. Simply forget about this man."

He told me, "I could not believe that he was not even ready to listen to anything about you. He did not even inquire, just for manners' sake." On the contrary, from that day the king kept a certain distance from him. Whenever there was a meeting of the Nobel Prize committee, he did not allow him to come close to him; he showed absolutely that a certain China Wall had arisen between himself and the poor Nobel Prize winner. And the only crime he had committed was that he had mentioned my name.

Indira Gandhi, who was a very powerful woman, had made at least six appointments to come here to see me, and every time, just one day before, a phone call would come, "An emergency has arisen and the meeting has to be postponed."

In fact, now the meeting is postponed forever! My secretary asked Indira Gandhi, "Why do you do this? If you don't want to come, we are not asking you to come. You ask us, that you want to come."

She had met me once in Delhi and had said afterward, "Since then that man's eyes have been haunting me and I want to see him again. And whatever he has said has changed the whole of history. I want his advice on other problems."

My secretary said, "Then why do you go on canceling? Because this is absolute nonsense, that every time on the same day, some emergency arises."

She said, "To be honest with you, there has been no emergency, just my colleagues, my cabinet stands in the way. Everyone says, 'Don't go there, you could even lose your prime ministership. There will be so much turmoil – just avoid going there.'"

Just by going for a meeting with a man who has no power, who is not interested in politics! But I can understand, those politicians were right. If she had come here the Mohammedans would have said, "We are not going to vote for you." The Hindus would have said, "That man has spoken against our Vedas, we are not going to vote for you. That man has spoken against our *shankaracharya*."

A powerful woman like Indira Gandhi is so cowardly that she cannot come when she wants to come because of the fear that the voters may start objecting, "You have been to a man for some advice. And any advice that man gives is going to be dangerous. In the first place you will be hypnotized." And she, an intelligent, well-educated woman asked my secretary, "Is it true that whoever goes to meet Osho becomes hypnotized?"

People like Goenka are noncontroversial, kindergarten school teachers. They don't understand the complexity of meditation.

*Vipassana* comes in the end; you cannot begin with *vipassana*. To begin with *vipassana* you will have to go through what you are saying – the dark night of the soul. And you will not find the dawn anywhere. The dark night will go on becoming longer and darker. It is a simple psychology: you are not prepared, you have not done your homework, and you have started a work which needs a tremendous background of experience.

They are all against me because I want you to live first as hotly as possible.

I used to go to Ahmedabad. One of my sannyasins, Jayantibhai, would pick me up from the airport or from the railway station, and suddenly on a bridge he would accelerate the speed of the car. And I would say, "What is the matter?"

He said, "The matter is that board."

Because I had been telling him again and again, "That board is very religious. You should once in a while go near the board and look at it."

It was an advertisement, but very beautiful. It said, "Live a little hot. Sip a Gold Spot."

I said, "I am not concerned about Gold Spot, but live a little hot!"

People live lukewarm; they live just at the minimum because from that minimum they are protected from many dangers. If you don't want to fall, crawl – you are safe! And that's what you are doing in your life. I say, live hotly while the season lasts. This season will not last forever. Don't hesitate because in that hesitation you are losing time.

A roseflower does not hesitate to open in the early morning sun, knowing perfectly well that by the evening the petals will fall and not even a mark will remain behind. Whether that roseflower ever existed or not, it will be the same. But while the sun is rising and the morning breeze is welcoming to dance, the rose dances. All the religions have destroyed your dance. They have made you crippled, they have destroyed your sensitivities. They have dulled your intelligence and then they say, "Do *vipassana*."

A man who has lived hotly is bound to do *vipassana* – but in the evening. He has seen the day. It was beautiful, but it was ephemeral; it is gone. Now begins the search for that which comes and never goes.

One of the great Hindu scriptures is Badarayana's sutras. The first sutra is: *Athato brahma Jigyasa* – now the inquiry into the ultimate. For almost two thousand years or more that "now" has been a problem. How to interpret it? Because this is the beginning. Books don't begin from now. It seems as if something has preceded it.

And now there are many commentaries on Badarayana's Athato, but no one has got the point. The man was saying, "You have lived hotly, you have loved deeply. You have done everything that you wanted to do, unrepressed, uninhibited. Now it is time for the inquiry into the ultimate. But only now. If you have not lived at the maximum, that which has been left unlived will go on lingering in your mind. That which has been repressed will go on asking for your attention. Your heart and your mind will be pulled by the unlived, the repressed, the denied, the condemned, and you cannot sit silently."

Otherwise *vipassana* is not an effort, it is a very simple experience. After the whole hot day of life, when you see the futility of it all... *You* have to see. You cannot see from other people's eyes; you have to see the futility with your own eyes. Then what is the problem? You sit silently, you settle silently within yourself, into your very interiority.

The word *vipassana* simply means perceptivity, clarity, seeing directly into truth. But if something you always wanted – it may be a small thing – is there in your unconscious, it won't allow your perception to be pure. It will try again and again: "I am still unfulfilled." First have the experience that you have denied yourself.

And all these religions have been teaching you to deny this, to deny that. They have driven the whole of humanity bananas; otherwise human beings are beautiful as they are. If they live naturally, one day they are going to ripen, one day they are going to mature. One day they are going to graduate from this so-called world of desires, ambitions, jealousies. After that graduation, *vipassana* is not a doing. It is a non-doing. You simply sit silently and it starts showering over you as if the whole sky is rejoicing in your silence.

One of the stories about Manjushri, a disciple of Gautam Buddha who became enlightened, depicts it correctly. He is sitting under his tree, silently, and flowers start showering on him. Those flowers are not visible, but they are fragrant, and they have tremendous power to transform your whole being.

It was in a way good that you went into "...isolation at Dhamma Giri practicing *vipassana* meditation as taught by S. N. Goenka." It has been a good experience. You say, "I have never experienced such pain..." You deserved it. Why did you go there?

You say, "I have never experienced such suffering and doubt ever before. Presently I feel exhausted, tired..." Very good. At least you are alive! Just a few days rest, a few days nourishment in my commune and all the pain, all the suffering, all the doubt and all the tiredness will disappear. If you have understood me correctly, it has already disappeared. You will be dancing and singing and rejoicing.

We have so many meditations here, but I have put *vipassana* at the very end. First go through all other kinds of experiences, purifying, so that you can become capable of entering *vipassana*. People want to jump into paradise directly, and they don't see the place where they are standing, that if they jump from there, they will have multiple fractures. One has to reach the steps and one has to move step by step, consciously, cautiously. It is a pilgrimage.

But this experience has been really good. You needed it. It will be easier now for you to see my arrangement of meditations. You are saying, "My interest in the meditation practice is passing away." Your interest in Dhamma Giri should pass away, not in meditations.

It is just too fresh. The wound is open. Just wait, and in a few days you will be doing *vipassana* here. But here *vipassana* is a juicy experience; it is not dry.

I have a few criticisms against the *vipassana* that is being practiced in Buddhist lands. They have all made it very dry, desertlike; nothing blossoms, no greenery; everything is simply businesslike. I want you to learn meditation as a play, as playfulness. Your meditation and your love should be synonymous. And that's what you are asking. You are asking, "I am yearning deeply to connect with my heart." That guy, S. N. Goenka, has disconnected you from your heart because in the Buddhist tradition there is no place for the heart. It is a very dry approach to reality.

Buddha never even mentions the word *love*. He was so afraid that for twenty years continuously he denied women initiation into his commune. Because women are impossible: they will bring some juice, whatever you do; something will start growing in the desert, some flowers. It is impossible for a woman not to be the heart. It is very easy for the man not to be the heart. The woman is the heart and the man is the head. And once you deny women, then there are only dry heads – coconuts!

My approach is that I never make any distinction whether someone is a woman or a man. Anyone who is a seeker of the path is welcome. Hence this is a totally different commune; such a commune has never existed before. Here you can sing and dance, here you can fall in love and fall out of love, there is no harm. Life is accepted in its totality. In this total acceptance arises the awareness that will enable you to meditate. And this meditation will be far richer than any *vipassana* of Gautam Buddha. This meditation may create songs in you, may create dances in you, may give a new impetus to creativity in all dimensions of life.

Your silence should not be the silence of a graveyard, your silence should be the silence of a garden. Once in a while a bird starts singing, but it does not disturb the silence, it deepens it. Once in a while the breeze comes with its song, passes through the pine trees, but it does not disturb the silence, it deepens it. I do not teach you the desert. I teach you the garden, the garden of the heart. That is where, with great respect, I differ from Gautam Buddha. I love the man, but that does not mean I have to agree with everything done by the man. His meditation is heartless, and a meditation that is heartless is not of any worth. I want a meditation that can laugh, that can dance.

You suffered well. This is what in the East people call the law of karma. You must have committed some grave sin in your past life; otherwise, why should you go to Dhamma Giri? Dhamma Giri of all places! But in a way it is good. That evil act and its punishment is finished. Now you can start afresh. I teach you a meditation which is totally different from anything that has ever been taught in the name of meditation.

Now a few things just to relieve your pain, your suffering, your tiredness, and to help you to forget that you have been to Dhamma Giri – you simply dreamed about it, there is no such place as Dhamma Giri. This guy S. N. Goenka does not exist; it was just a nightmare.

A man parked his car on a street in New York. But when he returned, he found that someone had smashed into the rear end of his car.

On the windshield he found a note that read:

Dear Sir, I just smashed into your car. The people who saw the accident are watching me. They think I am writing down my name and address, so you can contact me regarding the damage. They are a bunch of idiots!

Hymie Goldberg is stopped in the street by a neatly dressed salesman who says, "Sir, would you like to buy a toothbrush for ten dollars?"

"Ten dollars?" cries Hymie. "That's robbery!"

The salesman seems hurt. "Well then," he says, "how about a nice piece of homemade chocolate cake for ten cents?"

This seems fair, so Hymie hands ten cents to the man and unwrapping the cake takes a bite. Suddenly he screams and spits out the mouthful. "My God!" he shouts. "This cake tastes like shit."

"It is," replies the salesman. "Wanna buy a toothbrush?"

Tired of being a yuppie, Bogart decides to leave the city life and buy a small farm. He goes to a sale of farm animals and asks to buy a rooster.

"Out here," says the salesman, "we call them cocks."

"Okay," says Bogart, "give me a cock. And can you sell me a hen?" he asks.

"Out here," says the salesman, "we call them pullets."

"Okay, give me a pullet," says Bogart. "And what else do you have for sale?"

The salesman explains that he has a jackass for sale, so Bogart buys that too. As he is leaving, the salesman warns Bogart that sometimes the jackass stands still and won't move until he is scratched between the ears.

Sure enough, on his way home the jackass stops and does not move, and Bogart has forgotten what the salesman had said.

Grandma Feigenbaum happens to be walking nearby and stops to ask if she can help. Just then Bogart remembers about scratching the jackass between the ears.

"Ah, yes, you can help me," says Bogart. "Would you hold my cock and pullet while I scratch my ass?"

## 29

# Everything Is as It Should Be

Osho,
A few months ago I had what seemed to be a great realization: that all you have ever been teaching is witnessing. At the time I was very excited about it but this has faded, leaving me after twelve years of sannyas still with the question: What am I doing with my time here? And the feeling that there is some dimension that I am not yet experiencing or that somehow I am still missing you. Would you say something about this, and maybe a prayer for me?

To expect is to be disappointed. Jesus says, "Seek and you shall find it." I disagree with him absolutely, categorically. I say unto you, "Seek and you will never find." Because the searching mind cannot be silent, the searching mind cannot be at ease. The searching mind is always looking into the future; it is never herenow. The searching mind distracts you from reality.

Jesus again says, "Ask and it shall be given to you." And I say unto you, "Ask and you have missed it." Because the asking mind is the mind of a beggar. This beautiful existence belongs to the emperors, not to the beggars. You don't have to have an empire to be an emperor. Just look at me: I don't have any empire, but that does not destroy my being an emperor. In fact, the people who have empires are not emperors, they are imprisoned in their own empire, worried, continuously afraid of being invaded – a thousand and one worries. What kind of being an emperor is this?

Jesus also says, "Knock and the doors shall be opened unto you." I don't want to disagree with the poor carpenter. He would have been a beautiful sannyasin. He was just a little eccentric, but that is not a bad quality; it gives some color to life. The statement "Seek and the doors shall be opened unto you" is again the same repletion; between you and the future. You seek, then the doors shall be opened.

I say unto you, "Don't seek. Don't ask. Don't knock and disturb the neighbors! The door is open – enter."

I have spoken about one of the most beautiful women, al-Adabiya, a Sufi mystic of very rare quality. She was passing by the side of the mosque. She never went into the mosque. If this whole existence is not his temple, then man-made houses will be too small; he cannot be a guest in those small houses. They are going to remain empty and waiting.

She had heard many times of another seeker, who finally became a master. And he became a master because of al-Adabiya. There is a limit… He was continuously praying, sitting outside the mosque, "God, open the door, let me in." She tolerated him for a few days, but the point came when she could not tolerate it. She hit him hard on his head and said, "You idiot, open your eyes! The doors are open, and there is no need to pray for it."

A crowd gathered. Hassan, the seeker, was very respected as a religious man, a man of prayer, and al-Adabiya was thought of as something crazy; she was always doing crazy things. Now she had done the last crazy thing. But something happened to Hassan. He looked into the eyes of Adabiya, touched her feet and said, "I am sorry, please forgive me. The doors are open."

How can existence close the doors to its own children? You expect and you create a tension in your being: somewhere, someday, in some life, you will become enlightened. But if I say to you, "I am ready to make you enlightened right now." You will say, "Just give me a little time to think. I have to ask my wife. And just to conceive of myself enlightened seems impossible. I am an ordinary man, living in the ordinary world."

But the people who became enlightened are also living in this world. This world is not ordinary. You cannot find any other world which is more extraordinary. In this vast universe, this small planet is very tiny. Just our sun is thousands of times bigger than this earth, and this sun is considered to be a mediocre star; there are stars millions of times bigger. And the expanse of the universe is infinite.

This earth is blessed: blessed with life, blessed with love, blessed with the possibility of your becoming aware, alert, conscious, enlightened. And no one is preventing you. But so many problems are arising in your drunkenness, in your unconsciousness.

A drunkard reached his home. His wife was tired; every night he would come home late, completely drunk, and disturb the whole house and all the people. The wife finally gave him the key, saying, "You don't have to disturb anyone. We know we cannot change you. The more we make the effort to change you, the more you drink. So keep this key and when you come, open the door silently and go to your bed. Don't disturb anyone's sleep and don't create the quarrels that we have been having through for years."

The drunkard was very happy. That day he drank as much as possible; there was no fear now. And then he staggered toward his house. On the way, two things happened. The first was a lamppost: he got struck by the lamppost. He looked all around, could not believe it. He had always known that there was only one lamppost, and he was surrounded by twelve lampposts! He went this way and that way, but he would get hit again by the lampposts.

A policeman was watching from the road, he felt mercy for the poor man – he had hurt his whole face, scratched it – so he came to rescue him. The drunkard asked, "Just this evening when I left the house, there was only one lamppost. Who is the idiot who has made twelve lampposts? And they won't let me out. Whichever way I go, the lampposts are preventing me."

The policeman said, "Don't be worried. Look again in the morning, when you are awake. Right now, go to your home and go to sleep."

The drunkard followed the policeman to his home, and now another problem arose. He could not manage to put the key into the hole of the lock. His hands were trembling, the lock was trembling. He managed this way and that way, but the hole of the lock and the key behaved as if they were conspiring against him.

The policeman laughed and said, "Can I help you?"

The drunkard said, "It will be great if you can help. Just hold the house steady; it seems there is an earthquake happening."

While all this was going on, from the first floor, the wife opened the window and asked, "What is the problem? Is the key not working? Should I throw down another key?"

He said, "No, the key is perfectly right, just throw me another lock!"

Somehow the policeman and the wife managed to get him into the house. He was worried because he knew that there were scratches and blood on his face, and in the morning the wife was going to find out. So first he went to the bathroom to clean off the blood, and he saw himself in the mirror.

He said, "My God! Those posts… I have never done anything harmful to them and they have been so nasty with me. Let morning come and I am going to go with an ax and cut down all those twelve lampposts completely to the ground. There was no need, even in darkness I was moving perfectly well. Those lampposts…" And then he thought, "If my wife sees me there will be trouble, so somehow the scratches have to be covered with some ointment." He looked for some ointment and he found, instead of ointment, his wife's lipstick.

He said, "This seems to be perfectly good ointment," and he put it on every scratch. In the morning, the wife shouted from the bathroom, "Who has destroyed my lipstick? Not only the lipstick, but who has painted the whole mirror?" Obviously he was looking at his face in the mirror, and wherever there were scratches...

Man is living in a very unconscious state, and whatever he does goes wrong.

Your question is useful for everyone. You are asking, "A few months ago I had what seemed to be a great realization..." After a few months, you will again feel that some great realization is happening. These realizations are just projections of the mind. It is because of the poverty of language that it is difficult to say that one day you find that every moment is a moment of realization.

Is not this moment a moment of realization? Aren't these birds and this sky and this silence a realization? Is not this intensity of thousands of people waiting for the unknown not a realization? Don't make realization a special treat; make realization your usual life. Everything that you have to pass through is a realization. But you have been blinded by all the vested interests. They have been using self-realization like a carrot, hanging far away. Once in a while you find a glimpse of the carrot and you say, "My God, this is it!" But the moment you have said, "This is it!" all realization is finished. Realization has to be synonymous with life, not something like an extracurricular activity.

I cannot see why you cannot understand this simple point. Waking in the morning, fresh, rejuvenated after sleep is a realization. Chopping wood, carrying water is a realization. Looking at the stars, looking in the eyes of people, holding hands with people and feeling the warmth is a realization. Even being tired is a beautiful space, but you have made it ugly by giving it an ugly name. Your tiredness simply means you have lived your day, now is the time to relax. And relaxation is a beautiful realization – a silent sleep.

My approach is to bring down your gods, your goals, your realizations to this moment, and to make everything that you do an act of love and creation. Unless your whole life is a beautiful flow of experiencing the millions of mysteries which surround you, you are just being befooled by the priests, by hanging some fictitious carrots before you. Even the carrots are not real because they are so far away, you will never reach them; so you will never know whether they are real or not.

But those carrots keep you worried, tense, expecting, concerned. It is a miracle that once in a while you believe you have realized. Perhaps you are tired of expecting and you imagine that you have realized. But how long is your imagination going to last? Soon it will fade away, and then comes a deep failure, a feeling of utter frustration.

You say, "A few months ago I had what seemed to be a great realization – that all you have ever been teaching is witnessing. At the time, I was very excited about it, but this has faded, leaving me after twelve years of sannyas still with the question: What am I doing with my life here?" Do you think I know what I am doing with my life here? I am enjoying talking, you are enjoying listening. What else do you want? Do you want to become Alexander the Great? Only then you will be satisfied? But even Alexander the Great died in utter frustration. He had conquered the known world and then he realized that he did not know even himself. He said to his people, "When you carry my casket to the graveyard, let my hands hang out."

They said, "This is not done." He said, "It is my order and whether it is done or not is my last will. But it has to be done with me."

They said, "But what strange idea is this?" He said, "It is not strange. I want people to see... Because thousands of people will participate in the last procession of my life. I want them to see that I am dying with empty hands. Conquering the whole world has not even filled my hands, what to say about my inner being. I am dying like a beggar."

Unless you understand a very simple thing, that it is none of your business to bother about what you are doing here... You will have to do something somewhere. The question will be there – what are you doing here? The trees don't ask, they just dance in the breeze. The flowers don't ask what they are doing here. The birds are saner than man.

A man reached his home earlier than expected. His wife was lying naked on the bed and there were shoes by the side of the bed. He recognized the shoes – they belonged to his best friend. Angry and frustrated, he looked all around, in every nook and corner. Finally he found him hiding in the closet, and asked him, "What are you doing here?"

And the man must have been a man of utter sanity. He said, "Everyone has to be somewhere. The question is not meaningful. I am standing here!"

Now, what to do with such a man?

Philosophers, theologians, thinkers have created hundreds of questions to torture you. I don't want you to be unnecessarily in a self-torture. Just to be here is so beautiful, it does not need any other reason to be here. Just watch for a moment, just remember what I had said about witnessing that has given you great excitement. That excitement was wrong; excitement is not understanding. If you have heard my word *witnessing* peacefully, silently, allowed it to sink deep into your heart, there will be no excitement.

The birds are singing, the sun has risen, the trees are basking in the sun rays, and we are here in one of the most unique gatherings of people: silent, not asking for God or anything, not asking, not desiring, not being ambitious, just simply enjoying being whatever we are. And who is going to answer your question? So the question will torture you your whole life, wherever you are: What are you doing here? Even if by chance you meet God himself, you will have to ask, "What am I doing here? And what are you doing here?" It is not a question of doing, it is a question of being – relaxed, joyous for no reason at all.

We *are* the universe. These kinds of questions create more questions. Questions are Indians – they don't believe in birth control. They are very religious people. They go on creating only one thing: more questions.

Now first, "What am I doing with my time here?" Who told you it is your time? "And the feeling that there is some dimension that I am not yet experiencing..." These are ways of torturing yourself. "...or that somehow I am still missing you." Strange, I am missing you, you are missing me; it is hilarious. And what will you get by not missing me? The question will persist: What are we doing here together? Be simple and get out of these self-torturing questions. I answer your questions to destroy them not to answer them, because any answer will bring new questions.

Everything is as it should be. No one is missing anything. But if you want to crucify yourself, then create such questions: that you must be missing something. But what gives you this idea that you must be missing something? And everyone in the world has that question lurking in their mind: we are missing something. Have a good laugh, jog and jump. If you cannot dance, do anything bizarre, and enjoy! Life is in itself the answer. No one is missing anything.

Your heart is beating perfectly – otherwise take a cardiogram. I become puzzled. I don't have any of my own puzzles, just your puzzles: Why are these people always running in some direction to find something? There is nothing to be found. What you will find is already within you; it is your life energy. Let it sing, let it dance, let it experience peace, let it enjoy blissfulness. And you will start blossoming, and your spring has come.

But people go on thinking that something is missing. Why do they think that something is missing? Because they have not been allowed to know the art of life. On the contrary, they have been told everything that is against life. That has created the problem. Certainly, you are missing God, but I promise you, God is not missing you. And after all, who is this god that you call "God"? Why should you miss him? What are you going to gain by not missing him? It will be very boring company. Just think for a moment that you are with God for twenty-four hours. That will be the most boring and anguish-creating thing. You don't have anything to say to him and he has nothing to say to you.

I used to travel in India continuously for twenty years. And I enjoy all kinds of things. One day, I got on the train in Mumbai and many people had come to see me off. As I entered my air-conditioned coupe, there was another man inside also. From the window, he was watching all the people outside. He certainly thought that I was a very important person – so many rich people touching my feet. As I entered inside the coupe he fell flat on the floor and touched my feet.

I said, "What are you doing? I am a Mohammedan." And he was a high cast brahmin.

He said, "My God! No, it cannot be true, you must be joking."

I said, "I never joke."

He became very fidgety. I sat there. After two minutes he again said, "No, you are just joking."

I said, "I am not joking, I am a Mohammedan."

He said, "My God, I will have to take a bath in this cold night."

I said, "Go and take a bath."

So he went and took a cold bath and came back shivering, and I started laughing. He said, "Why are you laughing?"

I said, "I was just joking." And he fell again at my feet.

He said, "I knew from the very beginning."

I said, "No, not that time. This time I am joking. I am a Mohammedan."

He said, "You will drive me crazy! Now I have to take another shower."

I said, "It is up to you, I don't say anything. You are doing all these things on your own."

He said, "That's true." He took another bath and came in. I closed my eyes and did not say anything to him. But he could not sit restfully. He again asked, "Tell me the truth. Were you joking?"

I said, "If I tell you the truth, you will have to take another bath. So it is better I keep my eyes closed."

But he could not, because it is such a sin for a high cast brahmin in India to touch the feet of a Mohammedan. He said, "But if you are a Mohammedan, then why did all those people – none of them was Mohammedan – come to see you off?"

I said, "I am a Mohammedan mystic. I tell people which horses are going to win in the race."

He simply jumped up again and touched my feet. He said, "Forget about Mohammedanism or Brahmanism, just give me a number. I am in financial difficulty."

I said, "You don't understand at all. You again will have to go to the shower. It is not easy for me to give the number of the horse that is going to come first in the coming race, and I cannot give it to someone who mistrusts me."

He said, "No, I will trust you. If you say, I will not take a shower again."

I said, "Promise?"

He said, "I promise."

I gave him a certain number – just any number. He said, "But what is the guarantee?"

I said, "When the race happens, then you will know the guarantee. Right now, it is just a fictitious number. That is my business – I cheat people."

He said, "What? So this horse is not going to win?"

I said, "In my whole life, I have not been in contact with any horses. I don't understand their language, they don't understand my language. But if people want to be exploited, I go on giving numbers. And before the horse race I move to another place."

He said, "My God, so this is useless?" He threw the number he had written out of the window. "I will have to take another bath."

I said, "You promised. As a high cast brahmin, breaking a promise is a sin."

He said, "You will kill me! And we have to travel for twenty-four hours together."

People have been cheated by the priests, by the politicians, by the pedagogues for centuries. They were giving them fictitious numbers; those horse races don't happen. You are not missing anything. The moment you realize, "I am not missing anything," all your problems will disappear. It is up to you. There are only two alternatives: either get it right now and become blissful, or postpone and remain miserable. My preference is, get it right now.

And what I have said to you about witnessing is nothing but a simple art of seeing. You are breathing, you are seeing, your heart is beating, you are surrounded by a beautiful universe. What more do you want? Are you certain that even if something more is added, you will not want more again? The realization is instantaneous. It is not from point *A* to point *B*. It need not go anywhere – to Mecca, to Moscow, to Kashi, to Lhasa. Wherever you are, just enjoy the moment. I cannot conceive a better situation than this.

The trees must be laughing at you. Do you think the crows are doing it for some purpose? Just clearing their throats – early morning clearings. Do you think anyone is telling the flowers to open and release their fragrance? No, it is all intrinsic. Only man has forgotten the language of being intrinsic. And the language of being intrinsic is the language of religion. Any moment decide, "This is enough" – and become enlightened.

It is not a question that you have to become enlightened after arduous disciplines. It is a question only of deciding: "From this moment I am going to enjoy totally and fully whatever is available." And witnessing will follow on its own accord.

And finally you are asking, "Would you say something about this, and maybe a prayer for me?" Prayer to whom? There is no one to listen. The universe does not understand human language, but it understands love, it understands laughter, it understands peace, it understands silence – not the words, but the experiences.

I cannot pray for you because there is no God who is going to answer your prayer. But I can make a device in which prayerfulness happens, not only to me but to you too.

Paddy is a drunkard and yet Maureen has never tasted alcohol in her whole life.

"Hey, you drunk," she says one day, "give me that bottle. I want to taste whatever it is that has made you the bum you are."

Taking the bottle of cheap whiskey, she takes a good gulp from it. "Yuk," she gasps, "that's the most vile-tasting liquid that has ever passed my lips. It tastes terrible."

"You see," says Paddy, "and all these years you thought I was having a good time."

Different things make different people feel insecure. For instance, to make a German feel insecure, tell him a joke.

To make an Italian feel insecure, agree with him.

To make an Australian feel insecure, talk to his girlfriend in German.

To make a Polack feel insecure, invite him home to play with the dog.

And to make a sannyasin feel insecure, tell him he is enlightened.

Outside the classroom it is snowing hard. "Boys and girls," says Mrs. Goodbody, "you must be very careful not to catch colds in this weather. I had a dear little brother, only seven years old. One day, he went out in the snow with his new skis. He caught a cold, pneumonia set in, and three days later he was dead."

A hush falls over the classroom and then little Ernie jumps up to his feet and asks, "Can I have his skis?"

Moishe Finkelstein goes into a jewelry store to buy his wife Ruthie a present. "How much is that?" he asks the clerk, fingering a silver crucifix.

"That is five hundred dollars, sir," replies the clerk.

"Nice," says Moishe. "And how much without the acrobat?"

Kowalski, the Polack farmer, is struggling to hold a pig above his head while the pig eats apples from a tree. A man passing by watches this for a moment and says, "Why don't you pick some apples and put them in a trough? It will save you time."

"Don't be a dummy," snorts Kowalski. "Pigs don't care about time."

30

# God Is a Fiction to Exploit Humanity

Osho,
What is your concept of God?

Rahul, before I answer your question, I would like to say something about you. Unless something is said about you, the question will not have a proper context. You belong to the Krishnamurti Foundation of India.

In the first place, during his whole life, Krishnamurti tried to say that no one should be his follower, that there should be no doctrine in his name, that there should be no organization around him, that he is not teaching you some belief system, but only sharing his experience. Now, unfortunately, he is dead. Even if you want to share his experience it will be very difficult. It was difficult when he was alive; it is now impossible. And everywhere – what he had been fighting his whole life – mushrooms have sprung up, and the same story: different names, different bottles, but the same wine.

What in the hell are you doing in the Krishnamurti Foundation? I can tolerate a follower; I can even love a follower – everybody knows I am contradictory. But Krishnamurti is a very consistent thinker. He will be tossing and turning in his grave that now organizations are organized, followers are gathering, making plans how to continue the tradition. And he was fighting against all traditions.

My own conflict with him was that you cannot avoid a tradition; it is beyond your hands. Once you are dead, you cannot prevent what people do. Rather than leaving it in the hands of the ignorant, it is better you should give the right guidelines.

There should be no Krishnamurti Foundation and there should be no teaching about him, around him. If you have understood him, he should disappear, just as a signature on the water disappears. That will be the greatest homage to him. But the disease is so old that it grips the minds of people. The more you say, "I don't want any followers," the more followers think, "This seems to be the right master."

And, Rahul, do you know the meaning of your name? Before you inquire about God you should at least inquire about your name. I don't think you know that your name is a condemnation. In Hindu mythology, when there is an eclipse of the moon, it is two mythological figures, Rahu and Ketu, who are trying to destroy the moon. They have been trying for millions of years, but they have not succeeded – that is another matter. That proves they are Americans; they believe in the philosophy of try and try and try again.

Rahul is not a good name. It is the name of a monster. Gautam Buddha gave his son the name Rahul, and since then people have forgotten the derogatory sense of the word, although Buddha had given that name particularly for that purpose. He was afraid that the birth of this son was going to prevent him from his search for truth: "He is just like a Rahul, who is trying to destroy the moon – he is trying to destroy me." To condemn the child, he named him Rahul. He had not even seen his face; he had given the name before his birth. He wanted to escape before the birth because he was worried. One can understand: a father's heart and the first son. It was dangerous, the attachment might at least delay, if not prevent…

But life does not follow stars, nor does it listen to the astrologers; the child was born one day before all the predictions. That was the night Buddha was going to escape. You can understand the natural feeling and instinct – before moving into the mountains, perhaps forever, never to return, he wanted at least to see the face of his son. In the middle of the night when the whole palace was asleep, he went into his wife's chamber. But she had covered the child all around with a blanket, and it was lying close to her heart.

For a moment Buddha thought just to remove the blanket a little and see the face. But then he became afraid: if the wife wakes up then there is going to be trouble. Then the whole house will be awakened, then the old father will freak out. It is better not to see the son. He simply stepped back, silently. He had given the name not in an appreciative way; it was a subtle condemnation. But because Buddha's son was named Rahul, then thousands of other people have been named Rahul. And no one inquires what the meaning of Rahul is. It is not a good name.

Instead of inquiring about yourself, you have put ten questions before me. That shows not only your stupidity, but also the stupidity of your foundation. What are you doing there, if you have to come here to torture, asking stupid questions like, "What is your concept of God?" There is no God! The question of any concept does not arise. And you being in the Krishnamurti Foundation, not just an ordinary member but a lecturer... Have you not understood a simple thing? – that God is a fiction created to exploit humanity; it has no truth in it. It is the greatest lie. It needs to be exposed to every human being because without its exposure man remains a puppet.

If God exists then our life is absolutely meaningless, without any dignity, with no freedom; we are just made out of mud. And if God makes us – he seems to be whimsical – he can kill us at any moment. He didn't ask us whether we wanted to be created, nor will he ask us whether we want to be destroyed. You don't count. If God is, man is meaningless. God is one of the ugliest ideas that has dominated humanity. But it served the purpose of the priests, of the politicians, the preachers, the philosophers.

I don't have any concept of God. I cannot have, by the very fact that there is no God. The moment you realize there is no God, a tremendous dignity arises in you, a freedom and a responsibility: that you are your own creation, that this whole existence is autonomous, it is not under the slavery of any whimsical God. And it is very creative; it does not need any creator. I teach creativity and I want to destroy the very idea of a creator, because that idea of a creator is taking away your freedom of creativity.

The world has remained so poor in every dimension for the simple reason that we are helpless, our strings are in the hands of God. Whatever he wants, happens. Without his will, not even a leaf moves in the wind. Do you see the implication of it? – it means that it is a prison and we are slaves under a God whose intentions are not known; who himself has not been courageous enough to appear in the MG marketplace, to declare, "I am here, do you have any questions?"

Christians believe he created the world six thousand years ago. My question is, what was this fellow doing before that? Just doing nothing for eternity? I used to think I am the laziest person, but this God seems to be the ultimate in laziness. Then what was the need to create this world with desires which will not be fulfilled, which will bring frustration; with love which is impure, polluted by jealousies, hence it will never blossom. And with ambitions which, even when fulfilled, will leave you utterly empty, frustrated.

Do you know that as man becomes more and more civilized, more and more people commit suicide, more and more people become mad. Buffaloes never commit suicide, at least I have never heard of any buffalo doing that in the millions of years. They are so contented, chewing the same grass every day, utterly fulfilled, so saintly – no hurry, no competition, at home, at ease.

But as consciousness grows, as man starts moving upward from the world of animals, he finds himself in hell: thousands of desires and no possibility of fulfillment. This is not the world a God who is proclaimed to be love will create. This is a world which has been created by the universe accidentally, unintentionally. And it was not created six thousand years ago, it has always been here. Forms go on changing, but that which is the inner content of existence remains eternally the same; it knows no death.

To ask a question about God after Friedrich Nietzsche declared that he is dead is impolite. I respect Friedrich Nietzsche more than your God. But my respect never makes me blind. Only one thing is wrong in Friedrich Nietzsche: he thought that once God was alive and now he is dead. He has never been there. It was a fiction which has become exposed; the soap bubble has burst.

Rahul's second question is:

> Osho,
> When you say that truth can only be realized and can't be described, what do you actually mean?

Exactly, that's what I mean! Watch a beautiful rose, experience the beauty and then try to describe it. No one has been able even to define what beauty is. Love… Millions of people have loved, but when the question arises, what is love? They start looking here and there; perhaps someone knows. You can love, you can experience it, but you cannot say a single word which will be a definition of your experience.

And these are our everyday experiences; what to say about truth, which is not our everyday experience. Once in a while, after thousands of years, someone realizes the truth. He can sing it, he can dance it, he can live it, but he cannot describe it. It is not his fault. Language is very poor; it cannot describe such precious experiences, it is not made for that. Language is a marketplace thing. It can be used perfectly in the ordinary world, but the moment you move within, you are alone and only silence prevails. You feel it, you rejoice in it, you radiate it, but you suddenly become dumb.

A Zen master, Rinzai, whenever asked, "What is truth?" used to do one thing: he would not even say that it cannot be said. A philosopher had come to see him, and when he asked and received the answer he said, "But you can at least say that it cannot be said."

Rinzai said a very pregnant statement, "Even to say that it cannot be said, you have said something about it. That's why I use the finger. I cannot descend from the heights of the experience to the dark valley of language. If you want to know the truth, I can hold your hand, but you will have to travel unknown paths. Are you ready?"

The philosopher said, "I have not come here to follow any path. I am a professor, I teach in the university, and I wanted to know what the attitude of a Zen mystic is."

Rinzai said, "Then you will have to go as empty as you have come. Although you have come very close to the well, you will go as thirsty as you have come."

The realization of truth is an inner experience. Even to say "experience" is not absolutely right, only approximately right. Truth is your being; either you know it or you do not. But no one can say anything about his being. It is so tremendous, and words are so small; it is so vast and words are so small. If your hands cannot reach the stars, that does not mean that the stars don't exist. It simply means your hands are very small and the stars are very far away.

Our language is very small. Its approach is very limited and our being is the unlimited, the unbounded; nothing can be said about it. And to say that nothing can be said about it – yes, even this much is to concede, is to be compassionate.

I consider Ludwig Wittgenstein the most important philosopher of this century. He has not written much, and he is the only Western philosopher of all time who has written only in maxims, what we call *sutras*. In the East that has always been the case. Those who had any glimpse, any taste, have written sutras – telegraphic, using as small a quantity of words as possible.

Ludwig Wittgenstein, in his famous book, *Tractatus*, has one sutra which makes him not only a philosopher but also a mystic. But he commits the same mistake which Rinzai was trying not to commit. The sutra is: that which cannot be said should not be said. When he was alive, I wrote him a letter saying, "You have said it. At least one quality of it you have brought into language."

He was sick and he died very soon. His brother answered me: "He received your question with great respect, and he said to me, 'It is true that if nothing can be said, then even to say this is to say something. I am sick and I am tired. If I get well, I will answer, but if I die you answer for me: in the second edition of *Tractatus* we will leave this sutra empty, just a space.'"

If you experience only things which can be explained, described, defined, then your world is very small and your mind is very childish. You go beyond the mind only when you start experiencing things which the mind finds itself incapable of bringing to language. To transcend language is one of the most significant things for anyone who is intelligent enough; otherwise, as far as idiots are concerned, they can express everything. They have never experienced anything which goes beyond the mind. The truth is beyond the mind; the truth is beyond language. That's why, Rahul, it can be experienced, but it cannot be described.

Chuang Tzu was one of the most absurd and most loving mystics of China. If Rahul had gone to Chuang Tzu… He used to forcibly push sweets into people's mouths. And you were asking, "Why can truth not be described?" And after you had swallowed the delicious sweet he would ask, "Now describe the sweetness that you have experienced, write it down." Even such an ordinary experience of sweetness is beyond. All that you can say is that it is sweet, but that is understood by people because they also have experienced it. If a man has never experienced sweetness and you talk about sweetness, he will simply say, "Don't deceive me, don't talk nonsense." Talk to a blind man about light and you will know or talk to the deaf about the beauty of music and you will know.

As far as the ultimate truth is concerned, all our senses are very small. If you ask me, I can say, "Look into my eyes, or hold my hand and feel the warmth and the love." More than that is this silence. If this silence can penetrate your heart, you have heard that which cannot be said, and you have received that which cannot be given. This silence will give you an indication of truth, but truth is a millionfold deeper. This silence is just a little fragrance of the flower.

His third question is:

> Osho
> Is there any state of mind which has never been programmed at all? Or are there any techniques to decondition our brain?

There has never been any consciousness which has not been programmed. The programming comes in the very upbringing. Even if the child is not brought up by you but by wolves in the wild, the wolves will program the child. There have been cases… Just a few years ago a twelve-year-old child was found in the forest in north India; he had been brought up by wolves. He could not even stand on his two feet. He ran like a wolf; even the best runner could not manage to keep pace with him. He had been programmed by the wolves.

The problem is that you have to bring the child up. And someone has to take care, and whoever is going to take care is going to, knowingly or unknowingly, condition the mind of the child. It is not a question that you have to program consciously. But how will the child learn the language? It is a program. Every language is called the mother tongue because the child never finds the father speaking in the presence of the mother. Naturally he is conditioned by the mother. There is no possibility of anyone being brought up unprogrammed.

And you are asking, "Are there any techniques to decondition our brain?" There are techniques to decondition, but that is reprogramming. You can call it deconditioning, but in fact, what are you doing? You are putting *B* in place of *A*. The only possibility is meditation; that's why meditation should not be called a technique. It is simply relaxing into your own inner world, alone – without a guide, without scriptures – and becoming so silent that not a single ripple of thought remains. That's the only way of canceling all programming.

Meditation is the only way – not the technique – in which you can find your self-nature, your buddha nature in its purity, in its virginity, untouched by anyone. But there are people who are trying to deprogram; in fact they are simply reprogramming.

There have been cases, strange cases, where young people have been abducted by their parents and taken to psychiatrists where they deprogram them, because they have gone out of the Christian fold, or the Jewish fold. They have gone outside the society that has brought them up. The society cannot tolerate this revolt. Parents abducting their own children and paying for their deprogramming... But it is not deprogramming, it is again programming, making the Catholic again Catholic. But the Catholicism itself was a program.

Except meditation, even if you are a Hindu, a Mohammedan, a Christian, a Jew – some kind of program will be there. Only the meditator rises above all programs, becomes a simple, innocent consciousness, on which nothing is written. But this gives such clarity of vision, such intensity of perception, such great joy of being that one becomes part of the eternal dance of existence for the first time. Those who are programed by anyone – Christian, Communist, Mohammedan, Hindu – it does not matter who programs you; he destroys your purity.

Now, what are you doing in the Krishnamurti Foundation? You will teach people a certain program; of course, you will think you are deprogramming people, but you are programming them according to J. Krishnamurti. Even deprogramming can be a part of a certain programming. Things are very complex. I have been meeting with many people who have listened to Krishnamurti for fifty years, forty years, and still they say, "We are Krishnamurti-ites." That poor man was continuously trying to deprogram you for thirty years, but he has really programmed you again. First you used to be a Hindu, a Christian or a Mohammedan. Now you are a Krishnamurti-ite.

Any doctrine, any effort of teaching about things which are not your experience is going to spoil your purity. For ten thousand years there has been only one way: its name is meditation. What Basho says:

> Sitting silently,
> doing nothing,
> spring comes and the grass grows by itself.

The fourth:

> Osho
> Is there anything permanent in the universe?

Except change, nothing is permanent.

Fifth:

> Osho
> Krishnamurti says that there is a psychological gap between being and becoming. Is there any way to bridge this gap?

Now, this is what I was saying. You are programmed by Krishnamurti. Now what Krishnamurti says becomes your problem. In fact there is no gap: being is becoming. Have you ever thought whether a tree inquires, "How to grow?" It grows. But in its being and in its becoming there is no gap. Have you ever thought about how you have been growing? Is there any gap between your being and your becoming, is there any need to bridge it? This is how a philosophical attitude destroys people's perception.

Krishnamurti is absolutely wrong on this point. Being is becoming; there is no difference. The moment you are not becoming you are dead; you are alive only while you are becoming. The river is flowing; is there any difference between the river's being and its flowing? The moment the river stops flowing, it is no longer a river. It becomes a pond, the river has died. The river was continuously rivering, moving, growing, reaching the ocean.

Sixth:

> Osho,
> How can we know that a person has realized the truth?

Only by realizing the truth. Otherwise, how can you know? Truth is not something objective, that a man can show, "Look, I have realized the truth." Only by realizing it will you start seeing its qualities. And those qualities will make you aware of all those people who have realized it, because the same qualities will be radiating: the same beauty, grace, honesty, truth, courage, integrity.

But right now you can only believe, and I am not a person to support any belief. All beliefs are blinding. When the truth can be realized, when the truth is in your very being, why bother about whether someone else has realized it or not? Someone may be pretending, someone may be acting. There are many actors, not on the stage, in the drama, but on the vast stage of life. Someone is acting as a saint, someone is pretending to be a mahatma, someone is declaring, "I have found it."

And certainly I can understand your question: how to make a distinction between who is authentic and who is inauthentic. In fact there is no criterion, objective criterion, because everything can be pretended, acted. One can walk just like Gautam Buddha – perhaps even better.

It happened…

There was a competition on a certain birthday of Charlie Chaplin. His friends arranged a competition all over England, that whoever can perform the act of Charlie Chaplin… There were three prizes. Hundreds of actors joined in. Charlie Chaplin, just to surprise them all, entered the competition from a different place. But rather than surprising them, he was surprised himself – he received the second prize, someone acted better. And when it was known, everyone was amazed that the real Charlie Chaplin got the second prize.

There is nothing amazing about this; the real one had not rehearsed well. He need not rehearse; he is spontaneous, he is himself. So he never bothered, he knew that his was the first prize. But all those other competitors had worked for months, and the man who came first had labored hard to walk like Charlie Chaplin, to talk like Charlie Chaplin. Even before the distribution of the prizes Charlie Chaplin had started being afraid, because the man was doing so well that he started suspecting, "Am I really Charlie Chaplin or is this fellow Charlie Chaplin? Have I gone crazy or…"

And there are saints pretending, posing, who look far better than any Jesus or any Buddha. It will be very difficult for you to find a criterion. The first difficulty is that the truth is not objective. The second difficulty is that each time it has been found by anyone its expression is different, because each individual has a uniqueness and the expression will be according to that uniqueness. For example, you cannot expect Gautam Buddha to dance like Meera. People will simply laugh. They will say, "It is better you sit under your bodhi tree; it doesn't look right. You look very good just sitting under your bodhi tree with your eyes closed, silently."

But Meera dancing… If you force her to sit under a bodhi tree you will reduce her to an ordinary woman. Her uniqueness is expressed in her dance, her song, her love. She is so beautiful. She knows nothing of dancing; she has not learned in a dancing school, she has not learned how to sing under a teacher. But even great singers cannot manage to bring that beauty and that juice which is flowing spontaneously in Meera. Just look around.

Bodhidharma entered China fourteen hundred years ago with one shoe on his head and the other shoe on one of his feet. And his fame had reached there long before he did. It took three years for him to travel from India to China. Emperor Wu was waiting at the border to receive a great saint, and when he saw the great saint he said, "My God! Now what to do?" But he was a very cultured man; he behaved as if he had not noticed anything: the shoe on the head. But however he tried, the shoe was there. He wouldn't look at the shoe, but the question was continuously there, "What kind of man are you receiving – a great emperor? And this man seems to be mad."

Finally, he could not contain himself and he said, "What kind of madness is this? Why are you carrying that shoe on your head, and one shoe on one of your feet?"

Bodhidharma said, "For you."

He said, "For me?"

Bodhidharma said, "Yes, for you, just to see whether you are really interested in truth or in stupid things. You are interested in the shoe, you are not interested in me. Take this shoe and be gone, be contented."

The emperor could not understand – what to do with this man? But he was immensely impressed because that man's eyes, that man's authority… And Bodhidharma did not cross the boundary into China. He said, "I will remain outside. What is the point? When even the emperor is interested in shoes, what about the ordinary people? I am not going to waste my time!" But only Bodhidharma can do that. You cannot expect Buddha to do such an act. You cannot expect anyone else in the whole history of mankind, because Bodhidharma is not born again and again.

There is no way. You will have to find your truth, and perhaps finding your truth you may be able to see different expressions in different people, but with a certain quality which joins them all.

I have heard a story…

Gautam Buddha, Confucius, Lao Tzu, all three are sitting in a restaurant in paradise and a naked woman comes with a jar and tells them, "I have brought the juice of life, would you like to taste it?"

Buddha immediately closes his eyes, but Confucius says, "First I will taste a little because without tasting a little I cannot make any judgment."

He was a very calculative, mathematical man, so he just tasted a little and said, "No, it is all illusory, made of the stuff dreams are made of. I am not interested."

She looked at Lao Tzu. Lao Tzu said, "Give me the jar."

She said, "The whole jar?"

He said, "Unless I have drunk it completely, I cannot say anything about it. I am a man of totality." And he drank it before…

Buddha and Confucius looked at each other: "Look at this fellow!"

And after drinking the whole juice he said, "It is great! Now, let us celebrate. You fellows, what do you want?" Now he was completely drunk.

All are men of truth. Different aspects are expressed through their individuality, but you cannot make a formula, a criterion to measure.

Seventh:

Osho,
How can we be aware of the content of our whole consciousness? Is there any kind of awakening process?

What I said about meditation is also the answer to this. Meditation will make you aware that there is no content in your being; your being is sheer emptiness; that you are not and only existence is. And in this nothingness flowers the rose of awareness.

Eighth:

> Osho,
> Is it possible to know the structure of our thought?

There is no need. You have to get rid of your thought, not to know the structure of your thought. The structure of your thought is not different from dreams. Just as the West has become entangled in the psychoanalysis of dreams, the East has never bothered about dreams. There is no need.

Again, I will have to tell you about Chuang Tzu…

One morning he said, "I am very disturbed because last night I dreamed that I had become a butterfly."

The disciples said, "That is not a problem, everyone dreams and becomes many things."

Chuang Tzu said, "That is not the problem. The problem is that if Chuang Tzu can become a butterfly when he sleeps, why can't the butterfly become Chuang Tzu when she sleeps? Now the question is, who am I? A butterfly dreaming of being Chuang Tzu? I am very disturbed, just find the way…"

The disciples said, "He has gone absolutely crazy! We always knew that he was a little bit outlandish, but this is too much. And now we have to find the way… How to find the way? Whatever we say is going to be refuted because his question is such that if Chuang Tzu can become a butterfly, what is the problem, why can't the butterfly dream of being Chuang Tzu?"

The chief disciple of Chuang Tzu was Lieh Tzu. He had gone out; they all waited for him. They said, "Let him come, perhaps he can manage to do something. He is also crazy."

Lieh Tzu came and heard the story, and said, "Don't be worried." And he took a bucket and went to the water well.

The disciples said, "What are you doing? We have told you to go to Chuang Tzu – he is in great despair!"

He said, "Don't bother me." He pulled up a bucket of ice-cold water – it was winter – and went inside with the bucket. Chuang Tzu was in his bed, and he poured the whole bucket of water on his head.

Chuang Tzu said, "Wait! The problem is solved."

Lieh Tzu said, "If something has remained, I can bring another bucket."

Chuang Tzu replied, "No, it is too cold. I *am* Chuang Tzu, a butterfly would have died!"

All the disciples said, "This is strange."

But such a crazy man was bound to be succeeded by another crazy man, Lieh Tzu. A simple solution... He did not want to discuss it. What is there to discuss? Just wake him up. A bucket of ice-cold water in the early winter's morning and he forgot all about his philosophy. Chuang Tzu said, "Where have you been? If you had been here before, I would not have even opened my mouth because I know you are dangerous. Things have to be discussed, this is not a way to behave – and you are my disciple."

Lieh Tzu said, "I am your disciple, but I had to bring you out from your dream and free you from the illusion of being a butterfly. Promise me never to do such a thing when I'm not around because all the disciples are sitting outside, very sad."

Don't be worried about what the structure of our thought is. Just be silent, go deeper than the waves of thought and they will all disappear. And in the depth of your being there is no thought, no dream.

Rahul, you need an ice-cold bucketful of water poured on your head. You will immediately come to your senses!

Ninth:

> Osho,
> What is your message to the new world?

Where is the new world? And in the first place, why should I give a message to the new world? First let me destroy the old! I am too much engaged in destroying the old. When the new comes, I am not going to give any message to the new because that will be programming. I will leave the new world to find its own way.

Tenth:

> Osho,
> Krishnamurti says that our brain has been programmed for millions of years, and we function according to that kind of conditioning. Is it possible to have an unconditioned mind?

Do you have any questions of your own? Or has Krishnamurti conditioned you so much that even he questions and you repeat his question? Are you a gramophone record? You may have dreamed the whole night, but just a hit on your head and all dreams will disappear. The room in your house could have been dark for millions of years, but bring a small candle in and all darkness disappears. It does not say, "I am too old. I cannot go so easily with just a small candle. Don't make me afraid."

The conditioning is old, but it is just like darkness: just a small flame of meditativeness, a small flame of silence and it will disappear. It does not matter whether you have been programmed for millions of years, you can be freed in a single moment. But this is not the way to attain freedom. Now you are caught in the thoughts of J. Krishnamurti. You don't have even a single question of your own.

Rahul has tortured you too much. Just a few herbal medicines to heal your wounds...

During army camouflage, private Paddy Murphy, disguised as a tree trunk, makes a sudden move and is spotted by the general.

"You idiot!" yells the officer. "You are supposed to be a tree. Jumping and screaming like that, you could endanger the lives of the whole platoon."

"Yes, sir," replies Paddy. "But sir, I must tell you, I stood quite still when some pigeons used me for target practice. And I never moved when three dogs thought I was a latrine. But I could not bear it when two squirrels ran up the leg of my pants and I heard one of them say, 'Let's eat one now and save the other until winter.'"

Ronald Reagan steps down from the plane and goes into the airport in Mexico. He is very full of his own sense of self-importance and keeps snapping instructions to his attendants.

A sleazy-looking Mexican man sidles up to him and whispers, "Hey, Americano. I get what you like – feelthy pictures, marijuana, girls, boys."

"Who let this man in here?" asks Reagan, pushing the Mexican away. "My business is with the president."

"I can fix that," replies the Mexican, "but for a president you will have to pay a little extra."

# About Osho

Osho defies categorization. Mystic and scientist, a rebellious spirit whose sole interest is to alert humanity to the urgent need to discover a new way of living. To continue as before is to invite threats to our very survival on this unique and beautiful planet.

His thousands of talks cover everything from the individual quest for meaning to the most urgent social, political and environmental issues facing society today. Osho's books are not written but transcribed from audio and video recordings of his extemporaneous talks to international audiences. And he tells them, "Remember: whatever I am saying is not just for you...I am talking also for the future generations."

Osho has been described by *The Sunday Times* in London as one of the "1000 Makers of the 20th Century" and by American author Tom Robbins as "the most dangerous man since Jesus Christ." *Sunday Mid-Day* (Mumbai) has selected Osho as one of ten people – along with Gandhi, Nehru and Buddha – who have changed the destiny of India.

About his own work, Osho has said that he is helping to create the conditions for the birth of a new kind of human being. He often characterizes this new human being as "Zorba the Buddha" – capable both of enjoying the earthy pleasures of a Zorba the Greek and the silent serenity of a Gautama the Buddha.

Running like a thread through all aspects of Osho's talks and meditations is a vision that encompasses both the timeless wisdom of all ages past and the highest potential of today's (and tomorrow's) science and technology.

Osho is known for his revolutionary contribution to the science of inner transformation, with an approach to meditation that acknowledges the accelerated pace of contemporary life. His unique OSHO Active Meditations® are designed to first release the accumulated stresses of body and mind, so that it then becomes easier to experience a stillness and thought-free relaxation which can be taken into daily life.

Two autobiographical works by the author are available:

***Autobiography of a Spiritually Incorrect Mystic***, St. Martin's Press, New York (book and eBook)

***Glimpses of a Golden Childhood***, OSHO Media International, Pune, India (book and eBook)

# OSHO International Meditation Resort

Each year the Meditation Resort welcomes thousands of people from more than 100 countries. The unique campus provides an opportunity for a direct personal experience of a new way of living – with more awareness, relaxation, celebration and creativity. A great variety of around-the-clock and around-the-year program options are available. Doing nothing and just relaxing is one of them!

All of the programs are based on Osho's vision of "Zorba the Buddha" – a qualitatively new kind of human being who is able *both* to participate creatively in everyday life *and* to relax into silence and meditation.

**Location**
Located 100 miles southeast of Mumbai in the thriving modern city of Pune, India, the OSHO International Meditation Resort is a holiday destination with a difference. The Meditation Resort is spread over 28 acres of spectacular gardens in a beautiful tree-lined residential area.

**OSHO Meditations**
A full daily schedule of meditations for every type of person includes both traditional and revolutionary methods, and particularly the OSHO Active Meditations®. The daily meditation program takes place in what must be the world's largest meditation hall, the OSHO Auditorium.

**OSHO Multiversity**
Individual sessions, courses and workshops cover everything from creative arts to holistic health, personal transformation, relationship

and life transitions, transforming meditation into a lifestyle for life and work, esoteric sciences, and the Zen approach to sports and recreation. The secret of the OSHO Multiversity's success lies in the fact that all its programs are combined with meditation, supporting the understanding that as human beings we are far more than the sum of our parts.

**Cuisine**

A variety of different eating areas serve delicious Western, Asian and Indian vegetarian food – most of it organically grown especially for the Meditation Resort. Breads and cakes are baked in the resort's bakery.

**Night life**

There are many evening events to choose from – dancing being at the top of the list! Other activities include full-moon meditations beneath the stars, variety shows, music performances and "meditations for daily life."

**Facilities**

At the Meditation Resort you can buy all of your basic necessities and toiletries in the Galleria. In addition, the Multimedia Gallery sells a large range of OSHO media products. For those who enjoy shopping, Pune provides all the options, ranging from traditional and ethnic Indian products to all of the global brand-name stores.

**Accommodation**

You can choose to stay in the elegant rooms of the OSHO Guesthouse, or for longer stays on campus you can select one of the OSHO Living-In programs. Additionally there is a variety of nearby hotels and serviced apartments.

www.osho.com/meditationresort
www.osho.com/guesthouse
www.osho.com/livingin
Facebook: osho.international.meditation.resort

# OSHO Books (English)

(OSHO books are available in Printed book and eBook formats, and most of them in audio format too. If a book is not available in one format, you can look up and buy it in another format.)

**Early Talks**

The Art of Living
Astrology
Breaking All Boundaries
Compassion and Revolution
Dimensions beyond the Known
The Eternal Quest
From Sex to Superconsciousness
The Great Challenge
Hidden Mysteries
I Am the Gate
The Independent Mind
Into the Void
Keys to a New Life
New Dimensions of Yoga
The Psychology of the Esoteric
Religion's Expiration Date
The Search for Peace
Woman and Rebellion
Work Is Love Made Visible

**Meditation**

And Now and Here
Body/Mind Balancing (Book & Audio)
Falling In Love with Darkness
In Search of the Miraculous
The Inner Journey
Just a Small Step
Meditation: The Art of Ecstasy
Meditation: The First and Last Freedom
The Path of Meditation
The Perfect Way
Silence: The Message of Your Being
Three Steps to Awakening

**Buddha and Buddhist Masters**

The Book of Wisdom
The Dhammapada: The Way of the Buddha (Vols 1-12)

The Diamond Sutra
The Discipline of Transcendence (Vols 1-4)
The Heart Sutra
The Great Secret
The Guest
The Path of Love
The Revolution

**Indian Mystics**

As if a Tree Starts Running (Yari))
The Beloved, Vols 1 & 2 (Baul Mystics)
Bliss:Living beyond Happiness and Misery (Shiva)
Die O Yogi Die (Gorakh)
Enlightenment: The Only Revolution (Ashtavakra)
Geeta Darshan Vol. 1 (Adhyaya 1-2)
Geeta Darshan, Vol.2 (Adhyaya 3)
Krishna: The Man and His Philosophy
The Last Morning Star (Daya)
Showering without Clouds (Sahajo)
The Song of Ecstasy (Adi Shankara)
The True Name (Vols 1&2) (Nanak)

**Kabir**

The Divine Melody
Ecstasy: The Forgotten Language
The Fabric of Life
The Fish in the Sea Is Not Thirsty

**Western Mystics**

The Art of Dying *(Hasidism)*
Come Follow to You, Vols 1-4 *(Jesus)*
Guida Spirituale (*Desiderata*)
The Hidden Harmony *(Heraclitus)*
I Say Unto You, Vols 1 & 2 *(Jesus)*
The Mustard Seed *(Jesus)*
The New Alchemy: To Turn You On (Mabel Collins)
Philosophia Perennis, Vols 1 & 2 (*Pythagoras*)
Reflections on Kahlil Gibran's *The Prophet*
Theologia Mystica *(Dionysius)*
The True Sage *(Hasidism)*
The Voice of Silence (Mabel Collins)
Zarathustra: A God That Can Dance (Nietzsche's *Thus Spake Zarathustra*)
Zarathustra: The Laughing Prophet (Nietzsche's *Thus Spake Zarathustra*)

**Sufism**

Just Like That

The Perfect Master, Vols 1 & 2
The Secret
Sufis: The People of the Path, Vols 1 & 2
Unio Mystica, Vols 1 & 2
Until You Die
The Wisdom of the Sands, Vols 1 & 2

**Tantra**

The Book of Secrets (Vigyan Bhairav Tantra)
The Tantra Experience (Saraha)
Tantra: The Supreme Understanding (Tilopa)
Tantric Transformation (Saraha)

**The Upanishads**

Behind a Thousand Names (Nirvana Upanishad)
Finger Pointing to the Moon (Adhyatma Upanishad)
Flight of the Alone to the Alone (Kaivalya Upanishad)
The Heartbeat of the Absolute (Ishavasya Upanishad)
I Am That (Isa Upanishad)
The Message beyond Words (Kathopanishad)
Philosophia Ultima (Mandukya Upanishad)
The Supreme Doctrine (Kenopanishad)
That Art Thou (Sarvasar Upanishad, Kaivalya Upanishad, Adhyatma Upanishad)
The Ultimate Alchemy, Vols 1 & 2 (Atma Pooja Upanishad)
Vedanta: Seven Steps to Samadhi (Akshaya Upanishad)
The Way beyond Any Way (Sarvasar Upanishad)

**Tao**

The Empty Boat (Chuang Tzu)
The Secret of Secrets (The Secret of Golden Flower)
Tao: The Golden Gate, Vols 1 & 2 (Ko Hsuan)
Tao: The Pathless Path, Vols 1 & 2 (Lieh Tzu)
Tao: The Three Treasures, Vols 1-4 (Lao Tzu)
When the Shoe Fits (Chuang Tzu)

**Yoga (Patanjali)**

Yoga: The Science of the Soul, Vols 1-10
- The Path of Yoga (Vol.1)
- The Heart of Yoga (Vol.2)
- Yoga: The Mystery beyond Mind (Vol.3)
- The Alchemy of Yoga (Vol.4)

- Yoga: A New Direction (Vol.5)
- Essence of Yoga (Vol.6)
- Yoga: The Science of Living (Vol.7)
- Secrets of Yoga (Vol.8)
- Yoga: The Path to Liberation (Vol.9)
- Yoga: The Supreme Science (Vol.10)

**Zen and Zen Masters**

Ah, This!
Ancient Music in the Pines
And the Flowers Showered…
And the Grass Grows By Itself…
A Bird on the Wing
Bodhidharma: The Greatest Zen Master
The Buddha: The Emptiness of the Heart
Christianity, the Deadliest Poison and Zen, the Antidote to All Poisons
Communism and Zen Fire, Zen Wind
Dang Dang Doko Dang
The First Principle
God Is Dead: Now Zen Is the Only Living Truth
The Great Zen Master Ta Hui
Hsin Hsin Ming: The Book of Nothing
I Celebrate Myself: God Is No Where, Life Is Now Here
Kyozan: A True Man of Zen
The Language of Existence
Live Zen
The Miracle
Nirvana: The Last Nightmare
No Mind: The Flowers of Eternity
No Water, No Moon
One Seed Makes the Whole Earth Green
The Original Man
Returning to the Source
The Search: Talks on the 10 Bulls of Zen
A Sudden Clash of Thunder
The Sun Rises in the Evening
Take it Easy
This. This. A Thousand Times This
This Very Body the Buddha
Turning In
The White Lotus
Yakusan: Straight to the Point of Enlightenment
The Zen Manifesto: Freedom from Oneself
Zen: The Diamond Thunderbolt
Zen: The Mystery and the Poetry of the Beyond
Zen: The Path of Paradox, Vols 1-3

Zen: The Quantum Leap from Mind to No-Mind
Zen: The Solitary Bird, Cuckoo of the Forest
Zen: The Special Transmission

**Osho: On the Ancient Masters of Zen**

Dogen: The Zen Master
Hyakujo: The Everest of Zen – With Basho's haikus
Isan: No Footprints in the Blue Sky
Joshu: The Lion's Roar
Ma Tzu: The Empty Mirror
Nansen: The Point of Departure
Rinzai: Master of the Irrational

**Responses to Questions**

Be Still and Know
Beyond Enlightenment (Talks in Bombay)
Beyond Psychology (Talks in Uruguay)
Come, Come, Yet Again Come
The Diamond Sword
From Bondage to Freedom
From Darkness to Light
From Death to Deathlessness
From Ignorance to Innocence
From Misery to Enlightenment
From Personality to Individuality
From the False to the Truth
From Unconsciousness to Consciousness
The Goose Is Out
The Great Pilgrimage: From Here to Here
The Invitation
Light on the Path (Talks in the Himalayas)
My Way: The Way of the White Clouds
Nowhere to Go but In
The Osho Upanishad (Talks in Bombay)
The Path of the Mystic (Talks in Uruguay)
The Razor's Edge
Sermons in Stones (Talks in Bombay)
Socrates Poisoned Again After 25 Centuries (Talks in Greece)
The Sword and the Lotus (Talks in the Himalayas)
Transmission of the Lamp (Talks in Uruguay)
Walk without Feet, Fly without Wings and Think without Mind
The Wild Geese and the Water
Yaa-Hoo! The Mystic Rose
Walking in Zen, Sitting in Zen
Zen: Zest, Zip, Zap and Zing

**Osho's Vision for the World**
The Golden Future
The Hidden Splendor
The New Dawn
The Rebel
The Rebellious Spirit

**The Mantra Series**
Hari Om Tat Sat
Om Mani Padme Hum
Om Shantih Shantih Shantih
Sat Chit Anand
Satyam Shivam Sundaram

**Personal Glimpses**
Books I Have Loved
Glimpses of a Golden Childhood
Notes of a Madman

**Interviews with the World Press**
The Man of Truth: A Majority of One

**Meetings with Individuals**
Above All Don't Wobble
Hammer on the Rock

**Quotation Books**
Gold Nuggets
More Gold Nuggets
Words From A Man of No Words

**Letters and Writings**
A Cup of Tea
Earthen Lamps
Flowers of Love
Life Is a Soap Bubble
Love Letters to Life
Seeds of Wisdom

For any information about OSHO Books, please contact:

**OSHO Media International**
17 Koregaon Park, Pune – 411001, MS, India
Phone: +91-20-66019999 Fax: +91-20-66019990
E-mail: distribution@osho.net
Website: http://www.osho.com

# For More Information

The official website of OSHO International is www.OSHO.com

www.OSHO.com/AllAboutOSHO is a comprehensive portal to all things OSHO.

www.OSHO.com/AllAboutOSHO
www.OshoTimes.com
shop.OSHO.com
iOSHO.OSHO.com
YouTube: OSHO/OSHOinternational
Twitter: OSHO
Instagram: OSHOinternational
Facebook: OSHO.international
Facebook: OSHO.international.meditation.resort

ALSO IN THE MANTRA SERIES